Gentle Black Giants
A History of Negro Leaguers in Japan

Gentle Black Giants

A History of Negro Leaguers in Japan

Kazuo Sayama *&* Bill Staples, Jr.

Foreword by Kenso Zenimura

To Alex,
Peace, Love & Baseball!
Enjoy!
Bill S. Jr.

Nisei Baseball Research Project Press
Fresno, California

LIBRARY OF CONGRESS CATALOGING-IN-PUBLICATION DATA
(APPLICATION IN PROGRESS)

Sayama, Kazuo, 1936 –
Staples, Bill, Jr., 1969 –
Gentle Black Giants: A History of Negro Leaguers
in Japan / Kazuo Sayama and Bill Staples, Jr.
foreword by Howard Kenso Zenimura.
p.   cm.
Includes extensive appendices and index.

ISBN: 978-0-578-50133-8
softcover : chlorine-free black ink on 55# acid-free interior white paper
supplied by a Forest Stewardship Council-certified provider.

1. Negro Leagues baseball – History
2. Japanese baseball – History
3. U.S.-Japan relations – History

On the Cover: O'Neal Pullen of the Philadelphia Royal Giants
with Japanese Baseball Hall of Famer Shinji Hamazaki, 1927.
(Photo courtesy of the Negro Leagues Baseball Museum)

Manufactured in the Unites States of America

Nisei Baseball Research Project Press
www.niseibaseball.com

When WWII ended, I was a third grader in Wakayama city. American soldiers soon arrived and they were especially kind to us kids. I later learned that they were members of the all-black 93rd Infantry Division of the U.S. Army. Like us, they loved baseball and some even coached and umpired in our games. One day, one of the soldiers said to me, "Someday you'll be a great pitcher!" Sadly, I never did fulfill his prophecy, but his encouragement fueled my love for the game, and I became a baseball writer instead. *Gentle Black Giants* is my "thank you letter" to that soldier. — Kazuo Sayama

This book is dedicated to the unsung heroes of the Negro Leagues, Nikkei (Japanese American) Leagues, and Japanese Leagues who helped build baseball's "Bridge to the Pacific" between the U.S. and Japan. — Bill Staples, Jr.

Table of Contents

Table of Contents

Acknowledgements

by Bill Staples, Jr.

I would like to thank the following people who helped make the English translation of *Gentle Black Giants* possible:

Kazuo Sayama, award-winning author and baseball historian, for his support and encouragement to translate his wonderful book about the Philadelphia Royal Giants' goodwill tours of Japan. Kaz and I first connected in early 2014 through our mutual friend, umpire-extraordinaire, Perry Lee Barber. At the time, Kaz was writing a book about Satchel Paige at the 1935 National Baseball Congress and needed some research assistance on the Japanese American players who also competed in that semi-pro tournament. As a token of his appreciation for my help, he sent me a copy of *Gentle Black Giants*.

Doris Asano is a friend and fellow board member with the Arizona Chapter of the Japanese American Citizens League (JACL). She is a life-long supporter of projects that celebrate Japanese heritage and promote cultural diversity. Upon learning about the importance of the tours of the Philadelphia Royal Giants, and my three years of failed attempts to have Sayama's book translated, Doris stepped up to the plate and provided both the support and social network to make the translation possible.

Shimako Shimuzu is a native Japanese speaker and educator who lives in Arizona. With the help of her son and husband, who are both passionate baseball fans, Shimako served as the primary translator (Japanese-to-English) on *Gentle Black Giants*. Without her attention to detail, insight and thoughtful approach to Sayama's story, this translation would not have been possible.

George Nakamura is a native Japanese speaker, writer, photographer and publisher who lives in Arizona. George served as the secondary translator on the project (comparing and validating the new English text against the original Japanese). Throughout this project, George embodied the Buddhist sentiment, "If anything is worth doing, do it with all your heart."

Kyoko Yoshida is a professor of writing at Ritsumeikan University in Kyoto, Japan. For more than a decade she and I have collaborated on U.S.-Japanese baseball research projects. Her shared passion, energy and interest in this topic helped bring this project to fruition.

Raymond Doswell, Vice President and curator at the Negro Leagues Baseball Museum, shares a passion for the Philadelphia Royal Giants, and researching the great untold stories of baseball. A special thanks to Raymond for his support over the years, and for granting permission to use Royal Giants photos in this and other related projects.

Gary Ashwill, fellow baseball historian and author, who not only served as an assistant editor on this project, he also inspired it many years ago when he wrote on his blog Agate Type, "it would be really nice to get some Japanese baseball books translated into English."

A special thank you to several baseball historians who have collaborated over the years, and/or have contributed an article in the appendices of this book. They are Yoichi Nagata, Ralph Pearce, Ronald Auther, Bob Luke, Dexter Thomas, Rob Fitts and Ted Knorr.

A sincere thank you to Prestige Collectibles and Sotheby's for granting permission to use images from their collections for *Part II: A History of Negro Leaguers in Japan*.

Kerry Yo Nakagawa is an award-winning baseball historian and the authority on Japanese American baseball history. Kerry was good friends with Buck O'Neil, and although I never got the chance to meet the Negro Leagues legend, I sense that the spirit of Buck lives on in Kerry. The Buck O'Neil stories that Kerry has shared over the years helped fuel the fire behind this project. Also, a special thanks to Kerry for allowing this book to be published by the Nisei Baseball Research Project.

And finally, a sincere thank you to Howard Kenso Zenimura for signing on to write the foreword to this book. He was born in 1927, the same year the Philadelphia Royal Giants and his father's team, the Fresno Athletic Club, toured Japan. He remembered watching several of the Royal Giants play in Fresno when he was a young boy. Kenso is a Nisei baseball pioneer who saw first hand how the game of baseball can break down barriers and help build bridges between people of different backgrounds. I am sad that he passed away before this project was completed, but I feel blessed to have been a part of his life. I considered him a friend, family, mentor and role model, and I truly appreciate him sharing his memories, perspective and passion related to great game of baseball—our "international pastime."

野球

Contributors

Co-Author

Kazuo Sayama is a historian and author of more than 40 books on baseball in both Japan and the United States. He was born in 1936 in the Wakayama Prefecture and currently lives in Tanabe. He holds degrees from Keio University Faculty of Literature and American Literature. He was employed by the Wakayama Prefecture Tanabe High School and founded the independent Tanabe English Academy. He is a member of the Society for American Baseball Research (SABR) and Sports Literature Society. He is the winner of numerous awards, including the Ushio Nonfiction Award, Wakayama Prefecture Culture Award, Mizuno Sports Writer Award, Joseph Astman Award, and the SABR Tweed Webb Award.

Co-Author & Executive Editor

Bill Staples, Jr. is a member of SABR in Arizona with a passion for researching and telling the untold stories of the "international pastime." He is chairman of the SABR Asian Baseball Research Committee, board member of the Nisei Baseball Research Project, board member of the Japanese American Citizens League (Arizona Chapter), and a past speaker at the Cooperstown Symposium on Baseball and American Culture at the National Baseball Hall of Fame. He is the author of the biography *Kenichi Zenimura, Japanese American Baseball Pioneer* (McFarland, 2011), winner of the 2012 SABR Baseball Research Award. He is also a contributing author to the following academic endeavors: "Black Giant: Biz Mackey's Texas Negro League Career" in Black Ball: A Journal of the Negro Leagues (McFarland, Spring 2008); and "Japanese American Baseball" in *Asian Americans: An Encyclopedia of Social, Cultural, and Political History* (ABC-CLIO, 2013). Bill is a graduate of the University of North Texas (BA), and Arizona State University (MBA) and lives in Chandler, Arizona.

Translators

Shimako Shimizu was born and raised in Yamaguchi, Japan. At age 19 she moved to the U.S. where she studied English and then graduated with Bachelor of Science degree in business from University of Texas at San Antonio. Shimako also holds two masters degrees, one in Elementary Education from Plymouth State University, and another in Curriculum and Instruction from Grand Canyon University. Professionally, she works as a certified teacher in the Scottsdale Unified School District. Prior to that she was human resources professional with JVC in New Jersey. She is also an award-winning writer who has been recognized for her work in local creative writing and art contests. She considers it an honor to "help bring such an amazing story to audiences who otherwise would not be able to read this important chapter of baseball history." Shimako currently lives in Scottsdale, Arizona, with her baseball-fanatic family, where they attend numerous Cactus League games each spring.

George Nakamura was born in the Nagano prefecture of Japan. After graduating from Soka University in Tokyo, he worked for a Japanese trading company. In 1980, he moved to the U.S. to study at Arizona State University and majored in history. After graduating from ASU in 1984, he served as a Japanese-to-English translator in the information technology industry. In 1989 he started own business, publishing a print and digital Japanese-language magazine *OASIS* for Japanese readers in Arizona. In addition to his role as writer and editor of the publication, he has established himself as a skilled, award-winning photographer. George currently lives in Phoenix, Arizona and enjoys capturing the beauty of Arizona's landscape, as well as many live events throughout the Grand Canyon State.

Associate Editors

Kerry Yo Nakagawa is the author of *Through a Diamond: 100 Years of Japanese American Baseball*. He is also the founder and director for the non-profit Nisei Baseball Research Project (NBRP), curator of the Diamonds in the Rough: Japanese Americans in Baseball exhibition which was displayed at the National Museum in the summer of 2000, a consultant to the prestigious Baseball Hall of Fame tour entitled Baseball as America, and an independent producer/filmmaker, actor, researcher, and writer. Kerry also served as associate producer of the major motion picture *American Pastime* (2007) produced by Rosy Bushes Productions and ShadowCatcher Entertainment, and distributed by Warner Bros. He currently lives in Fresno, California. His uncle, Johnny Nakagawa, toured Japan in 1927 with the Fresno Athletic Club and competed against the Philadelphia Royal Giants.

Gary Ashwill is a baseball author, researcher, and analyst, particularly of Minor League, Negro League, and Cuban baseball, probably best known for his baseball history blog Agate Type: Adventures in Baseball Archeology (agateype.typepad.com). He also contributes to the Hall of Merit at Baseball Think Factory, and is co-founder with Kevin Johnson (KJOK) and Dan Hirsch of Seamheads.com's Negro Leagues Database. He is the author of the 2014 edition of *Sol White's Official Base Ball Guide* (Summer Game Books Baseball Classics). Gary is a member of SABR and is a past winner of the John Coates Next Generation Award from the Jerry Malloy Negro League Conference. Originally from Kansas City, he now lives in North Carolina. He is a freelance editor. Before creating AgateType, he was part of the Negro League Researchers and Authors Group (NLRAG), contributing statistics from the 1928 and 1934 seasons of Negro League play.

Contributing Authors

Kyoko Yoshida was born and raised in Fukuoka, Japan. Herr first Nippon Professional Baseball (NPB) game was a preseason game between the Crown Lighter Lions and the Yomiuri Giants at Kokura Baseball Field. She studied in Kyoto (the Hanshin Tigers) and Milwaukee (the Brewers), taught in Yokohama (the Baystars) and Tokyo (the Swallows), and now teaches American Literature at Ritsumeikan University in Kyoto (the home of the Kyoto Flora of the Japan Women's Baseball League, the only professional women's league in the world). She writes fiction in English and translates from/into Japanese. *Disorientalism* (Vagabond Press, 2013) is her first collection of short stories. She's been researching on the trans-Pacific baseball exchanges between the United States and Japan before World War II, particularly focusing on African-American baseball players. She has an essay on the Keio University baseball team at home and abroad in the 1920s and '30s, titled "Nichibei yakyû no ôgon jidai—San'itsu shita Fujita korekushon" in Keiô Gijuku Toshokan no zôsho (the Golden Age of US-Japan Baseball—Through the Fujita Collection at the Sotheby's Auction" in Collections at Keio University Library, Keio University Press, 2009). Her other interests in the American pastime include how baseball is represented in literature, film and other cultural media, which she explores in *Bêsubôru wo yomu* (Reading Baseball, Keio University Press, 2013). The essay included in this volume is based on her talk at the International American Studies Association 7th World Congress in Seoul in 2015.

Dexter Thomas is a scholar of cultural identity, studying the intersection of youth, music, black, and Japanese cultures. He currently works as a correspondent for *Vice News Tonight* on HBO, where he has received an Emmy nomination for his coverage of the heroin epidemic in the United States. He previously wrote for the *Los Angeles Times*, where in 2015 he contributed to Pulitzer Prize-winning coverage of the shootings in his hometown of San Bernardino, California. He is also a PhD candidate in East Asian studies at Cornell University, and is writing a book about Japanese hip-hop. His personal website is: whatupdex.com.

Ralph M. Pearce works at the San Jose Public Library's California Room assisting in state and local history research. He has written two books, *From Asahi to Zebras: Japanese American Baseball in San Jose, California* (2005), and *San Jose Japantown: A Journey* (2014). He is currently working on a book about the first Americans in professional Japanese baseball.

Bob Luke's life-long passion for baseball reached its peak on the field when he captained his Montgomery Blair High School's baseball team as a center fielder in Silver Spring, Maryland. After graduating from Colgate University and earning a PhD in sociology from the University of Maryland, he turned to a career in Human Resource Development. In retirement his interest in the history of baseball, especially the history of the Negro leagues, led to two biographies of Negro leaguers, Willie Wells and Effa Manley, one book on the history of the Baltimore Elite Giants, and, most recently, a book about the integration of the Baltimore Orioles. His first book traced the life and career of his childhood next door neighbor, Bill McGowan, an American League umpire from 1924 to 1954. He has also published a book about the role that African American soldiers played for the Union in the Civil War.

野球

Foreword

by Howard Kenso Zenimura

I am a second-generation Japanese American, also known as Nisei. I was born in Fresno, California on May 16, 1927. I've been blessed with a beautiful family, a long life and a lot of wonderful memories—many of them involve the great game of baseball.

The day I was born my dad, Kenichi Zenimura, was on his second tour of Japan with his team, the Fresno Athletic Club. Touring Japan at the same time was a Negro League all-star team from California called the Philadelphia Royal Giants.

My dad first met Royal Giants' manager Lon Goodwin when their teams played each other in September 1925 in Los Angeles. Goodwin's team was called the L.A. White Sox then. The next year they scheduled a two-game series on the Fourth of July weekend in Fresno. Plans for my dad's second tour were already in motion, and that's when he encouraged Goodwin to take his ball club to Japan. As they say, the rest is history.

My dad was born in Hiroshima, Japan, and raised in Honolulu, Hawaii. The island was a multi-cultural baseball paradise. Because of his early exposure to different races and cultures in Hawaii, he embraced people from all walks of life. We learned from his example.

Japanese Americans and African Americans faced similar struggles because of racial discrimination in the U.S. Ballplayers in our communities were forced to play in their own leagues. Many times, black and Japanese American teams competed against each other.

Some of my earliest memories as a kid are of watching my dad's team play at his Fresno Japanese Ballpark. Most often the teams were Japanese American, but occasionally African American teams played there too.

I remember watching the Bakersfield Colored Cubs play there. Their manager and catcher was O'Neal Pullen, the same player shaking hands with Japanese Baseball Hall of Famer Shinji Hamazaki in the famous photo from 1927. Pullen scheduled games at my dad's ballpark many times throughout the 1930s.

That photo of Pullen and Hamazaki is symbolic of the special relationship between black and Japanese ballplayers. We are baseball brothers—before, during and after WWII. It also represents the important role of black and brown ballplayers as goodwill ambassadors in U.S.-Japanese baseball relations.

In May 1945, I left the Gila River Japanese American Incarceration Camp in Arizona after graduating from high school. I moved to Chicago to live with my uncle Bob Yamasaki, who had relocated years earlier to work at a battery factory. Uncle Bob was a huge baseball fan and he bought us tickets to attend the Negro League East-West All-Star game at Comiskey Park.

The game featured future Hall of Famers like Buck Leonard, Willie Wells, Martin Dihigo, Roy Campanella and a rookie second baseman named Jackie Robinson. I also played second base, so it was inspiring to watch Jackie. It was even more inspiring when he crossed major league baseball's color line a few years later.

In 1953 my brother Kenshi, pitcher Ben Mitsuyoshi, and I went to Japan to play for the Hiroshima Carp. We were the first Americans to play for Hiroshima. That same season manager Shinji Hamazaki of the Hankyu Braves signed two others from the U.S., infielder Larry Raines and pitcher Jonas Gaines, both African Americans. The year before Hankyu signed Negro Leaguers John Britton and Jimmy Newberry. I believe that Hamazaki's interaction with the Royal Giants in 1927 greatly influenced his desire to have African American players on his team.

According to the Nisei Baseball Research Project, prior to WWII there were roughly 100 goodwill baseball tours between the U.S. and Japan. Of those teams, few captured the minds and hearts of Japanese fans and opposing teams like the Royal Giants.

In the book *Gentle Black Giants*, we learn that former player Yasuo Shimazu, a shortstop with the Diamond Club in Japan, thought that many of the white teams visiting from the U.S. during the 1920s and 30s were disrespectful. They often mocked the opposing players who were still learning the finer points of the game. But not the Royal Giants. Instead of being arrogant and acting like experts of the game, they interacted with Japanese players with the spirit of, "hey, we are friends, let's play ball together."

Gentle Black Giants author Kazuo Sayama believes that the tours of the Royal Giants played an important role in the start of Japanese professional baseball in 1936. He said, "There is no denying that the major leaguers' visits (of Babe Ruth and Lou Gehrig) were the far bigger incitement to the birth of our professional league … but if we had seen only the major leaguers, we might have been discouraged and disillusioned by our poor showing." He adds, "What saved us were the tours of the Philadelphia Royal Giants, whose visits gave Japanese players confidence and hope."

I like to think that this same positive sentiment applies to Japanese American ball clubs touring their mother country as well—like the Seattle Asahi, Honolulu Asahi, Fresno Athletic Club, San Jose Asahi, Aratani Guadalupe Packers, Stockton Yamato, L.A. Nippon and Kono Alameda All-Stars.

Roughly 80 years after the start of pro ball in Japan, the confidence and hope instilled by the tours of African American and Japanese American ball clubs have resulted in:

- Four World Baseball Classic (WBC) medals for Team Japan—two gold and two bronze medals in four WBC tournaments;
- Three Olympic medals for Japan—one silver and two bronze medals in five Olympic Games (1992-2008), and;

- Roughly 70 players from Japan have entered MLB and transformed the game, including stars like: Masanori Murakami, Hideo Nomo, Ichiro Suzuki, Daisuke Matsuzaka, Hideki Matsui, Masahiro Tanaka, Yu Darvish, Kenta Maeda and Shohei Ohtani.

I am extremely proud of both my Japanese and American roots. Therefore, I consider it an honor to invite you to learn more about the Philadelphia Royal Giants—a great American team who played a key role in the formation of professional baseball in Japan.

Baseball historian and author Bill Staples, Jr, and his team of interpreters do an excellent job of presenting Kazuo Sayama's *Gentle Black Giants* to English readers for the first time. This new edition lets fans around the globe learn more about the important role the Philadelphia Royal Giants played as goodwill ambassadors.

Jackie Robinson once said, "A life is not important except in the impact it has on other lives." The Philadelphia Royal Giants positively impacted and inspired the start of pro baseball in Japan through the power of love and respect for their fellow man.

My hope is that baseball fans around the world develop a greater appreciation for the Philadelphia Royal Giants and the positive impact they had in helping to make the great game of baseball the "International Pastime" that it is today.

Kenso Zenimura
Fresno, California
April 18, 2018

Howard Kenso Zenimura
Born: May 16, 1927, Fresno, CA
Died: December 13, 2018, Fresno, CA
Height: 5' 7"   **Weight:** 136 lb.
Bats: Left   **Throws:** Right
Positions: Second base, outfield, pitcher

Teams: 1944 Gila River All-Stars, 1945 Butte High Eagles, 1946-49 U.S. Army Baseball Teams (Fort Monroe, Virginia; Monterrey, California), 1948 San Jose Zebras, 1950-51 Fresno State, 1950-54 Fresno Nisei, 1953 Hiroshima Carp (Japan), 1955 Regina (Canada)

Kenso Zenimura first held a baseball in his hands long before he could walk or talk. His father Kenichi taught young Kenso, a natural righty, to bat left-handed so he could get down the first-base line quickly. In 1942 the Zenimura family was sent to the Gila River Incarceration Camp in Arizona, and there Kenso was among the internees who helped his father build a baseball field. The Block 28 diamond (aka Zenimura Field) provided a sense of hope for the community unjustly imprisoned behind barbed wire. After the war Kenso became a star player with the Fresno College Bulldogs. In 1951 his team-leading .424 average carried the Bulldogs to a 36-4 record and the conference title. In 1953, he and his brother Kenshi were the first Americans to play for the Hiroshima Carp in Japan. After a career in teaching, Kenso became a coach for the Fresno team in the International Boys League (Shonen Yakyu), a tournament for players ages 14-15 in the U.S., Japan, Mexico and Brazil. He was inducted into the Fresno State Baseball Hall of Fame as both an individual player and as part of the 1951 team.

野球

Preface

by Bill Staples, Jr.

It is an honor to share with you the English translation of the award-winning book, *Gentle Black Giants*, by Japanese baseball historian, Kazuo Sayama.

When it was first published in 1986, Bob Davids, the executive director of the Society of American Baseball Research (SABR), called it "a new dimension to baseball research" and said that the Philadelphia Royal Giants' tours "undoubtedly contributed to the decision in 1936 to launch the Japanese Professional League."

I currently serve as the chairman of SABR's Asian Baseball Research Committee, a group dedicated to preserving Asian baseball history and sharing it with others. You don't have to be a member of SABR or well-versed in Japanese baseball history to appreciate the Royal Giants. Anyone who loves baseball, or has a passion for Negro Leagues history, U.S.-Japan relations, civil rights, or cross-cultural encounters, will enjoy reading this book.

I received a copy of *Gentle Black Giants* as a gift from Kazuo Sayama in the spring of 2014. I flipped through the pages filled with beautiful kanji characters wishing I could read it. I could not. I wrote Sayama and thanked him for the gift, and suggested that maybe I could someday help translate his book for English readers.

He responded, "I quite agree with you in your idea (for an English translation). It is kind of a raw material. It's all up to you to decide how to cook it. It is written for Japanese readers, and I think I will have to add some explanation for foreign readers when it has an English version." He later explained that the book was originally published as a series of articles that appeared in the Japanese baseball magazine *Yakyukai (Baseball World)* between December 1985 and April 1986. "The publisher later made it in a book form, but it was kind of an appendix, bounded very poorly." After receiving the green light from Sayama to proceed, I turned to a team of translation experts for assistance.

The Translation Process

Much like individual players who contribute to the success of a baseball team, it took the unique skills and effort of several individuals to complete this project. The process and the people involved are as follows:

1. Original research and writing, by Kazuo Sayama
2. Primary Japanese-to-English translation, by Shimako Shimizu
3. Interpretation and editing of English, by me—Bill Staples, Jr.
4. Secondary English-back-to-Japanese translation, by George Nakamura
5. Editing, additional research, and annotation of English copy, by me
6. Proofreading, editing, fact-checking and additional research, by Gary Ashwill
7. Final editing, file preparation, layout, design, and publishing, by me
8. Post-layout proofing, by several readers

Steps 2 through 4 involve "translation and interpretation." Through this process, I learned that there is no such thing as a true Japanese "translation," as many words and phrases do not have a one-to-one English translation. A more appropriate term for the process would be "trans-terpretation"—a hybrid of translation and interpretation.

It should be noted that our team strived to maintain the integrity of Sayama's original intent. In fact, his English-language article, "Their Throws Were Like Arrows" that appeared in the 1987 *SABR Research Journal,* was used as the model for Sayama's English-speaking voice throughout the entire translation of his book. And as Sayama suggested, footnotes with background information were added so that those unfamiliar with foreign names, places, and players could better understand his references.

An editorial decision was made to keep to Japanese era name for years. Even though this is an English translation, I wanted the reader to be reminded that the events took place in Japan, and the story is being told by a Japanese author, Sayama. For those unfamiliar with the concept, the Japanese era name (nengō, "year name") are eras that correspond with the reign of a new emperor. The four eras during baseball's existence in Japan are:

*   Meiji (1868–1912)
*   Taishō (1912–1926)
*   Shōwa (1926–1989)
*   Heisei (1989–2019)

The Japanese era year consists of two elements, the era name and the number since the era began. For example, the first year of the Meiji period was 1868, so in the Japanese calendar, it is known as Meiji 1. Therefore, the year 1872—the year baseball was first introduced to Japan—is known as Meiji 4. With that, you will see multiple references to Showa 2 (1927) and Showa 9 (1934) throughout this book, the years of historically important goodwill baseball tours in Japan by American teams. Note that the Japanese era year will not be used when referencing events that occurred outside of Japan.

This book is divided into two sections, *Part I: Gentle Black Giants*, and *Part II: A History of Negro Leaguers in Japan*. Because the original book was a compilation of weekly articles, you will notice that some key points and events are repeated from one chapter to the next in *Part I*. This was intentional by Sayama so that he could educate those readers who were new to his weekly series. For the English translation, we kept Sayama's repetition to maintain the integrity of each chapter. Plus, it does help to reinforce learning when exposed to information multiple times.

Part II is a collection of stats, articles, essays, newspaper clippings, maps and photos from the multiple tours of the Philadelphia Royal Giants. Sayama had many unanswered questions in his original book, and fortunately 30 years later we now have the answers. The information in *Part II* provides new insight and interesting perspectives on the tours, some from the players themselves.

In addition to presenting information related to the Royal Giants' three tours to Asia (Japan, China, Korea, and the Philippines), *Part II* also includes information on their three separate tours to the Hawaiian Territories. Prior to U.S. statehood in 1959, the baseball-rich environment of Hawaii played an important role in the development of what I call "Baseball's Bridge to the Pacific." The Royal Giants' tours to Hawaii often involved games against visiting teams from Japan, so it is important to consider when discussing the influence of the Philadelphia Royal Giants on Japanese baseball.

Above all, the primary objective when translating *Gentle Black Giants* was to maintain the integrity and accuracy of Sayama's original intent for Japanese audiences, while also creating an enjoyable experience for English readers.

The Heart and "Honne" of this Book

Almost all that has been published about U.S. baseball tours to Japan has been written by English-speaking and Western-thinking authors. What makes Sayama's book special is that we now have an insight into the Japanese perspective on goodwill tours to Japan—and it's fascinating.

Since 2004, I've studied and written about Nikkei (Japanese American) baseball history. Over the years I have gained some insight into the unique aspects of Japanese culture through my interaction with the Japanese American community. One fascinating concept that I've learned about is called honne (inner truth) and tatemae (outer face). It is quite common in the Japanese culture for individuals to not speak the truth in order to maintain harmony with others.

What does this have to do with Sayama's book? As the English version of *Gentle Black Giants* started to take form, I began to see that through his interviews with former Japanese ballplayers who competed in the 1920s and 1930s, Sayama was able to harness the honne (inner truth) about the previous visits of American ball clubs to Japan.

Based on his interviews with these players, Sayama presents the truth (as seen through their eyes) about both the positive and negative attitudes and behaviors of different teams and players from the U.S. An eye-opening list comparing and contrasting the tours of the white professional ballplayers versus the members of the Philadelphia Royal Giants is presented in *Chapter 17: Underappreciated Value of the Team in the Shadow.* Once you read and reflect upon this list, you will understand why Sayama believes that the tours of the Royal Giants helped make it possible for professional baseball in Japan to start in 1936.

In addition to my work as a baseball historian, I also coach youth baseball and softball. I know that it is the coach's responsibility to fill the "emotional tank" of developing athletes and help motivate them to grow, learn and be successful on and off the field. According to The Positive Coaching Alliance, a non-profit organization that provides education for youth-sports coaches, the fuel for an athlete's emotional tank is a special blend of ingredients—a ratio of five parts positive reinforcement and one part constructive criticism. With this 5-to-1 ratio in mind, it is helpful to think of the Royal Giants as the coaches who provided the positive fuel that filled the "emotional tanks" of early Japanese ballplayers and encouraged them to stay on the path of progress.

Japan's all-time home run king, Sadaharu Oh, incorporated aikido into his training to help him become a better ballplayer. A concept from aikido called the "uke-nage relationship" is also helpful to understand how the Royal Giants helped develop ballplayers in Japan. According to Dorian Ealy, a respected health and fitness professional who incorporates Eastern philosophy and martial arts into his training with clients, the "uke-nage relationship" is a scenario where a more skilled sensei (teacher) enters into an agreement with a student to not exert maximum force for training purposes. The teacher (nage, literally "the thrower") is in a position of sacrifice and compassion for the greater good of the student (uke, literally "one who receives"). Without this understanding, it is no fun for the student to suffer embarrassing defeats over and over, which could eventually lead to discouragement.

The members of the Royal Giants might not have been trained in aikido, but they intuitively embraced the compassionate "uke-nage relationship" when they stepped on the field with their Japanese counterparts. With this in mind, we now see why the Japanese ballplayers referred to the visiting Negro Leaguers as "gentle, black giants."

Other countries rejected baseball because the visiting professionals left fledgling players disillusioned with the game through defeat. "We were lucky enough to have the chance to neutralize the shock," said Sayama. "The Royal Giants' visits were the shock absorber." He concluded, "Baseball has in it many elements that appeal to the Japanese mind, and it may safely be said that professional baseball would have been born in the course of time. Without the visits of the gentlemanly and accessible Royal Giants, however, I don't think it would have seen the light of day as early as 1936."

I have one final observation on the comparisons between the tours of the Royal Giants and those of the major league All-Americans. Professional baseball is a business model that relies on two key components for survival: 1) highly-skilled ballplayers to create a quality product (the supply), and 2) the fans who pay their hard-earned money to watch the game (the demand). The debate about which tours inspired the start of professional baseball in Japan—the Royal Giants or the major league All-Americans—is not a zero-sum game (i.e. for one side to be right, the other side must be wrong). I think there is a degree of truth in both perspectives. The Royal Giants played a key role in helping to create skilled ballplayers, whereas the All-Americans played a key role in generating excitement among the media and fans. Thus, professional baseball grows and/or survives with only the right mix of player talent (supply) and fan interest (demand). It is a yin and yang relationship—one does not exist without the other. So when it comes to the debate about which teams or tours inspired the start of professional baseball in Japan in 1936, I do not think it is wise or productive to debate which is more valuable, the yin or the yang. Having said that though, it is critically important to preserve the history of both sides of the story, which Sayama demonstrates has failed to occur when it comes to the celebrating the Philadelphia Royal Giants—whom some of their former opponents in Japan consider the "other fathers of Japanese baseball."

These Guys Could Play

Last but not least, the translation of *Gentle Black Giants* provides a fascinating insight into the details of the games played by the Royal Giants in Japan. One thing quickly becomes apparent—these American tourists had talent. In reading *Gentle Black Giants* and the comprehensive appendices in *Section II: A History of Negro Leaguers in Japan*, we learn that there were three separate tours to Japan by the Royal Giants—in 1927, 1932-33, and 1933-34. Each time the roster of players was comprised of three levels of talent: semi-pro caliber players, major league quality players, and future Hall of Famers.

As of 2018, there are three members of the Philadelphia Royal Giants who are enshrined in the National Baseball Hall of Fame (HOF): "Bullet Joe" Rogan, Biz Mackey, and Andy

Cooper. Rogan was inducted in 1998, while Mackey and Cooper were both inducted in 2006 with 15 other Negro Leaguers. Based on the caliber of performances depicted in *Gentle Black Giants*, three other players who deserve consideration for Cooperstown are Rap Dixon, Frank Duncan, and Chet Brewer. On the field, Dixon, Duncan and Brewer stood head and shoulders above all others, just like Rogan, Mackey and Cooper.

In my opinion, another candidate worthy of Hall of Fame consideration (in either the U.S. or Japan) is manager Lon Goodwin. He was once a teammate of Rube Foster's with the Waco Yellow Jackets, and arguably is one of the most active and influential managers for the international game. Goodwin's biggest disadvantage in receiving HOF recognition is that his career played out on the West Coast during an era when the spotlight for Negro Leagues baseball shined brightest on the East. Despite oversight, I think that time will treat Goodwin's legacy well. He and the other "Trans-Pacific Barnstormers" who traveled by steamship and spent over 500 days on goodwill tours to Asia (See *Appendix O: Trans-Pacific Negro Leagues Barnstormers Summary*) will be viewed in the same light as the bus-traveling barnstormers of the East Coast and Midwest like the Kansas City Monarchs and Pittsburgh Crawfords.

Another important figure in the story of the *Gentle Black Giants* is Kazuo Sayama himself. To some degree, this story is also about him and his relationship with the Royal Giants. Although he never met any of the players, it is clear that he feels a personal connection to them and responsibility to preserve their legacy for future generations. As I read *Gentle Black Giants*, Sayama reminded me of Ray Kinsella, the Iowa farmer in the movie *Field of Dreams* who was compelled by "cosmic forces of the universe" to build a baseball diamond in his cornfield. Sayama's passion for the ballplayers he researches is evident, and the responsibility he feels to bring their story to life is palpable.

And finally, speaking of connections, I must disclose that I have distant family ties to this story. My wife's great-uncle, Robert Bailey, played second base with the Dallas Black Giants and Fort Worth Black Panthers in the Texas Negro Leagues and was once teammates with several members of the Royal Giants, including Biz Mackey, O'Neal Pullen, and William Ross. I want my children to be proud of their family ties to Negro Leagues baseball history. Therefore, like Sayama, I too feel an obligation to help preserve the legacy of the Philadelphia Royal Giants, a ball club comprised of African Americans (and many from Texas) who played a key role in laying the foundation for professional baseball in Japan—a legacy to be proud of and worth celebrating.

野球

PART 1: GENTLE BLACK GIANTS

Introduction

By Kazuo Sayama

Editor's Note: This introduction first appeared as an article in the 1987 *SABR Research Journal after the publication of Sayama's book* Gentle Black Giants *in 1986 in Japan. This early work provides a comprehensive overview and serves as a solid introduction for his seminal classic about the Philadelphia Royals Giants' tours of Japan.*

*   *   *

*Two visits by Philadelphia's gentle Royal Giants convinced
the Japanese that baseball could be both exciting and harmonious.
The seed was planted for pro ball in the Orient.*

There were no professional baseball teams in Japan before 1935. Baseball had been introduced into this country long before that, but our teams were all amateur. Why were professional teams born in quick succession in 1936?

Quite simply, the visits of major leaguers. In 1931 an all-star team including Lefty Grove, Mickey Cochrane, Lou Gehrig, Rabbit Maranville, Lefty O'Doul, and Al Simmons visited Japan. Baseball fans were astounded at their overwhelming superiority: They played seventeen games, and won all of them.

Three years later, another American team arrived with Babe Ruth on it. Streets were crowded with people welcoming them. They won all eighteen games, and created a strong enthusiasm for baseball in Japan.

But these visits alone did not create professional baseball in Japan. Another professional team—a black club called the Philadelphia Royal Giants—had visited in 1927 and then again in 1932. It seems quite strange that this team has scarcely been mentioned in Japanese baseball books. The reason may be that the white Americans' visits were sponsored by the Yomiuri newspaper, which had one of the biggest circulations in Japan. Yomiuri was already thinking of having the first professional team in Japan. They gave the major league tours nationwide publicity, with the result that all Japanese knew about the visits and adored the team's stars.

On the other hand, the Philadelphia Royal Giants were not sponsored by any newspaper. They seem to have arrived through the efforts of a Japanese promoter named Irie, who lived in America, and he must have done little publicity work.

It was only by chance that I became interested in the team. Negro League historian John Holway wrote me a letter, asking for information on Biz Mackey's hitting the first home run ever in Jingu Stadium, Tokyo. I was surprised to hear about this, because we have often been told that the first home run in the stadium was hit by the premier college slugger of the time, Saburo Miyatake of Keio University. After doing some research, I found that Holway was accurate. This was the beginning of my probe into the visits of the black team.

It was lucky for me that I was able to meet some people who had games with the Giants more than fifty years ago. It was fortunate, too, that the Japanese Baseball Hall of Fame still preserves some of the news articles about their games, though they are not detailed.

The Philadelphia Royal Giants were a big surprise to the Japanese players. Saburo Yokozawa, who played second base on a Japanese team, says, "I still remember how surprised we all were. I can even call back some faces of the Giants. I can't forget the big hit by Rap Dixon at Koshien Stadium. It flew well over the centerfielder and hit the fence on the fly. The park was far bigger then than it is now, and you must bear in mind that the balls used then were still dead balls."

No Japanese player could expect to hit that far. In Dixon's honor, a white mark was painted at that point of the fence, with his name on it. This mark remained there for a long time before the fence was torn down to make a bleacher.

Biz Mackey's home run, the first in Jingu Stadium, should be been more celebrated. The stadium had been completed in October of 1926, and no one had hit one over the fence. Mackey did it in a game against the Fresno, California team, which happened to be here at that time. It was a semipro team, made of Japanese players who lived in Fresno. The hit flew over the fence, bounced off the grass bleacher, and disappeared beyond it. Altogether, Mackey hit three over the fences in Jingu during the 1927 tour.

Dixon's drive to the Koshien fence and Mackey's home runs established the power of the black players, since these were the biggest parks in Japan. The Giants' fielding and throwing also astonished the Japanese. In the words of old Japanese, "Their throws were like arrows."

Their running was another phenomenon. They stole bases every time they needed to. The records show that they won all but 1 of their 48 games.

As the days passed, black players attracted much respect from Japanese players and fans for their gentle behavior. They never even complained about their one loss – a controversial 1-0 victory for the Japanese team. In fact, it should have been at least a draw. As Jyukichi Koshiba, who played on the Japanese team, explained: "The record might read that the Daimai team won in the game, but it was a win unlawfully acquired. There was one out. Runners were on third base and first base. The next batter hit a big fly to right field. We got two outs. But after the catch, the runner on third base scored. And the other runner was still running. He tried to go back to first. The ball was thrown by the right fielder to the base before he reached it [but after the runner on third had scored]. Three outs. As you know, one run should have been given to the Giants. Nevertheless, the umpires admitted no score. Their assertion was that it was a double play. But the judgment was wrong."

Said second baseman Yokozawa, "The black players well knew that it was a misjudgment. A runner reached home before the third out was called. Double play? It was out of the question. They knew it. But no black player got angry at this, and soon allowed that wrong call. They seemed to be saying, 'It's okay. If you say it's a double play, it is a double play.' We Japanese players, too, knew it was the umpires' fault. But the Giants were too clean-cut. We lost the chance to make it correct." In checking the record of the game, I found that the third base runner was Rap Dixon, and the other was Pullen. The batter was Cade.

This is not the only example of the Giants' gentle attitude. In the game against the Tomon club of Waseda University, Mackey was hit by pitcher Wakahara. Mackey made a face. The pitcher felt small, and, taking his cap off his head, bowed politely to Biz Mackey. In turn, Mackey made a Japanese bow in the same polite way. A happy mood prevailed.

The Giants were gentle and kind-hearted, both on and off the playing field. After expressing surprise at the Giants' size, Takeshi Mizuna wrote in the June, 1927 issue of *Baseball World*:

But their behavior is quite gentle. In the hotel, they keep quiet. The voices they use with each other are calm, and hardly audible. You would hardly know of their existence. When I asked them about the games in this country, they gave me some comments but in a very humble way. They are modesty itself. You'd think the voices of housewives in the back street of the hotel are far noisier. When there is no game, they enjoy billiards, or walking in the neighborhood. They show great love for children and play with them happily. I heard that they sometimes go to cafes where young girls serve tea or alcoholic drinks, but they never become rude. Not even a quarrel has arisen between them in these long months of travelling, I heard. I asked them about their impressions of Japan. Their first answer was they are really happy, and appreciated Japanese hospitality. In Kyoto, they enjoyed watching Miyako-Odori, traditional dances by geishas. In

Tokyo, too, they visited the Shinbashi-Enbujyo Theater, and enjoyed AzumaOdori dancing. They seem to be entranced by their beauty. One of them said, 'I feel very happy. I am fortunate. We came here to play games, and had the chance to see many beautiful things. I wish I could tell my family and friends how happy we are. I wish they all could see this country of Japan.'

The Giants sent a message to Japanese baseball fans. I found a Japanese translation of it in *Asahi Sports* of April, 1927. Having no way to find the original, I've tried to put it in English again. This is not the exact message by them, but it should give you an idea of what they wanted to say.

After playing some games against Japanese baseball teams, we felt our respect growing. The biggest surprise we had here was the fact that Japanese baseball has already got the very essence of the game. Before we came over here, we often wondered, and talked between ourselves about baseball in Japan. Our conclusion was that Japanese baseball would still be immature. But when we had games against teams here, we could not help being stricken dumb by the wide difference between our surmise and reality.

While at sea, we dreamt of the country of Japan, which we were approaching, and talked about it many a time. One of our greatest concerns was—what kind of parks do the Japanese have? We were unanimous in deciding that Japanese ballparks would surely be very small, poorly equipped ones. They would be no bigger than Class D ballparks in the States. When we found ourselves in the magnificent Jingu Stadium, which is situated in the outer garden of solemn Meiji Shrine, and in the grand and imposing Koshien Stadium, we had to admit that we had had a double misunderstanding. Particularly, Koshien Stadium is grandeur itself. It has a capacity of more than 50,000 people, and is as big as any in the United States.

In the games, we marveled at the dauntless plays by Japanese players. The offense was not only brave but also understood inside baseball. Our team has so far lost one precious game against the Daimai Club. It was the game in which ace pitchers of both teams—Ono of Japan and Mackey of the Giants—showed a keen competition. Though we were defeated in the game, we feel proud that we played baseball of the highest level. We feel admiration for the crafty pitching Ono showed. But more than that, the team play shown in the game by the Japanese called forth our unbounded admiration.

We do believe that baseball will have prosperity here. And our admiration should not be confined to the techniques Japanese players have. Their sportsmanship, too, was worthy to be praised. Frankly speaking, no other people in the world play the game so joyously, disregarding the result of the game. Fans, too, we find sportsmanlike and gentlemanly. We would like to say true enjoyment of sports is to be gotten only by people like the Japanese. We do hope that

Japanese baseball will have permanent prosperity. And at the same time, through *Asahi Sports*, we would like to extend our hearty thanks for many kindnesses shown us since we arrived here.

April 8, 1927, Philadelphia Royal Giants

Has any other team left such a courteous message to the baseball fans here? I don't think so. A member of the Giants, Frank Duncan, told John Holway; "We sailed out of San Pedro, California, to Yokohama, Japan. Went on *La Plata Maru* boat. Took us nineteen days going over. The people were wonderful over there. I loved them. I hated to see them go to war. Wonderful people, the most wonderful people I've come in contact with. We played all over—Osaka, Kobe, and into Nagasaki. They had some nice teams over there in Japan, but they weren't strong hitters. Pretty good fielders, fast, good baserunners ..."

A former Japanese player, Yasuo Shimazu, writes: "Several baseball teams visited Japan in those days from abroad. College teams, semi-pros and professionals. Each impressed us. We could hardly expect to defeat any one of them. So it would have been too much expectation to hope for their uttermost sincerity in all games. To be sure, one team showed quite strange sights. All the players, except the battery and first baseman, took off their gloves when they were on defense. Some infielders turned the backs to batters, and showed their faces between their legs. These kinds of deeds might have been intended for the enjoyment of spectators. But we could not feel happy at them. In this respect, the Royal Giants played in a right way. They, too, might have felt nothing of Japanese competency inwardly, but they showed no sign of it. They kept on playing in a sincere manner. One of the examples was the case of Mackey's throwing. While they were practicing before the games, he threw from home to second base in a sitting position. We were simply surprised at his hard throwing. But once the games began, he didn't do that. After catching balls, he stood up and threw in quite a fundamental way. They had no signs of negligence.

"Some players of other teams made several kinds of funny shows. Some danced around before the spectators, and made strange sounds like those made by fowls. The players themselves! Those were the last acts we expected of players. The Royal Giants didn't display these kinds of deeds. Nor did they play pranks outside the park, which players of other teams often did. A member of the Giants, whose name I forget, said to me, 'I like Japan and the Japanese people. There is no racial barrier here. What a good country! I'd like to come back here again.' I believe that this was the manifestation of his true heart. Putting this and that together, I'd like to emphasize that the players of the Royal Giants were real Gentlemen."

Shimazu reminds us of the visits by major-league teams. In a game held in the rain at Kokura in 1934, Babe Ruth took to the field as a first baseman with a Japanese umbrella over his head, and Lou Gehrig, who was playing as a left fielder, had rubber rain shoes on. In another game, when Lefty Grove was pitching, left fielder Al Simmons laid himself on the field to show he had nothing to do but lie down and watch what Lefty was doing. They may have been intended their actions to be a show, but many Japanese fans weren't altogether happy.

The Royal Giants did put on a show one time. It was at Jingu Stadium after their last game in Tokyo in 1927. The Giants performed not in a mocking, but in a sincere way. Everything they did had something to do with baseball itself. No singing, no dancing, Rap Dixon threw a "straight" ball directly to the bleacher from home plate. Biz Mackey knocked balls into the bleacher from home. Rap ran around the diamond in fourteen and one-fifth seconds, and Frank Duncan in fifteen seconds. These displays helped Japanese fans gain additional respect for the black team.

Barnstorming black teams often sang and danced. Why didn't the Giants? I think the reason is quite simple. They had no need to act like clowns. Japan has had no segregation. We have had a practice of welcoming every visitor from abroad as an honored guest—even if he is here for commercial reasons. The Royal Giants were guests, and they could act quite naturally. They felt no stress. So ... "Was it a double play? Oh, yes, if you think so, it's a double play."

I think this relaxed mood was very important to the history of Japanese baseball. The major leaguers played like textbooks, but they were too much for the Japanese players. Japanese baseball was only a baby, delicate and fragile. Everything the big leaguers had was too big for the baby. Every play, every show the major leaguers made could not help making the Japanese player recognize how small he still was. If he had seen, at that time, this big textbook alone, he might have been killed by the weight. David Voigt makes a similar point when he speaks of the attempts to plant baseball in Great Britain in *America Through Baseball*:

> ... the three great baseball missions were all undertaken under the mistaken notion that baseball could best be spread by professional advocacy in the form of a spectacular display of the game as played by skilled professionals. While by no means a total failure, the results of these displays were disappointing and sometimes even counter productive ... the very polish of the American professionals hurt the spread of baseball in Britain.

It goes without saying that Japan had quite a different sporting and historical background from that of England, and the relationship between Japan and America is not the same as that between Britain and the United States. Nonetheless, Voigt's point is well taken.

Why did the transplanting of baseball succeed in Japan? In my opinion, the reason was that the Japanese had a good shock absorber. "Spectacular display" by a "great baseball mission" could have been counterproductive here, too. But we were lucky enough to have the chance to neutralize the shock. The Royal Giants' visits were the shock absorber. Baseball has in it many elements that appeal to the Japanese mind, and it may safely be said that professional baseball would have been born in the course of time. Without the visits of the gentlemanly and accessible Royal Giants, however, I don't think it would have seen the light of day as early as 1936.

Another letter from Shimazu includes these very sentiments:

We heard that, though they [the Royal Giants] were not major leaguers, they were as strong as, or stronger than, the majors. I myself played in some games against them, and saw many of their games here. I know it was true. But I'm still in wonder. I have been thinking of it in my sickbed since I got your letter. Why was it that we felt we could nearly win? We had the feeling after the game against the Giants that if we had tried a little harder, we could have won. In the games against the major leaguers, we were treated like children. We were at their mercy. We could do nothing. Babies against grown-ups—that was the impression we had. But in the games against the Giants, the whole impression is quite different. Of course, the All-American team was a star-packed team, and the Royal Giants wasn't. But as a whole, they could not have been so far away from the major leaguers. Then why was it that we almost always had close games? Was their batting not so good? Look, they blasted long hits when they were needed. They seemed to be able to hit as they wished.

Here I'd like a jump up to a bold conclusion. Didn't they have abundant showmanship? In games they could have scored many more runs. But they took—or tried to take—the least runs needed. They never tried to take too much score. In so doing, they attracted the interest from the spectators, as well as from the opponent players. Even if a Japanese team didn't win, the hope remained. More spectators visited the next day. . . .

Regretfully, not all games were reported in detail. In the scarce records we have, we can see proof of Shimazu's remark. When the Giants scored many runs, the Japanese team scored some runs, too. When the Japanese didn't score, the Giants often didn't score many, either. (To be sure, wide margins occurred in some games in small towns. The Giants were probably unable to keep the score close against really inferior opposition.)

The Giants seem to have let Japanese teams score some runs in the last inning if it didn't affect the result. This reminds us of the attitude of Satchel Paige, Josh Gibson, and other Negro League players in games against the Marine Corps; they deliberately gave the opponents a run to save face.

The Giants didn't push their powers too far. They were reserved, and their reserve might be said to have been for commercial purposes. But even so, how fortunate it was for Japanese baseball.

There is no denying that the major leaguers' visits were the far bigger incitement to the birth of our professional league. We yearned for better skill in the game. But if we had seen only the major leaguers, we might have been discouraged and disillusioned by our poor showing. What saved us was the tours of the Philadelphia Royal Giants, whose visits gave Japanese players confidence and hope. It is unfair that no words of gratitude have been spoken by the Japanese to this team.

Source: Kazuo Sayama, "Their Throws Were Like Arrows": How a Black Team Spurred Pro Ball in Japan, SABR Research Journal, 1987, p. 85-88. Courtesy of Kazuo Sayama.

野球

Preface
By Bob Davids

May 23, 1986

I congratulate Kazuo Sayama on the completion of his book "Kuroki, Yasashiki, Giants". It is a timely literary composition considering that this is the 50th anniversary of professional baseball in Japan. The visits of the Philadelphia Royal Giants, including such stars as Biz Mackey, Rap Dixon, and Frank Duncan, to Japan in 1927, and two other visits in 1932 and 1933 undoubtedly contributed to the decision in 1936 to launch the Japanese Professional League. The visits of these black players smoothed the way for black American players to compete in the Japanese league in the 1950s (Larry Raines led the Pacific League in batting in 1954). Mr. Sayama is one of the most active members of the Society for American Baseball Research and contributes significantly to the work of the Negro League Committee. His book on the visits of the Philadelphia Royal Giants to Japan add a new dimension to baseball research and publication.

L. Robert Davids

Bob Davids

野球

1

The Void in Baseball History

History is imperfect and often incomplete. The stories that are celebrated and frequently talked about live on, whereas events that are rarely mentioned risk the possibility of disappearing from the stage of history forever.

And because no story teller is truly impartial, I suspect that no history is entirely free of biases either. All history contains a touch of dramatization, exaggeration, sympathy, prejudice and politics.

Therefore, it's no surprise that some historically significant events are treated as though they never occurred, simply because they lacked a voice and were never passed on for future generations.

The history of baseball is no exception.

This year (Showa 61, 1986) marks the fiftieth anniversary since professional baseball was established in Japan. Yet, since the founding of the Japanese Baseball League (JBL) in Showa 11 (1936), little to nothing has been shared about an important team that played a critical role in the development of professional baseball in Japan.[1]

The team is the Philadelphia Royal Giants, comprised of black all-stars who played professional baseball in the Negro Leagues in the United States.

I believe that these ballplayers should be remembered and celebrated for their sportsmanship and humanity, for their gentle yet strong, and refreshing, approach to the game.

Furthermore, I agree with the opinions of the Japanese ballplayers who competed against them—the Philadelphia Royal Giants are important enough to be considered "The Other Fathers of Japanese Baseball."

Therefore, the purpose of this book is to give a voice to their story, to celebrate their contributions to the game in Japan, and to fill this void in our baseball history.

So, who were the Philadelphia Royal Giants, and why did they come to Japan in the first place? The answers to these questions are the core of this book.

But before I address these and other matters, let me first explain how I came to learn about this important ball club.

In late July 1983 I attended the annual meeting of the Society for American Baseball Research (SABR) in Milwaukee, Wisconsin. It was a three-day meeting held at Mashuda Hall on the campus of Marquette University. As the only person from Japan in attendance at the meeting, I was indeed a stranger in the crowd.

Even though I was new to SABR, I was quite familiar with the organization's activities. At the time SABR's membership was over 3,000, but only an estimated 300 people attended the annual meeting. Attendees included scholars, researchers, members of the media, former ballplayers and fans. Their backgrounds varied, but they shared a common passion for the game.[2]

As a lifelong baseball fan, I could talk forever about my wonderful three-day experience in this great environment. But I won't.

Instead, I want to talk about one particular incident that occurred at lunch time during the first day of the conference. It was quite memorable for me because it is the beginning my relationship with the Philadelphia Royal Giants, and how this story came to be.

Shortly after I checked in at the registration desk for the convention, I visited with my good friend Clifford Kachline, a former librarian with the National Baseball Hall of Fame. He was the person who first encouraged me to join SABR.[3]

After our conversation ended, Cliff moved on and I was left alone in what appeared to be a very lively cafeteria full of people joyfully meeting with one another. I must have looked lonely standing there by myself. Suddenly, a man appeared in front of me, smiled, and stuck out his hand to greet me. "Hi, my name is John, John Holway."[4]

After I introduced myself he said, "I know your name. I saw it on the list and was looking forward to meeting you. By the way, I'd like to sit and talk with you over lunch. Is that okay?"

It appears that there was a list of attendees distributed to everyone at the convention. In addition to my name, the list also included my address and a note that I was the person who traveled the longest distance to attend. John, on the other hand, lived two blocks from the convention location.

My initial thought is that he wanted to talk about our geographic proximity to the conference, but as he started to speak I quickly learned that he had something more important to discuss.

John said, "Because you are a SABR member and from Japan, I have one question that I want to ask you. I am a baseball researcher and have written articles for several magazines. Right now I am writing about the Kansas City Monarchs, one of the strongest teams in the history of the Negro Leagues. My question is this: have you ever heard about the Monarch players who went to Japan and played a few games? Have you come across any information about them in Japanese books or magazines?"

"When did this tour take place?" I asked.

"It must be around the end of the 1920s and the beginning of the 1930s," John answered. "They went to Japan at least twice. "

I dropped my knife and fork on the table after he spoke. If true, this is a very important story, I thought to myself.

"You're talking about THE Kansas City Monarchs, the team that won the first Negro Leagues World Series? The team that became even more famous after signing the legendary Satchel Paige?" I asked.

"That's right," John said. "They were among the elite teams in the Negro Leagues. But at the time of their tour to Japan, Paige had not yet joined the team. Instead, their ace pitcher was Bullet Rogan, and they had one of the leagues' greatest hitters, Frank Duncan."

"Bullet Rogan?" I inquired.

"Yes, His real name was Wilber but no one called him by that name.[5] Instead, everyone knew him by his nickname, 'Bullet Joe.'"

John clarified. "Not all those players who visited Japan were members of the Monarchs. Some were players on other teams. So, I am not 100 percent sure they played under the team name of Monarchs or not. Could you help me learn their name?" he asked.

"The top players recruited for the Japan tour were Biz Mackey and Rap Dixon. They were great players, so I could only imagine what kind of numbers they put up in Japan," said John. "Do you know anything about them?"

"I've heard of Rogan, but I don't know anything about him playing in Japan," I responded. During the late 1920s to the early 1930s, the professional Japanese Baseball League had not been established yet. Around that time, major league all-star teams came to Japan, but I have never heard of an all-black team coming to Japan. You must be mistaken."

I was concerned that my disbelief would dampen his enthusiasm, but Holway was sure of it.

"I lived in Japan for a little while. Two years in Kyushu, and three years in Tokyo. It was in the 1950's and my favorite player was Masaichi Kaneda of Kokutetsu Swallows. I still remember his distinctive pitching style," said John. He added, "I've written a book about Japanese baseball, and while I was doing research, I remember seeing the win-loss record of this Negro League team in Japan. They won most of their games, only lost one or two. I can't be sure, but I remember reading that Mackey was the one to hit the first home run at

Meiji Jingu Stadium, and Dixon hit the longest-hit ball in the history of Koshien Stadium. Could you help me with the research and confirm this?"

"Hold on." I had to stop him. "I think the first home run at Meiji Jingu Stadium was hit by Keio University's Saburo Miyatake. It was in a game against Tokyo University, known then as Teidai. He hit it over left field fence. You are saying that there was a home run hit by a black player before that?"

"I think a couple, or several home runs," John replied. "The Negro Leaguers were still using a dead ball then, unlike the major leaguers, who had switched to a 'live' ball. They had the power to hit it out of the park at that tiny Jingu Stadium, no doubt. I'm not sure who it was, though, Mackey or Dixon—I need to know this," exclaimed John.[6]

I could tell that he was disappointed that he didn't know who exactly hit that first home run. He was a meticulous guy, who even corrected my pronunciation of his name when we first met. He made sure that I called him "John" with an "a" sound instead of an "o" sound (the latter, coming from a speaker with a Japanese accent, made it sound more like the woman's name "Joan"). He cared that things be correct.

John continued, "Mackey was the best of the best in the Negro Leagues. He was primarily a catcher, but because of his athleticism and strong throwing arm he also played shortstop. And, as I mentioned already, he was a tremendous power hitter. He is not as famous as Josh Gibson, but he may have been a more all-around player than Josh."[7]

"In addition, I've heard that he was also a good person. The most important qualities for players who travel far distances were having a well-integrated personality and an ability to play multiple positions. It could be said that Biz Mackey was a perfect fit, having both qualities."[8]

"What about Rap Dixon?" I asked.

"Rap Dixon had also become a star player in the Negro Leagues. His foot speed, arm strength, and batting were outstanding. In Japan, he played center field and batted third or fourth in the lineup. I assumed that he also had many stolen bases. Oh yes, I remember that he showed off his arm strength for the fans in Meiji Shrine Stadium. You know … for the entertainment of fans, a player often throws a ball from the home plate to the outfield bleachers."

"To the outfield bleachers?"

I was trying to recall the history of the Meiji Shrine Stadium. If I was not mistaken, the outfield fence was brought in twice. Anyway, it must be correct that the original fence was deeper than it is now. If this was true, their arm strength must have been incredible. Only a few current outfielders in the Major Leagues can accomplish this feat.

"I'm not asking to find out about all the details of the trip, all I want to know is the name of the team that went to Japan, and their win-loss record," said John. "If you can find out who else was on the team that would be great. Do you think you can help me research this?" he asked.

"I will try my best and will respond. I'm not sure what will be involved in finding those things out, so it may take some time, but I promise to get back to you."

I ended the conversation with him, but I was still skeptical about the story.

The early 1920s to the late 1930s was the beginning of the Showa era in the Japanese calendar. During that time, the biggest events in Japanese baseball were the two visits from the major league all-stars. Needless to say, the team was filled with only white players. During the Showa 6 (1931) tour, the pitching performance of Lefty Grove and popularity of Lou Gehrig were well documented and discussed in the press. In Showa 9 (1934), it was all about the popularity of Babe Ruth.

However, I'd never heard of an all-black team that visited Japan during the same time period. I did know about American teams made up amateur and college players who came to Japan. Who was this other all-star team? There might not have been any records left of this mystery team. Even though I had my doubts about the accuracy of the story, I now felt a responsibility to learn more. So I gathered my thoughts and prepared some questions for John's inquiry:

- In the early Showa era—before professional baseball began in Japan—did a black team from the U.S. compete against Japanese teams?
- If so, when was it exactly? And how many times did they visit Japan?
- What was the team name?
- What was their win-loss record?
- Do any statistics from their games in Japan exist?
- How were they perceived by Japanese players and fans?
- What was their impact on the start of professional baseball in Japan?

This was a quite an assignment that I got myself into, and all because I attended a SABR meeting. I took on the great challenge, and also felt a great responsibility.

However, after I returned home, when I opened the door of the Japanese Baseball Hall of Fame and Museum located in front of Korakuen Baseball Stadium, I thought to myself that I was pushing open the door to an unknown territory of baseball history.[9]

野球

2

A Black Team Was in Japan

It wasn't difficult to find the answer to the question that John asked me at the SABR conference. In fact, it was rather easy. I found the information in the first Japanese baseball history book that I picked up. It was called the *Official Baseball Guide* and it contained information about the mysterious team of black players. They were known as the Philadelphia Royal Giants.

On page 193 of the *Official Baseball Guide* (Showa 58, 1983 edition) was the list, "American Pro Teams That Visited Japan and their Records." It reflected all known professional teams from America to visit Japan.

Upon closer inspection, the list revealed that during the ten-year period prior to the start of professional baseball in Japan (Showa 1-11, 1926-1936), only four pro teams came to Japan. Two of the tours were by major league all-stars, and the other two were Negro League teams. The information that John shared with me was correct.

As I list the order of the four teams and their tours to Japan below, notice that they alternate between teams of black players and teams of white players:

YEAR	TEAM	W-L-T
Showa 2 (1927)	Philadelphia Royal Giants	23-0-1
Showa 6 (1931)	Major League All-Stars	17-0-0
Showa 7-8 (1932-33)	Philadelphia Royal Giants	23-1-0
Showa 9 (1934)	Major League All-Stars	17-0-0

American Professional Teams in Japan and Results

YEAR*	TEAM	GAMES	W-L-T
'08 (Meiji 41)	Reach All Americans	17	17-0-0
'13 (Taisho 2)	Major League World Tour vs. Keio	1	1-0-0
'20 (Taisho 9)	All American National	20	20-0-0
'22 (Taisho 11)	Major League All Stars	16	15-1-0
'27 (Showa 2)	Philadelphia Royal Giants	24	23-0-1
'31 (Showa 6, Yomiuri)	Major League All Stars	17	17-0-0
'32 (Showa 7)	Philadelphia Royal Giants	24	23-1-0
'34 (Showa 9, Yomiuri)	Major League All Stars	17	17-0-0
'49 (Showa 24, G.H.Q)	San Francisco Seals	7	7-0-0
'51 (Showa 26, Yomiuri)	Major League All Stars	16	13-1-2
'53 (Showa 28, Yomiuri)	Fall: New York Giants	14	12-1-1
'53 (Showa 28, Mainichi)	Fall: Major League All Stars	12	11-1-0
'55 (Showa 30, Mainichi)	New York Yankees	16	15-0-1
'56 (Showa 31, Yomiuri)	Brooklyn Dodgers	19	14-4-1
'58 (Showa 33, Mainichi)	St. Louis Cardinals	16	14-2-0
'60 (Showa 35, Yomiuri	San Francisco Giants	16	11-4-1
'62 (Showa 37, Mainichi)	Detroit Tigers	18	12-4-2
'66 (Showa 41, Kyodo)	Spring: Mexican Tigers	13	0-13-0
'66 (Showa 41, Yomiuri)	Fall: Los Angeles Dodgers	18	9-8-1
'68 (Showa 43, Yomiuri)	St. Louis Cardinals	18	13-5-0
'70 (Showa 45, Orions)	Spring: San Francisco Giants	9	3-6-0
'71 (Showa 46, Yomiuri)	Baltimore Orioles	18	12-2-4
'74 (Showa 49, Yomiuri)	New York Mets	18	9-7-2
'78 (Showa 53, Yomiuri)	Cincinnati Reds	17	14-2-1
'79 (Showa 54, Suponichii)	N.L. vs. A.L. All Stars	7	N.L 4-2-1 A.L. 2-4-1
79 (Showa 54, Suponichii)	A.L. All Stars vs Japan	2	1-1-0
'81 (Showa 56, Yomiuri)	Kansas City Royals	17	9-7-1
'84 (Showa 59, Yomiuri)	Baltimore Orioles vs. Hiroshima	5	4-1-0
'84 (Showa 59, Yomiuri)	Baltimore Orioles vs. All Japan	9	4-4-1

*Japanese organization that invited the team noted in parenthesis.

We now have proof that a professional team of Negro League players came to Japan at the beginning of the Showa era (circa 1926). This official publication supports this fact.

This evidence now leads us to the next question: Why is it that everyone in Japan knows about the Major League All-Star tours, but no one talks about the Negro League tours? Why the disparity? How can it be that a team visited Japan twice, was officially recorded by historians, yet remained neglected by researchers for over 50 years?

Despite the historic oversight, I feel fortunate to have confirmed their presence in Japan. We now know their team name, and how well they performed in Japan.

Back then, the team name was written as "Ro-yal Giants" in Japan, but today it is written correctly as "Royal Giants." And we know that during their two tours combined, they played 48 games, won 46, lost one and tied one.

Amazingly, the Major League All-Stars went undefeated in their 34 combined games.

The major leaguers had a better winning percentage, but the Negro Leaguers played more games. Before professional baseball was established in Japan, the top players in Japan played in more games against black players than white players. I suspect that the Japanese players benefited greatly from these additional games.

To confirm this hypothesis, I needed to know more about the specific games—which Japanese teams participated and played against the Royal Giants. Without that information, I could not sufficiently answer John's questions.

So like any good baseball historian, I wandered into a wilderness of archival documents. Of course I knew that it would be almost impossible to locate game details in a baseball history book. And if they did contain any information, it would only scratch the surface.

In a book titled *100 Years of Baseball* (Kyuji Yamato: Jiji Press Co.) I located the following:

> In the spring of Showa 2 (1927), the Waseda University baseball team toured the U.S. Afterwards, many teams from America came to Japan, one after another. They included: a black American team called the Philadelphia Royal Giants, the Fresno Japanese American team, and California State University. The black American team performed exceptionally well, with 23 wins and a tie in 24 games. They returned to America undefeated.

The book *100 Years of Baseball* was a gigantic almanac. It contained over 700 pages, but had only three lines of text about the Showa 2 (1927) tours, and part of that was dedicated to a college team. Nonetheless, the Royal Giants were mentioned by name, and the description emphasized their dominance against the competition in Japan. I think this is very important.

In another book, titled *Japanese Baseball History* (Kenzou Hirose: Japanese Baseball History Publication Society, Kankokai Inc.), I located a team roster and a description that detailed how baseball fans in Japan viewed these powerful players:

> In Showa 2 (1927), the "Philadelphia Ro-yal Giants" arrived in Japan!
>
> The first game was against the Mita Club on April 1, at Meiji Jingu Stadium. They returned to the U.S. with wins in all games except one draw with Daimai (the Osaka Mainichi Shimbun team).
>
> The Japanese fans were mesmerized by, just to name a couple, a great defender, the shortstop Mackey, and a strong-armed left fielder, Dixon. The black team did not have any problems with the Japanese-American team from Fresno, who themselves had made a clean sweep against the all Japanese college teams. The result was 9 to 1, the black team winning without any doubt.

I found several brief records of home runs and longest hits. A book titled *Celebrating a Half Century of Glorious Jingu Stadium* describes the following:

> In Showa 2 (1927), Saburo Miyatake of Keio University hit the first home run. On April 29, which was Emperor Hirohito's birthday, Miyatake of Keio University hit a ball that was thrown by Azuma of Tokyo University on 1-0 count to the mid-left grandstand in the 8th inning. He recorded the first home run in Jingu Stadium in the Big Six college league. However, before that day, Mackey, a player of the Philadelphia Royal Giants (a professional Negro League team) that visited Japan in April, hit a home run on April 20. This is the first one by a foreign player. Miyatake holds the record for the first home run by a Japanese player.

In the book *Twenty Five Years of Pro Baseball* (published by Houchi Shimbun), I was able to learn more about Rap Dixon's prodigious hits in Koshien Stadium.

> The power alley from home plate in Koshien Stadium at that time was 417 feet (127 meters). Because of that, there were no players who were able to hit the ball into the outfield seats. Two players who recorded a home run over the outfield fence at Koshien were Dixon with the Negro baseball team (he hit it on April 6, Showa 2 (1927), against Daimai's pitcher Watanabe) and Larry Dihel from the University of Southern California (on June 10, Showa 3 [1928], against Keio University pitcher Ueno).[1]

Additionally, in Showa 6 (1931), [Ralph] Shinners of the Major League All-Star team hit a ball from Date (a pitcher with Waseda University) and [Al] Simmons hit a line drive ball from Ueno (pitcher from Keio University) off the wall. Simmons was honored to write his name and the date on the wall that he hit. He also received a cash prize of 100 yen. The original fence at Koshien Stadium was demolished and replaced in Showa 11 (1936) when the stadium was remodeled with new outfield seats.

With that, we not only have proof that a professional Negro League team visited Japan, we now know about their powerful hitting ability as well. Unfortunately, the books referenced above do not mention anything about the Royal Giants' visit to Japan in Showa 7 (1932).

This tour followed the visit of Lou Gehrig and other major league players that created a sensation in Japan in Showa 6 (1931). Even though the Negro Leaguers proved themselves to be the same caliber of players as the Major League All-Stars, the Japanese fans did not give as much attention to the Royal Giants.

Therefore, to learn the details behind their records, I needed to research the archives from Showa 2 (1927). I knew the name of the team, and the scores of the games. And in my mind I could only imagine how they played. I thought to myself that I am now becoming the team's historian.

For the first time I discovered the players' names and ages in a copy of the *Japan Times and Mail* (now known as the *Japan Times*). The newspaper also described their arrival in Japan and their schedule. The following is from the sports section dated March 30:

The Black Baseball Team Arrives!

The first overseas team to arrive in Japan is the Philadelphia Royal Giants. They arrived in Yokohama on the ship *La Plata Maru*. They stayed in "Hosenkaku," which is an inn located in Kanda. There are 14 players with a manager, Lon Goodwin. All of them are well-experienced players. Before they came to Japan, they competed in the California Winter League. They must be in very good condition. Although the game schedule is not yet determined, today (Wednesday) they will practice for the first time in Meiji Jingu Stadium. They will watch a championship game between the Mita Club and the Tomon/Inakado Club. This will be the first time for them to watch Japanese teams. This team's visit was made possible through a contract arranged by George Irie. As the team manager, he is responsible for arranging all games in Japan and is currently trying to set up one game in Honolulu for their return trip back to the U.S. During their stay, the team will tour several cities and play at least 20 games against the first-class teams in Japan. The names and ages of the Philadelphia Royal Giants are as follows:

Pitcher	A. J. Johnson (23)
Pitcher	A. L. Cooper (26)
Pitcher	A. Evans (28)
Pitcher	E. A. Tucker (26)
Catcher	O'Neal Pullen (27)
First base	Frank Duncan (25)
Second base	Robert Fagan (24)
Third base	Jesse Walker (18)
Shortstop	J. Riddle (24)
Left field	Herbert Dixon (23)
Center field	Joe Cade (25)
Right field	Green (23)
Captain	Raleigh Mackey (27)
Manager	L. Goodwin (44)

As you could imagine, I was extremely pleased to discover more details about the team's schedule and travels throughout Japan. I did not, however, see the name "Bullet Rogan," which John shared with me when we first met.[2]

I had also heard that the majority of the visiting team were members of the Kansas City Monarchs, but this article only mentioned Philadelphia. I am certain that Philadelphia was the top place for a black American baseball team in those days. However, I believe that the top Negro team in Philadelphia at that time was Hilldale. I had never heard of the Royal Giants of Philadelphia before.[3]

Furthermore, they had only 13 players on their roster, which seems small for a full team.[4] And it seemed strange to me that they were looking for teams to play against after they arrived in Japan.

While there were many unanswered questions, it was clear to me that they were passionate about playing baseball, as they started practicing the day after they arrived in Japan.

I located additional information about the games in a "specialty publication" that I thought was the last place I would find anything about the Royal Giants. According to this book, the first game occurred on April 1, one day after their initial practice. The game appears to be the result of successful negotiations by tour manager George Irie.

I gather that the Japanese media did not fully understand who these guests from America actually were. An article from *Yakyukai* (17th edition, No. 16) refers to the players as "American Indians."

The following is an excerpt from the article about the Negro team playing against the Mita Club from Keio University:

Black Players Visit Japan

The "Philadelphia Royal Giants" sounds like a magnificent name. This team of American Indians became very famous and the entire stadium was almost full except the first-class seats. The first game started at 2:43 pm on April 1 and they played against the Mita force in the Gaien Stadium.

The stadium was jam-packed because people had heard that the black players had the reputation of being a powerful team. While the Mita Club were practicing on the field, the Royal Giants entered with big smiles and were welcomed by loud applause from the crowd. They wore off-white jerseys just like the Sundai uniform. The Royal Giants started to entertain the fans. They began light warm-ups and batting practice. They hit very well for sure. All their hits looked like line drives. They were well-built and physically much stronger than Mita's batters. During fielding practice, the shortstop, Mackey, showed off his strong arm. The speed of the ball was like a bullet. The first baseman (Duncan) also performed well with his slick glove work. Both Mackey and the first baseman shined among the infielders. However, some flaws in their fielding skills were noticeable. If the Japanese team were to stand a chance, they needed to take advantage of the Giants' weak points. Now came game time. It was 2:43 pm. There were two umpires, Ikeda and Oki. The game started with the Mita going to bat first. The pitchers were Sei and Cooper.

野球

3

Unknown Power

Now let's focus on the games! This will tell us how well the Philadelphia Royal Giants, the team made up entirely of professional black players, performed in Japan.

According to an English-language newspaper in Japan, the Royal Giants first played in the California Winter League and came straight across the Pacific Ocean. It was not uncommon for the major leaguers to seek warmer climates to continue playing after the regular season ended. It is easy to imagine that professional players who struggled financially in the Negro Leagues would seek similar off-season opportunities out west.

But when they arrived in Japan not all the players looked like all-star caliber players from the Negro Leagues. The black team assembled for this tour of Japan appeared to be more of a mixture of players with different skill levels.

With that in mind, I wondered how this scratch team comprised of players from different teams performed against the best teams in Japan.

According to available documents, the Mita Club from Keio University put up a good fight, even though the Royal Giants won by the score of 2-0.[1]

Score by inning:

Mita   0 0 0 0 0 0 0 0 0 = 0
Royal Giants   1 1 0 0 0 0 0 0 A = 2A

The difference in power was evident based on the offense displayed in the first and second innings. Shinji Hamazaki, who later became a manager of the Hankyu team, was the first batter for the Mita Club. He struck out against Cooper's fast ball. The second batter, Sugai, grounded out to first base. The third batter, Nagai, also grounded out to the shortstop. Mita could not get a rally going.

On the other hand, the offense of the Royal Giants started off strong. The first batter, Duncan, lined a single to centerfield. After one ball, Duncan stole second base while the second batter, Fagan, executed a successful hit and run by placing a ground ball between the first and second basemen. Runners were now on first and third. Mackey grounded out to the shortstop, but he was able to drive in Duncan from third base for the first run of the game.

In the second inning, both teams displayed their distinctive qualities. The fans must have really enjoyed the game. The fourth batter, Nomura of Mita Club, lined a clean hit to right-center field. The next batter was a famous player, Michimaro Ono. He hit softly to the pitcher Cooper, who attempted to get the force out at second base, but the runner beat the throw. The fielder's choice resulted in runners on first and second base.

Two runners were on and nobody out. Perhaps the Japanese baserunners became a bit overzealous and lost their focus? Pullen, the catcher with a strong arm, picked off the runner at second base. The next batter, Okada, grounded to shortstop Mackey for an inning-ending double play.

In the bottom of the second inning, outfielder Hamazaki executed a fine play which excited the whole stadium. The Royal Giants' offense started with Mackey's walk. When Cade hit a long drive out to the right-center gap, Hamazaki ran and reached out to catch the ball. He quickly threw the ball to first base. Although Hamazaki was unable to get the double play, the fans showered him with applause and cheers. However, on next play, Hamazaki misplayed Evans's fly ball and it rolled all the way to the fence, allowing Pullen to score from first base.

After the third inning, the Mita pitcher Nagai controlled the game and limited the damage of the Royal Giants' offensive attack. They continued to mount rallies, getting several hits, but could not convert any of their chances to score. Despite Nagai's brilliant pitching performance, Mita's offense produced only three hits and drew zero walks, so they had little opportunity to win.

> The team was as powerful as I expected and played up to their reputation. Their fielding ability was indeed fantastic, but their batting was inconsistent. Even though there were a few amazing and skillful hitters on the team, their offense paled in comparison to their fielding. If we played against them again, as long as we use good pitchers, we might be able to make it an interesting game. In short, I think that the Negro team is a defense-oriented team.

This commentary was offered in the *Yakyukai* by Yutaka Ikeda, of the Tomon Club. Other writers agreed with his opinion.

Because the final score was 2-0, many felt that the Royal Giants' batting was not as strong as expected. Interestingly, the black team seems to have left an impression of being unbalanced, skill wise. In the same magazine, another editorial argued that:

> ...Today Mita's offense had no chance to win. However, if I were asked by someone whether or not this Negro team is as outstanding a team as rumored, I would hesitate to say "yes." I saw them hit and field and noted their fine plays here and there, but somehow they lacked refined skills. Their game strategy was limited. Their poor base running was especially noticeable. Of course, my conclusions could not be definitive after watching just one game, but this is what I observed. However, I do think that if the Japanese teams had stronger bats and more offensive power, they might not be able to beat the Royal Giants, but maybe they could make it a tie game.

Clearly, the review was mixed. On one hand it was positive, pointing out "impressive batting and fielding plays," and at the same time negative, with the observation that in some areas the players "lacked certain skills." I think that what he meant was that this team lacked "refined harmony."[2] This observation would later become very significant.

Based on the 2-0 score of the first game, one could easily leave with the impression that they were both defense-oriented teams. However, this notion did not last long, judging from the second game.

*   *   *

Let's look at the second game, played on April 2nd between the same teams—Mita versus the Royal Giants. Here are the highlights:

- 10 to 6 – The Negro team won again.
- The total number of hits (for both teams) was 25.
- Mackey hit a big triple!

As the headlines in the magazine *Yakyukai* showed, the second game was a high-scoring affair. The Japanese players hit well and scored six runs, but it was not enough to match the Royal Giants, who scored ten. What kind of game was it? Here is the line score:

Score by inning:

Mita   2 0 1 0 0 1 2 0 0 = 6
Royal Giants   1 3 0 1 0 1 4 0 A = 10A

In the first inning, after Murakawa of Mita walked, Sugai hit safely to left field. After two outs, Hamazaki lined a double to left field, driving in two runs. As for the Royal Giants, Mackey and Dixon recorded back-to-back hits to load the bases. The next batter walked to bring in a run.

The Royal Giants continued to pile on more runs in the second inning. With one out and two runners on, Fagan knocked a base hit to right field, driving in another run. After Mackey got a free pass with a base on balls, Dixon hit the ball hard between third and short, to bring the run total to three for the inning.

Afterwards, both teams scored bit by bit. By the top of the seventh, the score was finally tied at 6-6. The home fans must have been really excited, but their excitement didn't last long. The black team battled back and put the game out of reach with their explosive offense.

> As soon as the game became tied, the bench of the black team got more excited, started to fight back and launched a powerful attack. Cade ripped a knock to third base. Green bunted for an infield base hit. The next batter was shortstop John Riddle, who made his first appearance in the game and hit a sharp ground ball that deflected off the pitcher's (Hamazaki's) glove into right field. As the ball rolled to the outfield, Cade and Green scored safely. Afterwards Duncan hit a fly ball to left field for the second out. Fagan then rolled a base hit past the shortstop and Riddle came in to score easily. Mackey then lined a base hit to left field. Dixon followed with a double and Fagan came in to score. The Mita Club sent in a relief pitcher, Machida, to replace Hamazaki. Pullen then hit a grounder to the shortstop, who forced Dixon out at third base on a fielder's choice.

After that, both teams continued to hit and put runners on base, but in the end, the Japanese team lost by four due to their weaker hitting. It was amazing to see three hitters in the game have perfect 3-for 3 days at the plate. They were:

Hamazaki: 2 2B, 1B, BB (single, two doubles, walk)
Mackey: 3B, 2 1B, 2 BB (two singles, triple, two walks)
Dixon: 2B, 2 1B, SF, BB (two singles, double, sac fly, walk)

ROYAL GIANTS

	AB	R	H	BB	SO
3 Duncan	4	2	1	1	0
4 Fagan	5	3	2	0	0

6,1 Mackey	3	1	3	2	0
8 Dixon	3	0	3	1	0
2 Pullen	4	0	0	1	0
7 Cade	5	1	1	1	1
9 Green	5	1	1	0	2
5 Walker	4	0	1	0	1
1,6 Evans	2	1	1	1	1
6 Riddle	1	1	1	0	0
Totals	36	10	14	7	5

	MITA				
	AB	R	H	BB	SO
5 Murakawa	4	1	2	1	1
4 Kirihara	3	2	1	2	1
8 Sugai	5	1	1	0	1
9 Nagai	5	1	2	0	1
1 Hamazaki	3	0	3	1	0
1 Machida	1	0	0	0	0
3 Ono	2	0	0	0	0
3 Mitani	3	1	1	0	0
2 Ito	2	0	0	0	1
2 Okada	3	0	0	0	2
7 Nitta	2	0	0	1	0
7 Nomura	1	0	0	0	1
6 Kato	3	0	1	1	0
Totals	37	6	11	8	8

By the way, Mackey's triple bounced off the center field fence, and would have been a home run in any other ballpark. At that time, it was the record for the farthest ball ever hit at Meiji Shrine Stadium.

To tell the truth, this second game against the Mita Club might not have been on the official schedule for the Royal Giants. After arriving at the Yokohama port, the players rested a few days in Tokyo to recover from their long journey.

While the team was resting, Mr. Irie, the tour organizer and promoter, must have wanted to set up games with teams in the Kansai region. However, the Mita Club was unexpectedly willing to play, delightfully resulting in two exhibition games. Playing more games meant more money for the black players. They must have been happy to add the game to the schedule.

After the second game, the Royal Giants went straight to Tokyo Station to catch a night train for the game scheduled at Koshien Stadium the next day.

The two extra games in Tokyo were a great opportunity to introduce the Royal Giants to the public. Several baseball magazines and sports newspapers wrote about their impression of the Royals' power.

For example, I would like to refer to an article by Mr. Aomine in the May, Showa 2 (1927), issue of the magazine *Undo Kai*. The original article is very long. Even though I have chosen select quotes, they are still somewhat lengthy. They demonstrate his curiosity about the foreign team (the Royal Giants) and his sincere interest for the game of baseball. The article is well written and I regret that I can share only a portion of it.

Impressions of the Negro Team

Rumors about the black team spread quickly throughout the Japanese baseball community. Everybody was talking about the arrival of the black squad with their exceptional skills and capabilities. In fact, no one really knew much about their true abilities. There must be varying levels of talent in the Negro Leagues. According to one person who knew a lot about American baseball, if they were actual Negro League all-stars, they would easily dominate the Japanese teams. But if the team were made up of a bunch of untalented players and worse than the previous visitors, the Sherman Indians, then the games would be unimpressive. So until we saw them play, we didn't know how good they were. So, we thought, let's just enjoy watching the Negro players perform. After seeing the actual games, I thought the way they played on the first day was greatly different from the second day. Either way, the team was very talented, without a doubt.

Strong Arms

On the first day, I was shocked to see how strong their arms were. Every player had one. Especially shortstop Mackey's "bullet ball." He had a cannon for an arm, as did Duncan, the first baseman. The catcher Pullen's powerful arm was beyond our imagination! If I may be allowed to use hyperboles, I'd say that they throw a ball so hard that you cannot even see it. They could throw a ball from second to home, first to third, home to second – straight to its target on a line without a crow hop. Furthermore, they threw with amazing velocity. The Japanese players might not be able to catch their throws.

(text omitted)

I heard that Mackey and the left fielder, Dixon, boasted that they could throw a ball over the center field fence, out of Gaien Stadium, and all the way to the bank of the river. For the Japanese players, this would be an impossible task even with a fungo bat. People often exaggerate in their stories, but in this case, it was true about the difference between the two arm strengths. It was like comparing a gun to a bow and arrow. Furthermore, their strong pitching with pinpoint accuracy was astonishing as well. The combination of their strong arms and effortless accuracy left me speechless.

Defense

With their strong arms, they were good defenders. Rather than being skillful and agile like dogs and rabbits, they were big and powerful like cows and horses.

(text omitted)

A remarkable play occurred in the sixth inning of game two when the hot-hitting Hamazaki ripped a curve ball down the first base line. He made great contact, but the first baseman, Duncan, dove and used his body to stop the tricky ball and then picked it up with his bare hand. He got up and slid back to first base. Hamazaki flew down the line like a bullet trying to beat Duncan at first. As they both collided violently at first base, their cleats clashed almost bringing about sparks. Even though the runner was safe, it was still an exciting play by Duncan.

Another fine play was made afterwards. Mitani was pinch-hitting for Ono, and with a 1-1 count, Mitani pulled an inside pitch. It looked like a line drive to the outfield, but the third baseman, Walker (18 years old), stretched his body up high to rob Mitani of a hit. Walker quickly threw it to second base to double up Hamazaki. He made the play so skillfully and naturally. It was unbelievable. The Negro team's defense is indeed strong.

Batting

… It was hard to believe the black team lacked hitting ability, given their outstanding skill, speed, and power on the defensive side. The Mita's stunning defense might have affected their batting, but the Negro team seemed to have great potential. Undoubtedly, they must be able to hit.

Pitchers

With regards to pitching, Cooper threw on the first day, which seemed to indicate that he was the ace of the team. His performance confirmed that he did indeed have the skill of an ace. The rest of the pitching staff didn't compare to Cooper. Due to the fact that everything else was solid except for their pitching, the Giants were regarded as a mysterious team.

Although this quotation seems very long, I only included the main points in each section, and had to omit the sections on "Base Running" and "Game Details." Hopefully I was able to convey how Japanese people were impressed by the power of this team.

It was interesting that he described the team as "mysterious" just because the pitchers were not as great as the other players. Why was the pitching so weak? At this point, this question could not be answered. Later on, after the black team played more games, the answer to the question would become apparent.

The most prominent writer of *Yakyukai* magazine, Mr. Hoshuu Hida, also had a hunch that the visiting black team was talented, but imperfect. Later, he wrote an interesting essay with comments and predictions about the visiting black team, which appeared in *Asahi Sports*. This will be featured in later chapters.

While these fanatic baseball writers were sitting at their desks and writing from their passionate hearts, the 14 black visitors headed down to the western region of Japan on the Tokaido line.

野球

4

Are They Pro or Semi-Pro?

A black professional baseball team arrives in Japan!

Prior to the fall of Showa 58 (1983), I had the opportunity to meet some former players of the Mita Club who competed against the Royal Giants. I was eager to stroll down memory lane with them, but they did not remember as much as I hoped. As a result, I nearly gave up looking for a first-hand source. These games occurred over 50 years ago. Perhaps getting vivid, eyewitness testimony was expecting too much?

Then I met Mr. Saburo Yokozawa, a former Japanese ballplayer who competed against the visiting black team. He played for Meiji University and then for the Daimai Club, the best team in Japan near the end of the Taisho era (1920s). When his playing career ended, Mr. Yokozawa became the first manager of the Tokyo Senators in Showa 11 (1936), and later became a lead umpire for the Pacific League. When the all-black team from American arrived in Japan, his Daimai Club faced them at Koshien Stadium.[1]

"Was the black team called the Royal Giants?" I asked Mr. Yokozawa.

"Yes, I remember them well. During my lifetime no team was more memorable. I can still vividly picture the faces of some of the ballplayers. Well, there were Dixon ... and Mackey, wasn't that their names?"

He spoke with a distinct voice and a lively smile beamed from his golf-tanned face. As he nostalgically recalled his experiences with the Royal Giants, I finally was able to set my mind at ease.

Even though some of the information about the Royal Giants was available in publications and archives, I needed to have first-hand testimonies from people who actually met them. Hearing their stories made the legend of the Royal Giants more real to me.

"What do you remember about the team?"

Mr. Yokozawa reflected for a second. "It was a mysterious team. Their power left a strong first impression on me. In addition to their strength, they were quick and moved with a graceful fluidity. Perhaps this was most impressive because compared to them I was not as skilled. But as time passed, I started to think that they were indeed an imbalanced team."

His words and expressions were surprisingly sharp and articulate. In addition, the accuracy of his memory was remarkable. I wondered if this was because he had been an umpire for a long time.

> To tell the truth, I knew something about the caliber of black baseball players at that time. It was in the fall of Taisho 12 (1923) that Meiji University won the first league championship. The roster of this team was fantastic. Yuasa, Amachi, Tanizawa, Umeda, Nidegawa, Hayashi, Daimon, Inaba, and myself. In the spring of the following year we were sent to America and Hawaii for exhibition games. We missed the Spring League season to make the trip, which took us about four months. Our opponents were mainly semi-professional and college baseball teams.[2] I don't recall the names of the places, but I remember we played against a couple of black teams. We always thought that the baseball in America was for white people, so at first we were really confused by their presence.

What about the scores?

> I recall that we had some wins and losses. As for the Royal Giants, we had anticipated that this team would be at the same level as the black teams we played in America. But once we saw them practice on the field in Koshien, they appeared to be totally different from what we expected. Especially the power of three or four key players. I had never seen anyone like them before. Just watching them practice put us in awe of their extraordinary strength. The difference in their power was amazing … We all sighed helplessly. This is no use. We are not going to win against them. In fact, it was just after this when we realized that they were a special team. Let me tell you what I mean …

He held back a grin on his face, as he pondered and tilted his head.

> Once we started playing, it was a great game. We were afraid, but as it turned out we had no reason to be. Of course we played hard. The real difference in their strength did not appear in the score, so we grew relaxed and enjoyed the game. We had thought that we were going to be destroyed, but the outcome was much different. It was a bittersweet loss. Despite the fact that they were a superior team, their attitude towards us was not one of arrogance. In fact, they were quite gentlemanly. We were surprised by their kindness. We wondered

why we were able to play a good game. It was really unexpected because they were not, by any means, worse than the major league all-star team that came to Japan a few years later.

By the way, I wondered if it was true that the caliber of the top black players matched that of the white players at that time.

The history of black baseball was not short at all. Jackie Robinson had become the first black major leaguer in 1947, but prior to that baseball was an integral part of black America. The National Negro Baseball League was founded in 1920 and considered "another major league."

There is a widely-held theory that the Civil War (1861-1865) was the reason for the quick, widespread popularity of baseball in America, even in the black community. It all started with the Union and Confederate armies, with each side playing baseball for entertainment during the breaks in the fighting. After the war, the soldiers went home, formed teams, and played games everywhere. This was how baseball first became popular in America.

At the time of Showa 2 (1927), it was undeniable that the black teams had reached the same level as the major league teams.[3] Black baseball was well established and reaching its peak performance. If this team, the Royal Giants, was made up of players from the Negro Leagues, it was understandable that the Japanese players should have been mesmerized by their remarkable talents.

Mr. Yokozawa's assessment that the Royal Giants were all as good as the major leaguers, made by a person who had played against the black team, was not shared by everybody. I found a critic who had some knowledge of the Negro Leagues. It was Mr. Hoshuu Hida of Waseda University. He was known to be rather influential within the College Baseball Association. In his essay in *Asahi Sports*, dated April 15, Showa 2 (1927), he speculated, based on two games that he watched in Tokyo, that not every one of the Royal Giants was an elite player.

At the same time, though, he thought it was difficult to evaluate their hidden talents. He also developed an opinion of their sportsmanship, along with other thoughts intertwined through his essay. It was very valuable information. It is worth comparing his comments to those of Mr. Saburo Yokozawa, about an event that occurred more than a half century ago.

> We welcomed the Philadelphia Royal Giants from America to Japan ... I had heard that members of this black professional team had also impressed the New York Giants in the past. In fact, when I visited America last year, I truly enjoyed watching the Negro League games in Indianapolis. Only black spectators filled the stadium. There must have been

over 30,000 people there. The roar of the excited fans rumbled throughout the stadium. The noise was deafening.

With the velocity of the strong pitching and the hits crashing into the outfield bleachers like meteors, the games were just like the major leagues. The only difference was the color of the ballplayers' skin. Because blacks were once slaves, the whites were perceived as superior in America. And eventually people with yellow skin were discriminated against as well. I suspect that the increasing population of the black race must be viewed as a threat to the white community. It would be especially disruptive to the white baseball community. It is odd that American Indians are allowed to join the major league teams, but players of African descent, who are citizens of the country, are not allowed to join. Just because of the color of their skin, they are not treated as equal human beings. They face so much discrimination back home in America—I heard the players say that if a war took place between the U.S. and Japan, they would cheer for Japan. Life is not as simple as baseball. When they say that they would cheer for Japan, they are saying that we are a colored race, too.

Does their sympathy for Japan come from the idea that we are in the same boat? Having watched Japanese players on the baseball field during the game against the black team, I think that, from a distance, the color of the Japanese seems closer to that of the white players. Only half of the players of the Royal Giants team have dark skin, while the rest appear to be mixed race. Those players of many races, whose gloves and hands are the same color, must be considered "All-Americans."

The team is not only mixed race, they are mixed talent as well. Many of the players have the appropriate skills to be considered semi-pros, but not all of them can be considered elite, professional ballplayers.

First of all, the team is not consistent in their batting skills, and their base running is poor. Second, the pitching staff as a whole is weak. Only the left-hander, Cooper, is a skillful pitcher. Evans and Johnson cannot match his pitching skill.

(omitted text)

As for the batters, Mackey, Dixon, and Fagan all have excellent abilities, as does Duncan. Fagan is an interesting case. He is a skillful batter. The rest of the players are not as good, and are not worth discussing here. Mackey and Dixon clearly are the sluggers of this team and they must have looked like a big threat to the Japanese pitchers.

As for fielding, the shortstop Mackey is outstanding. He is a great fielder and throws the ball in a straight line. Unfortunately, there are no Japanese players like him. His build is enormous. He is even a lot bigger than the sumo wrestler Tochigiyama when standing side by side.[4]

The black team is too predictable, as their strategy is almost non-existent. It is simply a power game, so to speak. However, they can still dominate against the Japanese teams because of the shortage of pitchers in our baseball community. If we had played three to four years ago, when Ono, Taniguchi, Yuasa, and Takeuchi were in their primes, and they joined our lineup, then the yellow versus black game would have been an exciting one.

(omitted text)

The Royal Giants never made us feel inferior. They played hard in those two games against the Mita Club. They were much better than the semi-pro team from the Philippines that came to Japan last year.

From these statements, it becomes evident that the Royal Giants were indeed an unusual team—even though many people rightly praised the players for their power, the black team was clearly comprised of mixed levels of talent. How this unique team of ballplayers was formed had not yet been revealed in my research. I needed to locate a profile of the players detailing their reasons for coming to Japan.[5]

What's most interesting is the fact that they left a good impression, as Mr. Hida's last comment demonstrates. Unfortunately, he did not illustrate with any particular examples from their games.

Mr. Yokozawa described the Royal Giants as gentlemanly. In fact, he remembered them more for their kindness than for their power. Could he provide any examples?

He suggested that I look at their second game in the Kansai region. I decided to check all the games in chronological order, using *Yakyukai, Undokai* and *Asahi Sports* as my sources.

In Koshien, their first game took place at 2:10 pm, on April 3, Showa 2 (1927). The black team's first opponent was the veteran Japanese team called the Diamond Club, made up of Keio and Meiji University alumni.

The pitcher for the Diamonds was Nagai, who had also pitched in the first game in Tokyo. Green was the starter for the Royal Giants.

In the first inning the Diamonds' offense was relentless. Takahama reached base on an error. The next batter, Nagai, hit, and Takahama ran to third base. As Nagai advanced to second base on the play, Takahama came home. The Diamonds had scored first. It was thought that in order to win against the black team, the Japanese teams must get an early lead to startle them. This game was going according to plan.

However, the Royals' offense countered with their own blows in the bottom of the first inning.

Duncan led off with a walk, and the second batter, Fagan, bunted and advanced Duncan to second. After that, Duncan tried to steal third. The flustered catcher, Koshiba, made an errant throw past third, leading to a run for the black team. Next, Mackey drew a walk from the distressed pitcher, Nagai. The following batter, Dixon, smashed a single to center field. With the runners now at first and third, Dixon proceeded to steal second base. Pullen then hit a triple to right. Two runners came home. The total runs for that inning were three.

In the third inning, Takahama doubled between left and center, which drove in a run for the Diamonds. But they were again attacked by the Royal Giants' offense in the bottom of the inning. Mackey lined a base hit to the shortstop. Dixon followed with a double to right field, putting runners on second and third. Pullen then hit a ball to center, driving in both Mackey and Dixon.

After the fourth inning, the Diamonds failed to score, while the Royals added more runs. In the fifth inning Dixon smashed a triple over the center fielder's head. Pullen hit a sacrifice fly and Dixon scored. In the sixth inning, Green also hit a triple to right field and Duncan then brought Green home.

At the beginning, the Japanese team played vigorously, but by the end of the game they were totally defeated. The score was 7A to 2.

Score by inning:

Diamonds   1 0 1 0 0 0 0 0 0 = 2
Royal Giants   3 0 2 0 1 1 0 0 A = 7A

In Tokyo, the Royals showed their strong defense, but in Kansai their extraordinary offense really shined, especially the fourth batter, Dixon, and the fifth batter, Pullen, who showed some amazingly destructive hitting power. Dixon had five at bats with one triple, one double, and three singles.[6] Pullen had one triple, one single, and one sacrifice fly.

*   *   *

Let's take a look at the second game. It took place the next day, again at Koshien. Expectations for the powerful Daimai Club were immense.

The pitcher for the Japanese team was the highly-respected star Michimaro Ono.[7] He had pitched well against the black team in the first game in Tokyo, giving up only two runs. He had been known as a fastball pitcher since his time at Keio University, where he shared popularity with another pitcher, Goro Taniguchi of Waseda. After his graduation, he pitched against a major league all-star team led by Herbert Hunter in Taisho 11 (1922). Ono won the game 9-3. It was the first win for a Japanese pitcher against major league players. He joined the *Mainichi Shimbun* newspaper and continued to perform as a core player on the Daimai Club. Later on, in Showa 34 (1959), he became one of the first Hall of Famers for his distinguished service in developing the National Intercity Amateur Baseball Championship Series. He was 30 years old when he pitched against the Royal Giants team. He must have been past his prime, but he pitched competitively.

As for the Royals, they countered with captain Biz Mackey as their pitcher. This second game left the Japanese hosts with a good impression, as it was a pitcher's duel. There was barely any offensive action all the way up to the latter part of the game.

By the eighth inning, no Daimai batter had reached second base, but the Royals had also failed to create any scoring opportunities. They had six hits, but no one came home to score.

The winning run was scored in the ninth inning. The Japanese squad was on offense. It was with two outs.

When Yokozawa smashed a single to left field and got on base, nobody thought it was going to be the winning run. When the next batter, Sugai, hit a fly ball to right, it seemed clear the game was headed to extra innings as a 0-0 tie.

However, the right fielder, Evans, dropped the ball. Yokozawa came home and the game was over.

Score by inning:

Royal Giants	0 0 0 0 0 0 0 0 0	= 0
Daimai	0 0 0 0 0 0 0 0 1	= 1

"Is that so? Does it say in the magazine that the Daimai won the game?"

The man of the hour, Mr. Saburo Yokozawa, who scored the only run in the game, could not help but smile wryly. He confessed:

> No. That is a mistake. Actually the score was corrected to a tie game, 1-1. Even we, the ones who played against them, did not think that we actually won the game.
>
> To tell the truth, everybody in the media was trying to figure out which Japanese team could upset the Royal Giants. Everybody thought that we would be the ones. It might have affected the umpires' thinking. Maybe they were hoping for the first win by a Japanese team to occur as soon as possible.

However, the Royal Giants were big-hearted about the situation. Reflecting on the game, we were ashamed. In fact the Royal Giants had also scored a run, but the umpires failed to give them credit for it. Most people will argue or try to fight back when this sort of thing happens, but the black players did not.

野球

5

Quiet Giants

Typically, teams from the U.S. were arrogant. They were full of pride because they believed America was an advanced baseball country. The attitude of most teams was, "Let us teach you!" instead of "Let us enjoy baseball together!"

This arrogance was not only revealed in the way they played, but in their attitude about the rules of baseball as well.

However, when it came to the Royal Giants, everything about them was the opposite.

The catcher Mr. Shigeyoshi Koshiba, of the Diamond Club, was watching the game between the Royal Giants and the Daimai Club with the scoring error.[1] He shares his memory of what happened:

> It was certain that they scored one run, but it was not counted. It was clear that the umpires made a mistake interpreting the rule. I could not believe how the Royals quietly allowed the umpire's controversial call to go uncontested. This was how the problematic run was scored.
>
> I am not sure which inning it was, but there was one out with a runner on third when the batter smashed a big hit to right field. The outfielder ran far and made a great play. The runner on third, of course, tagged up to ensure a run. The ball was thrown to the catcher from the right fielder, but it was too late. After that, the catcher threw the ball to first. The runner on first base was trying to run to second and quickly returned back to first, but he arrived late and was tagged out.
>
> It was the third out and ended the inning. That was okay, but the umpires should have counted the runner who tagged up from third. The run was made before the third out. However, the umpire mistakenly called 'no run,' thinking it was a double play.

According to the record, it happened in the fourth inning. After one out, Dixon hit a single. Later, Pullen smashed a hit to right field, and the runners were now at first and third.

It was Cade who hit the big fly ball to right field. The runner on third base was Dixon, who had great speed, so the sacrifice fly must have been easy to execute.

"A strange thing occurred after that." Mr. Yokozawa remembered the details vividly:

> They [the Royal Giants] did not argue with the umpire's call that "due to the double play, no run was in." Initially, they showed their dissatisfaction with unhappy faces, but they quickly accepted the decision. "If that's your call, we will agree with you." They accepted easily, just like that. We were the ones in shock.
>
> Although some players from the Japanese team tried to point out the erroneous call to the umpire, Tomigashi-kun, he did not change his ruling. During this time, the black players started to run onto the field to take their positions, saying, "That's okay!" I could not believe what they did. I have never seen a team act like them before. The result should have been corrected and revised later to a tie of 1-1.

As for Mr. Yokozawa, he remembered the Royal Giants as a team with unknown, seemingly limitless powers, and at the same time as a team full of gentlemen.

By the way, their relaxed attitude toward competition, their open-heartedness and their friendly nature, were not just evident because they were playing in Japan. Rather, it was said that this was their "true form." It is safe to reach conclusions about their innate qualities, because the same kind of situation was seen in Hawaii, where they stopped on their way home. This article was printed in the *Hawaii Hochi*, dated June 6, Showa 2 (1927):

> The black baseball squad, the Royal Giants, is as strong as rumor states it to be. It was amazing that they effortlessly won against the Asahi baseball team and the Standard [Oil] squad. Everybody was mesmerized by the skills of the shortstop Mackey. His speed and quickness on defense and his strong throws were remarkable.
>
> The Japanese can learn from both their technique and their outstanding sportsmanship. Jim Mann, who was the home plate umpire for the first game against the Asahi team, said: 'I have been a home plate umpire for many games, but I have never seen such a respectful team. In this game, I accidently called Cooper's excellent strike as a ball, so I told the catcher Pullen about it and he replied, 'Such a little mistake does not matter.' He did not seem to care about it one bit.'
>
> I believe that his words fully describe one of their most admirable characteristics.

Mr. Takeshi Mizuno talked about the gentleness of the Royal Giants in the *Yakyukai* magazine for June, Showa 2 (1927). Under the headline "The Gentle Baseball Players," he wrote:

> Even during the game, they were relaxed. Their actions and behavior in the hotel after the game were mellow as well. The volume of the conversation among themselves was kept to a minimum. Nobody could tell if they were there or not. During the interviews after the game, they responded with humility. The gossip by the women in the rear tenement was noisier.
>
> Mr. Irie shared these qualities. Their personalities were very calm and they were cordial. Because they lived in a white-dominated country and were not treated equally in America, the blacks related more to the Japanese American side in America, and liked the Japanese Americans. In this tour to Japan, they all enjoyed themselves, and they received a big welcome everywhere they went. They were uncomfortable at times because they were not used to this sort of positive treatment, but they had big smiles on their faces.
>
> When they were not playing baseball they liked to shoot billiards and go for walks for enjoyment. They also adored children and played with them gleefully. When they played billiards in the hotels, which they did often, they respectfully took turns to shoot. They also went to cafes and such, without any special agenda...

Most observers in Japan could not have guessed how the average black person was treated in America at that time. The Royal Giants simply came to Japan as they were. Of course, the Japanese must have recognized their humility through their actions.

The Japanese did not discriminate against the blacks. In fact, they displayed a rather sentimental feeling toward these visitors who had come from such a far distance. They also had enormous respect for them as people from America, the home of baseball.

When Japanese people treated the black players with respect, they must have felt the true sentiments of Japan. I wonder if they enjoyed a sense of freedom, even if it was only temporary. It was at the height of spring, a time full of positivity and joy. It is natural to think that a relaxed and harmonious feeling developed.

*   *   *

One more thing ... the following is a pivotal point on how they played ... It was lucky for Japan that these Royals Giants were a team made up of players with different skill levels—semi-pros, with a few professional all-stars. The reason for this can be shown when comparing their tour to the "exhibition games" played by the major league all-stars who visited Japan several times. I would like to point out that the black players paid their own expenses, so they did not act full of pride, like a "baseball mission team," nor did they act like "instructors" who believed they were superior to the Japanese players. This made the Japanese players feel relaxed and they were able to play in an eased manner.

It is very interesting how "the tie game after revision" demonstrated the true colors of the black team. However, the score of the game was only revised for the Japanese teams' records. The black team simply took it as a loss, according to their statement in the magazine *Asahi Sports.*

At the same time, they not only stated how happy they were that they had come to Japan but also how surprised they were by the level of play in Japanese baseball. They fully explained their feelings in their farewell message. At first glance, it might be reasonable to think that it was written by a Japanese reporter, but from its context, it appears that it was written in English and later translated into Japanese by *Asahi Sports.* In the paragraphs below, the capacity of Koshien Stadium is exaggerated, and must have been heard mistakenly. Even though I felt embarrassed about that, I did not see any other critical mistakes or false information.

Japan Observed from the Baseball Field—A Noble Sports Nation

Dear Japanese players and fans from the baseball field, although we had admired the Yamato race for some years, our respect for you grew immensely after being treated so well by the Japanese people.

In this tour to Japan, our biggest surprise was the quality of Japanese baseball, which is improving and becoming closer to that of a real league. Before we came here, we used to talk about Japanese baseball. We came to the conclusion that the Japanese had not reached the professional level yet. However, to our surprise, once we came here and watched the Japanese baseball teams, not only were we amazed, we realized that our prediction was way off from reality.

Even on our way to Japan, we continued to discuss the same topic, and dreamed of Japan as the ship came closer to land. We were most interested to find out what kind of baseball fields there were in Japan. We decided that the Japanese fields must be very tiny, poorly equipped, perhaps the same as Class D fields in America, or promenade-like places. However, after observing the Meiji Shrine Stadium with great earnestness and then seeing the gigantic Koshien Stadium, we realized we were wrong again. Especially Koshien Stadium—it was larger and more splendid than the stadiums in America. The capacity of

80,000 spectators in Koshien Stadium was beyond that of Yankee Stadium, which is proudly said to be the number one stadium in the world after having millions of dollars spent on it. In comparison to Koshien Stadium, Yankee Stadium would be dwarfed.

The difference between the two stadiums is that Yankee Stadium is privately owned by a rich club, while Koshien is used by everyone. This should be emphasized, so that Koshien Stadium stands proudly.

Throughout the games against the Japanese teams, we could not help but be amazed by the aggressive nature of their defense. We reckoned that they knew how to play inside baseball. Up to today, we lost one important game to the Daimai team, but this was a scoreless game to the end and a fantastic fight between our captain Mackey and the ace pitcher, Ono-kun, of the Diamonds. Unfortunately, it became our first loss since we arrived in Japan. However, we truly enjoyed the game that was played by the Yamato souls. We not only admired and praised the skillful pitcher Ono, but we also thought that the Daimai Club were not any lesser than a major league team in the way they fought back with Ono as a leader in that day's game.

We believe that Japanese baseball will continue to thrive greatly in the future. However, our admiration for Japanese baseball is due not only to the skills that were shown in the Daimai game, but also to the respectable sportsmanship that the Japanese players demonstrated.

Frankly, we think there is not any other country where we could play and enjoy games while not paying any attention to wins or losses. We especially admire the passionate baseball fans, who are well educated and watched the games with respectful manners. That left us with a great impression of Japanese baseball. The more we thought about the dilapidated American stadiums, the better and nobler the Japanese stadiums appeared. We think that the stadiums are used by all the fans, and are for the Japanese people to enjoy real sports.

We wish great success and a promising future to Japanese baseball society, and we also express thankfulness for their hospitality and kindness from the bottom of our hearts to our Japanese hosts through *Asahi Sports*.

Lon Goodwin
Manager, Philadelphia Royal Giants
April 8, Showa 2 (1927)

I was certain that this must represent the honest, true feelings of the Royal Giants. Their reflections on their mistaken, preconceived ideas of Japanese baseball, their unexpected positive impressions of the stadiums, and their respect for the Japanese fans all represented what they really thought of Japan.

A very important point from this letter was the undeniable pleasure they felt being in Japan and playing baseball. This was a revelation for them. They really had a fun time playing the game itself. Their attitudes influenced the souls of the Japanese players, and the games became more friendly and enjoyable. "We tasted the pure enjoyment of sports for the first time in Japan."

I wanted to learn more about their other important games. After the two games at the Meiji Shrine Stadium and two at Koshien, where the black team had one win and one loss (which they gracefully accepted), how had their other games progressed?

*   *   *

On April 6th, the second game against Daimai took place at Koshien, just like the previous day. The Royals Giants were planning to take revenge, having lost the first game. They attacked early and scored heavily from the beginning.

In the second inning, Green and the following three batters got three hits and a walk and scored four runs almost immediately. In the third inning, Dixon's long distance hit, followed by a squeeze play, resulted in another run. In the sixth inning, the star batters put on a hit parade, resulting in five runs. They finished with a total of ten runs.

Daimai changed pitchers, bringing on Ono in the seventh inning to try to keep the score down, but they were themselves held scoreless till the eighth inning. In the ninth Nakagawa and Takasu finally hit and produced two runs, but this did not lead to a win.

Score by inning:

Royal Giants	0 4 1 0 0 5 0 0 0	= 10
Daimai	0 0 0 0 0 0 0 0 2	= 2

Judging only by the score it seems to have been a dull game, but the fans were satisfied with the contest. In the second inning, Dixon hit a triple that was the farthest ball ever recorded at Koshien. The fans were ecstatic with the breathtaking blast.

野球

6

Dixon's Record Breaking Hit, Good Fight by Japan

Dixon's great hit that smashed the outfield fence at Koshien Stadium was one of the stories that I needed to confirm for the baseball researcher John Holway, whom I had met during the SABR meeting in the summer of 1983. Also, I was personally intrigued by the fact that nobody ever talked about the black baseball squad that visited Japan.

To tell the truth, when I first heard about it, I could not believe that a black player from the Negro leagues had made the first hit to reach the fence at Koshien Stadium since it opened in August, Taisho 13 (1924). However, after confirming it to be true with concrete evidence, I started to wonder why nobody seemed to remember it.

Here are the details again. It happened on April 6, Showa 2 (1927). It was the second inning in the first game between the Royal Giants and the Daimai Club. Dixon hit it off the pitcher Tairiku Watanabe.[1] The ball rocketed out to left-center field. The speed of the ball was such that after it hit the outfield fence it bounced off the wall back toward the infield, allowing the speedy Dixon to reach third base.

It is necessary to explain just how big Koshien Stadium was back then to appreciate how great the hit must have been to strike the outfield wall.

The field was not only used for baseball—the vast outfield space was also used for rugby and soccer. It was built as a multiple purpose stadium. As such, the name was "Koshien Dai Undojo."[2] It was 110 meters (361 feet) down the left-field foul pole and right-field foul pole. From home plate, it was 119 meters (390 feet) to straightaway center. The gaps were extremely deep. It was 128 meters (420 feet) to the left-center gap and the right-center gap. It was often said that visitors who came to the construction site wondered whether it would be possible to see the ball in such a big field ("The Koshien Story," *Mainichi Shimbun*, May 15, Showa 59 (1984)).

After renovations in Koshien Stadium, the farthest point in the current ballpark is now 120 meters (394 feet) to deep center. The triple that Dixon belted in Showa 2 (1927) would have been easily over the current fence for a home run. This kind of hit had never been made before. In Taisho 14 (1925), the prodigy batter Minoru Yamashita of the First Kobe Shinkou Commercial High School hit the outfield wall on one bounce in a game against Nagano Commercial High School.[3] At the time it was considered the record for the longest hit in Koshien. This was during the dead ball era, when the ball did not carry well.

The spot where Dixon's blast hit the wall was painted white to commemorate his great hit for future generations. The excitement of the baseball people of Koshien can be seen in their desire to preserve this great record. In fact, anyone who had known the old Koshien still remembered the white mark vividly. Although they did not recall the name of the particular player, they remembered the white spot. It is not difficult to confirm this fact.

Unfortunately, the outfield fence of Koshien was demolished and the white mark was erased. In time the name of Rap Dixon was also forgotten. And since nobody remembers forgotten names, people are now ignorant about the history of Dixon. This has not changed even to today.

With that in mind, how much was known back then about this record holder, Rap Dixon? There were many baseball reporters who could write about the games in detail, but not many of them knew about his personal history.

According to American records, his legal name was Herbert Dixon. He was usually known by his nickname, "Rap." It is not uncommon in America that a ballplayer's nickname is used in place of his real name. A great example of the use of nicknames is how George Herman Ruth was commonly known as "Babe."

I wonder, how did Herbert Dixon's nickname "Rap" come about? Maybe it came from the adjective "rapid," because he was very fast—although this is just my wild guess. "Rap" itself can mean to hit, to strike, to whack. He was known as a fast runner and as a slugger, and for having a strong arm.[4]

Even in America, there are not many currently known documents about his baseball experience prior to his tour in Japan. Dixon was born in Georgia in 1902. After his high school graduation in 1922, he joined the Negro Leagues. He was just 19 years old. In the next five years, he consistently played as an outfielder for the Harrisburg Giants. During that time, Oscar Charleston, who was known as the best outfielder in the Negro Leagues, was the centerfielder on the same team. Later on Charleston became a Hall of Famer. Young Rap must have learned a lot from this veteran teammate.

In 1925, Dixon hit .354 in the official season and became known as an outstanding player in the Negro Leagues. During the off-season of the following year, he played extremely well against a major league team, which made him even more of a standout player. He hit a double in his fourth time up at the plate off a good pitcher, Herman Pillette of the Detroit Tigers. This was a confidence-boosting performance for the young player.

That was all we knew about Dixon prior to the Japan tour. Later on he left his name in the Negro League history books for his outstanding performance during the tour of Japan. He also was celebrated as one of the top players for the Pittsburgh Crawfords, and for his contributions that helped the Baltimore Black Sox win a championship. I will explain more about this in later chapters.

In summary, when Rap Dixon came to Japan, it was five years after he joined the professional Negro Leagues. In a way, it was after he had finished his "apprentice time" in the league. While he was still in his developmental stage, he was about to become a star in the Negro Leagues.

*   *   *

The captain of the Philadelphia Royal Giants, Raleigh "Biz" Mackey, put himself in the third spot of the lineup and let the younger player, Dixon, be the cleanup hitter. This move tells us that Dixon was viewed as a reliable batter. So it was not unexpected that this powerful black player from Georgia would establish a record for the longest ball ever hit at Koshien Stadium.

Now, let's continue with the story of their tour. How did the black visitors play in the rest of their games in the Kansai region?

Considering the difference in their skill level, the Japanese teams played relatively well. Let's see the results of the games. We'll look at how the individual players performed later.

April 7, Koshien Stadium (Umpires: Hirano, Tomigashi)

Score by inning:

Kansai Univ.   0 0 0 0 0 0 0 0 0 = 0
Royal Giants   0 2 0 0 4 0 0 0 A = 6A

Kansai Lineup:

3B	Kawamura
C	Kageyama
2B	Toyota
LF	Kawanishi

P   Morita
SS   Miki
RF   Nose
1B   Kodera, Danjo
CF   Konishi

	Royals		Kansai Univ.
	31	AB	32
	8	H	5
	1	SAC	1
	2	SB	0
	4	K	4
	4	BB	7
	2	E	2

Kansai had five hits and seven walks, but it resulted in zero runs. It was unfortunate for the Kansai ball club. They could not take advantage of their opportunities to score. The Royals had the same number of men on base (12). The great difference between the two teams was that the Royals were able to hit with runners on base.

April 9, Doshisha Stadium (Umpires: Iida, Ikematsu)

Score by inning:
Doshisha   0 0 0 0 0 0 0 0 0 = 0
Royals Giants   0 1 1 0 0 0 0 0 A = 2A

Doshisha Lineup:[5]
RF   Sugiura
2B   Aise
SS   Hiroshi Hasegawa
C   Ikuno
3B   Kanda
1B   Yamane
CF   Kiyoshi Hasegawa
RF   Ohta
P   Ito

ROYALS		DOSHISHA UNIV.
31	AB	31
10	H	7
2	SAC	0
3	SB	0
5	K	2
2	BB	4
3	E	2

The previous year the Doshisha team had been powerful, but four of the best players had left, leaving Takada as the team's only star. Because the newcomer pitcher, Ito (from the Kyoto Nichu ball club), pitched well, the game was close. Here's how the Royals scored their two runs. In the second inning, the number nine hitter got on base due to the third baseman's error. The leadoff batter, Duncan, hit a double and drove in one run. In the third inning, Mackey, who got on with a single, came home on Cade's knock to right field.

Doshisha had about the same number of men on base, but it was understandable that they could not capitalize on their opportunities, because they hit into four double plays. The pitcher for the Royals was Tucker.[6]

April 10, Kyoto Okazaki Stadium (Umpires: Tokugawa, Ikematsu)

Score by inning:

Diamond   1 0 1 0 0 0 0 0 0 = 2
Royals Giants 0 0 0 0 0 1 2 1 A = 4A

Diamond Lineup:

CF	Nidegawa
LF	Takahama
P	Nagai
C	Hashimoto
1B	Nagahama
3B	Hamazaki
RF	Yoshioka
2B	Uchimi
SS	Shimazu, Nishizawa

ROYALS		DIAMOND
36	AB	32
10	H	4
1	SAC	2
1	SB	0
4	K	6
2	BB	4
3	E	3

This is the only information located about this close game. Other details are unknown. Even though the starting pitcher was Cooper, the Diamond Club fought well and built a two-run lead in the early innings. In the sixth, seventh and eighth innings, the Diamond Club allowed runs and lost the lead.[7] It must have been a great game.

April 11, Koshien Stadium (Umpires: unknown)

Score by inning:
Takarazuka Club   0 0 0 0 0 0 0 0 3 = 3
Royal Giants   0 0 2 1 0 0 0 1 A = 4A

Takarazuka Club Lineup:
SS	Kodama
3B	Oide
2B	Nohara
LF	Ozaki
RF	Son
1B	Shimizu
C	Ikeda
PH	Ohnuki, Yamaguchi
P	Tamura
CF	Tomizuka

ROYALS		TAKARAZUKA
31	AB	34
10	H	11
2	SAC	0
2	SB	0
5	K	0
1	BB	3
3	E	2

The official name of the Takarazuka Club was the Takarazuka Athletic Association. They were the first Japanese professional team, and were sometimes referred to as the Nippon Athletic Association. They were founded as the Shibaura Association. Kazumi Kobayashi bought the team and combined it with Hankyu Railway. Of course, it was the best team in Japan. Based on the data shown here, they could have beaten the Royal Giants.

In the ninth inning, Takarazuka fought hard. It is not certain whether they finally figured out the pitcher or not, but I would like to find out. Unfortunately, no further records about this game were found.[8]

April 12, Koshien Stadium (Umpires: Hirai, Tomigashi)

Score by inning:

Royal Giants	0 2 4 0 1 2 0 0 0 = 9
Braves	2 1 2 0 0 0 0 1 0 = 6

Braves Lineup:

2B	Kawagoe
SS	Yokozawa
1B	Umeda
LF	Daimon
3B	Watanabe
RF	Nakagawa
CF	Kobayashi, Nidegawa
P	Yasui
C	Amachi

ROYALS		BRAVES
31	AB	40
11	H	13
6	SAC	1
3	SB	3
1	K	4
6	BB	1
3	Errors	4

In the beginning, it was a back-and-forth game. The Braves had 13 hits. From the details of the game, it could be said that the Braves played better than the Royals. It's hard to believe that they lost.[9]

That was all. There were many great games in the Kansai region. Overall, the Royal Giants won seven and tied one. After that, they returned to Tokyo, where they continued to play against strong teams from the Kanto region.

*   *   *

I wondered how many of the Japanese players remembered the games. The Royal Giants' tour must have been a big event at that time, but it had been 50 years, without any opportunity to talk about it. It seemed inevitable that most of the stories had been forgotten. Those players who played only one game against the black professional team might need something to help jog their memories. Also, the immense impression made by the major league all-stars who came to Japan shortly thereafter (Showa 6, 1931) must have caused the memory of the black players to fade.

With all of the above in mind, the vivid memories of Mr. Yasuo Shimazu were exceptional—and quite valuable.

In a brightly lit room in a nursing home built on a quiet hill in Tondabayashi, Mr. Shimazu still cheered on many of his students on television and radio.[10] He was a renowned shortstop. He was with the Diamond Club when he played against the Royal Giants. Later on, he trained umpires, mainly for the old Kansai Six Baseball League.

He was healthy, although he had a problem vocalizing due to laryngeal cancer, which had caused part of his throat to be taken out. His memories were surprisingly clear. Shimazu recalled:

We almost won ... we had a chance. Just a bit more and we could have had that powerful black team startled. After the last three games in Kansai, we had a real strong feeling of disappointment. The scores were 4-2, 4-3 and 9-6. We were all frustrated. Not only the players—the fans probably felt the same way, don't you think? We almost made it. It was so close.

Because the Royal Giants left a strong impression on us, we remembered them very well. It was not only because the team was made up of black players—it was also because they were nice guys and talented players. Back then, I don't know why but so many American teams came to Japan. There were many college teams and some semi-pro teams.[11] We were not sure who these Royal Giants were. Everybody was speculating that it might be a semi-professional ball club, but they were professional. The powerful batting, strong arms ... actually they were beyond our imagination.

I had a chance to talk to some of them. They said, "Because we are black, we cannot play in the whites-only major league. However, in the games against the major leaguers, we have played as well as them or better. We have a better record."

We were able to go up against that kind of team and play an excellent game. Looking back at it now, we gained confidence, even though we were greatly disappointed with our loss. But I should not dwell on my regrets. They were indeed professionals. They made the games fun.

野球

7

It Was Great Timing

Mr. Yasuo Shimazu continued with his story:

I wonder if the Royal Giants were purposefully making the game fun for the fans. Because of that, we were able to play great games … It was later when I started to think this way. While we were playing, we did not even think about it. We were just playing hard.

At that time, one of my cousins was living in America. I heard about the caliber of the Negro Leagues from him. I might have had preconceptions about them. He told me so many times about the level of black baseball and how it was not any lower than that of the major leagues.

We held our own against a team that was as good as a major league team … We were totally ecstatic. However, when I reflect on it now, this was not the case. The major league team came to Japan soon after, and compared to them we were like a little league team. The major leaguers must have felt that we were no competition, so they were goofing around on the field. I am not sure where the game occurred, but this is what I saw.

While Lefty Grove was pitching, the left fielder, Al Simmons, lay down at his position. The shortstop, Maranville, turned his back to the batter. He sometimes put his face under his crotch and yelled, "Hey, Come on!" In Showa 9 (1934), Babe Ruth played defense while holding an open umbrella during a rainy game. He also played with his rubber boots on. Although they were trying to be playful for the fans, it was not fun for us. We were disappointed in ourselves for the difference in our abilities, and at the same time, we could not hold our composure to endure their foolishness.

The black team, however, was not like that. They were trying to play a competitive game. They also provided fans entertainment, but they never made fun of anybody. What they did was show off their arms by making long throws, and show off their speed on the bases. As for the catcher, he threw the ball like an arrow down to second base on his knees, but during the games, he stood up and threw it down like a textbook play.

As for the black baseball team, they made their money from the spectators. They needed to do something fun in order to get as many people as possible to come watch the games. We did not think of that. We thought that we had close, competitive games because of our ability ... It was shown in their attitude, I think. They worked so hard to try to win. We were so amazed that we were competing head-to-head. They seriously made us think that we were as good as them. While they acted like they were playing hard, they were actually pretending in order to push us to play our best, which resulted in an entertaining game for the fans ... I wonder if this was what they were trying to achieve.

From the game scores, this could well be true. When the Japanese teams could not score many runs, the black team appeared to hold back and score only a few to keep the game close. When the Royal Giants had high-scoring games, it seemed that the Japanese teams also scored many runs.

How did they control their game this way? What was their secret? They must have been good actors.

I could not answers these questions only from the documents available in Japan. I would have to figure out how the players were put together to form this team. With this information, we could finally find out all the answers.

*   *   *

The organizer of the Royal Giants, Lonnie Goodwin, had started this team to compete in the California Winter League. As a successful businessman, he planned to put together the best possible team with the least possible expense. Obviously, the biggest cost was the players' wages. The salaries of the star players in the Negro League were smaller than those of the major leaguers, but a whole team was not going to be cheap. If all the players came from the Negro Leagues, the profits would be slim. Therefore, Goodwin decided to sign only four reliable—and expensive—players from the Negro League teams.[1]

The team was built around its leader, the multi-talented utility player Biz Mackey. He was the best fit to be the captain, based on his personality. Then Goodwin added a rising star in Rap Dixon, and the hard-working Frank Duncan from the Kansas City Monarchs, to form the core of their lineup. Duncan was a talented utility player who could play catcher, pitcher, and any position in the infield.[2] Goodwin might have thought that he needed a dominant pitcher in order to have a good framework for the team, but it was hard to find any available good pitchers. He did not have many choices, so he selected a mediocre pitcher, Andy Cooper, also from the Kansas City Monarchs.[3]

Goodwin might have thought that these four players gave him a strong foundation for the team. At that time, they had no intention of going to Japan and Hawaii. They judged that this was probably enough for the California Winter League.[4]

The rest of the positions could be filled easily. He just needed to get four more players from Negro League teams. Pullen, Fagen, Green, and Riddle fell into this category. However, that was only eight. What about the rest of the team? Goodwin was not worried. He could get local semi-pro players in California.[5]

In summary, this team was made up of three different groups: four players from Negro League teams equal to the major leagues; four players from black teams that were considered to be at a minor-league level; and five newly-hired players from semi-pro teams in California. The players of these three groups varied in their baseball skills and their experience levels From the beginning, the critics said that the Royal Giants were:

- A patched-together, unbalanced team;
- A "mysterious" team; that is, it was hard to accurately judge their quality.

These observations were right on point. If this quickly-constructed team wanted to intentionally "create" an entertaining game, their four best players would have been capable of doing so. They had to control their abilities, which were greatly above those of the Japanese players. When they needed to perform, depending on the situation, they could have doled their skills out, as it were, little by little.

The rest of the players did not have the ability to do this, especially the semi-pro players, who had to play and perform to their full capacity. They must have been quite preoccupied dealing with the Japanese teams, which played like they were fighting for their lives.

"The black team played seriously." This is what was said by the Japanese players and fans who watched the Royal Giants play. Even if the four main players adjusted their performances to produce entertaining games, their plan might not have been noticed, because the rest of the team held nothing back. Their competitive play was so undeniable that it left a good impression.

The main players hid their remarkable talents, waiting for "the right moment" to display them. It's quite possible that at times, they simply matched their play to that of their less-skilled teammates. Maybe that catcher who "could throw a ball to second like an arrow from his knees, but stood up and threw it properly during the games" was just doing it to support the less-experienced second baseman?

Regardless, it was fortunate for Japanese baseball that the intention of this black professional team, the Philadelphia Royal Giants, was to entertain and make money, and that as a result they played gentleman-like games. There were many Japanese players who had discovered a new respect for baseball and increased self-esteem through their games against the black players.

*   *   *

The arrival of the black team in Japan and their competitive games with the Japanese teams had a significant impact on Japanese baseball. In order to fully understand this importance, we need to look at the Japanese baseball situation at that time.

It was Showa 2 (1927). The popularity of baseball was starting to grow in Japan. About 50 years before, the American teacher, Mr. Horace Wilson, had first introduced the game to students at Nan-ko (South School). Baseball became rooted in this island country due to the efforts of several subsequent teachers.

Koshien Stadium was built in Taisho 13 (1924), and the Meiji Shrine Stadium opened in October Showa 1 (1926). Baseball was introduced as a school sport in high schools and colleges. The Koshien and Meiji Shrine Stadiums were established as meccas of scholastic baseball.

In Taisho 4 (1915), Japan's National High School Baseball Tournament began. Koshien Stadium hosted the tournament in its first year. The two stadiums helped cultivate the rise of baseball popularity in high schools throughout Japan. Baseball had achieved a fixed popular status in Japan.

College baseball also received much attention. The Big Six University Baseball League Tournament officially started in Taisho 14 (1925), 22 years after the first game between Waseda and Keio (Meiji 36, 1903). The popular college teams, staffed by elite players from high school teams all over Japan, showed that baseball's popularity extended beyond the Tokyo area. The construction of the Meiji Shrine Stadium, home for all Big Six games, meant a promising future for college baseball.

Baseball at the high school and college levels helped influence younger boys. There was a national tournament for elementary school kids too, even though they used softer balls. Many schools wanted to register for the tournament, and qualifying tournaments took place in almost every prefecture. The rising popularity of baseball made the Ministry of Education uneasy, leading eventually to the Baseball Control Order.[6] The elementary school tournament continued until Showa 6 (1931), when this law was passed.

Baseball prevailed among non-students too. Regional and national tournaments for industrial teams started in the Taisho era. Due to the booming economy after World War I, many corporations invested in amateur teams. In fact, the National Intercity Non-Pro Baseball Championship Series was created in the summer of Showa 2 (1927) to improve industrial league baseball.

Thus, when the Philadelphia Royal Giants set foot in Japan, Japanese baseball was not at a starting point, but was rather in the process of developing.

*   *   *

However, another form of baseball–professional–had not yet been organized in Japan. This did not mean that there had been no professional teams in Japanese baseball history. There had been, but the proper structure did not exist to support a professional league and to differentiate it from amateur leagues.

The first professional team appeared in Taisho 10 (1921), when Shinobu Oshikawa, Yatsushi Kohno, Shin Hashido, Fujio Nakazawa, and Tadao Ichioka formed the "Nippon Athletic Association," also known as the "Shibaura Association." However, unfortunate events happened to this team constantly. They suffered financial hardships, and lost their practice field after the Great Kanto Earthquake of Taisho 12 (1923), when it was used as a place to store materials for the recovery effort.[7] Subsequently, Kazumi Kobayashi bought the team and changed its name to the "Takarazuka Association."

Another professional team, "Tenkatsu Gumi," was established, but it folded after two years because it could not find a new sponsor after the earthquake disaster.

Therefore, in Showa 2 (1927) the Japanese baseball scene consisted mainly of college, amateur, and industrial leagues.

Had great all-stars from the major leagues suddenly arrived in Japan at this time, our elite players might have lost their desire for baseball. It might have made them think it would be a mistake to form a professional team in Japan. They could have been discouraged from building for the future of Japanese baseball.

In fact, in Showa 6 (1931), four years after the tour of the black team, the Japanese players who had started to gain confidence in Showa 2 (1927) were disappointed with their performances against a major league all-star team that played without any mercy. The reappearance of the Philadelphia Royal Giants in Showa 7 (1932) was very helpful for the discouraged Japanese players, as it helped them to regain their confidence and motivation for baseball. The black American ball club returned to Japan at the best possible time.

In Showa 2 (1927), the black players gave Japanese players an increased interest in baseball and gave baseball the possibility for a bright future in Japan. At the same time, the black team was able to showcase top-level American baseball for Japanese players.

Four years later (Showa 6, 1931), when a major league all-star team came to Japan at the invitation of the *Yomiuri Shimbun*, the Japanese players were very disheartened by the results of the games. But instead of feeling helpless afterwards, they had been "immunized" against that feeling by their experience with the Royal Giants four years previously. The visit of the black team helped the Japanese players prepare for and accept their losses with a positive attitude.

野球

8

The Good Fight

Once a sport is well established in one country, that sport can be introduced to other countries. The question is, how is the sport able to thrive in the new countries? First of all, the propagation of a new sport must start with a relationship between two parties: one to introduce the sport and the other to accept it.

According to the anthropologist Homer Barnett, there are four different kinds of mediators who helped spread the sport of baseball:[1]

1. Professional teams: major leaguers
2. Visitors/ambassadors: politicians, businessmen, religious missionaries, who live and play with locals and function as a part of a group.
3. Upper classes: baseball is first adopted upper-class people, then spreads to others.
4. Soldiers: allies or an occupying army, who may spread the sport to other soldiers.

Needless to say, all four mediators co-exist. In many cases, it happens in a combination of two or three, and the sport is spread effectively. In reality, the propagation of baseball in Japan prevailed by all methods.

The interesting notion here is that propagation carried out by professionals is not necessarily the best way to spread a sport. In fact, history has proven that it creates the opposite effect.

In the 19th century, America attempted to export baseball to its mother country, Great Britain, three times, but failed every time. The Americans' direct sale of baseball equipment was not a good idea. An even worse idea, though, was sending elite professional players as "baseball missionaries." The showcase of their excellence instead alienated the British people.

This did not happen only in Great Britain. The team that Spalding sent on a world tour in 1888 was an extreme case. Their enthusiasm was so great that they played games at the Pyramids in Egypt. In Italy, after demonstrating their exquisite skills, they asked the authorities for permission to play in the famous Colosseum. However, their polished baseball skills discouraged the locals instead of generating interest in the game.

These kinds of failures could have occurred in Japan. Of course, Japan was unique in many ways because of its situation and history. Japan and Great Britain differed greatly in their responses to American products. As far as the development of baseball went, Japan was quite advanced by Showa 2 (1927), so the situation was not the same as in other countries. However, had Japan lacked prior knowledge of the high skill level of the major leaguers, and lacked the experience of facing the black team prior to playing against the major league all-star team in Showa 6 (1931) and Showa 9 (1934), the Japanese might have been discouraged just like the locals in those other countries. It was right around this time that Japanese players started to become more confident, so their losses to the major league teams were not as devastating.

As I stated in the previous chapter, the Philadelphia Royal Giants came to Japan at the perfect time and served as a shock absorber, if you will, for the later experiences against the major league players.

* * *

Now, let's talk more about the games played by the Royal Giants. Two days after arriving in Japan, they played the Mita Club of Keio and won two straight, 2-0 and 10-6.

The powerhouse Royal Giants became the big talk of Tokyo before they left for the Kansai region, where they recorded seven wins and one tie in eight games.

They then returned to Tokyo to take on the popular Tomon Club and Sundai Club.[2] The Fresno Athletic Club were also scheduled as opponents, which really excited the fans.

The Royal Giants players were also excited and motivated, as seen in their message to Japanese fans, shared in the previous chapter. They were pleased with the positive attitudes of the players and the friendliness of the fans. They had never expected to play baseball in conditions where they felt so welcomed and were treated with so much respect.

From an article in *Yakyukai* magazine for June, Showa 2 (1927), we learn of the Royal Giants' return to Tokyo after their eight-game road trip in the Kansai Region:

> Prior to the Tokyo Big 6 university baseball spring championship, the Philadelphia Royal Giants excited the Japanese baseball world. They headed to the bustling town of Kanda-nishikicho in Tokyo to stay in the Hosenkaku Hotel.

The majestic, western-style hotel is built in the barracks of the earthquake recovery. The major street is Otsuka … the train to the Shinbashi station always runs back and forth, so it is very convenient for guests of the hotel and first-time visitors.

Most of the games against the Royals team were held in Jingugaien (Meiji Shrine) Stadium, so the players probably took a couple of cars and drove through Yotsuya and Akasaka while they enjoyed gazing at the cherry blossoms in full bloom.

Spring, the Sumida River full of cherry blossom
The petals of cherry blossom
Fall, fall, on my hands holding the oars.

Like that … The folk song was sung long ago like this, but now the soot has fallen down after the earthquake. The Royal Giants ball club not only saw Tokyo's cherry blossoms, but also they gazed at beautiful weeping cherry blossoms in Kyoto.

The results of the games at Jingu Stadium (Meiji Shrine) were all excellent. Mackey, the slugging captain – who smashed the first home run ever at the stadium – and O'Neal Pullen were both 27 years old. Their heights were over 6 shaku [71.58 inches, or approximately 5 feet, 10 inches]. They were big and tall. They weighed more than 20 kan [200 lbs]. I asked Mackey, "How much do you weigh?" He responded, "Two hundred sixteen kin" [108 kg / 238 lbs]. I also asked Pullen, "How about you?" He answered with a grin, "Two hundred eighteen kin" [109 kg / 240 lbs].[3]

They were asked what kind of impression they had of Japan … They said they were pleased with the welcoming gestures. During the breaks in Kyoto, they were invited to watch the Miyako Odori (a traditional spring dance festival). In Tokyo, they also enjoyed the Azuma Odori, an indoor stage show. They were pleased with the performances by the geishas, who moved swiftly, all legs and elegant, swaying hands. They were full of praises. "Oh, beautiful! Beautiful!"

In addition, they all said that they would share with their friends and family their impressions of what they had done, seen, and experienced. But what they really wanted was to bring their friends and family to experience Japan instead of just telling them about it … This showed that they really enjoyed their time in Japan.

After this, the team will play in Nagoya and the Fukuoka region. Next they will enjoy the hot spring baths in Beppu, then they will board the train from Kobe and head back home.

There is a picture taken in front of a traditional Japanese hotel. It must be from their visit to Kyoto. They look cheerful, with smiles on their faces. A banner reading "Welcome Philadelphia Royal Giants!" is hung in the front of the entrance.[4]

As the team developed friendships among themselves, how did their games progress in Tokyo?

During their second visit to Tokyo, the first team they faced was the Tomon Club. Usually, this match would have been an exciting game. Unfortunately, the star players from Waseda left for America on a goodwill tour and were not available to play.

These star players were all gone: (P) Sadayoshi Fujimoto, (C) Yasuhiro Itami, (1B) Narutoshi Nishimura, (2B) Shigeo Mori, (3B) Shinjiro Iguchi, (SS) Tokio Tominaga, (outfielders) Kiichiro Segi, Takeo Himuro, Yoshiaki Mizuhara. Only the veterans Yamazaki and Nagano were available; the rest of the roster needed to be filled out.

The game took place on April 16, at Waseda Totsuka field. They could not use the Jingu Stadium because on the same day the Fresno team that had come to Japan at the same time had a game against Hosei University. Because both popular foreign teams had a game, many fans must have struggled to decide which game to attend.

> The team called itself Tomon, but there were seven newcomers. It probably should have been called the Tomon backup team. The pitcher, Segawa, held the Royal Giants' offense down, but in the fifth inning and seventh inning, the black team was finally able to get to the pitcher. In the end, the pitcher's weapons were neutralized. Nonetheless, I would like to acknowledge his spirited efforts.

This comment about the game appeared in *Yakyukai*. The fan must have applauded with warm cheers for this backup team that gave up only seven hits. Looking at a picture of the game in *Asahi Sports*, I saw many fans, from the infield seats all the way to the outfield. I could imagine that the fans had high expectations for the Tomon team, at least judging by the look of one spectator with a derby hat who can be seen cheering enthusiastically.

Here are the game details.

The Tomon ball club had runners on base every inning from the first to third, but it did not lead to any runs. In the fourth the Royals scored one run. This occurred when Dixon hit a single and Pullen doubled over the left fielder.

In the fifth inning, the Tomon team fought back aggressively. After one out, both Uchigawa and Kamijo hit grounders through the infield and got on base. When Imai walked, the bases were loaded. As everybody hoped, Yamazaki got a hit past second base. Uchikawa came home. It became a tie game at 1-1. However, the next batter, Kuroki, failed to execute a squeeze play and could not get an additional run across.

During the sixth inning, the offense of the Royals was excellent as expected. The first batter, Riddle, drag bunted for a single. Mackey then grounded to Minagawa, who made a great play and got Riddle out at second base. Next, Dixon hit a long double to right field. Runners were on second and third. Pullen also hit a double to right field and drove in two runs. The next batter, Green, doubled between left and center field and added one more run. They scored three runs in total.

Tomon had not given up. In the seventh inning, Kamijo and Imai both had hits and scored one run but in the bottom of this inning, they were hit by Mackey and allowed two runs, and the deficit grew. At the end, the score was 6-2. The power difference was too drastic and Tomon was overmatched.

Score by inning:

Tomon Club	0 0 0 0 1 0 1 0 0	= 2
Royal Giants	0 0 0 1 0 3 2 0 A	= 6A

Tomon Club Lineup:

2B	Kamijo
LF	Imai
SS	Yamazaki
3B	Kuroki
C	Nagano
P	Minagawa
1B	Kubota
CF	Yamamoto
RF	Mori
PH	Kuroda
1B	Uchikawa
P	Tase

Royals		Tomon Club
32	AB	34
10	H	7
2	SAC	1
0	SB	0
1	K	5
2	BB	3
2	E	3

Next day on April 17th, the same teams competed against each other. The fans who had enjoyed yesterday's game came again to fill up the ball park. In fact, the first game had been so entertaining that the number of spectators increased from the day before.

However, the game did not turn out as everybody hoped. The fans had to watch the Tomon ball club lose again. The pitcher, Tase, who was known for his fast ball, pitched with huge expectations from the crowd. His weak point was that he did not have a breaking pitch, so he struggled from the beginning and was eaten alive by the black ball players' hitting.

As for the Royal Giants, again the main players, Dixon and Mackey, made long hits, which showed the great difference in power between the two teams. Dixon hit a home run over left field, as well as a triple. Mackey also hit a double between left and center. These two alone produced many runs. The pitchers for the Royals were Evans and Cooper.

Score by inning:

Royal Giants	2 0 0 0 0 1 5 0 0	=	8
Tomon Club	0 0 1 0 0 0 0 0 0	=	1

Tomon Club		Royals
34	AB	38
9	H	10
1	SAC	1
0	SB	2
5	K	2
2	BB	4
6	E	1

The lineup of the Tomon Club was almost the same as the previous day. The right fielder, Mori, was replaced by Kimitsugu Kawai, who was known as Waseda's Babe Ruth. The pitcher was Takahashi.

Speaking of Kawai, he worked as a bodybuilder for a long time, but now he lives quietly on a hill near Tabata Station on the Kokuden (National Railway). He is passionate about planting cherry blossoms and azaleas on the slope so that people can enjoy the view from the train.

I asked Mr. Kawai about the game, and at first he responded, "I don't remember anything about the game. It was 58 years ago."

However, he eventually started to talk about it, dredging it up from his memory:

> I don't talk about this nowadays. Yes, the team of all black players came to Japan. They played against Tomon. I remember I was on the team. We were all surprised that everybody was so dark. I remember that we joked around … we thought that if we played with them, the white ball would turn black. Once the game started, they were so strong.
>
> And one more thing. I heard that even though they were very good, they needed to earn money for their return ticket on the ship. At that time, everybody was so naive that no one thought about making baseball a job. We felt disappointment for them when we heard about their situation. We lost the games, but we fought back so hard. We did not feel that we were losers.

I remembered how in the magazine *Yakyukai* the writer praised Tomon's remarkable effort:

> Of course, the loss was due to the difference in their body sizes and powerful batting. Considering the differences in their physiques, skills, and ages, the Tomon ball club played well. Especially the pitcher, Tase. He is a promising pitcher. The relief pitcher, Takahashi, also pitched well. The first game with Tase pitching against the black team was excellent.
>
> The offense of the black team was certainly strong. Unfortunately, the current college teams would not have any chance. In order to win, the Japanese would need to have a dominant pitcher.

By the way, if this comment was accurate, it would have been difficult to find a team that could defeat the Royal Giants.

*   *   *

The Japanese fans, however, had high expectations for the Fresno Athletic Club, and understandably so. The majority of the team's players were Nikkei (Japanese Americans). They were a strong, good team that had not lost yet in Japan. Because it was their second time touring the country, they had many Japanese fans.[5,6]

The popular Fresno team was scheduled to play against the Royal Giants. Both teams played with pride, and both were undefeated. Interest started to grow around this decisive game, scheduled for April 20.

野球

9

Finally, the Real Power Appears

Fresno is located in central California, where many Nikkei (Japanese Americans) live. Baseball-loving Japanese Americans have formed teams and have enjoyed playing games for decades.

It has been said that many Issei (first-generation Japanese American) parents thought that baseball would be the best way for Nissei (second-generation Japanese Americans) to be able to return home and learn about Japanese ways.

The Fresno team in Showa 2 (1927) was sent to Japan, just as their parents may have wished. They were a team comprised of amateur players. However, because the players did sometimes join professional teams, they called themselves "semi-pro."

It is interesting to note that this team came to Japan at the same time as the Philadelphia Royal Giants in the early Showa era.[1]

In fact, the Fresno ball club was a strong team. The team was made up of talented Nikkei players and three white players. These white players were Hendsch, who was a relief pitcher for the staff ace Mamiya; Hunt, the second starting pitcher; and Simon, a catcher. Simon had played in the Pacific Coast League, and his assets were his strong arm and great bat.

Because of its solid pitching staff, Fresno had a winning record. In addition, they also boasted a sharp lineup of Nakagawa, Kunitomo, Miyahara, and Iwata. After their arrival in Japan, this team went undefeated against strong university and corporate teams.

Here are the results of the games:

Fresno	4A - 3	Meiji University
Fresno	3A - 2	Hosei University
Fresno	20 - 2	Sapporo Railways
Fresno	15A - 2	Sapporo Railways
Fresno	5 - 0	Hakodate Ocean Club

Fresno	1 - 1	Hakodate Ocean Club
Fresno	5 - 2	Hakodate Ocean Club
Fresno	15 - 4	Hakodate Ocean Club
Fresno	5 - 4	Morioka Toryo Club

The Fresno ball club won four consecutive games against the powerhouse team in the industrial league, the Hakodate Ocean Club, which must have added credibility to their name. With that, let's look at the details of the Fresno game against the Royal Giants.

*　　*　　*

The game between these well-traveled visitors was held on April 20 at Jingu Stadium. Because it received a lot of media attention a large crowd of spectators attended.

The Fresno players must have felt pressure from the crowd. As a Japanese team, they would have tried their best to win against the black team. The starting catcher was Yoshikawa, and the backup catcher Simon was used as a pinch hitter. The starting pitcher was Mamiya, as they kept the white pitcher on the bench. "We've got to win this game," said the Fresno players.

The Royal Giants were thinking the same thing. They used their ace, Cooper, as their starting pitcher.

It is tedious to write down all the game details on paper. However, this game was different from the previous games against the Japanese amateur players. This was a game between two semi-pro teams that came from the same place—America. As a professional team, the black team would have been able to use their full power for this game. I need to look at the game details and read the comments closely.

The offense of the Royals started quickly in the first inning. After two outs, the captain, Mackey, smashed a triple to left center field. The next batter, Dixon, continued with a hit between the first and second basemen, scoring a run.

After that, the Royals could not add any more runs due to Mamiya's pitching. He performed well, but began to falter in the sixth inning. It started with Mackey's home run. In the seventh inning, they put together an excellent combination of singles and extra base hits, which resulted in four more runs.

The seventh inning details are as follows: After one out, Walker hit a single to left. Cooper hit a single to the same location. Runners were on first and second base. Next, Fagen hit a single, and Mackey continued with a sacrifice hit. Dixon hit a triple to right. The end result was a total of four runs.

The black team tried to show that they were at their best and they continued to display their powerful offense in the eighth inning. After Cade's double, Green's walk, and Walker's single, Fagen hit a single. After this, Mackey smashed a double between left and center, which scored an additional three runs.

In the other dugout, Fresno was finally able to score a run, right before the end of the game in the ninth inning. After the pinch hitter Simon doubled, another pinch hitter, Yamasaki, hit a single between the first and second basemen to score Fresno's lone run.

The Fresno team was able to defeat the top-level teams in Japan, but they could not find their game against the Royal Giants, who competed without mercy.

The final score was 9-1. The game ended leaving with the impression of remarkable power on the part of the black professional team.

Score by inning:

Royal Giants	1 0 0 0 0 1 4 3 0 = 9
Fresno	0 0 0 0 0 0 0 0 1 = 1

FRESNO

	AB	R	H
6 Zenimura	3	0	0
2 Yoshikawa	4	0	0
3 Nakano	2	0	1
PH Simon	1	1	1
8 Nakagawa	3	0	0
PH Kawasaki	1	0	0
7 Iwata	2	0	0
PH Yamasaki	1	0	1
9 Furubayashi	4	0	1
4 Kunitomo	4	0	0
5 Miyahara	3	0	0
1 Mamiya	3	0	1
Totals	31	1	5

ROYAL GIANTS

	AB	R	H
3 Duncan	5	2	1
4 Fagen	5	1	3
6 Mackey	4	2	3
8 Dixon	5	0	3
2 Pullen	5	0	2
7 Cade	5	1	1
9 Green	3	1	0
5 Walker	4	1	2
1 Cooper	3	1	2
Totals	39	9	17

The details of this game were well described in the magazine *Undou Kai (Athletic Society)*, June, Showa 2 (1927). The name of the writer is unknown, but I would assume that it was Mr. Aomine, who wrote about the game against Mita. The original is very long. Even though I will quote only the main points, they are not short. But I would like to repeat his comments in order to convey the excitement of the game:

The Black Team! A Dominant Win by a Big Margin

- Fresno allowed 17 hits
- 9 – 1, Mackey records the first home run at Jingu

Except for the first game against Daimai, the blacks won against all the Japanese teams as if they were little leaguers. The Fresno team also easily beat the university teams. Both teams were stronger than the current Japanese teams, but between the blacks and Fresno, there was huge difference in skills and ability. As for Fresno, this team was a group of talented players with great offense and defense. However, they were different in their foundations. The power of the cat and dog cannot compare with that of the cow and horse.

(omission)

The game score of 9-1 demonstrated that it was no competition. The Fresno would have no chance of winning one game even if they played ten against the blacks.[2]

The Ability of the Pitchers: These undefeated teams prepared their best lineups as if they were trying to win a championship. The Fresno team used their starting pitcher, Mamiya, and the blacks sent out a big left-handed pitcher, Cooper, but there was no competition between the two. Mamiya had a sturdy, big body for a Japanese person and threw hard, but Cooper was like a hornless bull and threw fastballs from his shining, black, muscular arm. The velocity of their pitches was incomparable. No one from the Fresno team could hit Cooper's heavy, fast sinker. The power and speed startled Fresno. At times they could not even swing their bats.

On the other side, the pitches from Mamiya added fuel to the blacks' fiery offense. They hit his slow ball and curve ball without mercy. He gave up one home run, three triples, two doubles, and a total of 17 hits. This performance was evidence that his skill was not as great as Cooper's.

The Ability of the Batters: The symbol of the black squad's strength was its hitting ability. During the first two games against Mita, their hitting performance on the first day and second day were very different. This difference was as drastic as the contrast between the black team's offense against Mita and Tomon and their great offensive showing against Fresno. Their powerful swings sounded with a hard crack just like the sound it makes on a fungo bat's sweet spot. Their powerful shots soared through the air, blowing in the wind, going right, left, back and in, which confused the Fresno outfielders – especially the captain, Mackey, who tripled between left and center in the first inning off Mamiya's unexpectedly slow pitch. Then in the sixth inning he smashed a long hit to the river bank that passed through the middle of the center bleacher. In the seventh he hit a sacrifice fly between right and center, and also singled to center. In all, he drove in eight runs.

The clean-up hitter, Dixon, hit as well as Mackey. He had two triples and a single. His average was .600. Fagen also had three hits for a .600 average. The pitcher, Cooper got two hits. Everybody recorded a hit except Green. They displayed exceptional skills, such as a good eye at the plate and great swings. Their performance was nothing like the previous games, which they seemed to treat as exhibitions. They were a different team.

Even though the offense of Fresno also had shown remarkable power against the university teams, they could not show their ability against the black team. Perhaps this was understandable, given that it was challenging to hit against Cooper. Without any doubt, the difference in hitting between the powerful blacks and the Japanese was like night and day.

The Ability of the Base Runners: It became obvious that the speed of the black players had not been fully demonstrated in the games against Mita and Tomon. The catcher Pullen and the shortstop Mackey were not as fast as the others because of their size. But the center fielder Dixon, the first baseman Duncan, and the other outfielders were speedy runners. Dixon and Duncan in particular had long strides like horses, and ran quickly from base to base. Dixon's speed was the most mesmerizing.

As a center fielder, he could easily run down any fly ball to right field, showing off his great speed and fielding ability. In the ninth inning, with the count 2 and 1, he scooped up a low pitch and drove it over the center fielder's head all the way to the fence. He galloped easily to third base. As he watched the left fielder throw it to the shortstop, Zenimura, Dixon attempted to score, trying to catch the defense off guard. He underestimated the defense and was unsuccessful. Still, even though he was out, his speed was amazing.

The Ability of the Defenders: The gap between the two teams' defensive ability was like the difference between a soft ball and a hard ball. Fresno committed no errors and played well defensively, but they were playing a totally different type of baseball than the black squad was. Everybody on the Royal Giants had a strong arm. We fully appreciated all their skills and abilities on defense, but their bullet-like throws left us speechless.

(Omission)

In this report, the big surprise caused by the black team's unbelievable power is obvious. The black team was finally given a chance to show their true power in the game against the Fresno nine. They appeared to be a different Royal Giants team, compared to the games they played against Mita and Tomon. This seems to align with Mr. Yasuo Shimazu's statement: "They hid their true power from our team and tried to control the game by pretending they were on the same level as us."

Needless to say, the Royal Giants did not have any problems playing all out against their fellow Americans on the Fresno ball club.[3] Their undefeated record in Japan remained intact.

The difference in power between the two teams was shown in this battle. Mackey's home run especially symbolized it.

In fact, this home run was the first one ever hit over the fence in Jingu Stadium. We must also note that it was still the dead ball era. A dead ball does not carry well or bounce off the bat well. For this reason, Mackey's accomplishments are even more impressive.

The ball he hit passed over the head of the centerfielder, went over the fence, and finally bounced on the grass of the bleacher section before disappearing outside the stadium. How can we know the speed of the ball that he hit? An illustration of the scene was published in the magazine *Undokai (Athletic Society)*.

The caption attached to it reads: "He can hit it to right field or left field. In an emergency, he can smash it to the river bank. We want him for the Japanese team as a star." In the illustration, the giant Mackey is running the bases. Looking at it closely, I can see the ball flying over the outfield bleachers and the outfielder trying to climb the fence. The art museum that is still standing next to the stadium is shown in the picture, along with a single white cloud. In addition, the face of Mackey as he runs is illustrated without eyes and nose, only white teeth. This must be an honest impression of the black players as the artist perceived them.

It was believed that Saburo Miyatake of Keio had hit the first home run at Jingu Stadium during the Big 6 University baseball league season on April 29th. However, Mackey's home run in this game occurred 9 days prior to Miyatake, so the American's blast was the very first at Jingu. Miyatake, however, holds the distinction of hitting the first home run at Jingu by a Japanese player.

The home run against Fresno was not the only one that Biz Mackey hit at Jingu Stadium. He had a total of three in that stadium during the Showa 2 (1927) tour. Interestingly, Mackey's three home runs included one to right, one to center, and one to left field. Let's look at the details:

- The first: April 20 off the Fresno pitcher Mamiya, sixth inning, first batter, first pitch, over the center field bleacher. About 70 Ken (127 meters, or 417 feet).
- The second: April 25 off the Sundai Club pitcher Nakatsugawa, seventh inning, one runner on base, one ball and two strikes, hit to the left field bleacher. About 60 Ken (109 meters, 358 feet).
- The third: April 28 off the Saint Paul Club pitcher Nawaoka, third inning, first batter, first pitch, hit to the right field bleacher. About 60 Ken (109 meters, 358 feet).

By the way, in Showa 9 (1934), Mr. Matsutaro Shoriki was slashed with a sword by a member of a right-wing group because he had invited the major league all-star team to play in Jingu Stadium—and thus was "responsible for allowing foreigners to trespass the sacred Meiji Shrine." If the Jingu's purity could be violated by a visiting team of foreigners, then it had already been violated by the Royal Giants in Showa 2 (1927).

It would not have been a simple task for the famous Babe Ruth to hit home runs like a "comet" in three different directions in the spacious Jingu Stadium. Yet Biz Mackey accomplished this easily. Who was this powerful man who hit home runs so effortlessly? Who was this Biz Mackey?

野球

10

The Man Who Hit
the First Home Run at Jingu

Who was this player, Biz Mackey? He recorded the first home run at Gaien Stadium in the presence of the sacred Meiji Shrine. He hit not only one, but also a second, and then a third.

Information about this great player is surprisingly limited. What is available is gathered from some interviews with Negro Leaguers, and some findings from the baseball researcher, John Holway. The known history of Biz Mackey's career is sparse.[1] Even though the information is limited, it is obvious that he was superior to the average black player.

His real name is Raleigh Mackey.[2] It is not certain why he started to be called by the nickname "Biz." It might be from the slang term "biz," for "business," though this is just my guess. As a common colloquialism, "good biz!" means "good job!" or "excellent." It is used to express something wonderful. Biz was great on defense and hitting. The phrase "good biz" might have been shortened to become "Biz."[3]

He was born in the small town of Seguin, Texas, in 1897. The famous pitcher "Smokey" Joe Williams was also born there. Biz grew up looking up to this ballplayer, 11 years his senior, as a hero. "Smokey" Joe Williams was comparable to the legendary pitcher Satchel Paige. Williams was the number-one hero about a generation before Paige.

Like Williams, Mackey had a strong arm. As he had displayed in Japan, many fans thought he was primarily a great defensive player. However, when he started to hit, the power of his bat was astonishing. He could hit a line drive straight to the outfield bleachers, bounce it and make the ball disappear outside the park at Jingu Stadium. This made the fans surprised and ecstatic. It was obvious that Mackey and the cleanup hitter, Dixon, who hit the longest ball recorded at Koshien, played a critical role in the lineup for the Royal Giants.

Back in America, Mackey's primary position was catcher. Because he competed with Josh Gibson, the catcher who hit 962 career home runs and was called the "Black Babe

Ruth," Mackey's ability as a hitter was overshadowed. Even if Mackey was a great batter, he could not compete with the reputation of the great Josh Gibson. It was often said that it was not insulting to call Babe Ruth "the White Gibson"—rather, it was a compliment to Ruth.

As such, it was understandable that critics mainly focused on Mackey's defensive skills.

Teammate and pitcher Bill Foster said this about Biz: "Mackey's throws carried far. When I was working with Biz as a battery mate, I had to be extra careful with his throws to second base. That ball would come by my mound knee-high. Zing! It came right back by me. Because I am a left-handed pitcher, his throws went right behind my back. It was very dangerous."[4]

Webster McDonald, another dominant pitcher in the Negro Leagues, said:

> "Of all the catchers, I'd pick Biz Mackey as smartest of all of them. He was an artist behind the plate, he was the master. I loved pitching to Mackey.
>
> Santop and Gibson could probably outhit him, but I didn't call them catchers, as far as I was concerned. They used to drop too many balls. They'd take strikes away from pitchers. Mackey could help a pitcher steal a strike, the way he received the ball. He fooled the umpire sometimes if it was a little low or whatnot.
>
> His arm? Terrific. And he threw a light ball, the infielders could handle it. Those other guys threw the ball hard, but a heavy ball. You ever been catching when somebody threw a heavy ball, keep your hands sore? That's a heavy ball. Mackey's was just like a feather. It was a pleasure for infielders when Mackey was catching."

Santop, whom I have mentioned before, was a famous catcher in the Negro Leagues era before Mackey's. His height was 183 cm (6 feet), and he weighed 108 kg (238 lbs). Because of his size he swung a powerful bat. He hit for a .465 average.[5] Without his performance, the famous Hilldale ball club would not have flourished.

As for Gibson, he hit the most career home runs of all baseball players—black or white— from around the world. That is all I should say about him. Other information is unnecessary.

Among Mackey's characteristics, people would often talk about his toughness. The submarine pitcher Holsey "Scrip" Lee said in an interview with John Holway: "Mackey had more stamina than anybody on his team. When someone was doing batting practice, he was often at shortstop fielding the balls. He said that it was the best practice for him. During the game, he of course played catcher. Even though everybody was struggling with the heat, he was okay. I have never heard of him complaining about the weather."[6]

Lee added, "I loved pitching to him. I did not need to worry about the bunt play. Mackey picked up any bunted ball on the first or third base line and made the out. Maybe his practice at shortstop paid off."

In 1926, Mackey played in the California Winter League and accepted the title of team captain of the Philadelphia Royal Giants. It was after that season that his manager Lonnie Goodwin recruited Mackey to go to Japan. How did Mackey perform prior to that season?

In 1924, he played in the Negro League World Series as a member of the Hilldale Club, winner of the Negro League eastern region championship. After losing to the western region champion, the Kansas City Monarchs, there was not much written about his performance. The result for Hilldale was four wins and five losses in the nine-game series. They lost by a close margin.

In the next season, 1925, Mackey's team won the championship with five wins and one loss. He hit .375 in this series. He also hit a game-winning double over the right fielder in the last game.[7]

In 1926, his team finished in second place in their region, so they did not make it to the World Series. Instead, during the offseason they played an exhibition game against the renowned major league team, the Philadelphia Athletics. The Athletics were known as a strong team led by the best manager, Connie Mack. Nonetheless, Hilldale had five wins and one loss against them. The difference in power was obvious. The pitcher Lefty Grove, who came to Japan and threw great pitches in Showa 6 (1931), played for the Athletics, and he was eaten alive by the Hilldale offense.

In the final three years of Mackey's career, he hit .345, .354 and .333. Although he did not have a great home run record, these numbers are excellent proof that he was indeed a quality hitter.

Later on, Mackey became the manager of several black professional teams. He mentored the well-known catcher Roy Campanella of the Dodgers. At this time, I would like to make it clear that when Mackey came to Japan, he had already grown into a person with an amicable personality—and a complete set of baseball skills.

Let's now focus on the games again. Here are Mackey's second and third home runs.

April 25, Jingu Stadium

Score by inning:

Sundai Club	0	0	0	0	0	0	0	0	0	= 0
Royal Giants	3	1	0	0	0	0	4	0	A	= 8A

Sundai Club Lineup:

C	Okada
SS	Oku
1B	Matsumoto
RF	Sakurai
LF	Yonezawa (older brother)
3B	Kobayashi
2B	Yonezawa (younger brother)
P	Nakatsugawa, Nakamura
CF	Hasegawa

ROYALS		SUNDAI
32	AB	27
8	H	2
0	SAC	0
3	SB	0
2	K	7
6	BB	4
0	E	3

The energetic Sundai Club played hard and the manager Okada put himself behind the plate, but the newly assembled team could not keep up against the Royal Giants. They only had two hits. They could not figure out Johnson's pitches. Nobody was even able to get on second base.

As for the Royal Giants, the batters hit and scored as expected. In the sixth inning, Mackey smashed a home run to the left field grass section at Jingu Stadium.

April 28, Jingu Stadium

Score by inning:

Saint Paul	0 0 0 0 0 0 0 0 0 = 0
Royal Giants	4 0 3 1 1 3 0 2 A = 14A

Saint Paul Lineup:

CF   Saito

LF   Arai

2B   Takase

C   Hayami, Noda

SS   Mori, Ouchi

3B   Miura, Suzuki

RF   Ichimura, Katada

P   Tamura, Nawaoka

1B   Makida, Shoda

ROYALS		SAINT PAUL
41	AB	34
14	H	6
3	SAC	0
2	SB	0
6	K	3
0	BB	1
2	E	10

"The difference in their abilities was obvious," wrote *Yakyukai* magazine. The game was a devastating loss. With a 14-run deficit, the Saint Paul team was defeated. It was an unavoidable loss and it was expected." The Rikkyo University and Meiji University squads also ended up losing badly to the Royal Giants.

In fact, were it not for the big run difference prior to Mackey's blast into the right field grass section, his second home run would have been more memorable. The Saint Paul Club committed 10 errors, so not even the Royal Giants, who were always mindful to keep the scores competitive to attract fans for future games, could have kept the score close.

After the game, the Royals Giants decided to make it up to the fans who were disappointed with the result and still lingered at the stadium. It could be said that the Royal Giants had a good sense of customer service and tried to please the audience.

The entertaining performance that they subsequently put on was something the crowd had never seen before. First, Dixon showed off his arm by throwing one ball one after another from home plate beyond the left-field grass section. His performance was illustrated in *Yakyukai*, No 10, 17th Edition (see illustrations on pages 91-92). Two players stood in the outfield bleachers to catch Dixon's tosses. Everyone could see that Dixon's throws were right on target. It was amazing to see how far he could throw.

Not many contemporary Japanese baseball outfielders could throw to home plate from their positions. At that time, the outfield fence at Jingu Stadium was much deeper than it is now.

By the way, when the Royal Giants visited this stadium for the first time they were surprised by both its beauty and its size. They bragged to reporters that they "could throw a ball to the outfield bleachers." Their words were captured in the newspapers, and Dixon proved it in front of the fans.

Next, Mackey entertained the crowd by hitting a ball to the outfield grass sections. He tossed the ball up to himself and displayed his beautiful hitting form.

After that, Duncan and Dixon showed off their base running. They ran around the diamond in 14.02 seconds.[8] This time amazed the Japanese fans. It showed that they still had so much energy after the game, which must have made it even more astonishing.

It also showed their seriousness, which was one of the characteristics of the Royal Giants. At that time, teams who came to Japan usually entertained fans by acting goofy, making silly faces, or performing imitations of birds and running around mimicking bird calls. They also performed funny dances. Sometimes they danced during the games. Some fans were annoyed by these childish acts.

The kindly Royal Giants team did not indulge in such foolishness. Instead they entertained the fans by displaying their exceptional talents, which grabbed the attention of the serious Japanese baseball fans. It is safe to say that this was a smart move.

The total number of games that the Royal Giants had played up to this point in the tour was 13. They had traveled from Tokyo to Kansai and back to Tokyo. They had played against strong, elite teams, and had come away with 12 wins and one tie. They were undefeated.

In order to search for new fans in Japan, they now left for different regions.

野球

Dixon showed off his arm by throwing to the outfield bleachers.

Dixon said,
"I am here already."

Second base said,
"Next time, we will
get you out!"

Shortstop said,
"Ah, What is this?"

Speedy Dixon's stolen base.

Mackey can hit it to right field or
left field. In an emergency, he can
smash it to the river bank. We want
him for the Japanese team as a star.

From Undo Kai (Athletic Society)

The home plate umpire looked uncomfortable standing behind the massive catcher, Pullen. Can I bring you a stool?

Both Mackey's knock and Dixon's throw reached the outfield grass sections like a missile.

11

To Countryside Ballparks, then Hawaii

Having recorded a great hitting performance at Koshien and Jingu, the Royal Giants went through the Japanese baseball community like a tornado. How were their games after Tokyo?

They left Tokyo with a record of 14 wins and one tie against the elite teams of Japan to that point. It was inevitable that their unbelievable power would become more noticeable when they went to the countryside. The scores reflected this. Even though the business-oriented Royal Giants needed to make money, it was almost impossible to arrange a good game when there was a huge gap in the playing abilities between the Royal Giants and the Japanese teams in the countryside. Here are the scores for the final nine games in Japan:

Royal Giants	8 - 1	Zenshinshu
Royal Giants	17A - 1	Koryo High School
Royal Giants	11A - 4	Moji Railways
Royal Giants	12A - 4	Fukuoka Kyokai
Royal Giants	7 - 5	Kansai University
Royal Giants	14 - 5	Kansai University
Royal Giants	22A - 4	Korean Shokusan Bank
Royal Giants	6A - 0	Keijo Railways
Royal Giants	17A -2	Keijo Railways

The Royal Giants won a total of 23 games, counting all contests from the beginning of the tour. After this, we are certain that the team also went to the Korean peninsula. There they played two games against the "Busan All Stars" and won 11-1 and 11-0. However, these two games were not listed in the *Official Baseball Guide* issued by the Commissioner's office. If the Korean games are counted, the Royal Giants had 25 wins and one tie. It is unfortunate that no game details can be found from this part of the trip.[1]

Everywhere they went, this team of black players must have overwhelmed the locals. Their physical appearance, and power on the field, must have been a startling sight for the fans.

The most hot-blooded player was the first baseman, Frank Duncan. He said this when reflecting on his trip to Japan:

> In the Spring of 1927, I joined the Japan tour team and went to Japan, and we boarded the big Japanese steamship from San Pedro, California, and headed to Yokohama. It took us 19 days.
>
> The people were the most wonderful people I ever came in contact with. I loved them, I hated to see them go to war. We played all over—Osaka, Kobe, on into Nagasaki. They had some pretty nice teams, they weren't strong hitters but pretty good fielders and base runners, and they had some pretty nice-looking pitchers. But we didn't lose any games… (*Voices from the Great Black Baseball Leagues,* by John Holway.)

Duncan and his teammate Dixon entertained the crowd by showing off their speed on the bases after the last game in Tokyo. From this gesture it would seem that he really enjoyed his time in Japan.

Speaking of Frank Duncan, he was considered to be the leading troublemaker in the Negro Leagues at that time. In 1922, he was the instigator of a brawl that was known as "the worst incident in the history of the Negro baseball leagues." Let's talk about the incident. It happened at the Muehlebach Field in Kansas City. Duncan's team, the Monarchs, was playing against the Chicago American Giants. Duncan collided with the catcher at home plate, and they started to throw punches, leading to a bench-clearing brawl.

There were many instances of the hot-tempered, Alabama-born Duncan fighting on the field.[2] However, when he was in Japan, he was calm and quiet. He was a total gentleman, without any incidents. In his reflection, it was apparent that he really enjoyed his stay in Japan. It was during the cherry blossom season, which created a peaceful atmosphere. He must have felt a heartfelt appreciation towards Japanese people. The people of Japan opened their arms to the visitors from a distant country and treated them with respect and friendship.

In contrast, the star players on the Royal Giants had animosity and conflict waiting for them back home in America. After returning to his home country, Duncan became a manager in the Negro Leagues. He also became a part of history when he mentored Jackie Robinson with the Kansas City Monarchs, who later became the first black player in the major leagues. He must have told Jackie a story or two about Japan.

Biz Mackey also mentored a future star in Roy Campanella, who received the MVP award three times. Both Mackey and Duncan remained in the Negro Leagues, but their influence and contributions did eventually reach major league baseball.[3]

But long before that, their last-minute decision to visit Japan allowed them to contribute to the growth of baseball in Japan as well.

As I stated, it is very interesting to learn about their lives in America after Japan, but I must talk about their path going back to America.

* * *

After the Royal Giants left the Korean peninsula, did they go straight back to America? No they did not. After boarding the *Siberia Maru*, a Nippon Yusen Kaisha Line ship, they arrived at Honolulu, Hawaii, on June 4. They planned to play a couple of games there.

The day after their arrival, on June 5, they were in Honolulu Stadium for a game against a Japanese American team, the Hawaii Asahi, at 2 p.m. According to the press, the local fans were very excited to welcome the Royal Giants.

When they arrived at the ballpark, the first game of that day between the Braves and Filipinos was still underway. It was an official game of the Hawaiian League, and it was in the middle of the seventh inning. The spectators were no longer watching the game. Instead they started applauding, and sent welcoming cheers to the black visitors entering the stadium.

"Stop the game now at seven innings! Let's move on to the next game!" the local fans pleaded, demonstrating the great popularity of the Royal Giants.

Why were expectations so high even before they played their first game? The reason was obvious. An article in the *Honolulu Star-Bulletin*, one of the largest newspapers in Hawaii, introduced the team to the island with a big headline on the front page:

> The Philadelphia Royal Giants, an aggregation of negro baseball players of the first order, left the United States on March 9 for a tour of Japan and the Orient.
>
> After a very stormy 18-day trip and two days in which to get rid of their sea legs, they swung into a very strenuous schedule of games and travel against the picked teams of Japan and Chosen (Korea).
>
> Baseball in the Orient, Japan and Chosen, is very good, much better than one would expect, considering the short length of time that they have been playing ball there. They were not, of course, in a class with this aggregation of stars which includes among its personnel such men as Captain Raleigh Mackey, shortstop; Herbert "Rap" Dickson [sic], centerfielder de luxe; Andrew "Lefty" Cooper, pitcher par excellent [sic]; Pullen, catcher;

Duncan, first baseman; Green, pitcher and right fielder, and one of the hardest hitting little men in present day baseball.

Anyone of the above mentioned men could hold down a position on any of the numerous major league clubs in the United States if were not for the fact that the color line bars them from these leagues.

[...]

Dickson and Mackey are capable of swatting the ball along with such stars as Ruth, Muesel [sic], Cobb, Speaker or any of the great men in baseball you care to name, and they can fill their respective positions equally as well; while the rest of the personnel is not far behind these stars.

The Giants play a smart, peppy, flashy yet safe brand of baseball that is hard to beat ... While in Japan the Giants played 27 games, winning 26 wins and tying one. Truly an enviable record for any ball club, considering the fact that most of the time while off the ball field was spent in travel, and then too, quite a few of the games were played under some of the most adverse weather conditions which are absolutely foreign to American baseball.[4]

No wonder the local fans developed high expectations for this black team even before the games started. Would the Hawaiian teams be able to win against this strong team, or would they allow the Royal Giants to add to their undefeated record? This game would reveal the true level of Hawaiian baseball.

Of course, the level of Hawaiian baseball was not necessarily low. One of the more prestigious teams was the Hawaii Asahi, the defending league champions. However, they had not been winning lately. Many doubted that they were going to win the championship again, and their fans had started to lose faith in their ability. It was under these circumstance that the Asahi ball club welcomed the Royal Giants and hoped to win against them, in order to get back their fans' trust.

About 8,000 spectators gathered for the game. There had never before been that many people in the stadium. The ace Moriyama was announced as the starting pitcher for the Asahi squad. The Royals Giants started Cooper. However, there were slight changes to their lineup. Pullen was used as outfielder for a portion of the game. Perhaps this was a plan to allow some rest from the demanding position of catcher, or maybe it was just for a change of scenery. The real reason is unknown.

Let's look at the report of the game details featured in the June 6 *Honolulu Star-Bulletin*:

The Royal Giants are Truly Giants

They came on the field to fulfill a prediction that they composed one of the best teams of its kind playing on the mainland, and they apparently satisfied all of the spectators that they really deserved the reputation accompanying them to Honolulu.

Who won? Why, the Philadelphia Royal Giants won at a walk. I believe the final score was something like 10 to 0, and it was apparent that they held the Asahis well in hand.

And don't think that the Asahis didn't play some mighty good baseball. Of course, they were nervous—what team wouldn't be? And they made some costly errors, but taking them all in all, they played an exceptionally good game.

The game was ended almost as soon as it started—that is, the Asahi's chances of winning was [sic] ended when the Giants socked young Moriyama's offerings for three hits, and as the last one was a double, it scored two runs. [...]

The Giants kept right on getting runs during various innings, until they had harvested a total of 10 circuits....

[...]

The Asahis played some excellent ball....[Moriyama] struck out several of the Giant sluggers, and acquitted himself with much credit for his bearing and ability to puzzle the Giants' hitters.

The Giants displayed some of the best base running, and the fastest infield work ever seen on local diamonds. Evans, who caught for the visitors, certainly put the fear of his whip into the opposition when they saw him make one or two pegs to second base. Not a base was stolen by the Asahis during the entire game.

Cooper, the Giant pitcher, and his teammate [Mackey], who played shortstop, were the outstanding players of yesterday's game....[5]

[Mackey] is about the fastest player seen here in some time. His peculiar style of catching and throwing the ball, and his tremendous speed, enabled him to pull some stuff that is absolutely new in Honolulu, and while the fans could not help laughing, at the same time it left them open-mouthed to see the speed with which this big fellow scooped up and got rid of the old pill.

The Giants are a team of throwing demons....there will be very few stolen bases if they maintain the speed they displayed yesterday.

And how they can clout out the old apples. There were long drives, and short drives, and hot grounders, and perfect bunts—when they were needed. Their base running was perfect. Dickson [sic] …proved himself to be a whirlwind on base, and stole bases with apparent ease.

And not to forget the Giants' outfield. It's good….They went after everything—and caught it. No hesitation, no misjudgments—and no errors.

The best play of yesterday's game was pulled by Pullen, the Giant left fielder, who in the eighth inning, made a long and spectacular run after a fly ball hit out by an Asahi player. He was unable to keep on his feet and executed a very nearly perfect nose dive, but as he hit the ground he caught the ball, and slid along for at least 10 feet on his stomach, with the ball held in his hand where every fan could see that he had caught it.

[…]

The Giants team will be one of the most popular teams ever seen in action here. They are full of pep, fun, and good baseball….

The Hawaii newspapers did not mention anything about their disappointment in the loss of the celebrated local team; instead they were impressed with the plays by the visiting professional black ball club. Similar to the events detailed in Chapter 5, reporters were impressed by the open-hearted attitudes of the ballplayers and the refusal of the Royal Giants' catcher to complain about the missed calls of the locally-hired umpire. Here are the game details.

Score by inning:
Royal Giants   2 0 0 1 0 1 2 1 3 = 10
Asahi Squad   0 0 0 0 0 0 0 0 0 = 0

I should include a story about the relief pitcher of the Asahi squad, who pitched in the eighth and ninth innings and allowed the final four runs. Because the ace Moriyama gave up six runs in seven innings, a kid was called in to relieve him. This kid later attended Hosei University and became the ace pitcher of the Osaka Tigers. His name was Tadashi Wakabayashi.[6]

At that time, he was only 18 years old and had just graduated from McKinley High School. He was a popular kid and known by the nickname "Bozo," a name that had slowly morphed from "Bozu." He was called Bozu early in his life because he was cared for by monks in a Zen temple.[7] Later on, he became well-known as a phenomenal pitcher because he could throw "seven different colored magic balls" (types of pitches). After the end of his career, he was inducted into the Baseball Hall of Fame in Japan. As a young relief pitcher in Showa 2 (1927), Bozo could have never expected that he had such a destiny to fulfill.

Bozo fearlessly threw fastballs to the Royal Giants. His fearlessness backfired as he gave up many hits. Perhaps this was when Bozo, who later became the king of the breaking ball, realized that having only a fastball was not going to cut it.[8]

野球

12

After Leaving Japan

It was Showa 2 (1927), nine years before the Japanese professional baseball league was born. The Royal Giants came to Japan and went undefeated against our elite teams. How did they perform after they left Japan?

On their way home, they stopped in Hawaii and played against the Asahi ball club, made up of Japanese Americans. The Royal Giants accomplished a big, 10-0 win against the Asahi. Then the unexpected happened.

Did they keep their undefeated record throughout their tour?

The answer is "No." It was surprising to learn that they had lost.

Their undefeated record was broken during their third game in Hawaii, in a game against the All-Chinese ball club.

The Royal Giants looked fine in their second game when they defeated Standard Oil, 7-3. Standard Oil were the defending champions of the Hawaiian Commercial League. They featured a former major league pitcher, Johnnie Williams, so their level was quite high.[1]

Even with the former big leaguer, who gave up a long homer to Mackey—smashed between left and center—Standard Oil could not win the game as they were unable to hit Green. The Royal Giants continued to enjoy an undefeated record during their goodwill tour.

During their third game in Hawaii against the All-Chinese, the game was going as usual for the Royal Giants. In the first inning, Dixon hit a triple and came in to score easily on Pullen's sacrifice fly. The fans in the stands were wondering, "How many runs would the black team score today?"

However, unusual for the Royal Giants, they did not have another opportunity to score until the ninth inning. When you play many baseball games, sometimes things do not go according to plan. This seems to have been the case here.

A side-armer, Yu Chun, was pitching well for the All-Chinese team. His slow breaking pitches stifled the Royal Giants. He struck out nine batters. Cooper also had eight strikeouts, but he allowed one run in the first inning and two runs in the fourth. The other team was in control for the entire game.

When the Royal Giants started to rally, it was already in the last inning. Green started the rally with a hit to center. Fagan hit a grounder to the shortstop, who tried to turn a double play, but made an error. The opportunity to tie or take the lead arrived for the Giants.

With two outs, and two runners on, it was all up to the next batter, Walker. He hit a line drive to the first baseman, but unfortunately the ball stuck right into the glove. The game was over. The Royal Giants had lost their first game, 3-1.

The fans could not accept the loss. "The blacks let the Chinese win," they said. "They went easy on them!"

This rumor that the Royal Giants lost on purpose spread quickly and everybody was convinced that it was true. "After they won against the local popular teams, Hawaii Asahi and Standard Oil, they might have thought that if they won against the All-Chinese, they would have lost the interest of the spectators. They needed to let at least one team win."

The *Honolulu Star-Bulletin* responded quickly. On June 14, reporter Don Watson wrote:

> "The principal topic of conversation among local baseball fans since Sunday seems to be the victory of the All-Chinese over the Philadelphia Royals Giants.
>
> The reason for all the chatter is that the story is going the round that the Giants "threw" the game to the Chinese—that they "eased up" so that the locals could beat them and thereby draw a big crowd at a return game.
>
> Such a line of talk is certainly not to the credit of those who are spreading the report and who insist that the game was not "on the level." How they figure that the Giants "laid down" is more than we can see—and the only [reason for] the howl that is in sight is that some disgruntled gamblers are having a hard [time] parting with the money they lost.
>
> Some talk was heard a few days ago about sportsmanship in connection with the Giants' games. Certainly it is not treating the Giants fair to spread a rumor that they "threw" a baseball game. It is an insult to these visitors as well as to the local team that played "heads up" baseball to earn a victory.
>
> The Giants…would have no reason to throw the game to the Chinese even if they felt inclined to adopt such tactics.
>
> Here was a team with a long string of victories to its credit, playing its 31st game since leaving the mainland. Why break a long string of victories by "throwing" a game? Certainly such action would not have been taken…over crowds. All of the Giant games have been well attended and indications were that the crowds would continue to flock to the Stadium every time the visitors performed.

Watson mentioned some of the plays that were performed by the Giants players during the game, and wondered how the game could possibly have been fixed. A ball that usually would have landed between left and center was caught by an outfielder with a fine play. Dixon stretched a hit into a triple "by daring base-running." Mackey dove to field a potential base hit through the infield and threw it to first base like a bullet for the out. How could they make such fine plays, asked Watson, if they were trying to fix the game?

Ashman Beaven, the general manager of Honolulu Stadium, also responded promptly.[2] He expressed his anger about the rumor that it was a fixed game in the *Star-Bulletin* on June 14. He offered a $500 reward to anybody who could prove it was a fixed game.[3]

He also announced that if any game was proved to be fixed, then he would cancel the rest of the Giants' schedule. His announcement had such a big impact that the rumors completely disappeared.

I also need to add the game against the Braves on the 26th of June to the list of Royal Giants' losses. They won all their games in Hawaii except those two, ending with a record of eight wins and two losses. Here are the scores:

Royal Giants	10 - 0	Hawaii Asahi
Royal Giants	7 - 3	Standard
Royal Giants	1 - 3	All-Chinese
Royal Giants	5 - 3	All Stars
Royal Giants	2 - 0	Elks
Royal Giants	11 - 0	Filipinos
Royal Giants	13 - 5	Flyers
Royal Giants	0 - 1	Braves
Royal Giants	5 - 3	All-Chinese
Royal Giants	5 - 4	Braves

In addition, the newspapers wrote carefully about the second loss because it was right after the fixed-game incident. One of the headlines read:

"1 - 0 The Royal Giants proudly lost the game!"

The Philadelphia Royal Giants returned home in June after finishing the tour in Japan and Hawaii. It was a three-month long tour that had begun on March 9.

I wondered, what happened to them after the tour? The team name Philadelphia Royal Giants was used only for the tour to the Far East.[4] They were not even from Philadelphia. If they had registered their team in the Negro Leagues, they would have returned to the league and continued to play. The reality was different. It turned out to have been a temporary team formed by the organizer, Lonnie Goodwin.

I assumed that the team's main players, Mackey and Dixon, continued to play in the league, but what about the others?

Upon investigating, I was shocked to find out that even the Royal Giants' star players went through an ordeal after they returned. It is often said that "fact is stranger than fiction"—and the saying did actually apply to their lives.

After the Japan tour, they did not come home to a happy welcome or hugs from their friends. Instead they were threatened with fines and suspensions, including a harsh five-year ban from the Negro Leagues.

Mackey, Dixon, and Duncan were the players who faced punishment.[5] They were all from different teams, but they were real professional players from the Negro Leagues. After playing in the California Winter League, they left for Japan. They missed games of the official season that had started in April. Their appearance in the Winter League might have been forgiven, as it was an off season league, but it was reasonable to consider that missing the regular season was a breach of contract. However, the whole thing might have been the result of a misunderstanding.

The players may have assumed that the organizer, Goodwin, had arranged for their leave of absence from their teams. They might have thought that they had permission to leave the league. Otherwise, perhaps they wouldn't have gone to Japan if their status was in jeopardy.

Needless to say, the five-year suspension was extremely severe. Their baseball careers would have been over had they accepted this suspension. They appealed and pleaded for forgiveness.

The suspension was reduced due to their persistence and sincere attitude—and maybe because of Mackey's consistently cheerful personality and his serious attitude toward baseball. They were found to be innocent and not responsible for missing league games. They received a lesser penalty, but it was a suspension for 30 days and a fine of $200.00.[6] As soon as they served out their suspension, they returned to their normal lives and moved on with their baseball careers.

The most splendid career of all three players after the suspension was Rap Dixon's. Of course it would be him. He was only 23 years old at that time. In Japan, he astonished the fans with a homer to the outfield fence at Koshien. The total number of his home runs in Japan was probably comparable to that of Mackey's, even though records were not available. He also had a strong arm and speedy legs. He was at the rising point of his baseball career at that time, so he became very prominent in America.

After the suspension Dixon joined the Baltimore Black Sox, where he played well and shined. His improvements were remarkable and he became an outstanding player, but it might not have been considered important by the general baseball public because he was in the Negro Leagues. In order to demonstrate his true ability, it would be best to highlight a game he played against a major league team.

During the off-season in 1928, his team played against a major league all-star team. He got three hits in four at bats off Lefty Grove, including a home run, a double, and a single. He crushed the ball against this great pitcher.[7]

His powerful offense in the season of 1929 was also astounding. He played 60 games with the Black Sox and hit 16 home runs, with a .432 average. He greatly contributed to his team's championship in the eastern region. His ability was again revealed in a game against white major leaguers. He hit a triple and a double in four at bats against Jack Ogden.[8] Although he was held hitless by the pitcher Ed Rommel of the Athletics, he hit a double and a single off the A's' Howard Ehmke.[9,10] In these three games against major leaguers, he recorded a .500 average.

His performance on July 5, 1930, made his name even more famous in the black community. On that day, Dixon achieved a record that not even Babe Ruth accomplished. Yankee Stadium was the Babe's home—it was called "The House that Ruth Built." Yet Rap Dixon made a better record than the master of the house.[11]

Dixon hit three homers in one day at Yankee Stadium. Not only was it a record that Rap owned, it was also a special day for the black fans because it was the first-ever Negro League game played at Yankee Stadium.

Dixon and others played a doubleheader against the defending champion New York Lincoln Giants on this special day.[12] During the first inning of the first game, he hit a homer to the right field bleachers with a runner on base. This was the first home run hit by a black player in Yankee Stadium. The pitcher was the top-notch right hander Bill Holland. Dixon's team won 13-4.

In the second game of the doubleheader, Dixon hit two home runs consecutively off Connie Rector. The game ended in a 5-3 victory by Baltimore.

In fact, Dixon did not go along when the Royal Giants team visited Japan for a second time because he was in great demand in America.

Mackey, on the other hand, who had become a more incredible human being for having visited Japan, chose to make a return trip.

野球

13

Between the First and Second Visit to Japan

It was Biz Mackey's destiny to visit Japan again. The first time he visited Japan was in Showa 2 (1927) when he was with the other strong players, Dixon and Duncan.

He hit a home run in three consecutive games at the Jingu Gaien Stadium. They were straight over the outfield bleachers, which had never been done before. The Royal Giants won 24 games with zero losses in Japan before they went back to America. He was the backbone of that strong but gentlemanly team.

In Showa 7 (1932), five years after the first visit, Mackey visited again, leading the Philadelphia Royal Giants once more. Again they achieved great results, winning 24 games and losing one.

Before going into the details of the games, I need to talk about Mackey's five years in between the two visits.

In June, Showa 2 (1927), Mackey returned from the first Japan tour and rejoined the Philadelphia Hilldale club. However, he was suspended for 30 days and fined $200, as I mentioned in the previous chapter.

Though he played shortstop in Japan, he was actually a catcher in the U.S. With Hilldale he became known as a good backstop with a strong arm, and a strong leader for the pitchers.

His batting against major league pitchers was consistently good, though there were few records of his accomplishments.

In 1927, he had two hits in four at bats against Joe Pirrone's All Star team.[1] In 1928, in a game against Connie Mack and his Philadelphia Athletics, he recorded five hits, three against Bullet Joe Bush and two against Ed Rommel.[2,3] Mackey contributed greatly to the Negro League team, who won two out of three games against the Athletics.

In 1929, his team played against a major league team with Al Simmons, Jimmie Foxx, and Meusel.[4] In three games, he hit five for 13 (.385). In 1930 he contributed to his team's 8-5 win over another major league squad with a good hit off Roy Sherid of the Yankees.[5]

In summary, Mackey had flawless defensive and offensive skills, yet at the same time his most lovable characteristic was his kind and cheerful personality. It was understandable that many managers valued him as a team captain.

For these reasons, Raleigh "Biz" Mackey had established a consistently high mark of achievement in the Negro Leagues. Despite his positive energy though, he and his black teammates were still negatively affected by the devastating social situation that unfolded around them.

The Great Depression started with the crash of the New York Stock Market in 1929 and jeopardized the existence of the Negro Leagues. Even though the level of talent in black baseball was equal to the talent of the white major leagues, they were not as financially strong as the major leagues. In fact, several black teams disappeared due to the loss of their sponsors. The teams that managed to survive could not even pay salaries to their players, so the players wandered the streets uncertain about their future.

It was amazing to learn that Biz Mackey was in the center of this chaos, but he had prevailed against all odds and continued to be a star. It is uncertain how much of his salary was guaranteed.

In the fall of 1932 (Showa 7), Mackey accepted an invitation to join another long tour to the Far East, not only because of his love for Japan, but also because of the financial hardships caused by the Great Depression in America.

By the way, American society changed drastically during these five years (1927-1932), but Japan remained stable. The exception was the Japanese baseball community, which had experienced significant changes. Was Mackey able to notice these shifts?

The following are the causes of change in the Japanese baseball community:

1. The arrival of the American major league all-star team in 1931 (Showa 6).
2. The Baseball Control Ordinance was issued.[6]

Regarding #1—the Showa 6 (1931) major league tour—while there are many books that detail the major leaguers' tours in Japan and their influence on Japanese baseball, it is important to remember the Philadelphia Royal Giants and their influence.

The *Yomiuri Shimbun* invited a major league team from America in order to sell more subscriptions. It was four years after the Royal Giants came to Japan. In between, no professional teams had come to Japan. Therefore, the Japanese players and fans saw a black professional baseball team before they saw elite white players.

The difference between these two teams was obvious. It was not just the color of their skin. The contrast in the ways that they arrived in Japan after the long voyage across the ocean showed the true difference in their characters.

When the black team stepped on Japanese soil for the first time, I wonder if anybody was there to welcome them. Possibly the tour organizer, Mr. Irie, was the only person who met them. There were no welcoming cheers by fans or hanging banners. They were a traveling baseball team who came without an invitation. They were an all-black team wearing black hunting caps and wrapping themselves with thick black coats. This group of 14 men must have stood out from the waves of people at the Yokohama port.

By contrast, when the white major league team arrived in Japan, the atmosphere of the Yokohama port, No. 4 terminal, was cheerful and festive. As soon as they stepped foot on Japanese soil, a bouquet of flowers was placed in each of their hands. In the sky, the organizer's welcome airplane was trailing welcome signs. The regular train became a "charter train" from Yokohama port to Tokyo station.

I do not need to write about the cheering fans at Tokyo station and the parade to the Teikoku Hotel where they stayed. There is no Japanese baseball history book that does not mention the welcoming of the major leaguers. They were invited to Japan as "baseball missionaries." This formed a stark contrast with the all-black traveling team. The enthusiasm of the promoter, the *Yomiuri Shimbun*, was huge because the company's future depended on the success of this event.

Understandably, the baseball games that were held under these circumstances differed greatly from those played by the black team four years earlier.

The attitude of these "baseball missionaries" was consistently "to teach baseball," and not to "have fun together." First of all, they were full of confidence and arrogance because they were elite major leaguers with enormous power. In fact, the team was called "the best of the best of the American teams." It was an epithet that suited this team very well. The roster of stars included:

Pitcher	Lefty Grove	Athletics
Pitcher	Larry French	Pirates
Pitcher	Bruce Cunningham	Braves
Catcher	Mickey Cochrane	Athletics
Catcher	Muddy Ruel	Senators
1B	Lou Gehrig	Yankees
1B	George Kelly	Giants
2B	Frankie Frisch	Cardinals

3B	Willie Kamm	Indians
SS	Rabbit Maranville	Braves
LF	Al Simmons	Athletics
CF	Tom Oliver	Red Sox
RF	Lefty O'Doul	Dodgers[7]
RF	Ralph Shinners	Giants

They were all current major leaguers. It is reasonable to assume that Japanese baseball society must have felt an obligation to bow down before them.

This visiting squad knew their mission in Japan very well. This can be seen in the actions they took upon their arrival.

On October 30, the day after their arrival, they visited Keio University's Nitta baseball field and displayed their skills. The next day, they went to Meiji University's Izumi baseball field. They invited the players from Waseda University to a baseball clinic. They visited a number of other colleges to host clinics, such as Tokyo University's Komaba field, Hosei University and Rikkyo University.

It was not only all-star players who provided instructions, but also an umpire, Beans Reardon, who instructed umpires from the Tokyo Big 6 university league. The team's athletic trainer, Dr. Leonard Knowles, enthusiastically taught people in the baseball community how to train players. They all understood what it meant to be baseball missionaries and what they needed to do. Their results:

Major League All Stars	7 - 0	Rikkyou
Major League All Stars	8 - 5	Waseda
Major League All Stars	4 - 0	Meiji
Major League All Stars	13 - 2	Sundai Club
Major League All Stars	14 - 1	All Japan
Major League All Stars	6 - 3	All Japan
Major League All Stars	11 - 0	All Japan
Major League All Stars	15 - 0	All Japan
Major League All Stars	2 - 0	All Keio
Major League All Stars	8 - 1	All Hosei
Major League All Stars	5 - 1	All Keio
Major League All Stars	10 - 0	Waseda
Major League All Stars	8 - 0	All Keio
Major League All Stars	17 - 8	Yahata Seitetsu

Major League All Stars	7 - 2	Kansai University
Major League All Stars	3 - 2	All Yokohama
Major League All Stars	11 - 5	Yokosho Club

It would be more accurate to call these games "baseball clinics" rather than games. It is easy to tell that the atmosphere differed from that of the games involving the black ball club. With the Royal Giants, the game was played in a relaxed mood, in the spirit of "Let's have fun!" With the major leaguers it was different. They were there to be role models, teachers and textbooks.

The Japanese players realized how big the skill gap was between them and the major leaguers when they played against this great team. The members of the All-Japan team were selected by a fan vote through the newspaper. Prior to the arrival of the major leaguers, the All-Japan players admired the greatness of the Americans. After the games, they were disappointed in themselves.

When they played against the black team, even though there was a big difference in power, they were able to play a good game and felt good about themselves. However, they struggled to play against the major league all-star team. Because the All-Japan team was considered an elite team, their embarrassing performance against the major league all-stars was even more disheartening. It would not be surprising if some of the players on the All-Japan team lost some passion for baseball.

It was a challenge for Japanese players to play against this great team. The fans, though, looked forward to these games because they came to watch the American players, not the Japanese players. Their textbook plays were a revelation. The Japanese fans were mesmerized by the Americans' display of power, which was obviously greater than the Japanese ball players. Sometimes the fans would applaud when the major leaguers ridiculed the Japanese players.

The fans, who once applauded the Philadelphia Royal Giants when they behaved like gentleman and displayed humility towards the games, had changed.

They watched top-notch play by white major leaguers who performed at an elite level. The major leaguers proudly and without hesitation showed off their power and polished skills. After watching this, the humility that the Royal Giants displayed faded from the memories of the fans. The major leaguers' power was about the same as that of the Royal Giants, but their approach to the game and how they treated the competition was so different.

When Raleigh "Biz" Mackey came to Japan for the second time, I wonder if he knew about this change in the fans. After five years, I wonder if he expected to receive the same level of respect and compassion from the Japanese fans?

There was one more big change in Japanese baseball society. I mentioned it previously: the issue of the "Baseball Control Ordinance."

What was the Baseball Control Ordinance? This rule was issued by the Ministry of Education. It applied to the world of amateur sports, and impacted all of baseball—from universities all the way down to elementary schools. In this ordinance, the biggest obstacle for Biz and the other black players was this rule: "Students are not permitted to play against any professional baseball teams."

The reason for this rule was that the *Yomiuri Shimbun* had made money on games between the major leaguers and university teams in the previous year (Showa 6, 1931). In fact, the profits went entirely to the American team, so *Yomiuri* actually ended up losing money on the tour. As a result, this criticism was unavoidable.

This new ordinance could be called a "souvenir" from the visiting major league all-stars. When the Royal Giants came to Japan for the second time in Showa 7 (1932), they were negatively affected by this ordinance.

Of course, Mackey and the other players did not know about the ordinance in advance. It was obvious from newspaper reports at the time, in which he stated that his team was planning to play against elite college teams, just like before. They thought they could find any number of teams in no time when they arrived in Japan. In fact, they had even bigger expectations and aspirations than five years before.

This was unfortunate for the black players, but there was no way they could have known beforehand.

In the fall of Showa 7 (1932), their passenger ship, *Chichibu Maru*, also carried Japanese Olympians on their triumphant trip back to Japan from the Olympic Games in Los Angeles, California. Biz Mackey was returning to Japan, once again leading the Royal Giants, but this time it was without his familiar teammates Dixon and Duncan.

野球

14

Before the Transformation of Japanese Baseball Society

7:40 a.m., September 7, Showa 7 (1932). The crowds of people who gathered in Yokohama port roared. They were looking forward to finally welcoming the *Chichibu Maru*, which had just entered the harbor. Many flags waved, and the crowd's singing got louder and louder. The festivities and excitement were as cheerful as when the major leaguers arrived in Japan in the previous year.

The flags made it obvious that the welcoming party was for the Japanese Olympians—the Japanese national flag, the Japan Swimming Federation flag, the Japan Equestrian flag. Of course they were not for the black baseball squad known as the Philadelphia Royal Giants.

They were travelling to Japan for a second time just as Japanese baseball society was in the middle of a transformation. As soon as they arrived at Yokohama, the Royal Giants got a sinking feeling that this was bad timing for a baseball tour.

Upon reflection, though it might have been bad timing for the team, ultimately it was good timing for Japan. Of course, the black team could have had no clue at that time.

"How can we attract more fans to come watch our baseball? … If the game is not fun, then we cannot get any fans to come to our games." The black team may have already predicted their eventual hardships.

It would be strange to see people pay special attention to the Royal Giants when they arrived at the same time as a group of accomplished Japanese Olympians returning home from Los Angeles.

The Olympic duo of Kusuo Kitamura and Shozo Makino were in the crowd. Kitamura won the gold medal in the men's swimming 1500-meter freestyle, and Makino won the silver medal in the same event. Also passing through the crowd were: Yoshiyuki Tsuruta, who had won consecutive gold medals in the men's 200-meter breaststroke; Yasuji Miyazaki, who won the gold for the men's 100-meter freestyle; and Masaji Kiyokawa, who won gold for the men's 100-meter backstroke. Lieutenant Takeichi Nishi, who won the gold medal in individual show jumping with his horse Uranus, was also there.

Welcoming these Olympians home, the Japanese people must have been ecstatic just to participate in the electric crowds. Their excitement could be seen in newspaper headlines:

> Kings of Water! A Conqueror on Horseback! Your accomplishments mesmerized the people of the whole world displaying the Island Nation Japan. Today, you proudly made a historic triumphant return to your country! Thank you! We, Japanese citizens, are all filled with sheer joy today … – *Tokyo Asahi Shimbun*, September 9, Showa 7 (1932).

The Royal Giants were fortunate to be included in a short newspaper article titled "The Arrival of the Black Baseball Squad," printed beneath the Olympic national team report.

It could be seen from the introduction of the ballplayers that the Japanese people had little interest in the black team. The pitcher Evans was mistakenly called "Evants," which could be viewed as a minor mistake, but writing Cooper as "Kuper" and Mackey as "Mackay" was awful. It showed the reporter's laziness, especially because these three players were arriving in Japan for a second time. A good reporter would have at least known their names from the previous tour.

The names of the rest of the players were mistakenly written as well. Perhaps the reporters of this renowned newspaper were too busy to pay attention to the details because of the Olympic national team.

In addition to all the sports celebrities, the famous opera singer Tamaki Miura, known for Madam Butterfly, was on board the same ship. She too was surrounded by many reporters. She was returning to Japan for a Tokyo performance, and was scheduled to leave for Italy two days later.

The second tour of the Royal Giants was rarely talked about in the press. However, their names (only surnames) were introduced at least in the English-language newspaper, *Japan Times and Mail.*

Pitcher	Cooper
Pitcher	Evans
Pitcher	Ross
Catcher	Mackey
Catcher	Baker
1B	Carr
2B	Perez

3B	Bland
SS	Harding
LF	Martin
RF	Chico
CF	Clemente

From the article written before the listing of their names, it was obvious that the black players were not aware of the new Baseball Control Ordinance that banned students from playing in games against professional teams. The article read:

> The black professional baseball team, the Philadelphia Royal Giants, arrived at Yokohama from Hawaii aboard the *Chichibu Maru* yesterday morning. They are stopping in Japan on their way to Manila. The manager is Will, who leads the team with 12 players.[1] If they manage to organize enough games, the length of their stay in Japan will be several weeks. As they negotiate to play games in Tokyo, they are planning to talk with university teams. (September 10, Showa 7 [1932])

In fact, when they had come to Japan five years earlier, they had mainly played against college teams and became very popular doing so. Because there were no professional baseball teams yet at that time, college baseball was probably the top level of baseball in Japan.

But now the government had issued the Baseball Control Ordinance. In the previous year, Showa 6 (1931), student players had participated in the games against the major league all-stars. Because of the unprecedented fan interest, it was decided that baseball needed to be better regulated. The law was officially issued on March 28. Even though six months had passed, the Royal Giants had arrived expecting the same situation as in Showa 2 (1927).

It ended up taking the Royal Giants four days to find their first opponents. If they could not play student teams, they needed to find corporate ball clubs. It was not easy. Luckily for them, they found club teams that were made up of alumni of universities and commercial/vocational high schools. Teams made up of alumni were very common. The Royal Giants were lucky that these alumni teams were willing to compete against a professional team.

*   *   *

The first game, against the Yokohama Commercial Club, took place at Yokohama Park Stadium on September 3. Start time was 3:15 p.m. This contest was obviously a game against non-students.

Yokohama Commercial Club was a strong team at that time. In the previous year, they played against the major league all-star team. They played well but lost 11-5. The players of this team might have thought that they had a chance to win against the black professional team, so they got carried away and failed.

Seiichi Ohashi, who had played against the major leaguers, had returned to his hometown, Kobe, to get a job, but was called back to join the club for the new game against the Royal Giants. They also added four current student players (which caused a big problem later on).

Score by inning:
Royal Giants   1 0 0 2 0 0 2 0 0 = 5
Yokosho   1 1 0 0 0 1 0 0 0 = 3

Yokosho Lineup:

LF	Mochizuki
CF	Ei, Nakajimasho
SS	Sugiya
3B	Kuroda
RF	Miyazaki
1B	Shiomi
C	Usami
P	Araki, Igarashi
2B	Ohashi

ROYAL GIANTS		YOKOHAMA CLUB
36	AB	32
12	H	6
1	SAC	0
4	K	7
5	BB	4
4	SB	1
3	E	3
1	HR	0
0	3B	2
4	2B	2

As I stated before, there is not much information about the Showa 7 (1932) Royal Giants in magazines and newspapers. Compared to their first visit, the reports of their second tour were written with less detail and lacked verve and style.

However, I was lucky to be able to hear first-hand testimonies and vivid memories from some of the former players in Japan. Mr. Chuzo Mochizuki, who was a left fielder, played in this game as the lead-off batter:

> Well, I remember that game very well. I played even though I was still a student at that time. Usami, Araki, and Igarashi were also students, but they also played, so it became a problem because of the Baseball Control Ordinance. Do you know what? A reporter at one of the newspapers wrote about it. We worried that we were going to be expelled from school. Principal Tajiri was really great. He talked with Mr. Ichiro Hatoyama, the Minister of Education, and the result was that there was no substantial penalty.[2] It was just a warning. Although we lost, it was a good game. We did not feel that our team was overmatched.

Mr. Usami, who was also a student, remembered Mackey's great skills better than his relief at not being expelled.

> I was a catcher, so I was focused on Mackey's fine abilities behind the plate. He was smooth, throwing the ball from his knees to second base like a string held taut. I have never seen an arm like his. The pitcher on the mound was forced to get low in order to avoid his throws [to second].
>
> I was surprised to see his glove as well. The mitt that we used was called a non-break mitt, which had a pocket and a round shape. We always caught the ball with our right hand next to the mitt. Mackey caught with only one hand …. It was impossible. If you did this with my mitt, the ball would bounce out.
>
> However, Mackey from this Royal Giants team was totally different. With only his left hand, he could easily catch the ball. His movement was so elegant.
>
> I thought to myself, "He must be using a first base mitt." Then I watched him closely. It was a catcher's mitt. My jaw dropped to the ground.
>
> When you think about it, it is logical. If you catch the ball by putting the right hand next to the mitt, the number of injuries will go up. That is why catchers sprain their thumbs from foul tips. In fact, it was said that two catchers were always needed for one game.
>
> It was the same in America. Proof can be seen in the history of jersey numbers in baseball. When they started putting numbers on uniforms, the number 1 was the pitcher and 2 was the catcher. The number 10 was also for a catcher. It was imperative to have two catchers

on the team. There were many injuries to catchers. Among the causes of catcher injuries were the shape of the old mitt and the way of receiving pitches.

When I saw Mackey's mitt and his receiving skills, I felt like blinders were being removed from my eyes. I was awakened to the truth. Later on, I saw the same catching style in Doigaki, a player for Hanshin.[3] I really think that Mackey had a huge impact on Japanese catchers.

The pitcher, Mr. Hachiro Araki, mainly remembered his own performance against the Royal Giants. He did not think that he pitched well that day, but according to the catcher, Usami, even though Araki allowed base runners, he held the game at a tie for six innings. He was pitching well. It was a see-saw game. It is possible that the Royal Giants were not playing at their best, or that they were trying to make it an interesting game, as they did five years earlier.

As for Mr. Araki, he remembered more about being a winning pitcher in a game against the Kono Alameda All Stars (a Japanese American semi-pro team from California) and in a big game against the Tomon ball club.[4] Even though he was unable to remember the details of the games against the Royal Giants, he did remember the black players.

His memory still contained scenes of striking out a couple of batters from the black team with a curve ball.

It was in January, Showa 60 (1985), when I met Mr. Araki for the first time. We were sitting in a café in the front of Tokyo Nakano station. He stood up and showed his pitching form in the middle of the café while recalling that scene. His windup was to stretch his back like a bow and snap back to throw his pitch. It was a very flexible pitching form.

I was convinced that this was how he threw his breaking ball. At the same time I learned how he and his teammates had a strong passion for baseball and spent an enormous amount of time on the game in their youth.

Baseball was always part of their lives afterwards. Araki and his battery-mate Usami joined the Mantetsu team and played in the Intercity Baseball Tournament.

Mr. Mochizuki joined the Nippon Life Assurance Co. and played for All-Osaka in the Intercity Baseball Tournament and won the championship.

Because of the intervention of his high school principal Tajiri, the Yokohama Commercial Club did not have any problems with the Baseball Control Ordinance. This was really fortunate for the student players on the team. It was also lucky for the Royal Giants.

Had these students been severely penalized under the Baseball Control Ordinance, the reputation of the Royal Giants might have been tarnished, because they would have been considered to be instigators. It was good they avoided trouble this time. However, in the next game against Tomon they faced the same problem again.

野球

15

Their Composure and Gentleness

On December 18, Showa 60 (1985), I had an opportunity to meet Mr. Shozo Waka-hara.[1] It was in the lounge of Osaka Waseda Club in Umeda, Osaka. I was fortunate that the pitcher, Mr. Masao Date, who pitched well against the major league all-stars, also sat with us.[2]

Mr. Wakahara was a freshman at Waseda University at the time, in Showa 7 (1932). It was right after he graduated from Yahata Commercial High School that he pitched against the Royal Giants. After being recruited by the alumni, he ended up breaking the newly passed law that "students cannot play against professional teams."

"I was the first one to be subjected to disciplinary action by the Baseball Control Or-dinance," Wakahara said rather cheerfully as he reflected on the past events.

> Before I knew it, I was in the game. Mind you, I was a freshman. It was imperative that I follow an order coming from the alumni. At that time, alumni had a lot of authority. Some were already well-known people. If they say "Go!", then of course I go.
>
> After that, I was suspended from playing baseball because I played in that game. Truly, I did not know what was going on.
>
> As a result, I was not allowed to play until the fall of Showa 8 (1933) although I had en-tered Waseda in Showa 7 (1932). I don't have any recollection of being angry or regretful—I just remember that I had a good experience playing in that game.

The Royal Giants' first game, after which Yokohama Kosho Club received only a warn-ing for using three student players, was just six days prior.[3] It makes me wonder why, even though both teams broke the rules and it happened only days apart, were only the players from Waseda disciplined?

Those subjected to disciplinary action were Mr. Munehiro Isao, Mr. Yutaka Fukuda and Mr. Wakahara. They were all freshmen. Mr. Masao Date, a Waseda alumnus, shared his recollection.

> At that time, club teams were made up of alumni from each university, but they usually added three active student players. During the game, as long as we kept this ratio, we could switch the players around at any time.
>
> The game between the Philadelphia Royal Giants and the Tomon Club was played as we normally did back then. We heard something about that ordinance, but nobody knew exactly what it was. Although it said that students were not allowed to play against professional teams, we assumed that having only three players would not be an issue ... if the students were starting members on the university team, then it would have seemed to be an issue. We were using alternates who were new freshmen ... this was our thinking back then. That was why those three ballplayers suited up for us. We never expected that it was going to be a problem. I actually knew about their Showa 2 (1927) tour in Japan. I knew there were some players who were as good as the white major leaguers even though they were from the Negro Leagues. If I remember correctly, the Tomon Club lost 10-1 or 10-2—they opened a big gap, right?

Let's look at this game. Was Mr. Date correct? The truth is quite interesting. Actually, it was a really good game.

Score by inning:

| Royal Giants | 0 0 2 3 0 0 0 5 0 = 10 |
| Tomon Club | 1 0 0 1 1 0 0 4 0 = 7 |

As I mentioned before, the Royal Giants drew less attention from the media in Showa 7 (1932)—the details for this game could not be found. My suspicion is that the game was not in fact a "real" game. Looking at the box score, there might have been some "fixing" by the black team.

Up until the fifth inning, the score was 5-3 and both teams were adding runs bit by bit. At least each team was playing well, but in the eighth inning, the Royals squad scored five runs and took a big lead. Right after that, the Royals let Tomon score four to make it even. The Giants' financial situation was worse than in Showa 2 (1927). Their best course of action would have been to be more business oriented. Considering their difference in abilities, it is possible that the final score should have been 10-1, as Mr. Date recalled.

The abilities that Mackey and the other black players displayed can be understood from the impressions that have stayed with Mr. Wakahara to this day.

> I have never seen such a strong team in my entire life. This does not mean only the teams that I have played against, it includes all the teams that I have watched too. They were the best. Mr. Date thinks that the Royal Giants team that came in Showa 2 (1927) was the stronger team. Unfortunately, I have no idea about them, so I cannot compare them. I think that this Showa 7 (1932) team was also strong.
>
> There was no comparison between our teams. First of all, their physique was different from us. Someone from our team exclaimed, "Wow, they are two times bigger than us!" They were really big.
>
> When we played against teams that were said to be strong, I always managed to focus and pitch fairly well. No matter how strong the teams were, I could avoid letting them overpower us. However, this black team was different. From the beginning, the difference was obvious. We could not escape their blows.
>
> They were well composed. They had good arms and they were agile. I envied them so much.

The following is not a memory of Mr. Wakahara, but from the scenes described we can tell that it was the game he played in. Given the limited information that was left about the Royal Giants' second tour, an article that appeared in the *Yakyukai*, Special Issue: No. 15, 22nd edition., Showa 7 (1932), is quite valuable. It was signed by a reporter named "Hasumoto."

> Need some money on the way to Manila!—No way, they are not that desperate! The kuronbo baseball squad is here again.[4] It's their second time. When they were here in the spring of Showa 2 (1927), the team had a powerful lineup with a left-handed pitcher, Cooper; a shortstop, Mackey; a first baseman, Duncan; a second baseman, Fagen; and an outfielder, Dixon …
>
> Anyway, I made a business trip to Totsuka to have a look on the 18th. Wow, I was surprised at their color. They were so dark. Their color was even darker than Japanese people with tans who have just come back from their summer vacation.
>
> By the way, speaking of their batting, I was impressed with their power. They could smash the ball to the outfield so easily. Fantastic! Their offense did a great job, and it resulted in a 20-0 blowout.

Tomon could even shut up crying children.[5] … I might be overestimating Tomon, but Takahashi, Itami, Kawai, and Imai are magnificent. One of the fans said to dark-skin Kawai Kimitsugu, "You look so pale." I felt sorry for Tomon.

In this game, Tomon used Jiki as the starting pitcher, but he was knocked out and removed from the game for a relief pitcher.

The relief pitcher was Wakahara. He was a pitcher from Hachiman Commercial High School in Oumi.[6] He had a great fastball. He pitched well and held the black team down. The fans were pleased to watch such a great game. But in the eighth inning, he gave up five runs in the blink of an eye.

The one who started this big rally was the clean-up hitter, Mackey. He got on when he was hit by a pitch that made a loud thudding noise. Even though he grimaced, he was okay because he had a body like armor.

When Wakahara promptly took his cap off to bow respectfully in apology, Mackey was somewhat embarrassed, and respectfully bowed back. He might have thought to himself, "Hey, it's not your fault. Don't worry about it."

Have you noticed the peaceful mood, consideration for others, and overall friendliness that marked this game? It was understandable for Mr. Wakahara, who hit Mackey with the wild pitch, to feel sorry. It was heartwarming to see Mackey's big, kind personality expressed through his playful reaction of bowing back respectfully, mimicking the pitcher's sincere apology.

This reminded me of a similar incident that happened in a game against the white major league team, but with the opposite outcome. One year before, in the fall of Showa 6 (1931), a comparable situation occurred in the fifth game against the major league all-star team, and brought huge excitement throughout Japan.

An unprecedented number of spectators were gathered in Shikishima Stadium in Maebashi to see the first game between the All-Japan team and the major leaguers. It was in the first inning. There was nobody out and the bases were loaded. The major leaguers' top hitter, Lou Gehrig, could not avoid an inside shuuto pitch by the pitcher Tsuji and was hit on his left wrist.[7] Gehrig was forced to leave the game and could not play for the rest of the tour.[8]

There was a reason that Japan felt deeply sorry for Gehrig. This might have kept him from breaking the record of consecutive games played. At that time, his record was 1,053 games. In the end, he achieved an amazing record of 2,130 consecutive games. Fortunately, this incident did not affect his career.

However, it was a big deal and caused a big ripple effect in the next major league tour to Japan. It was difficult for the organizers to convince Gehrig to participate in the Showa 9 (1934) tour to Japan, all because of that hit by pitch.

In retrospect, there was a big difference between these white and black teams that came from the same country. Their tours were carried out in different ways and their situations were also different, but I think that the hit-by-pitch incidents really epitomized the differences between them.

It is impossible to know whether Mackey could have dodged Tusji's shuuto, or if his injury might have been different if he did get hit by that pitch. On the other hand, if Wakahara of Tomon had hit Gehrig, would Gehrig have been able to take the pain and bow back respectfully? Setting aside concerns for preserving his consecutive-games record, how many people could deny that there was a clear difference between the black and white teams in their attitude towards the Japanese players?

There is another story about the umpire in the game between the Royal Giants and the Tomon Club.

The home plate umpire for this game was named Fuma. The black team had never complained about umpire calls in Japan. Here is a further passage from the previously quoted article:

> Today's umpire was Fuma. It was noticeable that he was not comfortable calling plays, which made it very funny to watch him. When it was a strike, he shouted, "Ball!" and then changed it to "Strike!" He gestured as if it was a strike, but shouted "Ball!" If he was umpiring in any other place, he would be in big trouble. But he is okay here because this is Totsuka and the players are all from Waseda. The fans were enjoying it and cheering on Fuma, saying, "Relax! You can do it." It was amazing!

Perhaps Mackey and the other black players smiled bitterly at this inexperienced umpire and thought it was okay, since the fans were enjoying themselves watching this funny umpire. The Royal Giants let the Japanese players and umpires do their jobs and ended the game with the score of 10-7. As Mr. Wakahara said, the Royal Giants were all composed. Certainly, they did not sweat over the small things.

This is a good example with which to compare the attitudes of the white major leaguers. It was Showa 9 (1934). The major league all-stars ignored Japanese umpires from the beginning, and they brought their own umpires to make final decisions. The games progressed by their rules.

The Royal Giants allowed Japanese umpires to make calls based on their judgement, and tried to have smooth games. By contrast, the major leaguers took authority away from Japanese umpires and followed only the calls made by their own umpires. This is another good example of the differences between the black and white teams. The next game, against the Mita Club, featured a similar incident.

Now, the Royal Giants came to Japan as a traveling team to make money, so it would have been impossible for them not to be friendly. The white team, on the other hand, was invited by the newspaper company. They were here to teach and give clinics. Their status was higher than that of the Japanese players from the beginning. Therefore, the white players did not have any tolerance for Japanese-style baseball.

Another thing that I needed to confirm was whether the characteristics of the black team had changed from the first tour.

Mr. Munehiro Jiki, the starting pitcher of Tomon, talked about the Royal Giants, even though his memories of the game had faded.

> They were all gentlemanly and kind. As far as skills went, we were like kids next to the black players. Despite the difference in abilities, the black team happily played against us and took us seriously. They were friendly, and true gentlemen. They kindly showed me how to throw a knuckleball. Everybody who played against the black team must have really enjoyed their company.

This travelling team made up of black players from different places was kinder and more gentleman-like than the white major leaguers. Testimony like this was given by many Japanese players. The black team had come to Japan at just the right time in the fall of Showa 7 (1932), because they served as a good shock absorber for Japanese players to remember when the major leaguers later came and crushed them in Showa 9 (1934).

野球

16

Two Types of Balks

I have already stated that the roster of the Royal Giants on the second visit to Japan was different from the one that visited in Showa 2 (1927).

Just by looking at the number of players who had stayed with the team, you could tell they were a totally different ball club. The team consisted of 12 players. Only three—Mackey, Cooper, and Evans—were also on the first team.

The manager, Goodwin, was replaced by "Will."[1] Who he was, how he came to know this team, and why he planned this second Japan tour is unknown.[2]

I would imagine that he thought he could make a competitive team with Mackey as his main player, Cooper and Evans from the previous team, and the rest of the roster filled with semi-pro or amateur black players.

In fact, the rest of the players on the team were relatively unknown. There is a book called *The All-Time All Stars of Black Baseball* by James Riley, which has a detailed list of black players. I found only two players from the team on the list. I would assume that the rest of the players must have been semi-professionals.

Regardless, the Showa 7 (1932) Royal Giants left an impression on Japanese players and fans of being a very strong team. The best players on the team performed at a higher level of baseball, one that was rarely seen in Japan.

Here is the limited information I was able to find about the player Carr. In Japan, he mainly played first base. His full name was George Carr. Because of his physique and his last name (which sounds like "car"), he was called "Tank." He played in the Negro Leagues from 1912 to 1934. When he came to Japan, he was at the tail-end of his career. Even though he mainly played first base, he also played catcher, third base, and outfield. He started his career with the Los Angeles White Sox, switched to the Kansas City Monarchs, and then moved to the Philadelphia Hilldale club. With Hilldale he contributed to league championships from 1923 to 1925. His results from the 1923 season included a .354 average with 21 home runs. He hit .316 in 1924 and .320 in 1925. A home run that he hit against the Monarchs in Game 5 for a 2-1 victory in the Negro World Series was a shining moment of his baseball career.

In the Cuban Winter League, Carr hit .416, and his career average in the Negro Leagues was .354. This demonstrates that he was a great hitter.

I was able to find some information about the cleanup hitter José Pérez from American records. His career spanned from 1911 to 1937, and he could play pitcher, catcher, and infield. He debuted with the Cuban Stars and played on prestigious teams in the Negro Leagues like Hilldale and the Homestead Grays. Based on this information, he must have been a great player.[3]

As for the pitching staff, William Ross was added. His baseball career lasted for only five years, beginning in 1925.[4] When he came to Japan, he must have been a semi-professional. Most likely whe was affected by the Great Depression when he was with Grays in 1929.

In summary, even though Mackey was the star of both teams, it could be said that this second team was not as deep as the first team, which featured sluggers like Dixon, Duncan, and Pullen.

Because of this fact, Mackey's great personality must have played an important role on the second team, and he was able to have a great impact. As a result, this second team, filled with semi-professionals, became a strong ball club with great chemistry.

Let's look at the fifth game after their arrival in Japan, played against the Mita Club, a team of Keio University alumni. The game took place at Jingu Stadium on September 20, Showa 9 (1932).

Until now, the black team had won every game against Yokohama Commercial High School Club, the Tomon Club, and the Kashima Club. The exact dates for the games are not always certain.[5] Anyway, according to available records, on the 18th of September the black team won 4-1 at Mikasa Stadium, on the Yokosuka Military Base, against the Kashima Club. The next day, the Royal Giants again beat the Kashima Club, this time by a score of 13-1, at Odawara Komine Stadium.

The Baseball Control Ordinance became a barrier once again in the game against the Mita Club. This team would have been stronger if the current Keio University players and all alumni were allowed to play, but the team was forced to fight without the young players. According to an article in *Yakyukai*, No 5, 22nd edition, the game between the Royal Giants and Keio's older players showed how much the game had progressed in Japan:

Mita cannot use the current student players today because Yokohama Kosho had a problem in their game against the black professional team.[6] Fans cannot seem to hide their concern for the Mita team. Are there players available?

When I got to Jingu, I was surprised to see Suzuki and Hasegawa. Even Doi was there. The oldest was Kan-chan Suzuki.[7] He entered Keio in Taisho 3 (1914). He was an older player, but today he was playing third base. He had not played baseball in a long time.

Another one was Doi, who was at shortstop. They have become so old, and their arms are so weak.

It is easy to imagine that these old guys weren't very good, but Saburo Miyatake, who graduated in the previous year, also joined this veteran squad.[8] He was a much-needed addition. Because of him, the team played well. He pitched and hit well, and the game was extremely close. The Mita Club turned out to be the Royal Giants' strongest opponent.

It was painful to watch the pitcher, Nagai, who was knocked out in the third inning, when the black batters waited and solidly hit his slow loopy pitches.

As for the next pitcher, the announcement was made. "The pitcher for Mita Club is Miyatake, Miyatake." The fans applauded crazily. Needless to say, the impact of Miyatake was remarkable. He pitched very well and shut down the black team. The bench player Koshimoto, cheered on his team, saying, "It's all right. It's all right. You can do it!"

I looked at the box scores. The Royals Giants did not appear to score much in the middle innings. Saburo Miyatake was known as a big star in college baseball for hitting seven home runs at Meiji Shrine Stadium. He was also one of the best pitchers. During his seven seasons (he went to America for one season), he was the key player on four championship teams.[9] His pitching record with Meiji was 39 wins and 6 losses. It was obvious that he had a strong arm.

Miyatake pitched well and also contributed with his fantastic offense. The stadium roared because it was near the end of the game.

In the eighth inning, Miyatake hit several foul balls. I am not certain but it seemed as if the pitcher Cooper was flustered. He threw an easy fast ball. Miyatake timed it perfectly and smashed a double over the right fielder's head.

The next batter was Doi. His sacrifice bunt moved the runner Miyatake over to third base. The score was tied at 4-4. Now it was all up to the next batter, Kan-chan Suzuki.

With two balls in the count, he watched the next pitch for a strike. His teammates cheered him on from the bench.

"You can do it. You can do it."

Kan-chan turned around and acknowledged them by raising his hand, tapping his chest, and saying, "It's all right. I can do it!"

This made the fans and the bench laugh.

In this high-tension game, there was still a peaceful atmosphere. Given this opportunity, how did the Mita offense perform? Were there any additional runs for the Mita Club or did the black team shut them down?

An unexpected event occurred. The count was one ball and two strikes. When Mita was about to do a squeeze play, the catcher Mackey missed the pitched ball. Here's the description of the play:

> Cooper had two strikes. When the catcher, Mackey, regretfully missed the ball, Miyatake rushed to home plate. Finally the Mita Club had scored, and it looked like the winning run. Kan-chan seemed rather surprised. He turned around and pretended like he was stroking down his chest with his hand and said, "Too close, too close," which made the fans laugh again.
>
> With the popular Miyatake running around the bases, and the comical Kan-chan Suzuki involved, this unexpected winning run must have caused much excitement on the bench and in the stands.

It is unfortunate that the description of the scene ends there. It is hard to tell what really had happened with Mackey's passed ball.

For those who have been reading this book up to now, you might be wondering whether or not it was possible that Mackey missed the ball on purpose and allowed Mita to score a run.

It was perfect timing, with the game now tied in the eighth inning. All the actors were in place. After each team had shown what they could do, now was the time for an exciting finish.

I would have liked to hear Mackey's side of the story, but he passed away years ago. I cannot ask him now. I looked at the plays that occurred after this passed ball incident in order to learn more about his agenda. With that thought in mind, I was amazed. Mackey must have thought that the Royal Giants could score to tie, or to take the lead, in the last two innings.

The proof could be found in the stats. In the bottom of the eighth inning, the Royal Giants must have decided to hit with full power in order to score one more run. The fifth batter, Pérez, hit a triple to right. The next batter was Martin. He hit it well to center for a sacrifice fly, driving in the tying run.

The next batter, Bland, tripled over the right fielder. The second baseman, Mitani, failed to get the runner out at home. The Royal Giants were easily able to take back the lead. They had allowed one run, but scored two more themselves. This was probably their plan all along.

Score by inning:

| Mita Club | 0 0 1 0 0 0 3 1 0 = 5 |
| Royal Giants | 2 0 1 0 0 1 0 2 A = 6A |

There is one more scene that shows the great character of the black team. It happened during Mita's last inning at bat, after they had given up the lead.

The Mita squad had the win in their hands after getting the one-run lead. They must have really wanted to win. They undertook the guerilla strategy of fighting until the end. Here is what happened.

In the ninth inning, with two outs, Kusumi singled, but thought he was too far away from home plate. He wanted to advance to second base to be in scoring position.

So he complained that Cooper had balked. It was uncertain how much a pitcher's movements were subjected to the rule. The black players listened to the umpire. They might have had something to say, but in the end they followed the Japanese umpire's call and continued to play.

This scene was briefly covered in an article in *Yakyukai*.

> In the eighth inning, Kusumi made his third hit and got on base. As soon as he saw the pitcher Cooper move his leg a little bit, he yelled, "Balk, balk," and proceeded to second. The black team took it calmly. They protested to the home plate umpire, Igawa, but he waved his hand left to right and said no. Kusumi advanced to second base.

The black team remained "gentleman-like," and continued to play against the Japanese team, who were making a rather pushy, aggressive claim in pursuit of the tying run.

This incident reminded me of the game that the Showa 2 (1927) Royal Giants almost lost to the Daimai Club. They were not credited with a deserved run because of the umpire's glaring mistake (see Chapters 4 and 5). As they had done then, they followed the umpire's call again. Even though they went to talk to the umpire for an appeal, they quickly accepted the call and peacefully continued to play the game like gentlemen. The Japanese players were shocked by their compliant attitudes.

Were the black players afraid of making the Japanese players and fans upset? When you are part of a self-financed travelling team, you must be mindful of the customer. If customers do not show up, the players are the ones who suffer. They were, in this respect, totally different from the white teams that came here with invitations.

This balk incident reminded me of a situation that occurred during the first game played by the All-American major league team in November, Showa 9 (1934). The sluggers Lou Gehrig, Jimmie Foxx, and Babe Ruth were all in the game, so the Japanese side treated them with absolute courtesy.

It was the first game against the champions of the Industrial League, the Tokyo Club. The first batter, Kiichi Masu, got a hit off the pitcher, Whitehill, and got on base.[9] What happened next is well-known. The runner left the base, trying to steal, while the pitcher threw to first. The first base umpire, Yutaka Ikeda, and the third base umpire, Toshikazu Amachi, both called a balk, but the American team ignored them. The home plate umpire, the American John Quinn, shouted "No balk," and overturned the call. The Japanese players were forced to accept it because they were ignored by the American players. This call left a bad taste in their mouths.

As always, the Royal Giants adopted a respectful attitude during the games. This was different from other teams.

The result of the game for Mita was a loss. The runner was allowed to advance to second due to the balk, but the next batter, Nagai, grounded to second and the game ended.

The last sentence of the article in *Yakyukai* summed up the game: "In the end, even the balk did not help. Mita lost as expected."

野球

17

The Underappreciated Value of
the Team in the Shadows

After the game against the Mita Club, the Philadelphia Royal Giants left Tokyo and headed to the countryside for more games.

As a result, the Royal Giants fell off the radar of the Japanese baseball community. Even the specialized baseball magazines did not write anything about them. The only signs of their presence in Showa 7 (1932) were the game results. They were:

> September 25 @ Star Stadium
> Royal Giants 8, Kumagai Star 4
>
> October 1 @ Takarazuka Stadium
> Royal Giants 5A, Osaka Railway 3
>
> October 2 @ Takarazuka Stadium
> Royal Giants 11, Star Club 1
>
> October 2 @ Takarazuka Stadium
> Royal Giants 5A, Kansai Mita Club 0
>
> October 4 @ Kurashiki Stadium
> Royal Giants 10A, Yonago Railway 2
>
> October 5 @ Chugoku Stadium
> Hiroshima Senbai 4, Royal Giants 3

October 8 @ Keijo Stadium
Royal Giants 3A, Korean Communication 1

October 14 @ Chofu Stadium
Royal Giants 5A, Moji Railway 1

October 15 @ Suizenji Stadium
Royal Giants 15A, Kumamoto Railway 2

October 17 @ Otani Stadium
Royal Giants 16A, Yahata Steel 2

October 18 @ Otani Stadium
Royal Giants 10A, Yahata Steel 3

October 20 @ Chugaku Meizen Stadium
Royal Giants 28A, All Kurume 5

October 22 @ Beppu Stadium
Royal Giants18A, Moji Railway 2

October 26 @ Kokura Stadium
Royal Giants 9A, Moji Railway 7

October 27 @ Shin Kashii Stadium
Royal Giants 19A, Yahata Steel 5

November 3 @ Neyagawa Stadium
Royal Giants 13A, Kansai Sundai Club 2

November 3 @ Neyagawa Stadium
Royal Giants 20A, Kansai Mita Club 0

November 5 @ Kobe Stadium
Royal Giants 8, Kobe Daiya Squad 3

Among all these games, details were preserved for only two games, both against Yahata Steel. An article about the game on October 17 appears in the *The History of Yakyu Club*, published by Yahata Steel Works in April, Showa 12 (1937):

> The practice by the black team was very entertaining. In the first game, the pitcher, Fujii, was knocked out by the black players' endless powerful hitting. The result was 16A-2. The Yahata were never a problem for the black team. On this day, when Baker was on second base, the next batter hit a fly ball to center field. This sacrifice fly allowed Baker to run through third base and head for home with an amazing slide.

There was a small report about the game on October 27 (19A-5). According to the write-up, the Royal Giants' first five runs were produced by three home runs in a row. The number three batter Carr, the clean-up hitter Mackey, and the number five batter Martin hit back-to-back-to-back home runs into the ocean behind the outfield.

Even the best teams in Tokyo did not stand a chance against the black team. It was inevitable for the teams in the countryside to lose by big run differentials.

Given the circumstances, it is worth noting the victory by the Hiroshima Senbai, who defeated the Royal Giants, 4-3. The winning run was finally scored in the 10th inning. Unfortunately, the details of this extra-inning game were not available.

In the end, the Royal Giants wound up with 23 wins and one loss out of 24 games in the Japan tour of Showa 7 (1932). This result was about the same as the previous tour.

Here is a summary of the game results of visiting foreign professional teams in the early Showa era:

- Showa 2 (1927): Royal Giants   23 wins, 1 tie
- Showa 6 (1931): Major League All-Stars   17 wins
- Showa 7 (1932): Royal Giants   23 wins, 1 loss

With this list, I need to include one more visitor, the All-American Team. This team featuring the famous Babe Ruth, was much stronger than any of the previous American squads, and destroyed the All-Japan Team:

- Showa 9 (1934): Major League All-Stars   17 wins[1]

The All-Japan Team, unable to use college players, was greatly discouraged by the overwhelming and powerful All-American Team. The disappointment of the players is well-documented in the book *Japanese Pro Baseball Unofficial History*, by Sotaro Suzuki (1976 Baseball Magazine Sha Co., Ltd.).

The All-American Team was also disappointed by the Japanese team because they appeared to have no spirit. Yet it was Babe Ruth who held an open umbrella while playing first base and Lou Gehrig who kept his rubber rain boots on while playing left field in the game at Kokura Stadium.

It is interesting to step back and take stock of the American professional teams that came to Japan before the birth of the professional Japanese Baseball League. Each team from each league came to Japan twice, and their contrasting narratives drew a vivid comparison between the two teams.

What they had in common included the time period of their tours and the unimaginable power that they both displayed. In everything else they were total opposites, like the contrasts of a shadow play. When I looked at the situation from the Japanese perspective, I saw that the disparities between the two teams must have been drastic.

To further convey this point, let's create a scenario where the white major league team is "Team A" and the black Royal Giants are "Team B." I am going to write the differences as they come to my mind:

- Team A was made up of only white players; team B was made up of only black players.
- A was invited by the newspaper; B was a self-funded travel team.
- A consisted of well-known players; no one knew about the players on team B.
- A was sponsored by politicians (including an ambassador) and commissioners; B had no sponsors.
- A played the games as baseball clinics because of their role as "baseball missionaries"; B embraced the motto, "Let's have fun together!"
- A often changed or ignored the calls made by the Japanese umpires when they didn't agree with them; B was always respectful to the Japanese umpires even when obvious calls were missed by unexperienced officials.
- A displayed their power without mercy; with B, it was sometimes hard to tell if the opposing team was good or bad.
- A often blatantly disrespected the Japanese players whose baseball skills were not up to their standards; B took the Japanese players seriously and treated them with dignity and respect.
- A was dissatisfied with the games against the Japanese teams and returned to America unhappy; B was satisfied with the games, truly enjoyed their stay in Japan, and left for America happy.

- The Japanese players who played against A were in awe, but they did not view them as friendly; the Japanese players who played against B were able to build friendships rather than simply being awestruck.
- A won many games against the premier teams in Japan by large scores; B seemed to make the games close.
- After the games against A, some Japanese players slammed their gloves on the ground and shouted, "I quit baseball!" because they were very disappointed in their skills; after playing close games against B, Japanese players gained confidence.
- Deep down in their hearts, A might have looked down on Japanese players and fans; whereas B breathed the air of freedom in Japan. They truly appreciated the country, which was displayed through their gentlemanly attitudes towards Japanese players and fans.

I received a phone call from Mr. Masuo Hayami as I was writing this book. He told me that when he was still a student at Rikkyo University, he also worked as an umpire when the Royal Giants played against Tomon. His story served as a testimony to the admirable character of the Royal Giants. It was similar to what Mr. Yasuo Shimazu and Saburo Yokohama shared with me. "I have never seen a baseball team that was this gentleman-like. "

"They did not just play to make the games entertaining, but also they were well-composed, and had a great temperament." The impression that the black team left in Mr. Hayami's heart was still powerful.

By the way, the comparisons between "Team A" and "Team B" may appear arbitrary and biased. However, there is a reason for each item. For example, it might seem unexpected that "A was dissatisfied with the games against the Japanese teams and left for America unhappy." In order to support this statement, one only needs to cite the comments of Lou Gehrig in the book *Japanese-American Baseball Exchange History: Baseball Crossed the Pacific Ocean* (Chuo Koron Shakan, Showa 51 [1976]), by Mr. Masaru Ikei. Gehrig said:

> I heard of the Japanese samurai spirit (Yamato-damashii), and I was looking forward to coming to Japan and learning about it. Unfortunately, I did not find the samurai spirit anywhere. Instead, I saw a player running to first base laughing after hitting the ball poorly. I wanted to punch him ... So much for the samurai spirit. (pg. 115)

To my surprise, Gehrig made this comment at the farewell party. These kinds of statements are not usually made in public. It looks like the greatness of the American team has been exaggerated.

If some of the items in the list of comparisons seem too extreme or harsh, then it might be because we have been ignorant of the truth about these tours.

The comment made by Lou Gehrig was the polar opposite of the message addressed by the Royal Giants' Lon Goodwin to the Japanese fans, previously featured in Chapter 5.

When I started to think about it more, I realized I failed to list the most important contrast between the two teams:

- Team A was praised greatly for its contributions to baseball in Japan, whereas nothing has been said about Team B for more than half a century.

The difference in the amount of information about Teams A and B in Japanese baseball history books, as shown in Chapter 2, was obvious. Even though there are a few articles about the Royal Giants, they are very rare. Most history books have no information about them.

Perhaps it would be easier to understand why this was the case if we recall what Mr. Shozo Wakahara said: "This is the first time I have been asked about the game against the black team!"

Even if Team B is not talked about in our baseball history, it is a fact that they came to Japan. It is also a fact that they played more games in Japan than the major league all-star teams.

The total number of Japan tours by Teams A and B was four. These visits took place before Japanese professional baseball was established in Showa 11 (1936). One team received great recognition and acknowledgement and left detailed records of their tours. The other team was not recognized for its accomplishments and left almost no marks in Japan. The differences are too extreme, and do not seem fair.

It could be said that the social impact that both teams made in Japan was different. Their operational styles were different. However, it could not be said that one team should receive a 10 for their performance, and the other should receive a zero. The fact that Team A had a major newspaper as their sponsor, and Team B did not, made their situations very different. Undeniably, the future of the *Yomiuri Shimbun* depended on the baseball tours it organized, so the newspaper made every effort to lend Team A more visibility.

By the way, some meaningful points about Japanese baseball history can be gleaned from the visit of the Royal Giants (Team B). I have organized them in bullet points:

- B was a black team composed of players who were banned by the major leagues. If this team was as arrogant as the white team, then the Japanese players might have been discouraged from playing baseball, and might not have become professionals after getting pounded by both teams.

- B had a couple of great players, but at the same time B had semi-professional players. The great players might have had the ability to manipulate the games at will, but semi-pro players could not. Because of that, there was no speculation about some of the close games being fixed.
- B had Mackey, who was the leader of the team. His big, kind personality influenced his teammates, and made the ball club a strong but gentleman-like team.
- B was a self-funded team, which influenced their desire to entertain fans and to support and encourage the Japanese players to do their best.
- When team B first came to Japan in Showa 2 (1927), there were almost no professional teams in Japan. By the time the great major leaguers arrived in Showa 6 (1931), Japanese professional baseball had started to propagate, and was quickly growing into maturity.

In the early Showa period, the Royal Giants crossed the ocean and came to Japan without any invitation or financial support and played 48 games. During their visits, they demonstrated a high level of baseball to Japanese players. At the same time, they taught others how to have fun and play the game in a respectful manner. They also enjoyed their stay in Japan. And before we knew it, these gentlemanly black ballplayers disappeared like the wind.

When they left Japan, there was no special event planned—just like when they arrived.

After the second tour, how did Biz Mackey's life turn out in America? How about the team's other members?

How did Dixon and Duncan from the first tour do after their experience in Japan?

Actually, I found out that a year later the Royal Giants added new members and landed on Japanese soil for a third time. Was this true?

野球

18

Post-Japan Tour of the Gentle Giants

What happened to those gentle black giants after they left Japan in Showa 7 (1932)? I will address that question now.

The first person to discuss must be the captain of the team who came to Japan twice, Biz Mackey—the man with the baby face and giant body.

He was a Texan who holds the record for hitting the first ball out the park at Jingu Gaien Stadium. He smashed a second and third home run there, too. I have already talked about Mackey in previous chapters. How about his later life?

He finally made it back to Philadelphia after leaving Japan and stopping at Manila. His teammates on the Philadelphia Hilldale ball club were not there to welcome him back. Surprisingly, the team had folded while he was gone.

Speaking of Hilldale, it was one of the strongest teams in the Eastern Colored League. In the Colored World Series of 1924 and 1925, they played against the Monarchs from the west for the championship.[1] Even though Hilldale was a popular team, they might have faced financial hardships during the depression.

Taking their place was the Philadelphia Stars, a team born under new management.[2] Biz, known for great skills on defense and offense as well as his leadership, did not have any problems finding a spot on this new team.

He played a total of three years with the Philadelphia Stars (1933-1935). Even though the team won the league championship in 1934, they too were unable to stay in business. After the Stars folded, Biz transferred to the Washington Elite Giants the following year.[3] The rise and fall of black professional teams was not new. Change was constant. And this new Elite Giants franchise eventually moved to Baltimore.

Mackey stayed on with the Elites and became their manager. In the end, he had greatly influenced American baseball society.

During this time, he met a 15-year old ballplayer named Roy Campanella, who years later became a famous catcher in major league baseball and earned the National League MVP (Most Valuable Player) award three times. At age 15 though, Roy had great catching skills but was still a student of the game. Mackey noticed his talents and often invited him to play with the Elites on the weekends.

The first thing about Mackey that surprised Roy was not his strong arm or his skill in handling pitchers, but rather his thick hands and bent fingers. Mackey had caught many pitches, in over 200 games a year, for 20 years.

The joints of his fingers were not only bent but they were so flexible that they moved in every direction. Young Roy could not fathom how Mackey was still able to catch and throw perfectly.

His cheerful personality must have also attracted the young Campanella. "Someday, I want to be like Mackey." The manager Mackey was a role model for the young 15-year-old ballplayer. Campanella said:

> As a manager and mentor, Biz Mackey was the best person. He rarely got upset. I think he never got thrown out from a game. He wasn't a mean mentor. When I did anything wrong, he always corrected me. I became a good catcher who doesn't make costly mistakes, which is all credited to him.
>
> It was only two years that I was playing around him, but it was a meaningful two years. He showed me how to block low pitches, block outside pitches, and helped me to have a short, quick throwing motion … Because of Biz, I mastered this all in my youth. (*The Artists with a Catcher's Mask*, by John Holway).[4]

After helping young Campanella establish his goals and direction in life, Mackey moved to the Newark Eagles and managed that club until 1947.

This was the same year that Jackie Robinson joined the Dodgers, becoming the first black player ever in the major leagues. After this milestone event, many black players joined the major leagues. Robinson's signing was a ringing bell of good fortune for great black players, but it was an evening bell—signifying the end—for the Negro Leagues.

Biz Mackey himself competed as a star player in the Negro Leagues during their peak, and he saw the end of the Negro Leagues as a manager. It became his last job to send the players he mentored to the major leagues.

In that regard, Mackey played a great role in the world of major league baseball world. The list of players he mentored included:

- Monte Irvin (the current MLB commissioner's assistant), a star with the Giants;
- Larry Doby, the first black player in the American League; and
- Don Newcombe of the Newark Eagles.

Some might remember that Doby and Newcombe played with the Chunichi Dragons in the Nippon Professional Baseball League in Showa 37 (1962). They were already past their prime, but they thought that they could still play. They finished the season with mediocre numbers. Doby hit .225 with 12 home runs. Newcombe hit .262 with 15 home runs. Was it due to aging?

Regardless, they still belonged to the elite group of black major leaguers who entered the game after Jackie Robinson, so they played important roles in American baseball history.

At the same time, it is worth noting that through them, Biz Mackey was once more connected to the Japanese baseball community.

Where did Biz go after his career in baseball ended? Fittingly, it was Los Angeles, the future home of the Dodgers. The Dodgers were the first team to show their acceptance of black players. It must have been his greatest pleasure to watch his players succeed in the major leagues.

In his later years, Mackey worked as a forklift operator and as a substitute teacher. He passed away at age 65 in 1962, the same year when Doby and Newcombe played in Japan. I wonder if Biz heard anything about their experiences in Japanese baseball from his former players?

There is an important event that occurred before Biz's death. It is a continuation of Campanella's positive words about Mackey. He invited his old mentor to a specially-organized event, "Roy Campanella Day."

> Yes, I invited Mackey to the event at Dodger Stadium.[8] I asked him to stand up, and I said to everyone, "This person taught me all the skills of being a catcher. I was able to play in many games from a young age. It was all because of him." He was very proud of me. I was happy that he came to the event. Soon after that, he passed away.

I tried many different ways to find out more about Mackey. I thought that if I contacted his family and researched his home town and the places where he lived, it might help. I continued with my efforts, but in the end, I could not collect any more information than I have provided here.

It was sad to accept that so little information is available on such a great player, but when I thought about it more I realized it was logical. The era when he played baseball was a difficult time for black players, and they were not allowed to play in the major leagues. During that time, he was not able to play even once in the major leagues. Of course, there would not be any information left about those who were not allowed in the major leagues.

However, the fever for Negro Leagues research has increased recently. I would expect that more facts will be found by many researchers.[9] Mackey, who came to Japan two times and played 48 games, might have shared his recollections of Japanese tours or about the Japanese baseball. I would love to hear about them.

*   *   *

After Mackey, the next person to highlight would be Rap Dixon. Prior to Showa 2 (1927), no one could smash a home run at Koshien. He mesmerized Japanese fans with his impressive batting, speedy legs and strong arm. How did life turn out for Dixon after the Japan tours?

When he returned home after completing the Japan and Hawaii tour, it was mentioned in the previous chapter that he, Mackey and Duncan were subjected to severe disciplinary action due to their absence from the league—they were suspended for 30 days and fined $200.

However, he was only 23 years old and this suspension did not cause any serious damage to his career. When he returned to the Negro Leagues after the tour, he began to play better than ever before. In 1930, he became the first person to hit three home runs in one day in Yankee Stadium. It was during a double header, the first Negro League games played in "The House that Ruth Built."

Dixon's great batting never stopped. During the off season, he also continued to play against major league players and recorded a high batting average in those games. (See chapter 12.) His speed also improved remarkably. He performed extremely well against Earl Whitehill, a pitcher for the Detroit Tigers. Rap had him in the palm of his hand, smashing a triple and stealing home. Rap completely frustrated Earl.

In 1932, when Mackey and the Royal Giants were about to leave for Japan for the second time, Rap Dixon joined the Pittsburgh Crawfords, a team that already had many good players. It would not have been easy for Dixon to join his friends on the second Japan tour. As one of the star players with the Crawfords, he probably had plenty of opportunities for baseball during the off-season. Even though times were tough, young all-around ball players did not have any problems finding a job.

The Crawfords of the early 1930s are considered to be among the best teams ever assembled in professional baseball, white or black. The 1927 New York Yankees are usually said to be the best team, but that is only in the white major leagues. If there were enough information about the Crawfords, fewer people would back the 1927 New York Yankees as the best team ever.

When the Royal Giants came to Japan for the second time (1932), the Crawfords were considered to be a strong team. Some people think that the 1935 Crawfords were the best team ever. For example, Rob Ruck, a professor from Chatham University, believes that the 1935 Crawfords were the best. I think the 1932 Crawfords were better. The '32 team had Satchel Paige, and the catcher was Josh Gibson, the "black Babe Ruth," who ultimately hit 962 career home runs.

Just looking at the battery of Paige and Gibson, it was obvious which team was the best. In addition, Oscar Charleston, a tremendous hitter, and Judy Johnson, the best third baseman in the Negro Leagues, were on the team. And the legendary Cool Papa Bell was in center field. The caliber of baseball they played must have been fantastic. All were selected to the National Baseball Hall of Fame in Cooperstown.

Considering that a total of ten players from the Negro Leagues are inducted into the Hall of Fame, it is surprising to note that five Hall of Famers played for the same team at the same time (1932 Crawfords).[10] Therefore, they were incredibly valuable.

How and why this strong team surfaced in Pittsburgh would be long story, too difficult to explain here. The quick version is that the owner of the Crawfords recruited great players to play against the powerful Homestead Grays, who were also located in the Pittsburgh area.

Rap Dixon kept his starting position with the Crawfords. He played right field instead of center field (as he did in Japan). Dixon's range as an outfielder must have been one step behind Cool Papa. However, on offense he reflected his skill by recording a .343 average in 1932, which was the third best on the team.

Dixon later moved on to Philadelphia and Baltimore. Those teams traded for him as a result of his strong performance. In 1935, he joined the New York Cubans and contributed to their run for the league championship.[11]

These are his career records as known to baseball historians. Two years later, he disappeared from baseball. He had suddenly become ill, but nobody knew what his diagnosis was at the time.

Rap Dixon passed away in 1944. He was only 42 years old.[12]

野球

19

These Men Have Passed Away

Crawford Street was the location of the "Crawford boom" that occurred such a long time ago. Yes, the name of the historic Negro Leagues ball club—the Pittsburgh Crawfords—came from the street.[1] I always wanted to see that famous street. I wonder how it looks today.

Was it still there? Did it have the same name? How about the Crawford Grill where many players gathered, drank, talked, and sang—was it still there? Was the restaurant, the one-time home of Cool Papa, Gibson, Paige, and Charleston, still there on the street?[2] Rap Dixon must have been taken to this place by those guys. Those powerful players used to spend time there, but now they were all gone … just like a dream. Was there anything left there that could remind one of the good old times?

An opportunity to find out arrived in June 1985. I needed to go to Puerto Rico, so I decided to stop by Pittsburgh.

The reality was totally different from what I had imagined. Crawford Street was there, but it was a deserted street. Many of the brick buildings that had once stood there were missing, and the neighborhood was covered with weed-infested emptiness. Even the buildings that were still standing did not seem to be used for anything. Some homeless people might have been using them for shelter.

There were a couple of cars parked on the right and left side of the road. The dreary asphalt was covered with a thick dust.

The street followed a slow downhill decline leading to downtown Pittsburgh. A big view of the blue sky appeared as you walked downward. New buildings abruptly appeared in the dusty, run-down town. I was only one block away from the campus of Duquesne University, a fairy tale-like castle located in the middle of a high-end residential area, surrounded by thick green landscaping. It made for a very peculiar contrast.[3]

A few unemployed people were hanging out on the eerie, quiet street. There was only one building left, its eaves stretching out into the road. It was the jazz club, the Crawford Grill.[4]

The old three-story building stood on the corner of an intersection with another small street. A white sign on the dirty faded green eaves read "Crawford Grill." Sadly, there was no sign of people, no sounds of the jazz music that used to play throughout the entire year. A tall, young black man passed by on his roller skates, moving his body like the wind. This was the only sign of life on the streets.

In the late 1950s, Roberto Clemente also used to visit this place, according to his biography. The jazz bar must have managed to keep its business running until at least then. However, once the era of the steel industry passed, the era of the Crawfords had ended as well. No sign of Dixon—not even one memory of the best team in baseball history—was here now. Their practice field now lay beneath the small houses that had been built randomly across the neighborhood.

One more thing … I learned that Frank Duncan also used to play with the Pittsburgh Crawfords. In the *Pittsburgh Courier* dated January 21, 1933, statistics for the Crawfords showed that in fact Duncan played with them briefly during the 1932 season. He played in 29 games and got 27 hits in 100 at bats. He must have played with another team that season as well.[5]

I feel I must explain a little bit more about Duncan. Here is what I know.

After his time in Pittsburgh, he moved to the New York Cubans with Dixon. He then moved on to Chicago. In 1940, he was called back to his former team, the Kansas City Monarchs.

However, he did not return as a player. Instead, he was welcomed back as a manager. It is interesting to note that Satchel Paige, who came back to his former team and accepted a role of a captain, asked Duncan to be the manager. Satchel had known Duncan for a long time and they became best friends. At that time, Paige, an outstanding pitcher, was the superstar of the Negro Leagues, and very popular. During the off season, this team was in great demand everywhere. So they changed their name to the "Satchel Paige All-Stars" and played games all across America.

Bob Feller, a famous and fast pitcher with the Cleveland Indians, also formed his own all-star team and to play against Paige's team. They played 22 games against each other. Each team had 11 wins, for a perfectly-tied record. These results were not vital for the baseball community or for Duncan himself. More importantly, he mentored a player who would later became a hero, like Mackey did with Campanella.

At that time, a young infielder from the University of California at Los Angeles (UCLA) joined the Monarchs. He was the man who later became the first black player in the modern major leagues. His name was Jackie Robinson.

Many people remembered him as a pioneering black athlete, or because he was a talented and powerful player, but not many knew about his first professional baseball team. Even though he was a star at UCLA, he remained in the shadows, like Paige and other great players, and did not receive equal treatment. He had to bide his time with the Kansas City Monarchs while waiting for his opportunity, but this eventually led to his success—with help from Duncan.

In 1947, Jackie joined the major league and hit .297 with 12 homeruns in his first year. As everybody knows, he was selected as the Rookie of the Year in the National League. Duncan retired at the end of that same year after watching Jackie get honored with this award. Duncan was known to be a stubborn guy, but he could not beat the inevitable process of aging. Also, Duncan owned a pub, so he did not want to leave town for road games. But the Monarchs' organization begged him to stay, so he became an umpire, a role that lasted for two years.

Duncan wore his uniform for the last time in 1965. It was at an all-star game played by the former stars of the Negro Leagues. Cool Papa Bell, Bullet Rogan, and many more legends gathered and played in the game. Duncan caught Satchel Paige. It had been a long time since he had last done this. Satchel pitched well, and gave up only one hit in four innings. Duncan must have felt his last joy as a player while he was catching Satchel. Afterwards, he continued to keep his pub, and enjoyed attending the yearly meetings of the Negro Leaguers. He died in December 1973 in Kansas City. He was 72 years old.

There is a transcript of an interview with Duncan by John Holway. He must have had a lot to say about being a Negro Leagues player during the time when blacks were discriminated against by the major league, but his words about his past were rather quiet. The date of the interview is unknown, but it was certainly conducted close to the end of his life.[6] Here's a portion of that interview:

> "I have a good reputation, a good name. I'm proud of that. I have nothing to regret. Lived a great life, thankful still to be living, a few of us living here and there, some dead and gone, both white and black, but that's life. Now you see the boys getting the breaks and playing good ball up there. We were among the pioneers who paved the way for them."[7]

Everybody already knows that Jackie Robinson was the first black player in the majors, but many others joined in his wake, one after another. The following facts show that their presence was integral to the peak years of American baseball.

Satchel Paige, Roy Campanella, Don Newcombe, Monte Irvin, Willie Mays, Ernie Banks, Hank Aaron, Roberto Clemente, Bob Gibson, Frank Robinson, Lou Brock ... the power of these black players is shown in the list of MVPs for the National League. Since Jackie Robinson received it in 1949, a total of 37 players have won the National League MVP award—and 21 of the recipients have been black. If the barriers of discrimination were still there, none of them would have played in the major leagues.

I wonder, what did the veteran players from the Negro Leagues think while they were watching the younger players succeed in the majors? Even though Duncan showed no discontent in his comments, it does not mean that he was not envious of the young black players. Actually, there were some honest responses which were not intended for the public.[8]

It was natural that older former Negro League players would begin to gather annually in special places and reminisce about their playing days. During the 1960s, they could still enjoy games together, swinging the bat and catching balls. However, the group started to lose its members, one by one each year. They embraced each other's company, knowing it would not last forever.

The destiny of these reunions was only to lose members without adding any new ones, but they did represent a pleasurable chance to cherish their past, and to remember how they had once fought hard and chased their dreams.

During their meeting in November 1980, the topic of establishing a Negro Baseball Hall of History was raised. An exhibit was opening in Ashland, Kentucky, and a search was underway for people who were still living as well as any baseball-related items they might still own. Companies who showed interest in Negro League history funded the exhibit. The venue was a borrowed corner of the Jean Thomas Museum in the American Heritage Park.

The sudden death of Satchel Paige in June 1982 triggered this project.[9] He was already a legendary hero when he was alive. When they lost him, they lost the main person in the black baseball community. The former Negro Leaguers must have thought strongly that "We must keep our history alive. If we don't do it now, everything will be gone forever."

On July 22, 1982, at the opening ceremony of the Negro Baseball Hall of History, former long-time Negro League player, Monte Irvin, assistant to the major league Commissioner, gave a speech. In it, he said:

> Strong discrimination existed towards people with different skin colors in this country. During that time, black baseball was not only our life, it was also an important part of American society. It was not as it was portrayed in the Hollywood movie, full of goofy, weak players.[10] Because I was a player in the Negro Leagues, I can tell you that our skills had reached the top level. When I reflect back, I can still visualize many thrilling moments.
>
> I am delighted that the presence of a black baseball league is no longer needed, yet at the same time, I remember well the many great black players and friends. I would also like to

keep alive memories of the excellent baseball we played. Our accomplishments were definitely part of American baseball history, and I am pleased with this effort to preserve our past...

I provided the records of the Philadelphia Royal Giants during their Japan tours, as Martha Baumgartner, one of the chairmen in the history museum, had asked. I think that they were very happy to receive this important piece of history. During the early Showa period, the gentleness of the black players made Japanese players relaxed and increased their interest in baseball. As for the black players, they felt a sense of freedom, and enjoyed their stay in Japan. I would like people to understand at least these two points from the documents.

By the way, having support from many people who are passionate about the Negro Leagues, I realized that there was one more thing about the Royal Giants that surprised and disappointed me. None of the strong players who had come to Japan for the first tour were still alive.

I have been able to detail the lives of Mackey, Dixon, and Duncan after their return from Japan, but they and the rest of players have all passed away. I felt strange about that now. When they played in Japan, they were so strong, and their power and speed were so superior to the Japanese players. Furthermore, they always kept their composure. But now they were all gone.[11]

When I interviewed some of the players from Japanese teams that did not even win one game against the Royal Giants, they were still somewhat regretful about those games. I could not believe how different their lives turned out to be. Maybe tough schedules under poor conditions took a toll on the Negro League players and contributed to shortened life spans?

As far as the members of the second Japan tour go, I don't have any information about their lives after Japan.[12] After the end of the Negro Leagues, they would have also disappeared from baseball. None of the players who came to Japan were on the lists of those who attended the yearly Negro Leagues reunion.

The Negro Baseball Hall of History exhibit was moved to the National Baseball Hall of Fame in Cooperstown, New York, in 1985. It was speculated that the financial hardship of renting the temporary location in Ashland, Kentucky, was the reason it moved. However, it is unlikely that Cooperstown embraced the exhibit for that reason alone. The Hall of Fame must have felt that it was appropriate to accept the Negro Leagues as a part of baseball history, and they did it willingly and with passion.

According to Tom Heitz, the National Baseball Hall of Fame librarian, more efforts are planned to keep the exhibit alive.[13] Heitz intends to move the black baseball exhibit from a small corner on the second floor to a larger space in the museum. The exhibit on "Japanese and American Exchange History" currently has a bigger space than the black baseball section.

As the movement grows to keep black baseball history alive, the publication of books about the Negro Leagues has increased. Previously, not many books on the subject had been published, but now more and more books reflect on the history of black baseball. Here is a list of a few recent books:

- *Baseball's Great Experiment*, Jules Tygiel (Oxford Press, 1983)
- *Invisible Men*, Donn Rogosin (Atheneum, 1983)
- *The Kansas City Monarchs*, Janet Bruce (Univ. of Kansas, 1985)

It's worth noting that all of these writers are white. The SABR meetings about the Negro Leagues are mostly attended by white researchers. I would like to see more African Americans researching black baseball.

In the course of my own research, I did hear of one black researcher who has been energetically investigating and tracking down old documents. His name was Phil Dixon, although he was not related to the famous Rap Dixon who came to Japan. His research, I was told, was thorough and he had amassed a remarkable collection of valuable artifacts left behind by the black players. I heard that he possessed the passport of the pitcher, Bullet Rogan, who used it for his visit to Japan.

Now I remembered—Rogan! In 1983, the question I was originally asked by John Holway at the SABR meeting in Milwaukee was about the pitcher "Bullet Joe" Rogan.

At first, I could not believe that a black professional baseball team had toured Japan. Then I started to investigate, and discovered it was true. I was continuously surprised by the story of the Royal Giants. In fact, I was so blown away that I completely forgot that John had asked about this pitcher. Now, as I reflected back on my research, I realized that I had not seen the name Rogan involved in the two tours in Japan. It was often said that there was a third tour to Japan by the Royal Giants. Maybe he was part of this third tour?

The passport of Bullet Rogan still existed. How could I not go see this? In June of 1985, I stopped by Kansas City to have a look at this historic document.

野球

20

The Third Black Team,
Who Were These Players?

There are two cities called Kansas City that exist on both sides of the Missouri River. One is located in the state of Missouri, where 450,000 people live, and the other is located in the state of Kansas, where 160,000 people live. The Negro Leagues baseball researcher and collector, Mr. Dixon, lived in Kansas City on the Kansas side.

He told me that he had just moved into a new place, a building that looked like the dormitory of an old school. His family lived in some of the rooms upstairs. The room he used for his office was full of pictures and books on Negro Leagues baseball. He had collected a great deal of information because he was going to write a book on Negro Leagues history. He was in the middle of this project.

He had about 7,000 pictures (3,000 were pictures of players before Jackie Robinson), and clippings from old newspapers. This must have been valuable material for his book.[1]

He had recently decided to write the book, but he had been collecting research and devoting his time and money to the project since he was a young child (his current age was 29).[2] His book, when published, promised to have more information and stories about black baseball than any other book on the topic.

Phil told me that he was not 100 percent comfortable with the idea of white researchers publishing books about black baseball. He felt that they did not have anything in common with the culture they were trying to understand. How could white people write about black baseball without knowing anything about the experience of the black players? Where they ate? Where they slept? How they felt about their lives? He repeated himself to reinforce this point.

Phil's father was friendly with many of the Negro League players, and he believed that he had something in common with the black players that the white writers would never have.

He was very excited to see the pictures and results of the Royal Giants that I brought him. He was glad that their box scores, games details and other materials could be used in his book.

It was great to share my research, but what I really wanted to know if it was true that the Royal Giants had come to Japan for a third time. One of the most famous Negro League pitchers, "Bullet Joe" Rogan, might have been a part of this team. If the rumor was true, if they did come to Japan again, they definitely must have left some trace. There were no documents in Japan that remained as proof. If there was any clue, it might have been in the United States ... maybe in the passport in Phil's possession.

First, what kind of the player was Rogan? This would be obvious to anyone who knew something about black baseball. His nickname, "Bullet," suggested that he had a really good fastball. His speed, plus his big-breaking curve ball, made him a star for the Kansas City Monarchs. It was well known that Smokey Joe Williams of the east and Rogan of the west were the leading pitchers in black baseball of their era. They were both in their prime just before the arrival of superstar pitcher Satchel Paige.

I could share more information about Rogan, but it would only add more support to the conclusion that he could pitch, hit and run. Considering all his talents, many people thought that Rogan was a better all-around player than Satchel.

There were many accounts of his greatness, but there was a specific example from the 1924 season worth highlighting. Rogan played in both the infield and outfield, and also pitched. As a pitcher, he won 19 games that season. During the Colored World Series, he played against Hilldale, the champions of the east. He played in seven games and also pitched. He recorded two wins, one loss, and one tie as a pitcher. When he was not pitching, he played center field, and he was proud that he did not commit one error. He recorded a .325 average at the plate, which was the second highest for the Monarchs.

If a player this great came to Japan, then there must have something about him in the records. But there was nothing. Were the rumors of Rogan's Japan tour a hoax? It seemed unlikely that it was all fake. In the book *Voices from the Great Black Baseball Leagues* (New York, 1975), there is an interview with Newt Allen. He talks about the long tour to Japan. Allen played infield with the Monarchs and was one of the best players of his era. He was also a member of the Royal Giants team that toured Asia. Allen begins his story in 1935 (1935 might be wrong. It must be 1933).[3]

> The winter of 1935 we made a trip to Japan, China and the Philippines. What a wonderful trip! We got $3,000 apiece before we left, and 40 percent of every game we played. That was split twelve ways, because we only had twelve ballplayers.

We left San Francisco and stayed about ten months in the Philippines, playing Philippine teams and Army teams. We were all in a league together. And we went up to sugar plantations and played clubs up there too.

After we left there we played a Chinese team over in Shanghai. Sure, they had a baseball league over there, mixed Chinese and Hawaiians, pretty well educated people. But most of those fellows were pretty small. We stayed there around a month.

[…]

Japan was different. The majority of them seemed to be decent, respectable, and they really had ball teams. They had some ball players. Sessue Hayakawa, the movie star, and a Japanese girl who was a star for Metro-Goldwyn-Mayer—I can't remember her name now—opened a movie studio in Japan and sponsored one of the best ball clubs over there. Japan was a fine country, full of fine people.

In Hawaii they had teams made up of all nationalities—Hawaiians, Japanese, two or three Negroes and a quite a few Koreans. A man named Yamashiro, a superintendent down at Dole Pineapple Company, offered Rogan and me a salary and the only thing we'd have to do was check crates of pineapples and play ball two days a week, Saturdays and Sundays. At the end of the ball season, the team split all the money. The factory just furnished us the suits and the name. But we decided to come on back home and play.

Reading this, it is hard to tell whether or not they actually played in Japan. He does mention a powerful Japanese team, so perhaps a game must was played. However, the length of their stay is not stated clearly. It would be all up to Rogan's passport. It would demonstrate how long they remained in Japan.

Phil Dixon was rummaging through his cabinets. He had tons of collections: old gloves, bats with faded autographs, and a "Satchel Paige All-Stars" pennant were casually tossed out.

"Here it is, I finally found it."

Phil removed two old passports. Both had red covers, but they looked blackish from the dirt. They were very thin compared to current passports.

Rogan's passport was No. 66217, and it was issued on October 26, 1933. The emergency contact was his wife Catherine, and her address was on Michigan Street in Kansas City. The details:

Name:	Wilber Rogan
Height:	5 feet 7 ¼ inches
Color of Hair:	Black
Color of Eyes:	Black

Characteristic: Scar on his left cheek

Date of Birth: July 28, 1889

Occupation: Baseball Player

Under the section "Transit Visa," dated November 13, Showa 8 (1933), was the signature of Japan's San Francisco Consul General, Shu Tomii. In his writing was a notation that read, "Length of Stay in Japan for two days."

The stamp underneath the writing was a light-greenish color. However, it was not a complete stamp—just half of it was visible. The words "Kanagawa Prefecture" was slightly legible in the half circle.

The truth was almost revealed.

It was certain that Wilber "Bullet" Rogan visited Japan—but only for two days.

Phil had another passport was from one of the members of the Japan tour. His name was Dink Mothell. His stamp was also faded and was not quite visible. On that page, the words "Shore Excursion" were written in pencil.

"Mothell was a player," Phil started to explain. "When I was young, he used to live near my house. I started to learn about baseball history because of him. He was with the Monarchs for 15 years. He also played in the Negro League World Series. His position was mainly outfield. Dink hit above .300 above in one of those years. He was a reliable hitter."

He added, "The first Royal Giants team that you have mentioned had great players, but as a team, the third one must have been better … Chet Brewer, Newt Allen, and T. J. Young were on the team."

He could be right. Chet Brewer was a fastball pitcher who competed on the mound with Rogan on the Monarchs. His long career lasted for 24 years. He is widely known for winning 16 games for Kansas City in 1934. However, his game against the Homestead Grays three years earlier was his most famous accomplishment and is still talked about today. At that time, Chet pitched against Smokey Joe Williams, who was recognized as the best pitcher in the Negro Leagues. The game went to the 12th inning and all the fans were engaged in the game. Brewer had 19 strikeouts, but he ended up on the losing side of a 1-0 loss. The opposing pitcher was better than he was that day. Smokey Joe struck out 27 batters and allowed only one hit to the Monarchs. Even though Brewer lost the game, his performance became legendary, and made him famous. These two pitchers, along with Rogan and Satchel, were called "The Big Four" throughout the league. Brewer and Rogan were on this Royal Giants team for their third trip to Japan.

Second baseman Newt Allen played for the Monarchs for 22 years. He had incredible speed and great hitting skills. He was a great switch hitter and especially good at bunting.

Another player, T. J. Young, was a catcher with a strong arm. He controlled Rogan and Brewer's breaking balls and had great framing skills as well. Besides the famous players, William Ross, who came to Japan in Showa 7 (1932), also may have joined the team for the tour. As such, this ball club was strong.

Dixon stated, "It was obvious that the third Royal Giants team was made up primarily of players from the Kansas City Monarchs. Oh, yes I have great stats to show how good they were. It was from 1929…"

He brought out a piece of paper glued to the mount in the file from the cabinet. It showed the results of three games against a team of major league all-stars that took place during the off season in the California Winter League. The black team's name was, of course, the Royal Giants. The result of this series was:

The first game:	12-8
The second game:	6-5
The third game:	10-3

The Royal Giants won all three games.[6] On this major league team were some of the players who had previously come to Japan. Al Simmons and Jimmy Foxx were familiar names. The clean-up hitter for the Royal Giants was Biz Mackey. Let's look at the details of the third game. In this contest, the major league team put in several pitchers to defend against the powerhouse Royals. Among the players with extra base hits in the game were Mackey, Foxx, and Rogan.

October 31, 1929 - White Sox Park, Los Angeles, CA

Game 3: Joe Pirrone's All-Stars vs. Royal Giants

POS.	ALL-STARS	AB	H	R
2B	Moorehart	3	0	0
SS	Haney	4	2	0
LF	Simmons	5	0	0
RF	Jolley	4	1	0
1B,P	Foxx	3	3	1
3B	B. Meusel	4	1	0
CF	Wingo	4	0	0
C	McMullen	3	1	1
P	A. Campbell	0	0	0

POS.		AB	H	R
P	Gould	1	0	0
P	Edleman	2	1	0
1B	Cotter	1	0	0
PH	Pick	1	1	1
Totals		35	10	3

POS.	*ROYAL GIANTS*	*AB*	*H*	*R*
2B	Mothell	4	1	1
SS	Allen	4	1	0
CF	Holloway	3	2	2
1B	Mackey	5	2	1
RF	Livingston	3	1	1
C	Young	5	1	0
3B	Joseph	3	2	2
LF	Taylor	4	2	1
P	Rogan	3	2	2
Totals		34	14	10

HR: Mackey, Pick, Joseph
3B: Holloway
2B: Foxx 2, Rogan
Umpires: Powell and Moore

For the third tour to Japan the Royal Giants had many of the same players, although with Chet Brewer as the replacement for Mackey. It is certain that not everyone on the team was an all-star in the Negro Leagues, but they were at the same level as the white major league team.

This team toured the Philippines, Shanghai, and Hawaii, and decided to stop by Japan. Did the team play any games during the short period of time they were there?[7]

Even if Rogan and the other players played in Japan, there could only have been one or two games.[8] This does not give me any disappointment. It does not matter to me. I have already learned many things while investigating Rogan. Having been attracted by the name "Bullet," I learned his story. Not only did I find the footprints he left behind, but I also encountered more than I expected.

I wonder why the story of "Rogan's Japan tour" has been passed on in the black baseball community for such a long time? Many people have mentioned the name of Rogan and his association with Japan.[9] One of the reasons I could think of was that when he talked about his long tour, he spoke passionately about Japan even though he was only there for a short stay. He received an unforgettable impression of Japan. Rather than talking about his other destinations he just talked about his time in Japan. Phil heard this from Mrs. Rogan when he received his passport, so the story was accurate.

Rogan spent a few days in Japan. He must have been welcomed by the Japanese people, or he must have heard about the great treatment accorded to Mackey and agreed with his claims. Otherwise, the legend of "Rogan visiting Japan" would not have lived on in the black baseball community of America.

By the way, Rogan has passed away, and his wife is also gone now. Both Mothell and Duncan are gone. Dixon and Mackey, who were described as "strong as horses and cattle" by Japanese writers, are gone too.

Because they were not sponsored by a Japanese newspaper, the Royal Giants did not have as many connections to market themselves. However, this did not mean that their footprints had completely disappeared.

The gentleman-like, black giants ... they live in the hearts of the Japanese players, the men who played against them using all their power from every inch of their bodies. The Japanese ball players saw the talent of the Royal Giants and appreciated their friendly, easy-going attitudes.

This year marks the 50th anniversary of the start of the Japanese Baseball League (Showa 11-61, [1936-1986]). For years nobody talked about the Royal Giants and the important role they played in the emergence of professional baseball in Japan. Now that the stories of the Japanese players who faced them are preserved for future generations to appreciate, the name of the black professional team—the Philadelphia Royal Giants—will live on forever as well.

野球

Afterword

An established theory—or popular way of thinking—is something that cannot be disrupted, even by divine forces. That is why it is called an established theory. Everyone viewed the writing of this book as a daunting task, for in it I have disrupted the established theories surrounding the origins of professional baseball in Japan. I might appear to be brave or extremely well-prepared. However, to be honest, I did not have the bravery or preparedness to challenge this theory. All I had was my recklessness.

In Showa 6 and 9 (1931 and 1934), Japan welcomed the American major league all-star teams. During the excitement of these visits, the seeds of the Japanese Professional League were planted, and the league was established in Showa 11 (1936). This established theory is certainly correct. In order to invite the major league teams, Japan needed to form the All-Japan Team, which became the Yomiuri Giants, and eventually led to the professional Japanese Baseball League.

This was exactly how it happened. These facts cannot be changed. As every book states, they are true. However, I think it is not accurate to claim that this is the *only* thing that happened, and nothing else. As such, what I have written here is simply an *addition* to the established theory … but it is a much needed addition that I think will be appreciated by many people. As an author, it is my pleasure to add this perspective to the conversation.

Although I just said I am the author, maybe I should be called an *editor*. And maybe even this title does not fit me.

Our old ballplayers shared with me their distant memories of the sounds of the game which they have not talked about for over half a century. Listening to their stories, I was moved by the spirit and passion that they still possessed. That is why I was able to complete this book. I would like to thank those old players who kindly shared their stories.

I would also like to say thank you to the people who supported me behind the scenes. Ms. Akiko Ogawa and Ms. Kiyomi Kimura, of the Japanese Baseball Hall of Fame, who patiently continued to find documents from piles and piles of old books and archives. Ms. Gwendolyn Shimono from Hawaii worked on clipping the old newspapers during her

Christmas holiday. Mr. Seiichi Ohashi continued to encourage me and supported me in finding the Japanese players and their addresses. Mr. Shigenobu Machida, Mr. Eiji Sugai, Mr. Shoichiro Tase, Mr. Nobuaki Nidegawa, Mr Shinsuke Tanada, and Mr. Shonosuke Fukumuro provided me with valuable documents and information. Thank you to all of you. I owe a lot to you.

Furthermore, I appreciate Ms. Shoko Tanabe, from the Third Technical and Research Library at Shin Nippon Seitetsu Corporation, and Mr. Gyo Hani, of *The Japan Times,* who supported me. Mr. Hani did not only provide me with the old microfilm, but he also kindly showed me how to use the machine even though he had a hectic schedule. This knowledge helped me later on. As for the American side, I thank all of you, Mr. Roy Campanella, Jim Olson, Rob Ruck, David Skinner, and Craig Davidson. In the book, I have mentioned Mr. John Holway and Phil Dixon, who also shared their valuable information.

Without every single person's help, I would not have been able to publish this book. I greatly appreciate all of you.

Finally, the black visitors to Japan are now able to take their place on the stage because of everybody's support, but they have not yet been fully described. I would expect that more people will trace the black players' footsteps and remember them and pass the knowledge on. I hope that from this book many more people will research the Philadelphia Royal Giants so there will one day be a more precise history.

This was written as a series for the magazine *Weekly Baseball* from December of 1985 to April of 1986. During that time, I received much support and encouragement from the readers, which kept me going. I don't know how to describe it in words. Thank you very much.

Lastly, I show my dearest gratitude to the President, Mr. Tsuneo Ikeda, and the Vice President, Mr. Ikuo Ikeda, of *Baseball Magazine Sha.*[1] Mr. Masao Yoshida, the Vice President in Osaka branch.[2] Mr. Yoshikazu Demura,[3] the former Editor-in-Chief of *Weekly Baseball,* and Mr. Hiroshi Harada, of the Publishing Office, gave me great guidance. I really appreciated the endearing support you provided to me, the inexperienced writer.

Kazuo Sayama
May 5, 1986

On April 16, Showa 2 (1927), the Royal Giants battle the Tomon Club at Waseda Totsuka Baseball Stadium. In the bottom of the 5th inning, Tomon scored a run to tie the game. The outfield bleachers were packed with fans. The atmosphere of the infield and outfield bleachers were shown by this valuable photo (From Asahi Sports).

Above: On June 5, Showa 2 (1927) the Hawaii Asahi (left) and Royal Giants (right) lined up in front of the camera at Hawaii Honolulu Stadium. Pullen and Johnson are holding the pennant. Mackey and Goodwin hold the trophy. Dixon and Duncan are among the others. The fourth from the right for the Asahi players was Tadashi "Bozo" Wakabayashi.

Biz Mackey shakes hands with former yokozuna (highest-ranked sumo wrestler) Tochigiyama Moriya. George Irie looks on in the background.

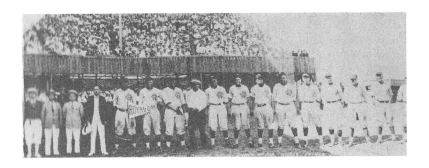

Biz Mackey and smaller Royal Giants teammates horseplay for the camera.

野球

Notes

Chapter 1

1. The Japanese Baseball League (JBL) reorganized in 1950 as Nippon Professional Baseball (NPB).

2. The SABR 13 conference occurred in Milwaukee, Wisconsin, July 15-17, 1983 at Mashuda Hall, Marquette University. According to the SABR website, "Hal Goodenough, a boyhood teammate of Mickey Cochrane and former member of the Braves' front office, was the guest speaker ... The players' panel consisted of Ken Keltner (also a SABR member), Andy Pafko, Mike Hegan, Fabian Gaffke, umpire Stan Landes and Negro Leaguers Lester Lockett and Ted 'Double Duty' Radcliffe." Source: SABR Convention History, http://sabr.org/content/sabr-convention-history.

3. "Clifford S. Kachline (1921-2010) left an indelible mark on the world of baseball research. For 24 years he worked at The Sporting News, writing hundreds of features and articles and editing many of their standard reference works. After the death of Lee Allen, in 1969 he became the official historian at the National Baseball Hall of Fame, a post he held for 14 years while working tirelessly with major league teams to secure archives and records that otherwise would have been thrown out. He also was a founding member of SABR in 1971, and became its first Executive Director in 1982. He was a stickler for the exactness of baseball records, and doggedly worked to get records corrected, from Rube Waddell's 1904 strikeout total to Hack Wilson's 1930 RBI figure. Cliff's contacts within the game helped countless researchers over the years, and he was helping them right up until his death in 2010." Source: http://www.sabr.org/about/clifford-s-kachline.

4. "John B. Holway (1929-) has been researching baseball since 1944, and he is still at it. Few may boast of as long and noteworthy a contribution to baseball research. Looking at baseball beyond America's major leagues, he wrote the first book in English on Japanese baseball, *Japan Is Big League in Thrills*, in 1954. Since then he has published many notable books on the Negro Leagues, most notably perhaps *Voices from the Great Black Baseball Leagues* (1975), a collection of interviews with the then virtually unknown Cool Papa Bell, Buck Leonard, Bill Foster, Willie Wells, and *The Complete Book of the Negro Leagues* (2000). Holway saw his first Negro League game—Satchel Paige's Monarchs against Josh Gibson's Grays—in Washington, D.C., in 1945. He has also researched intently and written frequently about Ted Williams, whom he saw strike two home runs in the 1946 All-Star Game. A former chairman of SABR's Negro

Leagues committee, Holway has received SABR's Bob Davids Award and the Casey Award for Blackball Stars, voted the best baseball book of 1988." Source: http://www.sabr.org/about/john-b-holway.

5. In the original Japanese text, Sayama incorrectly lists Rogan's legal name as Joe. The pitcher was born Charles Wilber Rogan, on August 28, 1893, in Oklahoma City, OK, and died March 4, 1967, in Kansas City, MO. "Bullet Joe" was inducted into the National Baseball Hall of Fame in 1998.

6. The dimensions of Meiji Jingu Stadium are: Left and Right Field Line: 297 feet (90.5 meters), Left and Right Field: 335 feet (102.1 meters), Left and Right Field Gap: 368 feet (112.2 meters), Center Field: 393 feet (119.8 meters). Source: Jim Albright / The Japanese Insider, Japanese Baseball Data Archive, Current Japanese Baseball Parks, Domes and Stadiums, http://baseballguru.com/jalbright/stadiums.htm.

7. Mackey was also a pitcher. See Appendices for more information about Mackey's pitching experiences in Japan and his early career.

8. See appendices for letters to Kaz Sayama from Monte Irvin and Leon Day sharing information about their personal relationship with his teammate, coach, and friend Biz Mackey.

9. The Japanese Baseball Hall of Fame and Museum first opened in 1959 next door to Korakuen Stadium in Tokyo, Japan. In 1988, the museum moved to the current site within the Tokyo Dome.

Chapter 2

1. In the original Japanese text, Sayama refers to a player with the 1928 USC baseball team as "Rixen". According to the records, there was no USC player by that name. Most likely, "Rixen" is the result of a translation and/or typographical error for USC player Larry Dihel, who went on to play briefly with the Portland Beavers of the Pacific Coast League in 1930.

2. According to Professor Kyoko Yoshida of Japan, the team roster that George Irie sent to Japan in advance of the tour reflected the complete roster of the Philadelphia Royal Giants squad who competed in the 1926-27 California Winter League—including Bullet Rogan, Turkey Stearnes, and other players who did not actually make the trip to Japan.

3. The Philadelphia Royal Giants were based in Los Angeles, California, not Philadelphia, Pennsylvania. There are a few theories for the unique team name: 1) Perhaps manager Lon Goodwin rebranded his Los Angeles White Sox in 1925 to the Philadelphia Royal Giants as an act of one-upmanship towards Rube Foster. Goodwin and Foster were former teammates with the Waco Yellow Jackets in Texas, and for some unreported reason, Lon Goodwin became a "persona non grata" in Foster's Negro Leagues in 1920. After leaving Texas in 1903, Foster became a star pitcher with several teams, including the Philadelphia Giants. In the Negro Leagues, it was common practice to add the term "Royal" to a team named "Giants" to declare a superior status to a similarly-named ball club; 2) Tour promoter George Irie lived in Philadelphia when he first arrived in the U.S. from Japan, where he married an American woman and had a son (b. 1908); 3) the name Philadelphia means "brotherly love" from the Greek (phileo) "to love" and (adelphos) "brother"; 4) Philadelphia was an important city for black baseball dating back to 1865 with the Pythian

Base Ball Club, one of the earliest Negro League baseball clubs. It is worth noting that Biz Mackey, the Royal Giants' biggest star, also played for a Philadelphia-area team, the Hilldale Club. In fact, several Hilldale players joined the 1927-28 California Winter League Goodwin's team. In 1928-29 Goodwin changed the name of his CWL team to Hilldale Royal Giants or just Hilldale Giants.]

4.   Thirteen or fourteen players was a typical roster size for a barnstorming team in the 1920s.

Chapter 3

1.   An "A" is used in Japanese line scores to indicate when the bottom half of the 9th inning was not played because the home team was ahead after the top of the ninth inning.

2.   Sayama's use of the word "harmony" means "balanced" in terms of the skill level and composition of the team.

Chapter 4

1.   Saburo Yokozawa (1904-1995) was from Taipei and attended Meiji University, where he participated in a tour of the U.S. in 1924. After managing the Senators, he became an umpire (1938-59) for the Pacific League in 1938. After WWII, he was the umpire-in-chief of the Pacific League. He was elected to the Japanese Baseball Hall of Fame in 1988. Source: Japanese Baseball Hall of Fame, http://english.baseball-museum.or.jp/baseball_hallo/detail/detail_090.html.

2.   Meiji University toured the U.S. in 1924. They played 37 games and finished with a 15-21-1 record (.405 winning percentage). Among their African-American competition, Meiji played Howard University in 1924, losing 4-3 in a ten-inning game. Source: "Japanese to Play Howard's Nine," *New Journal and Guide* (Norfolk, VA), May 30, 1925.

3.   From 1920 through 1926, Negro league teams played 56 games against major league teams (either intact or all-star teams), winning 29, losing 26, and tying 1.

4.   Tochigiyama Moriya (1892-1959) was the 27th yokozuna in sumo wrestling from 1918 until 1925. He is considered one of the pioneers of modern sumo, and remains the lightest yokozuna in the history of sumo with a weight of 104 kg. (229 lbs).

5.   See "Birth of the 1927 Tour" in the appendices.

6.   The 1927 source erroneously states that Dixon collected 5 hits in 4 at-bats. Most likely Dixon had 5 hits in 5 at-bats. The original reading has been corrected in the text.

7.   Michimaro Ono (1897-1956) was a star Japanese pitcher in the decade before the formation of the first Japanese professional league in 1936. Ono pitched for Keio, Mita Club, and Daimai. He later became a sportswriter and promoter of amateur baseball. In 1959, Ono was part of the first class of the Japanese Baseball Hall of Fame.

Chapter 5

1.   Shigeyoshi Koshiba (1908-?) toured the U.S. in 1929 with Meiji University baseball team.

Chapter 6

1. Tairiku Watanabe (1901-1955) was a pitcher for Meiji University. In 1922 Watanabe pitched against a major league all-star team during their tour of Japan. He went on to manage the 1950 Taiyo Whales of the Japan Central League. Source: "Japanese Would Learn Fine Points of Ball," *The Washington Times,* December 25, 1922, pg. 16.

2. Koshien was originally built for multiple functions, thus "Koshien Dai Undojo" translates literally to Koshien Large Playground. Most likely the name "Koshien Dai Undojo" was commonly understood as Koshien Athletic Field, Sports Grounds or Sports Arena.

3. Minoru Yamashita (1907-1995) was a first baseman and outfielder from Kobe, Japan. After graduating from Daiichi Shinko Commercial High School, he went on to play six seasons with Hankyu and Nagoya. Source: https://www.baseball-reference.com/register/player.fcgi?id=yamash000min.

4. Rap Dixon was a "five-point ballplayer who did everything with style … [T]he power-hitting outfielder was one of the better hitters during the 1920s and 1930s. The line-drive hitter never guessed on a pitch and was regarded as both a good two-strike hitter and a good curveball hitter. Although he could really "rap" the ball, his nickname derived from the Rappahannock River in Virginia. A complete ballplayer, Dixon also ranked among the best defensive outfielders." Source: James A. Riley, *The Biographical Encyclopedia of the Negro Baseball Leagues,* New York: Carroll & Graf Publishers, Inc., 1994.

5. The Japanese press inadvertently lists two players in right field for this lineup, Sugiura and Ohta. Most likely one of them played left field, the missing position from the lineup.

6. The Japanese press lists Tucker as the starting pitcher for the Royal Giants, yet other tour records indicate that pitcher Ajay Johnson recorded the win in the 2-0 victory over Doshisha on April 9, 1927. Incidentally, E.A. Tucker, a 26-year-old pitcher/outfielder, is listed on the incoming roster. According to passenger ship records, pitcher Eugene Tucker appears to have stayed behind in China, and did not play in Korea and Hawaii. Tucker was not among those listed on the passenger ship record with all other Royal Giants players returning to the U.S. from Hawaii

7. Andy Cooper was the starting pitcher, but Ajay Johnson was the winning pitcher of record, according to records compiled from other Japanese sources by Professor Kyoko Yoshida. Shared via email correspondence, December 28, 2006.

8. Julius Green was the winning pitcher of record, according to records compiled from other Japanese sources by Professor Kyoko Yoshida. Shared via email correspondence, December 28, 2006.

9. According to records compiled from other Japanese sources by Professor Kyoko Yoshida, Alexander Evans pitched in the Royal Giants' 9-6 victory on April 12, 1927. Shared via email correspondence, December 28, 2006.

10. Tondabayashi is a city located in Osaka Prefecture, Japan.

11. See appendices for complete list of US-Japan tours prior to WWII.

Chapter 7

1. See "1927 Tour Scrapbook" in appendices for Lon Goodwin's position on player salaries in the Negro Leagues.

2. In the Negro Leagues, Duncan was primarily a catcher.

3. At the time Cooper actually played for the Detroit Stars—he wouldn't join the Monarchs until 1928. Sayama is suggesting that Bullet Rogan was Goodwin's first choice as an ace pitcher to take to Japan. The use of the description "mediocre pitcher" for Cooper also reflects, to some extent, Sayama's personal admiration for the legacy of Rogan. In 1986 when *Gentle Black Giants* was first published, the average fan did not fully appreciate the career of Cooper. Twenty years later (2006), he was elected to the National Baseball Hall of Fame.

4. Members of the Philadelphia Royal Giants of the 1926-27 California Winter League (CWL) included Bullet Rogan, Turkey Stearnes, and other stars.

5. The Royal Giants squad that toured Japan in 1927 was comprised of four players from the CWL Royal Giants (Cooper, Mackey, Dixon and Duncan) and nine players from the semi-pro Los Angeles White Sox.

6. "… The risk of sports injury due to excessive activity had been warned (about) in the early years of Japanese sport history. Yet, there were a few periods that enthusiasm for sports got heated, namely the 'baseball poison theory period' in the 1910s and the 'baseball madness period' from the late 1920s to early 1930s. Concerned that enthusiasm for school baseball has gone too far, Japanese Ministry of Education issued 'Baseball Control Ordinance' in 1932 (Ministry of Education Directive No. 4; March 28, 1932). This control ordinance states that 'The school principal shall select only those who have both the permission of their parents to participate and a health certification issued by a school physician,' making medical examinations for baseball players mandatory." Source: https://www.med.or.jp/english/journal/pdf/2010_03/173_177.pdf

7. The Tokyo-Yokohama earthquake of 1923, also called the Great Kanto Earthquake, was a magnitude of 7.9 that struck the Tokyo-Yokohama metropolitan area near noon on September 1, 1923. The death toll from the quake was estimated to have exceeded 140,000. Source: https://www.britannica.com/event/Tokyo-Yokohama-earthquake-of-1923.

8. Gehrig was rushed to the hospital in Tokyo for treatment after the injury. Two months later his hand was still swollen prior to spring training for the 1932 season. Source: "It took the Japs to Prove Gehrig is Human," *The Brooklyn Daily Eagle*, Brooklyn, NY, Feb. 26, 1932, pg. 22.

Chapter 8

1. Sayama's source here is: Homer Barnett, *Innovation: The Basis of Cultural Change* (New York: McGraw-Hill, 1953), p. 186

2. Tomon was a team comprised of ballplayers from Waseda University who did not participate in the school's 1927 tour to the U.S. The Sundai Club was a team of Meiji alumni ballplayers.

3. Kilograms and pounds conversion added for English readers.

4. See appendices for "1927 Tour Scrapbook" and photo outside the hotel.

5. The Fresno Athletic Club (FAC) first toured Japan in the spring of 1924.

6. See appendices for list of all U.S.-Japan Baseball Tours prior to WWII.

Chapter 9

1. See appendices for "1927 Tour Scrapbook" and "Birth of the 1927 Tour" article for the backstory between Kenichi Zenimura's Fresno Athletic Club and Lon Goodwin's ball clubs in California.

2. See appendices for "1927 Tour Scrapbook" and article "Birth of the 1927 Tour" for a history of games between Fresno and Goodwin's ball clubs in California.

3. According Japanese press clippings from the 1927 tour available in the Harvey Iwata Collection at the National Baseball Hall of Fame archive, the Fresno Athletic Club and Philadelphia Royal Giants were scheduled to play a rematch a few days later. The rematch never occurred due to rain.

Chapter 10

1. See appendices for bio of Biz Mackey.

2. James Raleigh Mackey was born on July 27, 1897. In the original text Sayama spelled his name "Riley"; this is how his middle name was often pronounced, and this spelling appeared in the press early in his career. His birthplace is commonly reported as Eagle Pass, Texas, in Maverick County on the Mexican border. However, Mackey's World War I draft registration records his birthplace as Caldwell County, 70 miles northeast of San Antonio. And when returning from the tour of Asia in 1927, he told U.S. Customs his birthplace was San Antonio. Based on genealogy records of other Mackey family members, he was most likely born in the small town of Luling or Prairie Lea in Caldwell County. Source: Bill Staples, Jr., "Black Giant: The Early Career of Biz Mackey," *Black Ball: A Negro Leagues Journal,* Vol. 1, No. 1 (Spring 2008).

3. Other theories on the origin of the nickname "Biz" include: 1) Mackey was known for being talkative behind the plate, and some believe that as a catcher he gave hitters "the business" or "biz" for short; 2) Mackey was teammates with Bill Pettus (1884-1924) in the California Winter League in 1920-21. Pettus, a former boxer, served as a mentor for the young backstop. One of Pettus's boxing contemporaries was Frank "Biz" Mackey of Akron, Ohio (1883-1962). Some scholars believe that Pettus gave the young catcher the familiar nickname "Biz," and that Mackey the ballplayer embraced the moniker to honor his mentor, who passed away unexpectedly in 1924. Source: http://boxrec.com/boxer/10730.

4. Bill Foster was teammates with Mackey only in the California Winter League (Oct to April; 1926-27, 1930-31). The two were never teammates during the regular season (April to October). Source: CWL by William McNeil.

5. According to the National Baseball Hall of Fame, Santop was 6' 4" and 240 lbs. As a hitter, he was described as "a gifted slugger who hit mammoth drives in the Dead Ball Era ... also hit for extremely high averages in the upper .300s and lower .400s." Source: http://baseballhall.org/hof/santop-louis

6. Holsey Scranton Scriptus Lee, Sr. (1899-1974) was a pitcher in the Negro Leagues who played for several teams between 1921 to 1934. Before his Negro Leagues career, he served in the National Guard, fighting against Pancho Villa's forces at the Mexican border in 1916. He also served in the 372nd Infantry during World War I, earning two battle stars and a Purple Heart. Sources: Riley, James A., *The Biographical*

Encyclopedia of the Negro Baseball Leagues. New York, 1995; and Bruns, Roger. *Negro Leagues Baseball.* ABC-CLIO, 2012.

7. According to game summaries of the 1925 Negro Leagues World Series, in the fourth inning of Game 5 Mackey hit a double and scored the second run in a tight 2-1 victory over the KC Monarchs. In Game 6, Mackey drove in 2 runs with a double and solo home run to clinch the series with a 5-2 win.

8. Rap Dixon circled the bases in 14.02 seconds. For comparison, as of the 2018 season, only four major league players have recorded faster or equal times: Billy Hamilton, 13.8 on July 15, 2012; Byron Buxton, 13.85 on August 18, 2017; Dee Gordon, 13.89 on June 16, 2014; and Peter Bourjos, 14.02 on April 19, 2011. Sources: All-Time Quickest Inside-the-Park Home Runs, http://tatertrottracker.com/news/tater-trot-tracker-leaders-all-time.html, and https://www.si.com/mlb/2017/08/18/byron-buxton-inside-park-home-run-video

Chapter 11

1. See appendices for "Barnstorming the Empire: The 1927 Philadelphia Royal Giants in Colonial Korea," By Kyoko Yoshida.

2. The Frank Duncan (1901-1973) who participated in the 1927 tour to Japan was born in Kansas City, MO. There was another Negro Leagues ballplayer named Frank Duncan (1888-1958) who was born in Georgia. Historians often confuse the two, which might be the case here, despite listing the incorrect state.

3. See appendices for article, "Mackey was Born 30 Years to Soon," by Frank T. Blair.

4. "Rogan's Giants Make Fine Record During Japan Tour," *Honolulu Star-Bulletin*, June 6, 1927, 11.

5. The article in the *Honolulu Star-Bulletin* originally said that Rap Dixon (spelled "Dickson") was the short-stop, but the accompanying box score identifies Biz Mackey as the shortstop, with Dixon in center field. Since these are the positions they played for most of the tour, it seems likely that the shortstop described here is actually Mackey.

6. Henry Tadashi "Bozo" Wakabayashi was born in Wahiawa, Oʻahu, and graduated from McKinley High School in 1927. He first gained fame in Japan pitching Hosei University to two championships in the Tokyo Big Six University League Baseball Championships from 1934-1935. Following graduation, he joined the Hanshin Tigers in 1936. He won the Most Valuable Player award twice, as a pitcher of the Tigers in 1944 and as player-manager in 1947, the year the Tigers won the single league pennant. During his 16-year career, he won 243, lost 141 and had an ERA of 1.99. Wakabayashi is one of only 48 Japanese baseball players who is a member of the Meikyukai, an organization of professional players with 2,000 career hits and pitchers with 200 victories. Wakabayashi was the 17th player admitted to the Japanese Baseball Hall of Fame on December 2, 1964, and the first from Hawaiʻi. Source: http://www.hawaiisportshalloffame.com/wp/henry-tadashi-bozo-wakabayashi/

7. Bōzu means a monk, a Buddhist priest. Bōzu is also used as a term of endearment for addressing little boys. Source: *O-Lex Japanese–English Dictionary,* Obunsha, 2008. pp. 1681—2.

8. Wakabayashi wore uniform number 18. As a tribute to him, to this day the ace of the staff in Japan is given number 18.

Chapter 12

1. John Brodie Williams (1889-1963) was a major league baseball pitcher who appeared in four games for the Detroit Tigers in 1914, including three starts. Known as "Honolulu Johnny", he was the first player of Hawaiian ancestry to play in the major leagues. Source: https://sabr.org/bioproj/person/7a544ac1.

2. "J. Ashman Beaven arrived in Honolulu in 1910. In 1912, he established the Oʻahu Baseball League, Oʻahu Service Athletic League and the Catholic Youth Organization. In 1925, he purchased 14 fee simple acres at the ʻewa/makai corner of King and Isenberg streets and built the Honolulu Stadium. From 1925 to 1939, he was general manager of the stadium. He brought teams from Japan and Korea to play baseball in Hawaiʻi, and, between 1933 and 1934, brought baseball celebrities such as Babe Ruth, Lou Gehrig and Jimmy Foxx, to entertain Hawaiʻi's sports fans." Source: http://www.hawaiisportshalloffame.com/wp/j-ashman-beaven/

3. "'Faked Game' Stories Draw Hot Reply from J. A. Beaven," *Honolulu Star-Bulletin,* June 14, 1927, 8.

4. Lon Goodwin first used the team name "Philadelphia Royal Giants" in the 1925-26 California Winter League (CWL) season. It was last used in the CWL in the 1939-40 season, for a total of 15 years. In the early 1940s the team name changed to "Royal Giants" and by the mid-1940s the all-black entry in the CWL was known as the "Kansas City Royals." Source: William McNeil, *California Winter League.*

5. Sayama doesn't mention him, but Andy Cooper was the fourth Negro leaguer threatened with suspension.

6. Two hundred dollars in 1927 had the same buying power as $2,728.05 in 2017. Source: http://www.dollartimes.com/inflation/inflation.php?amount=200&year=1927.

7. Game details available at: "Black Sox Rout Lefty Grove Sunday," *New Journal and Guide* (1916-2003); Oct 20, 1928; ProQuest Historical Newspapers: Norfolk Journal and Guide, pg. 6.

8. Jack Ogden (1897-1977) pitched 16 season in professional baseball, five of them at the major league level with the New York Giants, St. Louis Browns and Cincinnati Reds. He finished his big league career with a 25-34 record (.424 winning percentage) and 4.24 ERA. Source: https://www.baseball-reference.com/players/o/ogdenja01.shtml.

9. Eddie Rommel (1897-1970) pitched 13 seasons with the Philadelphia Athletics (1920-1932). He finished his big league career with a 171-119 record (.590 winning percentage) and 3.54 ERA. He led the league in wins twice, with 27 in 1922 and 21 in 1925. Source: https://www.baseball-reference.com/players/r/rommeed01.shtml.

10. Howard Ehmke (1894-1959) pitched 15 seasons in the majors (1915-1930) with several teams including Buffalo (Federal League), Detroit, Boston (AL) and Philadelphia (AL). He finished his big league career with a 166-166 record (.500 winning percentage) and 3.75 ERA. He led the league in WAR for pitchers in back-to-back seasons (1923-24), and with 22 complete games in 1925. Source: https://www.baseball-reference.com/players/e/ehmkeho01.shtml.

11. Ruth did hit three home runs in one game on May 21, 1930, but it was not at Yankee Stadium. It was on the road in Philadelphia at Shibe Park. https://www.baseball-reference.com/boxes/PHA/PHA193005211.shtml

12. Dixon hit 3 home runs at Yankee Stadium on July 5, 1930, Source: *Negro Leagues Baseball*, by Roger A. Bruns, ABC-CLIO, p. 40. The Lincoln Giants were not the defending champions in 1930 (Dixon's Black Sox had won the American Negro League pennant in 1929).

Chapter 13

1. Nightclub owner Joe Pirrone was one of the major leaders of the California Winter League for decades. A local amateur player, he appeared briefly in the minor leagues in the early 1920s. From 1920 through 1945 he organized teams of major-league players and minor-league stars to compete with other local teams and black all-star teams. Some years Pirrone's All-Stars was the only white team in the 2-team California Winter League. His teams, despite having some Hall of Fame and other star talent, usually were no match for the Negro League teams. Players who played for his team included Babe Herman, Bob Meusel, Irish Meusel, Smead Jolley, Fred Haney, Willie Ludolph and Ernie Orsatti. Source: https://www.baseball-reference.com/bullpen/Joe_Pirrone

2. Bullet Joe Bush (1892-1974) pitched 17 seasons in the majors (1912-1928) with several teams including Philadelphia (AL), Boston (AL), New York (AL) St. Louis (AL), Pittsburgh and New York (NL). He finished his big league career with a 196-184 record (.518 winning percentage) and 3.51 ERA. He was a member of three World Series-winning clubs: 1913 Athletics, 1918 Red Sox and 1923 Yankees. Source: https://www.baseball-reference.com/players/b/bushjo01.shtml

3. Eddie Rommel (1897-1970) pitched 13 seasons with the Philadelphia Athletics (1920-1932). See Notes, Chapter 12, 9 for more career details.

4. The major league players competed against Mackey during the 1929-1930 California Winter League season as members of Joe Pirrone's All-Stars. Both Meusel brothers, Bob and Irish, played with the team. Mackey hit .352 that CWL season with the Philadelphia Royal Giants. Source: McNeil, California Winter League.

5. Roy Sherid (1907-1982) pitched 3 seasons in the majors (1929-1931) with the New York Yankees. He finished his big league career with a 23-24 record (.489 winning percentage) and 4.71 ERA. Source: https://www.baseball-reference.com/register/player.fcgi?id=sherid001roy

6. Concerned about the "baseball madness period" from the late 1920s to early 1930s, the Japanese Ministry of Education issued the "Baseball Control Ordinance" in 1932. Learn more about the Baseball Control Ordinance at: https://www.med.or.jp/english/journal/pdf/2010_03/173_177.pdf

7. Sayama indicates that O'Doul was with the Dodgers in 1931. Technically that is incorrect. In 1931 the Brooklyn ball club was known as the Robins. Source: https://www.baseball-reference.com/teams/BRO/1931.shtml

Chapter 14

1. Lonnie Goodwin was still the team manager during the 1932 tour, but William Ross, as the elder player at age 38, served as team captain. Most likely this reference to "Will" in the Japanese press is team captain William Ross.

2. Ichiro Hatoyama would later become the Prime Minister of Japan. Source: *Time Magazine*, March 14, 1955. http://www.coverbrowser.com/covers/time/34#i1672.

3. Takeshi Doigaki (1921-1991) was Japan's top catcher in the years following World War II. He broke in with the Hanshin Tigers in 1940. He missed three seasons due to the War. He won Best Nine honors as the JPBL's elite catcher in 1947, Doigaki switched to the Toei Flyers in 1954, and retired in 1957 with the Hankyu Braves. Doigaki later changed his last name to Wakamatsu. He coached for Hanshin, scouted for the Lotte Orions and was a baseball commentator. Source: https://www.baseball-reference.com/bullpen/Takeshi_Doigaki

4. The Kono Alameda All-Stars toured Japan in 1937 and were led by veteran captain Kenichi Zenimura, who had led two previous tours in 1924 and 1927. Zenimura was the California entrepreneur who in 1926 suggested to Lon Goodwin that he take his team to Japan. The 1937 tour was funded by Alameda businessman Harry Kono, who served as a scout for Dai Tokyo (precursor to the Shochiku Robins and Yokohama BayStars) and also negotiated the contract of James Bonner in 1936, the first African American to play professional baseball in Japan. See appendices for James Bonner article.

Chapter 15

1. Shozo Wakahara (1915-?), pitched for Waseda University and participated in their goodwill tour of the U.S. in 1936. Source: Ancestry.com; California, Passenger and Crew Lists, 1882-1959 for Shozo Wakahara.

2. Masao Date (1911-1992) was a Waseda University pitcher who competed well against the U.S. All-Stars. The one-time catcher turned strong-armed hurler of the Waseda nine was well-known for pitching in three consecutive games against Keio in 1931. He proved a strong opponent of the American All-Stars in 1931 and 1934. He was elected by special committee into the Japanese Baseball Hall of Fame in 1989. Source: http://english.baseball-museum.or.jp/baseball_hallo/detail/detail_097.html

3. "Yokohama Kosho" is a short name for Yokohama Commercial High School.

4. Kuronbo is a derogatory term used to describe people of African ancestry. This expression is the combination of two nouns, "kuro" and "bou"—the former being the proper term for the color black and the latter being an old-fashioned slang term roughly equivalent to "boy." While "kuronbo" literally translates to "black boy," the common usage of the applied expression and implied negative undertones could be loosely defined as the slang equivalent of the "N-word."

5. This is a Japanese idiomatic expression for being "ruthless" or "merciless."

6. Oumi is an old name for the Shiga prefecture. It is located next to Biwa lake.

7. The shuuto or shootball is a pitch commonly thrown by right-handed Japanese pitchers. The pitch is mainly designed to break down and in on right-handed batters, so as to prevent them from making solid contact with the ball. It can also be thrown to left-handers to keep them off balance. Good shuuto pitches often break the bats of right-handed hitters because they usually get jammed when trying to swing at this pitch.

Chapter 16

1. As stated in previous chapters, most likely "Will" is team captain and veteran pitcher William Ross.

2. According to passenger ship records, articles and photographs, Lon Goodwin was still involved in this tour as manager.

3. Sayama accidentally confuses Javier Perez with Jose Perez. In this chapter he describes Jose Perez's career, not Javier's. For Javier Perez's career summary, see Appendix P.

4. See Appendices for more information on William Ross's 25-year-career (1910-1934) in professional baseball.

5. See Appendices for 1932 tour game summaries, including dates and final scores.

6. This is a short name for Yokohama Commercial High School.

7. "Chan" is a term of endearment, suggesting that Suzuki was still loved and remembered by many people after many years.

8. Saburo Miyatake (1907-1956) is a former Keio slugger and hero of the Tokyo Big Six University League (TBSL). After leading the Keio nine with his pitching and batting (notably seven home runs and the first homer at Jingu stadium) to victory four times in the TBSL, he joined the Hankyu Braves in 1936 along with his teammate Minoru Yamashita. He was posthumously elected to the Japanese Baseball Hall of Fame in 1965. Source: http://english.baseball-museum.or.jp/baseball_hallo/detail/detail_022.html

9. Miyatake toured the U.S. in 1928 as a member of the Keio University ball club. Future Hall of Famer Shinji Hamazaki was also a member of the team.

10. Earl Whitehill (1899-1954) pitched in the major leagues with Detroit, Washington, Cleveland and Chicago (NL). During his 17 seasons (1923-1939), he compiled a 218-185 record (.541 winning percentage) and 4.36 earned run average. Source: https://www.baseball-reference.com/players/w/whiteea01.shtml

Chapter 17

1. To learn more about the 1934 tour, see Banzai Babe Ruth: Baseball, Espionage, and Assassination during the 1934 Tour of Japan, by Robert K. Fitts, University of Nebraska Press, 2012.

Chapter 18

1. Hilldale were champions of the Eastern Colored League in 1923, 1924, and 1925. The Kansas City Monarchs were champions of the Negro National League, the western circuit, during the same years. The two teams met in the World Series in 1924 and 1925.

2. Ed Bolden (1881-1950) had controlled the Hilldale Club for many years, but by 1932 he had been forced out. The following year he founded the Philadelphia Stars.

3. In fact, the Philadelphia Stars lasted until 1952.

4. No book by John Holway with this title has been located.

5. When Sayama wrote this book in the early 1980s, Monte Irvin was working as a MLB public relations specialist for the commissioner's office under Bowie Kuhn. The appointment in 1968 made him the first black executive in professional baseball. Irvin stepped down from his role when Kuhn announced his retirement in 1984.

6. See appendices for article "Mackey Born 30 Years too Late," for Biz's thoughts on baseball's integration.

7. In fact, Mackey died on September 22, 1965, several years after Doby and Newcombe played in Japan, so he undoubtedly knew about it.

8. Roy Campanella Day was held at the Los Angeles Coliseum, not Dodger Stadium.

9. See appendices for Biz Mackey biography by Bob Luke.

10. As of 2018, there are 35 individuals from the Negro Leagues in the Hall of Fame. According to baseballhall. org, "the defunct Committee on Negro Baseball Leagues selected nine men between 1971 and 1977 and the Special Committee on Negro Leagues in 2006, elected 17 Negro Leaguers."

11. In 1935 the New York Cubans won the second-half title of the Negro National League, but lost the league championship series to the Pittsburgh Crawfords.

12. Herbert Alphonso "Rap" Dixon (1902-1944) was an American outfielder in Negro League baseball for a number of teams. He was born in Kingston, Georgia. The accomplished Negro League legend died at age 42 in Detroit, Michigan.

Chapter 19

1. The Pittsburgh Crawfords were named after the Crawford Grill, a club in the Hill District of Pittsburgh owned by Gus Greenlee. Satchel Paige and Josh Gibson often hung out there and it became one of black Pittsburgh's favorite night spots. Black stars like Lena Horne and Bill "Bojangles" Robinson were some of the top-notch entertainers that the club regularly featured. Source: http://www.baseballhistorycomesalive. com/?p=9310

2. The original Crawford Grill (1933-1951) was located at 1401 Wylie Ave., at Townsend, in a former hotel called the Leader House that opened in the 1910s. The third floor of the three-story structure was for reserved for VIPs. Known as "Club Crawford," it served as Gus Greenlee's office. The audience was racially and socially mixed. Locals from the Hill District were patrons, as were Pittsburgh's powerful families, athletes and celebrities from out of town. Source: Knoch, Ashley (January 16, 2014). "Let's Learn From the Past: The Crawford Grill", *Pittsburgh Post-Gazette*.

3.   In the original Japanese text, Sayama (most likely) incorrectly refers to Chatham University instead of Duquesne University. Chatham University is located four miles away from the intersection of Crawford and Wylie, whereas Duquesne University is approximately one block away.

4.   According to Gary Ashwill, Greenlee opened several Crawford Grills, and in 1985 one still existed at the corner of Wylie & Elmore, several blocks east of the original locations.

5.   Duncan also played for the Homestead Grays in 1932.

6.   Source is possibly: Holway, John B. "Historically Speaking ... Frank Duncan, The Complete Catcher." *Black Sports Magazine,* December 1973, 22-23, 54.

7.   Quote later featured in John Holway's book, *Blackball Tales*, Scorpio Books, 2008, pg. 82.

8.   See appendices for article, "Mackey was Born 30 Years Too Soon," by Frank T. Blair.

9.   Satchel Paige died on June 5, 1982, shortly before the Negro Baseball Hall of History was dedicated. As Sayama mentions, the Hall of History was proposed in November 1980. According to contemporary accounts, former players Othello "Chico" Renfroe and Ted Page suggested a Hall of History due to their dissatisfaction with the displays on black baseball in the National Baseball Hall of Fame at Cooperstown. Paige's death did overshadow the Hall of History's dedication in 1982, and may have led Sayama to infer a causal link.

10.   Irvin is presumably referring to the film *The Bingo Long Traveling All-Stars and Motor Kings* (1976), which was widely criticized by Negro league veterans for portraying black baseball as mostly about clowning and comedy.

11.   There were five individuals associated with the Royal Giants' tours still alive in 1985-86, when the research for *Gentle Black Giants* was underway. They are: 1927 tour, Ajay Johnson; 1932-33 tour: Steere Noda; 1933-34 tour: Newt Allen, Chet Brewer, and James Brown.

12.   See Appendix P—Negro Leagues Trans-Pacific Barnstormers Summary & Bios for information on other players.

13.   Tom Heitz (1940-) was the National Baseball Hall of Fame Librarian for 12 years beginning in 1983. He oversaw a construction project that greatly enlarged the building and made it a modern facility, grew the collections and services, provided for the conservation of materials and expanded access to researchers. As Hall of Fame Librarian, he first proposed and then helped establish SABR's Seymour Medal, first awarded in 1996, to honor the best book of baseball history or biography published during the preceding calendar year. He now serves as general manager of Friends of Doubleday, a nonprofit organization dedicated to the preservation of Doubleday Field in Cooperstown, New York. Source: http://sabr.org/about/tom-heitz

Chapter 20

1. Phil Dixon published *The Negro Baseball Leagues: A Photographic History* in 1992. It won SABR's Casey Award for the Best Baseball Book of 1993.

2. For more information on Dixon, see: "The Tenacity of Phil Dixon," by Jay Berman, *435 Magazine* (Kansas City, MO), November 2016, http://www.435mag.com/November-2016/Phil-Dixon-Negro-League-Baseball-Kansas-City/.

3. This is Sayama's note, and he is correct. Some Royal Giants players departed from San Francisco while others departed from Los Angeles on November 12, 1933 on the *S.S. President Pierce*.

4. The Royal Giants' 1933-34 tour lasted approximately seven months, November 12 to April 6. The team competed in the Philippines for roughly 8 weeks (early Jan to Feb 10, 1934).

5. This game was played in Kansas City, Missouri, on August 2, 1930.

6. The final game occurred October 31, 1929.

7. The Royal Giants arrived in Yokohama, Japan, on Dec. 4, 1933, on the *S.S. President Pierce*. On Jan 1, 1934, they boarded the S.S. President Wilson in Yokohama and departed for Manila, PH. Source: Research conducted by SABR member Yochi Nagata, 2006.

8. According to Japanese baseball historian Yochi Nagata, bad weather prevented the Royal Giants from playing any games in Japan in December 1933.

9. Itaru "Rogan" Miyanishi (1903-1973), is a Nisei ballplayer from Hawaii who took on the nickname "Rogan" after watching Bullet Joe compete in Hawaii circa 1913-1916 with the 25th Infantry Wreckers.

Afterword

1. Tsuneo Ikeda (1911-2002) attended Waseda University. As writer and chief editor for *Baseball World* starting in the 1930s, he promoted baseball and was credited with introducing baseball to the Soviet Union. He founded *Baseball Magazine* in the 1940s. Ikeda was inducted into the Japanese Baseball Hall of Fame in 1989. Source: https://www.baseball-reference.com/bullpen/Tsuneo_Ikeda.

2. Masao Yoshida (1914-1996) was a Japanese amateur pitcher originally from Ichinomiya, Aichi. He had 23 wins at Spring and Summer Koshien. In the National High School Baseball Championship between 1931 and 1933, he won 14 consecutive games at Koshien Stadium and he became the only pitcher to win three consecutive championships. He never joined Nippon Professional Baseball, instead continuing to play as an amateur pitcher. In honor of his unprecedented pitching at Koshien, Yoshida was inducted to the Japanese Baseball Hall of Fame in 1992. No high schools have ever achieved three consecutive victories since Yoshida's team recorded the feat. Source: "Yoshida Masao". Japanese Baseball Hall of Fame.

3. Author of "Eigo de kitemiruka besuboru" (Let's Listen to Baseball in English). Tokyo: Gogaku Shunjusha, 1992.

野球

PART II: A HISTORY OF NEGRO LEAGUERS IN JAPAN

Appendix A:
U.S.-Japan Baseball Tours, 1905-2019

On 1905, Waseda University traveled across the Pacific to become the first team from Japan to play in the U.S. Led by manager Iso Abe, the Waseda nine barnstormed America learning the finer points of the game in 26 contests. In doing so, they laid the foundation for the building of the U.S.-Japanese "Baseball Bridge Across the Pacific." Since then, hundreds of teams at all levels—high school, college, amateur, semi-pro and professional—have journeyed across this goodwill baseball bridge.

The following section details the majority of the tours that occurred between 1905 and today (2019). The list includes roughly 140 tours across the Pacific, including stops in the Hawaiian territories—an important mid-point for U.S. and Japanese teams. This list is not exhaustive and most likely will be updated over time as more tours are identified, and exact win-loss records become available.

This information is included here because at the heart of Kazuo Sayama's *Gentle Black Giants* is a debate about the impact the Philadelphia Royals Giants had on the start of professional baseball in Japan in 1936. Prior to Sayama's book, the common narrative was that Babe Ruth and the All-Americans arrived in 1934, and two years later it resulted in Japanese professional baseball. The truth is more complex.

As addressed in the *Preface* of this book, there is no disputing the fact that Ruth and the All-Americans generated excitement among Japanese fans for high-caliber baseball. However, it would be inaccurate and disrespectful to ignore all of the other encounters that contributed to the improvement of Japanese baseball players' overall skill level.

Therefore, the following list honors the unsung heroes who in their own small way, helped build baseball's goodwill Bridge to the Pacific between the U.S. and Japan.

*   *   *

HIGH SCHOOL

YEAR	TEAM	DIRECTION	W	L	T	WIN%
1927	Wakayama High	to U.S./Can.				
1928	McKinley High (HI)	to Japan	10	3	0	0.769
1929	Shinko Shogyo Commercial	to U.S.				
1931	Shogyo-Hiroshima High	to U.S.				

UNIVERSITY TEAMS *(*estimated, based on newspaper reports)*

YEAR	TEAM	DIRECTION	W	L	T	WIN%
1905	Waseda	to U.S.	7	19	0	0.269
1908	Santa Clara College	to Hawaii	3	1	0	0.750
1908	Keio	to Hawaii	2	3	0	0.400
1908	Univ. of Washington	to Japan	6	4	0	0.600
1909	University of Wisconsin	to Japan	3	2	0	0.600
1910	University of Chicago	to Japan	9	0	0	1.000
1910	University of Wisconsin	to Japan	3	4	0	0.429
1910	Waseda	to Hawaii	9	10	0	0.473
1911	Keio	to U.S.	29	20	1	0.580
1911	Waseda	to U.S.	17	36	0	0.321
1913	Stanford University	to Japan	13	7	0	0.650
1913	Univ. of Washington	to Japan	9	3	1	0.692
1914	Keio	to U.S.	15	14	2	0.484*
1914	Meiji	to U.S.	26	28	2	0.464*
1915	University of Chicago	to Japan	13	0	0	1.000
1916	Waseda	to U.S.	10	19	0	0.345
1920	UC Berkeley	to Japan	7	3	0	0.700
1920	University of Chicago	to Japan	8	4	2	0.571
1920	Waseda	to U.S.	15	23	0	0.395
1921	University of California	to Japan	8	3	0	0.727
1921	Waseda	to U.S.	10	18	0	0.357*
1921	Univ. of Washington	to Japan	23	12	0	0.657
1922	University of Indiana	to Japan	2	7	1	0.200
1924	Meiji	to U.S.	15	21	1	0.405
1925	University of Chicago	to Japan	13	3	5	0.619
1926	Stanford University	to Japan	8	9	0	0.471
1926	University of California	to Hawaii	16	4	0	0..800
1926	Univ. of Washington	to Japan	9	10	0	0.474
1927	University of California	to Japan	4	7	0	0.364
1927	Waseda	to U.S.	22	12	0	0.647
1928	University of Illinois	to Japan	7	3	1	0.636
1928	Univ. of S. California	to Japan	27	15	0	0.556
1928	Keio	to U.S.	15	12	0	0.556
1929	University of Michigan	to Japan	13	11	0	0.846
1929	University of California	to Japan	6	6	0	0.500

1929	University of California	to Hawaii	6	4	0	0.600
1929	Meiji	to U.S.	17	11	0	0.607
1929	Hosei	to Hawaii	7	8	1	0.438
1930	University of Chicago	to Japan	7	7	1	0.467
1931	Hosei	to U.S.	6	20	0	0.231
1932	University of Michigan	to Japan	14	10	0	0.714
1932	University of Hawaii	to Japan	21	9	0	0.700
1932	Rikkyo (St. Paul)	to U.S.	11	10	0	0.524*
1935	Harvard University	to Japan	4	6	0	0.400
1935	Yale University	to Japan	4	6	1	0.364
1936	Waseda	to U.S.	15	7	0	0.681
1936	Kansai (Osaka)	to Hawaii	20	2	0	0.910
1952	Pacific Coast All-Stars	to Japan	10	5	2	0.588
1955	Univ. of S. California	to Japan	25	3	0	0.893

SEMI-PRO TEAMS

Year	Team	Direction	W	L	T	Win%
1912	All-Chinese (Hawaiian)	to U.S.	65	50	4	0.546
1913	All-Chinese (Hawaiian)	to U.S.	105	40	1	0.719
1914	All-Chinese (Hawaiian)	to U.S.	125	21	4	0.833
1915	All-Chinese (Hawaiian)	to U.S.	102	53	3	0.646
1916	All-Chinese (Hawaiian)	to U.S.	77	56	2	0.570
1921	Canadian Stars	to Japan	5	1	0	0.833*
1921	Suquamish Indians	to Japan	16	2	0	0.889
1925	Phila. Bobbies (female)	to Japan	4	9	1	0.286
1932	Athens (CA) A.C.	to Japan	24	9	0	0.727

NEGRO LEAGUE TEAMS

Year	Team	Direction	W	L	T	Win%
1927	Phila. Royal Giants	to Japan	23	0	1	0.958
1928	Clev. Royal Giants	to Hawaii	16	12	1	0.552
1929	Pullen Royal Giants	to Hawaii	13	2	0	0.867
1931	Phila. Royal Giants	to Hawaii	25	1	0	0.961
1932-33	Phila. Royal Giants	to Japan	40	2	1	0.952
1933-34	Phila. Royal Giants	to Japan	34	1	0	0.971

JAPANESE AMERICAN LEAGUE TEAMS

Year	Team	Direction	W	L	T	Win%
1907	St. Louis-Hawaii	to Japan	5	3	0	0.625
1914	Seattle Asahi	to Japan	2	4	0	0.333
1915	Honolulu Asahi	to Japan	8	6	0	0.571
1918	Seattle Asahi	to Japan	16	9	0	0.640
1920	Honolulu Asahi	to Japan	*Mgr., Unichi Takahashi*			
1920	Seattle Mikado	to Japan	*Coach, Tom Hedigan*			
1921	Hawaii All-Stars	to Japan	15	3	2	0.750

1921	Honolulu Nippons	to Japan	17	12	1	0.567
1921	Seattle Asahi (F. Miya)	to Japan	8	3	0	0.727
1921	Vancouver Asahi	to Japan	6	4	1	0.545
1923	Seattle Asahi / Mikados	to Japan	13	11	0	0.542
1924	Fresno Athletic Club	to Japan	21	7	0	0.750
1925	San Jose Asahi	to Japan	32	6	0	0.842
1926	Honolulu Asahi	to Japan	25	7	0	0.781
1928	Aratani Guadalupe	to Japan	25	4	1	0.833
1927	Fresno Athletic Club	to Japan	41	8	1	0.820
1928	Stockton Yamato	to Japan	18	6	0	0.750
1930	Seattle Taiyo A.C.	to Japan	*Mgr., Kenji Kawaguchi, returns Dec.*			
1931	Kono Alameda All-Stars	to Japan	18	8	0	0.692
1931	L.A. Nippon	to Japan	20	5	0	0.800
1933	Honolulu Asahi	to Philippines	10	3	0	0.769
1937	Kono Alameda All-Stars	to Japan	41	20	1	0.661
1940	Honolulu Asahi	to Japan	4	4	0	0.500

PROFESSIONAL TEAMS

YEAR	TEAM	DIRECTION	W	L	T	WIN%
1908	Reach All-Americans	to Japan	17	0	0	1.000
1913	MLB Giants-White Sox	to Japan	7	5	0	0.583
1920	MLB All-Stars (G. Doyle)	to Japan	20	0	0	1.000
1922	Herb Hunter's All-Stars	to Japan	15	1	0	0.938
1925	Osaka Mainichi (Daimai)	to U.S./Hawaii	7	14	1	0.318
1928	Ty Cobb	to Japan	6	4	0	0.600
1931	Hunter & Lieb All-Stars	to Japan	23	0	0	1.000
1932	Hunter, O'Doul & Berg	to Japan	*Instructional clinics*			
1934	All-Americans (Ruth)	to Japan	17	0	0	1.000
1935	Dai Nippon/Tokyo Giants	to U.S.	107	10	8	0.856
1936	Lefty O'Doul	to Japan	*Instructional, stadium consultant*			
1936	Tokyo Giants	to U.S.	45*	20	1	0.681
1949	San Francisco Seals	to Japan	7	0	0	1.000
1951	DiMaggio & O'Doul	to Japan	13	1	2	0.813
1953	Eddie Lopat All-Stars	to Japan	11	1	0	0.917
1953	New York Giants	to Japan	12	1	1	0.857
1953	Tokyo Giants	to U.S.	9	12	0	0.428
1955	New York Yankees	to Japan	15	0	1	0.938
1956	Brooklyn Dodgers	to Japan	14	4	1	0.737
1957	Yomiuri Giants	to U.S.	*Spring, 4 players, Dodgers, FL*			
1958	St. Louis Cardinals	to Japan	14	2	0	0.875
1960	San Francisco Giants	to Japan	11	4	1	0.688
1961	Yomiuri Giants	to U.S.	*Spring training, Dodgers, FL*			
1962	Detroit Tigers	to Japan	12	4	2	0.667

1963	Osaka Hanshin Tigers	to U.S.	Spring training, Tigers, FL			
1966	Los Angeles Dodgers	to Japan	9	8	1	0.500
1968	St. Louis Cardinals	to Japan	13	5	0	0.722
1970	San Francisco Giants	to Japan	3	6	0	0.333
1971	Baltimore Orioles	to Japan	12	2	4	0.667
1971	Lotte Orions	to U.S.	Spring training, Giants, AZ			
1971	Yomiuri Giants	to U.S.	Spring training, Dodgers, FL			
1972	Lotte Orions	to U.S.	Spring training, Giants, AZ, HI			
1974	New York Mets	to Japan	9	7	2	0.500
1978	Cincinnati Reds	to Japan	14	2	1	0.824
1979	AL & NL All-Stars	to Japan	1	1	0	0.500
1981	Kansas City Royals	to Japan	9	7	1	0.529
1984	Baltimore Orioles	to Japan	8	5	1	0.571
1986	Major League All-Stars	to Japan	6	1	0	0.857
1988	Major League All-Stars	to Japan	3	2	2	0.429
1990	Major League All-Stars	to Japan	3	4	1	0.375
1992	Major League All-Stars	to Japan	6	1	1	0.750
1993	Los Angeles Dodgers	to Japan	0	2	0	0.000
1996	Major League All-Stars	to Japan	4	2	2	0.500
1998	Major League All-Stars	to Japan	6	2	0	0.750
2000	Major League All-Stars	to Japan	5	2	1	0.625
2002	Major League All-Stars	to Japan	5	3	0	0.625
2004	Major League All-Stars	to Japan	5	3	0	0.625
2006	Major League All-Stars	to Japan	5	0	0	1.000
2008	Athletics & Red Sox	to Japan	4	0	0	1.000
2014	Major League All-Stars	to Japan	2	3	0	0.400
2018	Major League All-Stars	to Japan	1	5	0	0.167
2019	Athletics & Mariners	to Japan	3	0	1	0.750

野球

Appendix B: The Secret History of Black Baseball Players in Japan

by Dexter Thomas

Editor's note: This article first appeared on NPR.org in July 2015.

In the fall of 1936, a 24-year-old black baseball player from rural Louisiana stepped off a boat in Tokyo. His name was James Bonner. An ace pitcher with a vicious submarine pitch, Bonner, according to Japanese newspapers breathlessly heralding his arrival, once threw 22 strikeouts in a single game back in the States. Bonner had just been signed by a Japanese team called Dai Tokyo, which debuted the year before, lost nearly every game it played, and was desperate for new talent.

Not for another decade would Jackie Robinson be allowed to play an American Major League Baseball game, but in Tokyo, being black wasn't a strike against Bonner. Just the opposite. Local papers excitedly pointed out his color, running headlines like "Black Pitcher Rushes Onto the Scene, Excellent Fielder, Holder of Amazing Strikeout Record." News reports gushed about his personality, calling him "athletic" and "charming." His signing bonus included daily steak dinners, unusual and expensive fare at the time, and his salary at the time was 400 yen per month. That won't get you a hot lunch in Tokyo nowadays, but then, it was an extremely generous salary. The biggest Japanese pitcher at the time, Eiji Sawamura, made about 120 yen a month

But the tale of how a black American baseball player from the Deep South ended up a big shot in Japan in 1936 is bigger than Jimmy Bonner. It's a little-known story of friendship and mutual aid between Japanese-American and black baseball players at a time when both groups were shut out of organized baseball. It sprang up in California in the pre-war years, became part of "one of the boldest—and most overlooked—experiments in baseball history," made its way to Tokyo, and would end up shaping the future of baseball in Japan.

A Place Where 'Only The Game Mattered'

To start, we need to go back to the 1920s, when professional black baseball teams played around the country in a network collectively called the Negro Leagues. One of these teams was the Los Angeles White Sox, managed by a black railroad worker named Lonnie Goodwin who is recognized today as one of the greatest baseball managers of his era. His team was all black, except for one member—a Japanese second baseman—and it played in Central LA's White Sox stadium along with a local Japanese squad called the L.A. Nippons.

The L.A. White Sox had more contact with Japanese-American players in 1925, when they lost a match against a Japanese team called the Fresno Athletic Club. That squad was managed by a Hiroshima-born mechanic named Kenichi Zenimura, whom sports historians would later refer to as the father of Japanese-American baseball. Perhaps over the customary cold beers and cigars he liked to enjoy after a win, Zenimura pitched Goodwin a new venture. Over the previous few years, Zenimura had been rounding up groups of Japanese-American ballplayers to tour Japan to develop the game back home. Might Goodwin be interested in bringing some of his players along for the next tour?

At the time, the sport was still finding its footing in Japan. Baseball had been in the country longer than you might expect, introduced by a white Civil War veteran named Horace Wilson, who taught English at Tokyo University in the 1870s, but it didn't get its native Japanese word—yakyuu, meaning "field ball"—until 1894. The sport developed slowly for the next couple of decades, primarily among students. By the mid-1920s, when Zenimura and Goodwin were making their plans back in the States, Japan's most popular baseball teams were still college teams, and the country had just built its first steel-and-concrete ballpark.

Baseball historian Bill Staples has written a biography of Zenimura, and he estimates that for both Zenimura and Goodwin, the prospect of touring Japan was a timely opportunity. Zenimura knew that baseball was slowly gaining popularity in his home country and that the pair stood to make good money on ticket sales at exhibition games at universities and parks in Japan. This was especially important for Goodwin; making a living as a semipro ballplayer was difficult for blacks, meaning that funds for stadiums, uniforms and player salaries had to be secured through creative means. This seemed like a good shot.

Zenimura and Goodwin may have had ticket revenues in mind, but if you take a step back, the stakes were bigger than baseball or business. Anti-Asian racism was rampant across the country, and by 1920, a California organization called the Japanese Exclusion League was gaining influence. With the backing of powerful newspapers, the group successfully lobbied for the Immigration Act of 1924, effectively banning Japanese immigration to the

U.S. For some Japanese-Americans, baseball was a way to negotiate their Americanness on their own terms. As Takeo Suo, who played ball as a prisoner in a wartime internment camp, would later put it, "putting on a baseball uniform was like putting on an American flag." For Zenimura, who saw baseball as a way to break down barriers, expanding the sport in Japan may have been a way to ease tensions at home as well.

A Glowing Welcome

In the spring of 1927, Goodwin and Zenimura arrived in Japan for a joint "goodwill tour." Zenimura brought his own Japanese-American team, and Goodwin led a powerhouse squad of 14 all-star Negro League players he had sourced from other cities and dubbed the Royal Giants. One Japanese player recalled arriving at a match against the Giants and watching in a mix of fear and awe as his far more experienced opponents warmed up on

Shortstop Biz Mackey and manager Lon Goodwin during the 1927 tour (Negro Leagues Baseball Museum).

the other side of the field. Surely, this squad of foreigners was going to crush his team. But, as he reported years later, "We were extremely pleased to find that they did not take an overbearing attitude, but instead were quite gentlemanly. Unlike our games with the Major League players, we had an excellent match, and this heightened our love for the game of baseball itself."

(Those other games he's referring to were in 1934, when a group of white major league superstars, including Babe Ruth and Lou Gehrig, went to Japan for another "goodwill" tour. Japanese baseball historian Kazuo Sayama reports that the experience left their hosts with a bad impression. "The white players ... treated their opponents and the fans with contempt, running up scores against inexperienced opponents and insulting their hosts, both on the field and off," he writes. "On one rainy day, Ruth played first base holding a parasol. Gehrig wore rubber boots. Al Simmons lay down in the outfield grass while a game was in progress.")

Other accounts of the 1927 black Royal Giants goodwill tour are similarly glowing. They could have easily overpowered most of their opponents but refrained from running up the score. When a missed call from an umpire resulted in the single loss of their otherwise undefeated 24-game tour, the Giants accepted the results with a smile. Even an accidental beanball was met with a friendly bow. And for the Negro Leaguers in Japan, their kindness was met with more kindness, as a 2008 article at MLB.com about the 1927 Goodwill Tour recalls:

"The emperor of Japan presented a [trophy] cup to Negro Leaguer and Royal Giant Rap Dixon, quite a step up from life in a country where blacks were treated as second-class citizens."

"When they got over to Japan and Tokyo, they felt a sense of freedom," said Ray Mackey, the grandnephew of Biz Mackey (a famous Negro League catcher). "The Japanese people met them more or less with open arms and subsequently caused them to respond in a like manner."

Did the fondly remembered Royal Giants goodwill tour—and the negative experience of the Major League Baseball tour just a few years later—lay the foundation for Japanese interest in a man like Jimmy Bonner, the ace pitcher recruited by Dai Tokyo in 1936? It's hard to say for sure, but if he'd heard anything about the treatment of his predecessors, Japan surely would have sounded like a great opportunity for him.

But how did a Tokyo team find out about him in the first place? A clue may lie in the liberal, multicultural climate of baseball culture in 1930s Northern California, which was giving rise to "one of the boldest—and most overlooked—experiments in baseball history."

No Reason They Shouldn't Coexist

That experiment was called the Berkeley International League, a Bay Area baseball league founded by black radio host, wire journalist, car race emcee and all-around entertainment mogul Bryon "Speed" Reilly. As the *San Francisco Weekly* recounts, Reilly brought together a whole host of hardscrabble semipro and sandlot teams from around the Bay Area who were shut out of all-white organized baseball. His league had not only black teams but also Latino, Japanese and Chinese, with names to match — the Aztec Stars, the Fuji Club, the Wa Sung Athletic Club.

These teams shared stadiums and practice grounds and—crucially—competed against each other. This was unlike anywhere else in the country at the time. Even when minority teams were permitted to use playing grounds in other parts of the country, they almost always played along racial lines—black teams playing only other black teams, Chinese squads scheduling games against other Chinese. But as *SF Weekly's* Ryan Whirty explains, the various ethnic communities that came together for the Berkeley International League "really saw no reason why they couldn't and shouldn't co-exist."

The audiences for these games were also remarkably mixed, and regularly broke 1,000 —massive numbers for a semipro match at the time. In particular, Japanese-American teams seem to have been an important part of Bay Area baseball culture. Local historian and baseball researcher Ralph Pearce, who has been on Bonner's trail for nearly two decades, writes in his book *From Asahi to Zebras* that as early as the 1920s, teams like the San Jose Asahi received enthusiastic newspaper coverage and had a strong following, including many white fans.

To be sure, West Coast baseball wasn't some utopia of racial harmony. The legendary Pacific Coast League, for example, enacted a "color line" policy that forbade its teams to play black teams, or black teams to use its parks. But when discrimination stood in the way, there are notable instances of black players leaning on Japanese communities for help. For example, most people who are familiar with baseball history have heard of Rube Foster, the founder of the National Negro League. Five years before he founded the league, Foster was touring Oregon with a black team and, as often happened to traveling black entertainers and athletes at the time, he struggled to find a single hotel, or even a restaurant, that would serve his team. But as the *Chicago Defender* reported on April 11, 1914, they eventually found a Japanese restaurant where no "color line" existed. There, they were finally able to eat breakfast.

So given what minority players faced in nearly every other league in the country, the Berkeley International League was a truly remarkable institution in its time. "Reilly and his comrades openly defied the social mores of segregation that still dominated even the progressive Bay Area," writes Whirty, "and prompted residents, players, and fans of different cultures to learn about each other, as athletes and as people."

And it brought together people who would almost certainly never have met outside the ballpark, setting off unlikely domino effects. After all, it was while playing for a Berkeley International League team that Bonner, who had moved to California from Louisiana in the early '30s, was scouted by a Japanese-American baseball fanatic who put him in touch with his soon-to-be team in Japan.

Playing Ball, On Their Own Terms

So why have most baseball geeks—including dedicated historians—never heard of James Bonner, a black star player in Japan a whole decade before Jackie Robinson broke American baseball's color line? After all, newspapers of the day seemed excited about his arrival. He played a couple of unofficial matches soon after arriving, and things were looking good. His submarine pitch was hot, and one catcher remarked that he doubted that anyone would be able to hit it.

But as it turns out, Bonner never quite lived up to the hype. Once the season started, Bonner lost control of his pitches, walking 14 batters over the space of four games. In his third game, he made a fielding error that cost his team the match. His batting average of .458 was stellar, but he'd been hired to pitch, not hit. News reports went from glowing to confused to dismissive. After only a month, he was taken off the roster and sent back to America. Very little is known about his later years, including whether he continued playing baseball.

But while Bonner's career in Tokyo was short-lived, the impact of the institutions that helped get him there, from the black-led Goodwill Tours to the racially progressive Berkeley International League, continued to roll on. The cover of the May 1927 issue of *Yakyuukai (Baseball World)* featured a player named Shinji Hamazaki shaking hands with a member of the Royal Giants after a game at Keio University. Hamazaki would later go on to manage the Hankyuu Braves, and once foreign players became eligible to play in the Japanese leagues, he immediately recruited two black players—the first to play since Bonner. Scholar Kyoko Yoshida reports that when the president of the team expressed reservations about hiring these new recruits, Hamazaki stood by them, saying stubbornly: "If you don't want black players, then you don't want me."

Baseball historian Staples says there's no doubt that black and Japanese American baseballers helped shape the foundation of Japan's baseball culture. As he points out, Japanese-American managers and players served not only as a bridge between the U.S. and Japan but between communities within the U.S. as well. And for their part, black players worked respectfully with their Japanese counterparts, encouraging them to develop the game in their home country. One historian even suggests that the Japanese style of baseball is closer to the old Negro Leagues style, emphasizing "teamwork, finesse pitching, and the sacrifice bunt" over the more individualistic style of MLB.

As the two countries headed toward war in the late 1930s, baseball relations were cut off. The game turned inward—U.S. games continued as an expression of American wartime patriotism, and Japan's *Baseball World* magazine briefly shifted to include coverage of sumo wrestling. But as soon as the war ended, it was again a Japanese-American who bridged the two cultures through baseball. Immediately after the American occupation of Japan began, the U.S. government recruited Tsuneo "Cappy" Harada, a former semipro player from California, to help rebuild Japan's baseball spirit.

And soon enough, Japanese and black baseballers were once again interacting on their own terms. When I mentioned the story of the Royal Giants to my uncle, who's also black and spent part of his childhood on a Tokyo-area military base in the 1960s, he told me that his first baseball idol was a Japanese slugger named Sadaharu Oh, known as the "Home Run King" to my uncle and his mixed band of Japanese and American friends. They played ball around the base and every time my uncle went to bat, he'd copy the "flamingo" leg stance he'd seen Oh do at the big game. He'd lift his left foot high off the ground as the pitcher wound up, and as the ball came close, step-whack! He'd plant his foot forward and swing, laying into it just like his Japanese hero.

Source: Dexter Thomas, "The Secret History of Black Baseball Players in Japan", npr.org, July 14, 2015. Courtesy of Dexter Thomas.

野球

Appendix C: Letters to Sayama

by Leon Day & Monte Irvin

Leon Day
3036 Harlem Ave.
Baltimore, Md. 21216
Tel. (301) 945-5019

Jan. 21-85

Dear Kazuo,

I received your letter and was glad to know that you are writing about Negro baseball. I played with Bizz in 1946 with the Newark Eagles. He was our manager when we won the championship that year. He often spoke of how nice they were treated during their stay in Japan.

I don't know too much about "Bizz" because he was before me. I heard he was a good catcher, and from what I could see when he was going out, all they said about him was true.

I haven't read about him teaching Campanella to catch but he had a lot to do with it.

He was a good manager and knows base ball. He taught me a lot about hitters.

Sorry I can't give you more on him. Looking forward to seeing you in the spring. Thank you for the picture, I'll treasure it.

Sincerely,

Leon Day

Monte Irvin Baseball Group, Inc.
11 So. Douglas Ct.,
Homosassa, FL 32646
904/382-0228

June 16, 1992

Dear Kaz,

Please pardon my delay in replying to your recent letter. I'm glad Buck O'Neil gave you my address because Biz Mackey was my manager when I broke into the Negro Leagues back in the late thirties.

I think Biz was one of the most talented and smartest baseball men that I ever met. He could really hit, was a very smart catcher and had a rifle of an arm. Plus, he was a very good manager with a pleasant personality.

He passed away in Los Angeles about 20 years ago and his wife Lucille also died not too long afterwards. As far as I know he had no children. Originally he came from Texas. He must have some family there. A SABR member could do some research about that.

He and I were good friends. On those long bus rides he would talk about the good ole days and many of the stars that played with him. Rap Dixon was mentioned many times —said he was truly a great baseball star—good hitter and good fielder.

He mentioned the trip to Japan often. Said all of them had a wonderful time and talked about how nice the Japanese people were. He didn't say how much money was made. In those days the salaries were not very much. Could you send me some photos and the names of those that made the trip? Let me know if I can help you any further. I am interested in that trip—and was that the only trip that the black players made?

Keep well and keep in touch.

Kind regards,
Monte Irvin

野球

Appendix D:
Mackey Was Born 30 Years Too Soon
by Frank T. Blair

June 24, 1949
Long Beach California Press-Telegram

Graying George [*sic*] Mackey, fat and 50-plus, a great Negro catcher 25 years ago, sat in the grandstand at Wrigley Field, Los Angeles, Tuesday night as Booker T. McDaniel, first colored player ever to pitch in the Pacific coast league, shut out Seattle, 17 to 0. The usually genial Mackey was a sepia study in gloom as he turned to meet his old-time Long Beach friend, Bill Feistner, who managed the local Shell Oil clubs in the days when Mackey and Bullet Rogan were the star battery for the Philadelphia Royal Giants in Southland winter league contests.

"I was born 30 years too soon, Bill," said Mackey as he gestured toward the mound, where Booker T. of the Angels was flogging his cannonball pitch past a Rainier batter. "And that goes for Bullet, too. In our day, we didn't get the change that Booker is getting here tonight, and that Robinson, Doby, Paige and the others are now getting to show what they can do in the majors. What wouldn't Bullet and I have given to have had that chance."

There were tears in the eyes of the big man whom John McGraw, famed leader of the New York Giants, once called as good as catcher as any in baseball. The man who could have matched the catching prowess of Bresnahan, Kling, Schalk, Cochrane, Dickey and other headliners never got the chance because of baseball's invisible, but powerful, color line. The aging Mackey, long since past his prime, shook his head and repeated: "I was born 30 years too soon."

Mackey and Rogan gave some magnificent performances for the Philadelphia Royals more than a generation ago in Southland games against the Long Beach Shell Oilers, the

White Kings and the Pasadena Merchants. Mackey, at the plate, faced such pitchers as Ferdie Schupp, the once great southpaw of the New York Giants, the late Herman Bell of the Cardinals, and Herman Pillette, all of the Shell Oil club; and "Doc" Crandall of the White Kings, once a Giant hurling headliner. It was Schupp who used to recall that John McGraw often said of Mackey:

"There's a great catcher, as good as any in baseball today. If I just could 'whitewash' him, I'd like to have him on my club."

"Mackey had great power at bat," recalled Bill Feistner. "And what a throwing arm he had! He squatted on his haunches to receive a pitcher's slants and he's throw out baserunners without rising from that position."

I scored all the games at Shell Field in those days and marveled at the way Mackey powered the ball. He hit one tremendous homer over the far-flung scoreboard at Shell Field, while his battery partner, Bullet Rogan, also a formidable hitter, clouted a ball over the left-field barrier, which was seldom cleared by winter league batters.

The grizzled Mackey caught occasionally in semipro games in the Southland until two or three years ago when he retired. The man who was born 30 years too soon is planning to open a newsstand on Central Ave. in Los Angeles.

Source: Frankly Speaking: Mackey was Born 30 Years too Soon, by Frank T. Blair, Sports Editor, Long Beach California Press-Telegram, June 24, 1949, pg. A-13.

野球

Appendix E:
My Experience as a Baseball Manager
by Bob Fagen

Editor's note: The following article appeared as a series of weekly entries titled "My Experience as a Baseball Manager," by Philadelphia Royal Giants' second baseman Robert Fagen in The California Eagle, during the summer of 1924. Note that his last name is spelled three different ways throughout the articles: Fagan, Fagen, and Fagin.

*   *   *

My Experience as a Baseball Manager (Part 1 of 6)
By Bob Fagen

Editor's Note: Bob Fagen has been acting as manager of the All-Stars and was also Captain of the Carroll Giants. Fagen is one of the youngest managers in the country and has been very successful in winning ball games.

Says Bob Fagen: "The job is not what I thought it was and at this time I wish to give those old gray hair pilots who are managing ball clubs the credit that is due to them. The cry of "get some fight out there" has a new meaning to me. I realize what fight means on a ball club.

I have learned that many different kinds of ball players make up a ball club. There is one kind, the indifferent player. Some times his indifference is due to carelessness. He doesn't take his profession seriously. Sometimes it is due to friction with the manager and again a grudge against the owner due to salary differences.

There are lots of professional and semi-pro players, too many of them, who are not doing their best work.

Robert Fagen was a member of the 25th Infantry team in Hawaii and Arizona who joined the Kansas City Monarchs in 1920. He moved to the West Coast to manage the L.A. Colored All-Stars in 1924, and later joined the L.A. White Sox. He participated in the tour to Japan in 1927 with the Philadelphia Royal Giants, and barnstormed Hawaii with O'Neal Pullen's ball club in 1929 (Fort Huachuca Museum).

Such players are apt to excuse their conduct on the grounds that they do all that they are paid to do or that indifference is not detrimental. Some even consider their conduct smart not knowing they are holding their club back and cheating the public who is paying to see a player do his best.

Such players if they stopped to reflect would understand that a reputation is worth while to the ball player—a reputation for doing his best.

A manager is always ready to give special consideration to a player whom he knows is exerting himself to the utmost. The public likes to see a hard working player always in the game.

They will excuse him for errors, for they know he is trying.

This reputation is with the grasp of every ball player. It is strictly worth while."

*   *   *

My Experience as a Manager (Part 2 of 6)
By Bob Fagen

"Last week I wrote about the indifferent players, but this week I'm going off of the diamond and talk about owners as well as players.

First I will say that few owners know how to conduct a baseball club and treat baseball players and I am speaking about owners here in California.

How often have you seen an owner strut out to the playing field during the playing of the game and give some supposedly important instructions to his captain or players. And how many times have you heard the knowing fan remark, "That Negro wants to show who is boss".

The above has happened to me or my playing mates time and time again during my several years of playing in and around Los Angeles. I am quite sure that you know that I am telling the truth.

You will no doubt agree with me that the owner's place is at the gate or box office. I believe the owner should consult with his manager or captain before or after the game unless extreme emergency arises.

Lonnie Goodwin is Ideal

Hats off to Lonnie Goodwin. He is to my mind the smartest manager I have ever come in contact with and that is saying a lot.

I know that some of you would like to know why Lon is my choice as a great manager. First he lets a player work his own way so long as he's getting good results. Next he knows how to get everything out of his players and keep harmony among them. He makes them think and imbues the confidence in them that they can beat any club in the world.

The Fan

"The fan is a buoyant creature who frowns at disappointment and failure but the same frown speedily becomes a wide, bland smile when victory arrives. We all like a winner that is true."

Back To The Player

Now back to the player. There is a deep-rooted tendency in the human mind toward hero worship. The player who does something unusual is sure of an admiring audience. Nor does it altogether depend on what that achievement may be.

The player who can excel in the field can depend upon elaborate press notices, popular applause, and all the benefits of brilliant but fickle fame.

We have some players here who are now basking in the bright light of the public's worshiping. I could call the players' names, but I won't.

I say to these players tho, "Keep up the good work, every fan appreciates what you were doing and I hope to see you at the top of the ladder some day."

Good luck, best wishes.

Bob Fagan.

*　　*　　*

My Experience as a Manager (Part 3 of 6)
By Bob Fagen

I have written about owners, managers and fans. Now I'm going to give my opinion about umpires and individual players. I shall start with Tommy Shores.

When Tommy and I were playing on the same team I never thought that he would make the umpire that he is and was such little experience.

He is the best around local talent that I have ever seen in many a day. He excels many of the umps back east. "Keep up the good work Tommy, we are (happy) for you and I hope someday what you may be calling me out or rather safe in the big show.

Now folks my reason for saying this about Tommy is that he calls them just as he sees them and he doesn't favor anyone, you can prove that by me.

Individual Players

Now for the individual players. Spencer Butcher, that peppery catcher is my ideal for a catcher. He is already ready to try something. In other words he is in the game all of the time and his head is always up.

Next Riddle the third baseman. There isn't a whole lot to say about Riddle except that he is a coming star. There are lots of teams back East that would like to have him.

Adams now playing first base for the All-Stars has a way of his own playing that base but believe me he knows his stuff. Now I have a youngster at short, Hines. He has the making of a great boy if he is handled right. With a seasoned player or myself on his right I believe another Walter Moore can be made of him.

Whatever the past reverses have been I hope the fans will encourage these young ball-players and I am sure they will make a winning combination.

Next week I shall tell you about my pitching staff and the rest of my brother ballplayers.

Hope to see you again next Sunday.

*　　　*　　　*

My Experience as a Manager (Part 4 of 6)
By Bob Fagen

Now for the rest of my gang.

I'll start with Paul Wilson, the outfielder. He covers lots of ground and is fast on bases and some manager will get this boy and make a star out of him. What he lacks is hitting form. I have watched his hitting closely and I believe he should try changing his style until he gets the right one then stick to it. The saying of managers that one player looks better striking out then some players hitting four hundred somewhat applies to Paul.

Savage who is playing next to Wilson in left field is a coming player. A good hitter and a good fielder covers Savage entirely.

The Pitchers Next

Now for my pitchers. Evans, Munion and Jay Johnson compose a very good staff. First we will look over and tell about Evans.

He is an old timer and has the pitching brains. He also knows how to pitch. He is awful slow and that is why they call him slow time.

Next we have Munion another Rogan. He has a world of stuff, will listen and is willing and loves to pitch. There is no reason why he shouldn't turn in many winning games for the All-Stars.

Johnson is somewhat on the same order, always trying to outsmart the batter and make him go after something bad. With more experience he will be a star in any company and very much in the lime light.

While talking of pitchers I wish to say that pitching is sixty percent of the game and when a team gets bad pitching it looks bad as a whole.

Hitting counts too, but there are lots of players who don't hit like their brother teammates but are wonderful fielders. While that player can't hit he is going across second base knocking down balls that are labeled for hits. Don't you think he is just as viable a man to his team as some players who can only hit? Lots of ballgames have been won by sensational stops.

I believe young ballplayers get more encouragement from the fading stars and old-timers now than in the old days. The old-timers seem to take a more philosophical view of the situation then earlier school of players.

They now school the youngsters and teach them the fine points of their positions. I didn't find things that way when I was coming up. I had to teach myself and fight my way to the front.

*   *   *

My Experience as a Manager (Part 5 of 6)
By Bob Fagen

How I Made The All-Stars A Winning Club

I will first say that the club played in the Summer League and didn't win a game. Jasper came to me and asked if I could take the team over and make a winner out of it. I told him I did not know but that I would try. I played a game with them and right then I saw what the trouble was. Then I was made manager. The club wanted me. I haven't been manager long enough to get used to the idea. But I think I like it.

He told me not to worry. He was right. There's enough real trouble in the world without looking for imaginary bothers. It's a pretty strenuous job and it takes all your time. So long as a manager is blamed when a club loses. It is only justice, I suppose to give him credit when the club wins. There's always credit enough to go around in such cases. Both players and managers can get their share of what is coming to them if each gives full credit to the other.

As soon as we started to win people began to ask, how did we do it. I suppose that's a natural question but it's not an easy one to answer.

I believe the real explanation is the fact that the ball club developed a determination to win when a club really does this and mean it, they are a hard club to beat. That was what this club needed when I took it over. I suppose some of the boys are hitting a little better now but on the other hand the boys have learned more about the game and believe in me, and with all of us hustling, we will beat the best of them.

They say I possess all the sterling qualities of a real baseball leader. One thing I try to have a cool way of commanding respect from the players and at the same time getting the best work out of them.

I'll say come out and look at them now and see the difference in the club.

Bob Fagan

*   *   *

My Experience as a Manager (Part 6 of 6)
By Bob Fagen

I'll call this article "West vs. East."

How often have you heard Fans say, "Say if he is so good, why don't he go East"? I wish to say that I was born and raised in the East and have played all over these United States. There are just as good players here as there are back East. It is a fact that all of your stars come from the west and the south.

There are lots of reasons for this and the main one is that the boys in the west and the south have baseball twelve months a year, while the Easterners have but five good months.

The boys from the west and south are always in condition. You would be surprised if you knew how the good ball players who won't leave their home towns.

A good one and the best one is that managers don't want to pay sufficient salaries to beginners from the bushes. There are exceptions of course, ball player who would go anywhere to play ball just to say that he is a member of such and such a club.

Many Chances for Youth

If some of the promising young players would take a few minutes for some really deep thinking, they would realize that the chances they have been waiting for are here.

All of the veterans are showing signs of wear and tear and some one has got to take their places.

We have seen many boys come from the east out here who have caused the remark to come from fans, "Say how did he hold down a job back there?"

Professional baseball more than any other business or pursuit that I know is based on the law of the survival of the fittest.

Fortunately, great physical strength goes to hand in hand with a peace loving disposition. It is an interesting question to determine just how important physical strength is in a ballplayer. Most athletes are wiry and tough if they are not uncommonly strong. Theoretically strength is needed only in batting and even the part strength plays in slugging is somewhat problematical. Other things being equal, it is fair to assume that the heavier and stronger a batter may be, the harder he can hit the baseball."

Perhaps a line of advice would be in line here. To all baseball players stay at home at night.

Your second baseman,
BOB FAGEN.

Source: My Experience as a Manager, The California Eagle, Aug. 15–Sep. 26, 1924.

野球

Appendix F: Biography of Lon Goodwin
by Alfred Bland

Editor's note: The most complete biography of manager Lonnie Goodwin comes from the follow-ing article written by ballplayer Alfred Bland of the Philadelphia Royal Giants. He wrote the article as a graduate student in Manila, Philippines.

The Chicago Defender
April 14, 1934

We read from time to time of many baseball managers and their accomplishments but few or, perhaps, none of them can demand as much praise in presenting opportunities to ball players as Lon (Pop) Goodwin. He is the first and only Race manager on a tour of Hawaii and the Far East and as far as I know is the first to enter the emperor's palace at Tokyo, Japan.

"Pop" Goodwin was born in Austin, Tex., in 1879.[1] He began his baseball career as a pitcher in 1903 with the Austin Reds. After 1904 "Pop" went to the Waco Yellow Jackets where he met Rube Foster, who was just beginning baseball. With only two pitchers, Rube Foster and "Pop," the Waco team lost only four games and won 96 in 1905.[2]

After 1905 "Pop" went to Los Angeles, Calif., while Rube Foster went to Hot Springs, Ark. and later to the Cuban Philadelphia ex-Giants. "Pop" moved into a lovely house at 1424 E. Adams Blvd., Los Angeles, which he now owns. That same year he married Miss Lizzie Hugh Carrington, also of Austin, Tex.

In 1908 Mr. Goodwin became active in baseball again by organizing the Los Angeles White Sox and played around the sand lots until 1912. From 1912 to 1916 the team traveled up and down the Pacific Coast playing amateur teams. It is this team which Mr. Goodwin claims "never lost a game in four years." The players of that team were George Carr, who is now in Santurce, Cuba; Carlyle Perry, who has a news stand at Vernon and Central Ave.,

Los Angeles; Blue Washington, who is now acting in pictures in Hollywood, Calif.; Andy and Bill Kyle, Willie Carr, Tommy Shores, Frank Mooney, Sunny Brooks, Clarence King, Willie Simpson, Julius Baker and Roy Hammond. After 1916 the team disbanded and "Pop" retired.

In 1920 "Pop" reorganized the Los Angeles White Sox and Charlie Anderson and Will Johnson built a ballpark at Boyle Heights. The players of the reorganized White Sox were George Carr, "Bullet Joe" Rogan, Bob Fagen, Walter Moore, Lemuel Hawkins, McNair, Andy Kyle, Julius Baker, Rube Curry and Jaybird Wilkerson.

In 1920 the first Winter league was formed in Los Angeles. The White Sox players played a white major league aggregation and defeated them for the championship.

The White Sox ball park was moved from Boyle Heights to 35th and Compton Sts.

In the winter of 1925 Mr. Goodwin changed the name of his ball club to the Philadelphia Royal Giants. The club won the southern California championship in 1925 and 1926.

In 1927 "Pop" took his team to Japan, the first and only Race team to ever tour the Orient. The reception given them was indescribable. They were feted like kings by the Japanese people. All the upper dignitaries of the Japanese empire were on hand to greet the players. They were escorted to the palace of the emperor amidst great pomp and splendor. The members of the team were "Bizz" Mackey, Neil Pullen, Rap Dixon, Duncan,

Lon Goodwin (standing) and Alfred Bland during the Royal Giants' 1933-34 tour stop in Manila (Christie's).

Jesse Walker, Andrew Cooper, J. Green, Alex Evans, Bob Fagen, Tucker, Johnny Riddle and Joe Cade. This team played 46 games, winning 45 and losing one. Stopping in Hawaii on the way home the team played and won 12 games.

野球

Source: Royal Giants Complete Fourth Trip to Orient, Alfred M Bland, The Chicago Defender, Apr 14, 1934, pg. 16.

Notes

1. Alonzo Alfred Goodwin was born Alonzo Washington to parents Manchaca Washington and Louisa Freeman on March 15 1879. Lon assumed many names as a young man, including: Lonny Washington, Lonny Freeman, and Lonnie Graves (with the Waco Yellow Jackets). When he married Lizzie Hugh Carrington on Sept. 12, 1904, in El Paso, Texas, his name was Lonie Goodwin. Sources: US Census; Austin, Texas City Directories; Texas, Select County Marriage Index, 1837-1965, Ancestry.com.

2. Rube Foster left Texas in 1902; in 1905 he spent the season with the Philadelphia Giants. Bland or his source (most likely Lon Goodwin) is off by a few years here. Foster pitched for the Waco Yellow Jackets in 1898 and 1899. See Larry Lester, *Rube Foster In His Time: On the Field and in the Papers with Black Baseball's Greatest Visionary* (Jefferson NC: McFarland & Co., 2012), p. 6.

Appendix G: Biography of George Irie
by Kyoko Yoshida

Joji "George" Irie (入江讓治) was born Goichi Hajun Irie (入江兼市) on the island of Agenosho in Yamaguchi Prefecture on June 15, 1885, to parents Ryozo Irie (1856–1949) and Kiyo Wada (1868–1898). In 1905, he arrived in San Francisco at age 20 and went on to New York to study. He then moved to the University of Pennsylvania to major in law, but left before graduation. There, in 1908, he married a Caucasian woman named Catherine Reed and together they had a son George (1909-1997), who later in life would change the spelling of his last name to "Erie." Irie sought new opportunities at the 1916 San Francisco Expo and lived in Los Angeles for a year after the expo, until his wife passed away in 1917, leaving him their only son. Irie moved to Stockton of Northern California, where he served as a public translator for the local police and high court. In 1923, he moved back to Los Angeles to take up residence, and while working at a law firm and a bond agency called Bengi-sha, helping the Japanese immigrants to deal with legal matters in English, he held the secretary's position at the Japan-U.S. Film Exchange Company. The president of the company Yoshiaki Yasuda (who was assassinated by the yakuza in 1930) was in charge of every entertainment in Little Tokyo, including sumo, Japanese sword-fight theater, and gambling. Irie was known in Little Tokyo as an active agent of sports events, especially baseball, which was at the height of its popularity in the Japanese American community on the West Coast. It is said that Japanese baseball teams in California spent more than $100,000 per year during the period.*

In 1927, he took up the role of the traveling manager of the Philadelphia Royal Giants baseball team in their barnstorming tour to Japan. The tour was overwhelmingly successful, prompting the team to revisit the country in 1932.

So-Cal Japanese Who's Who published in 1928 describes Irie as "agile and enthusiastic, quick to weigh the interests, and daring enough to take any means to achieve his ends; his

George Irie (standing, far left) posses with Andy Cooper (front row, kneeling) and officials in Japan during the 1927 tour (PrestigeCollectibles.com).

In 1908, George Irie married Catherine Reed (above) and together they had a son, George (1909-1997). Later in life, George Jr. changed the spelling of his last name to "Erie" (Jay Erie).

inscrutable ability defies imagination for his swiftness and vehemence." He was tall for a Japanese man, "with an impressive mien and stature of such dignity."

In 1931, Irie managed Michio Ito, a pioneer of modern dance based in Los Angeles, during his European tour.

On February 16, 1932, Irie married Yukiye Kataoka in Los Angeles. Soon after, the couple moved to Uzumasa, Kyoto, where a new film studio had opened in 1927. Kyoto had become a new center of film production after the Great Kanto Earthquake of 1923 destroyed much of studios in the greater Tokyo area. Irie seemed to have been involved in film production in the thirties—there is one silent film "Ginrin no Hanakago" produced in 1934 in which Irie's name (as 入江譲二) is credited as screen writer.

Sources
「入江譲二」松本本光『加州人物大観　南加之巻』加州羅府昭和時報社, 1928. 471-2.

Notes from Jay Irie
羅府新報社編『羅府年鑑』羅府新報社, 1938.
* 「日本人の野球」加藤新一編『米国日系人百年史：在米日系人発展人士録』新日米新聞社, 1961. 245.

野球

Appendix H: Biography of William Ross
by Bill Staples, Jr.

The lack of published material about the career of pitcher William Ross is a prime example of the "East Coast" bias that has existed among Negro Leagues baseball historians for decades. If something occurred west of the Mississippi River or south of the Mason Dixon line, it just doesn't get the attention it deserves. Case in point: in *The Biographical Encyclopedia of The Negro Leagues Baseball Leagues*, James A. Riley sums up Ross' career in 47 words: "Pitching in the starting rotation for St. Louis Stars for four seasons, his best season was 1926 when he posted a 9-6 record. He closed out his career with the Homestead Grays, where he had a 3-2 work sheet against teams." (683)

Riley's summary reflects just a fraction of Ross' impressive and adventurous 25-year career that began in Texas in 1910 and ended with a tour of Japan, Korea, the Philippines, and Hawaii in 1934.

William Ross was born October 5, 1893, in Corrigan, Texas, 95 miles northwest of Houston and located next to what is now known as the Davey Crockett National Forest. He was raised by Callie Jackson, his widowed mother who was a well-respected midwife in the local community.

After an impressive outing for his high school in Diboll, Texas, young Ross was taught the finer points of pitching by Roy Locket, then considered one of the best black pitchers in the country. William began his professional career at age 17 with the Silsbee Black Cats where he posted an 11-4 record and 100 strikeouts. Also on the Silsbee club was catcher O'Neal Pullen, who would serve as Ross' batterymate numerous times throughout his career.

William caught the attention of the ball clubs in larger cities in Texas like Beaumont and Houston and Shreveport and Monroe in Louisiana. In 1911 he pitched in 42 games for the Beaumont Black Oilers, winning 36 and losing 6 while striking out 322 batters.

Between 1911 and 1916 he pitched for four different teams and even played on loan for series with the visiting Indianapolis ABC's in 1916. During this period a teammate asked him where he was from, and as he described his East Texas upbringing he was quickly given the nickname "Nacogdoches." This moniker stuck with him for the rest of his career.

In 1917 "Nacogdoches" Ross signed on with the Hot Springs Giants as a player-manager. He was only 24 years old. Racial tensions began to rise in Texas in the summer of '17, so it was the perfect time to escape the heat. Ross created the barnstorming Texas All-Stars and headed north where his ball club competed against well-known teams like the Chicago American Giants.

The following year he was hired to manage the Dallas Black Giants, however, the season was cut short due to the military draft for World War I. Ross answered the call to serve and in doing so also pitched for the Camp Travis Army baseball team.

After the war, he returned to the Texas Colored League and picked up with the Beaumont Oilers for the regular season, and the Dallas Black Marines for the post-season. Dallas was defeated by Biz Mackey and his San Antonio Black Aces in the championship, but Ross established relationships that would take him to the West Coast. A year later he joined the Alexander Giants of the California Winter League for the 1920-21 off-season.

He fell in love with the West Coast scene and decided to sign with Lon Goodwin's L.A. White Sox in 1921. With Rube Foster's National Negro League in full swing for its second season, Ross received an offer to join the Indianapolis ABC's for the 1922 season. Prior to joining Indianapolis, Ross compiled an impressive 318-87 pitching record (.783 winning percentage) between 1910 and 1921 and appeared to be destined for greatness on the national stage.

In his first season with the ABC's in 1922, he recorded a solid 26-10 record. However, in 1923 he unexpectedly began a ten-year trek as a journeyman, pitching for 12 different clubs and compiling a respectable 63-41 record.

With the close of the 1931 season, at age 38 Ross had a career 384-137 (.736) record. He not only amassed an impressive record, but

Pitcher William "Nacogdoches" Ross served as the captain of the Philadelphia Royal Giants as they toured Hawaii, Japan, Korea, China and the Philippines in 1932-33, and 1933-34. He went undefeated during these tours compiling a 39-0 record (Christies. com).

he also developed a reputation as a wise and respected team leader. In 1930 when a curious young rookie named Joshua Gibson joined the Homestead Grays, they gave him "the truthful and blond Master Ross for a 'roomie,'" according to the *Pittsburgh Courier*. "Ross is ready with an answer for any sort of question. His store of information is exhaustive, if not always accurate." *The Courier* added, "Master Ross defends himself in this fashion: 'If you ask a question, you don't know the answer. Therefore, if my reply is sometimes at fault, what difference can it make since you do not know that I am wrong?'"

In late 1932 Ross returned to the West Coast to join the Philadelphia Royal Giants and serve as the team's pitching ace and captain as they toured Hawaii, Japan, Korea, China, and the Philippines. He went undefeated during these tours compiling an impressive 39-0 record. Sadly, he returned from his final tour of Asia to learn that his mother had passed away while he was out of the country. He also discovered that he had missed her funeral back home in East Texas.

After the 1934 season, Ross officially retired as a player at the age of 41 with an impressive career pitching record of 416 wins, 134 losses (a .756 winning percentage) and just over 2,500 strikeouts. In retirement, he worked as a bartender at a jazz club in Los Angeles called Club Alabam. He married Edna Barrett, a singer/dancer at the club, and followed her to San Francisco when the new Club Alabam opened in the Bay Area. In 1940 he was employed as a porter at the St. Francis Hotel in San Francisco. Although no divorce records have been located, it appears that William and Edna separated sometime

Ross with the 1930 Homestead Grays (back row, 3rd from left) where he mentored rookie catcher Joshua Gibson. Ross pitched from 1910 to 1934. After a 25-year career he retired at the age of 41 with a record of 422 wins, 136 loses (a .756 winning percentage) and over 2,500 strikeouts (Negro Leagues Baseball Museum).

during the 1940s. Ross returned home to Diboll, Texas in 1950, where he took a job in the local creosote plant.

William "Nacogdoches" Ross died of a cerebral hemorrhage on December 22, 1964. Two days later he was buried in Corrigan, Texas, his birthplace. He was 71 years old.

*   *   *

Career Pitching Record of William "Nacogdoches" Ross, 1910-1934*

AGE	YEAR	TEAM	G	W	L	SO	PCT
17	1910	Silsbee Black Cats	15	11	4	100	0.733
18	1911	Beaumont Black Oilers	42	36	6	322	0.857
19	1912	Beaumont Black Oilers /					
		Houston Black Buffaloes	22	11	11	205	0.500
20	1913	Shreveport Smart Set	28	21	7	175	0.750
21	1914	Shreveport Smart Set	35	30	5	295	0.857
22	1915	Shreveport Smart Set	36	27	9	295	0.750
23	1916	Monroe Braves	38	33	5	209	0.868
23	1916	Indianapolis ABC's	6	3	3	0	0.500
24	1917	Hot Springs Giants	23	15	8	50	0.652
24	1917	Texas All-Stars	2	0	2	11	-
25	1918	Dallas Black Giants	5	5	0	30	1.000
25	1918	Camp Travis	36	34	2	4	0.944
26	1919	Beaumont Oilers	29	21	8	75	0.724
26	1919	Dallas Black Marines	2	1	1	8	0.500
27	1920	Alexander Giants	36	29	7	196	0.806
28	1921	Alexander Giants	28	23	5	155	0.821
28	1921	L.A. White Sox	1	1	0	6	1.000
29	1922	Bakersfield Club	6	5	1	50	0.833
29	1922	Indianapolis ABC's	36	26	10	4	0.722
30	1923	Washington Potomacs	4	1	3	8	0.250
31	1924	St. Louis Stars	17	7	10	53	0.412
31-32	'24-'25	St. Louis Giants (CWL)	12	7	5	67	0.583
32	1925	St. Louis Stars	10	3	7	49	0.300

AGE	YEAR	TEAM	G	W	L	SO	PCT
33	1926	St. Louis Stars	15	9	6	19	0.375
34	1927	Detroit Stars	6	3	3	14	0.500
35	1928	Grand Rapids (MI) Fox Giants	0	0	0	0	-
35	1928	Cleveland Tigers	7	2	5	13	0.286
36	1929	Buffalo Colored Cubs / Homestead Grays	6	5	1	8	0.833
37	1930	Homestead Grays	5	3	2	8	0.750
37-38	'30-'31	Nashville Elite/Royal Giants	6	6	0	29	1.000
38	1931	Philadelphia Royal Giants	3	3	0	0	1.000
39-40	'32-'33	Philadelphia Royal Giants	16	16	0	63	1.000
40	1933	Bakersfield Colored Cubs	2	2	0	0	1.000
40-41	'33-'34	Philadelphia Royal Giants	23	23	0	0	1.000
			G	W	L	SO	PCT
		CAREER TOTAL (25 seasons: 1910-1934)	558	422	136	2,521	0.756

Pitching performances between 1910 and 1921 are self-reported by Ross in a 1921 Dallas Express article. Records after 1922 were gathered through various newspaper sources and most likely are incomplete. Therefore, his career pitching stats are most likely higher.

Sources: Baseball-Reference.com; The Buzz Saw, Southern Pine and Lumber Company (Diboll, TX), California Eagle; California Winter League, by William McNeil; Chicago Defender; Dallas Express; Fresno Republican; Pittsburgh Courier; San Antonio Evening News; State of Texas Death Records; Washington Post; WWI Draft Cards.

野球

Appendix I: Jimmy Bonner, Japan's First African American Ballplayer

by Ralph M. Pearce

Eleven years before Jackie Robinson broke the major league color barrier, a star pitcher from Oakland, California, signed a contract to play for the newly formed Japanese Professional Baseball League. At the time, this ace dominated the Berkeley International League, an integrated circuit that historians have called one of the boldest and most overlooked experiments in baseball history. Although this player's time in Tokyo was brief, his presence would help shape the future of baseball in Japan and pave the way for other players of African ancestry; players like John Britton, Jimmy Newberry, Larry Raines, Larry Doby, Don Newcombe, Warren Cromartie, Greg "Boomer" Wells, Tuffy Rhodes and Wladimir Balentien (who now holds the record in Japan for the most home runs in a single season with sixty). For players of color in Japan, someone had to be the first, and in 1936 that person was Jimmy Bonner.

James Everett Bonner was born on September 18, 1906 in Mansfield, the seat of De Soto Parish, Louisiana. The son of Peter Bonner,[1] he was the fourth of five children born to Martha Ann (Lewis) Bonner Goldsmith. By the time Jimmy was four, his parents had divorced and his mother had remarried. His step-father, Rory Goldsmith, worked at a saw mill in the small, predominantly African American lumber town. Rory died when Jimmy was a child, and by 1920 the thirteen-year-old was working as a delivery boy for a drug store.

Baseball's "golden era" was under way in the 1920s, with teams and leagues flourishing across the country. Jimmy played ball in junior high, and continued to play after leaving school. Heading into the 1930s Depression era, Bonner was twenty-three years old and employed as a tailor, while his mother took in laundry to make ends meet. In the spring of 1932, he was a utility player for the nearby Shreveport Black Sports baseball team. Standing 5 feet, 10 inches, Jimmy threw right and batted left. The Black Sports had played in the Texas Colored League, the Texas-Oklahoma-Louisiana League, and more recently the

Texas-Louisiana League (Negro leagues). At the time, the Black Sports had just experienced the failed formation of a Tri-State league, and then in May their part-time ballpark (Biedenharn Park) burned to the ground.

Later that year, Bonner decided to move to West Oakland. This appears to be about the time that he married Lillian Victor of Waggaman (located roughly fifteen miles southwest of New Orleans). During the Depression, California was seen by many as a land of opportunity. Oakland was the last stop west along the first transcontinental railroad. By 1900, African Americans working as Pullman porters helped establish an ethnically diverse, middle class community in West Oakland.

Bonner played for the San Francisco Giants (also referred to as the San Francisco Colored Giants) in 1934. This was an independent, semi-professional African American baseball team that mostly played against Caucasian teams within the San Francisco Bay Area.

Jimmy Bonner in the October 6, 1936 issue of the *Kokumin Shimbun* (Ralph Pearce).

Though Bonner had previously appeared as a position player, he had been working on his pitching. On Sunday July 8, "Sunny" Jim Bonner pitched a no-hitter for the Giants in a 5-2 win over the Polk Athletic Club. His pitching was reported as stellar as he struck out sixteen men. The following Sunday, he pitched in relief against the Cosgrove All Stars. Though the game ended in an 11-11 tie, Bonner was commended for his pitching and for a triple in the seventh inning that brought in two runs. "Sunny" Jim was developing into a double-threat. An excerpt from *The San Francisco Spokesman* on August 9, 1934, called Sunny Jim a promising young ballplayer and said that he, "…possesses a million dollar arm, and with proper schooling, should become a headline pitcher with his speed ball."[2]

In 1935, Bonner joined the Oakland Black Sox. In one early-season game against Emeryville, he started in right field. When the pitcher got in trouble in the fifth inning, Jimmy was called in to replace him. Bonner allowed only two bases on balls, and struck out six, though the Sox were not able to recover and wound up losing 9-6. In 1936, Bonner pitched for the Berkeley Grays of the Berkeley International League (BIL). The BIL (Berkeley Colored League prior to 1935) was an ethnic mix of Bay Area teams that included the Athens Elks, the Berkeley Grays, the Golden Gate Buffets, the Tijuana Grill, and the Wa Sung Chinese. Their home field was San Pablo Park, where games would reportedly draw crowds of 2,000.

On April 19, 1936, Bonner whiffed seventeen batters in a contest against the Berkeley Cardinals (a Caucasian team).[3] This broke the previous BIL record of fourteen strikeouts. Then on May 18, Jimmy shut out the strong Athens Elks. He allowed only two singles to win 9-0. Bonner was referred to as "Satchel" Jim by both the *Oakland Tribune* and the *Berkeley Gazette*. He also led the team at the plate, hitting two for four appearances, and driving in a run. The win put the Grays in second place, a half game behind the Elks. This was significant because previous seasons found the Elks at or near the top of the standings, and the Grays in the cellar.

Towards the end of June, the Grays had battled their way into first place with a record of 6-2 behind the pitching of Bonner. Unforeseen scheduling difficulties caused a shortened second half and playoff season, which resulted in the Grays and Elks sharing the 1936 championship.[4] Based on his outstanding performance for the season, Bonner was selected to pitch for the Berkeley International League all-star team in the *Oakland Tribune*-sponsored California State Semi-pro Championship Tourney.[5] On September 5 and 6, Bonner led the Civilian Conservation Corp's San Pablo Dam team to the CCC championship. He accomplished this feat pitching three complete games in two days to take the series 3-1.

Bonner's success had caught the attention of Harry H. Kono, a successful Japanese American businessman based in Alameda.[6] On September 8, Kono, working as an agent for the Dai Tokyo Baseball Club, signed Jimmy to play in a newly formed Japanese baseball league.[7] The request to sign Bonner came from Kono's friend Hitoshi Tanaka, owner of the *Kokumin Shimbun*, the newspaper that sponsored the Dai Tokyo team.[8]

The Japanese Professional Baseball League had been established seven months earlier on February 5. The league was comprised of seven teams; the Giants (Kyojin), the Tigers, Nagoya, the Senators, Hankyu, Dai Tokyo, and the Nagoya Golden Dolphins. The Giants, the Senators, and Dai Tokyo were all based in Tokyo, the Tigers and Hankyu were both based in Osaka and Nagoya and the Nagoya Golden Dolphins were both based in Nagoya. The teams were owned by either newspaper or railway companies. The newspaper companies, like the *Yomiuri Shimbun* who sponsored the Giants, saw professional baseball as a means of advertising the company and increasing circulation. Railway companies benefitted from increased ridership to and from the ball parks, and had already been involved in the construction of stadiums such as the legendary Koshien Stadium in 1924.

Bonner's new team, the Dai Tokyo Baseball Club, had also been formed in February 1936. It was the sixth of the seven clubs to join the new league, and it suffered from a lack of talent. The Nagoya club experienced the same problem. Though it was the third team to form, Nagoya had trouble finding talent because it had begun recruiting later than other teams. One solution Nagoya found was to recruit talented semi-professionals from the west coast of the United States.[9] By the second half of the 1936 season, Dai Tokyo (0-1-13) was seriously looking for an infusion of foreign talent as well. They were hoping that Bonner would lift them from the depths of the cellar.

On September 17, 1936, a passport was issued, and on September 18, his thirtieth birthday, Bonner boarded the *S.S. President Pierce* and departed for Japan. His reputation preceded him, and newspapers recounted his exploits on the mound and at the plate, describing his "viciously fast and powerful submarine pitch."[10] His contract was for 400 yen a month, commencing on September 10. By comparison, the average salary of a Tokyo Giants player in 1935 was only 140 yen a month. The proven American catcher "Bucky" Harris McGalliard on Nagoya was receiving twice that at 300 yen a month. Dai Tokyo was willing to pay handsomely, but their needs and their expectations were great.

Bonner arrived in Japan on October 5. Soon after his arrival, he and an interpreter sat down with the team's general manager Ryuji Suzuki and player/manager Katsuzo Ito. Jimmy was very charming as he described himself as a pitcher who could also play infield. He said that his fastball was so fast that you couldn't see it. When asked how many strikeouts he made per game he replied, "I always make a lot of strikeouts, and my nickname is 'Bullet' Bonner." Jimmy concluded, "I'd like to win everything, and set a new strikeout record."[11] The meeting went well for Bonner, who even negotiated steak for breakfast every morning.

Less than two weeks after arriving in Japan, Bonner appeared in his first game, an exhibition game against Nagoya. He played first base in the 13-3 loss, hitting two in five at bats. Bonner played first base again in another exhibition against Nagoya three days later. In the first inning with a man on first, he hit a triple to left-center driving in the game's first run. He then tried to steal home, but failed which ended the inning. Bonner would go on to score twice during the course of their 5-4 win.

The third of six tournaments that made up the fall season began on October 23. Named the Osaka Tournament, it took place at Takarazuka Stadium in Takarazuka City near Osaka. Dai Tokyo's first game was against the strong Tigers. Expectations were high, and the team's catcher Yoshitake Tsutsui was warned that he should put extra padding in his glove to protect his hand from Bonner's powerful pitches. Before the game, the Tiger's Hawaiian pitcher and future Hall of Famer Henry 'Bozo' Wakabayashi had an opportunity to speak with the American. He asked him, "So, you're going to play the Tigers now, and the Tigers are a little bit better than Hankyu. What do you think?" Jimmy answered, "Oh, so the Tigers are a little bit better than Hankyu. I can shut out the Tigers." Wakabayashi replied, "Oh, that's interesting. Please do it! I'll see you at the plate."[12]

In the bottom of the first inning with a 1-0 lead, Bonner experienced control issues. He walked two batters and gave up a hit to fill the bases. With one out, Tiger's infielder Jungo Igaue stepped up to the plate and hit his first and only homerun for 1936, resulting in a grand slam for a 5-1 lead. Dai Tokyo scored two runs in the fifth (Jimmy knocked in one of them) and three runs in the sixth to take a 9-6 lead. In the seventh, Bonner started to walk batters again, and was immediately replaced by Hisashi Kondo. The Tigers were able to tie it up in the eighth. With the score still tied at the end of nine innings, the game was called because of nightfall. A new game was scheduled for the next day. Tying the Tigers was an achievement for Dai Tokyo, but Bonner's showing was a disappointment. When questioned, Jimmy blamed his performance on the chilly weather.

In the rematch against the Tigers the following day, Bonner faced another future Hall of Famer in Fumio Fujimura. The weather was warmer, so there was some hope that Jimmy's performance might improve. After Bonner walked the first batter, the crowd called for a new pitcher. After two more balls to the second batter, Manager Ito moved Jimmy to second base and put their best pitcher, Chujiro Endo, on the mound. The Tigers won the game 7-4, with Jimmy getting three hits, but making two critical errors at second base. That game concluded Dai Tokyo's appearances in the Osaka Tournament. A week later on October 31, Dai Tokyo played another exhibition game against Nagoya. Dai Tokyo lost 3-1, though Bonner performed well at second base with two put-outs and three assists.

The next tournament was the Tokyo League Tournament at the Tokyo Senator's Kami-igusa Stadium. Dai Tokyo played the Senators on November 3. Bonner once again took to the mound. He survived the first inning, but then gave up three walks in the second only to have the Senator's pitcher Akira Noguchi hit a base-clearing triple. Jimmy was pulled and moved to shortstop. He doubled in the sixth inning and eventually scored. In the ninth, Bonner singled, then advanced and scored off of two pitching errors. It was not enough to overcome the Senator's lead though, and Dai Tokyo lost 13-9.

The following day, Dai Tokyo took on the mighty Giants. The fans were excited to see the Caucasian pitcher Starffin against the African American Bonner. As Jimmy stepped up to the plate, Starffin tilted his head forward in a challenging manner. Bonner responded by smiling at him and shaking his hips. Jimmy singled in the fourth inning, and eventually scored by stealing home. By the ninth inning, Dai Tokyo had a 3-0 lead and was only two outs from victory. The Giants had a runner on first, and then hit a grounder to third base setting up a double play for Dai Tokyo's win. Bonner was playing second and failed to cover the base, so the runners wound up safe on both first and second. The runners went on to score, and then two additional runs gave the Giants the win.

On November 6, Dai Tokyo played the Tigers once again. Jimmy was on the bench that day, but a group of school kids in the stands had a banner that read "Bonna-chan!" (an endearing term for Bonner). The kids wanted Bonner to play, so in the seventh inning Ito put him in to pinch-hit. He singled to center, and then played shortstop for the rest of the game. Dai Tokyo lost the game 5-0.

Three days later Dai Tokyo faced the Nagoya Golden Dolphins. Bonner was brought in to pinch-hit in the eighth inning. He struck out and played second base for the remainder of the game. On November 10, the end of Bonner's monthly pay period, he played his final game in Japan. He played first base against Hankyu, securing three hits in four at bats. He appeared briefly as a pitcher as well. In the ninth inning, the first two Dai Tokyo batters flied out to center. Bonner then stepped up to the plate and tripled to left. His joy was fleeting, as he overran the third base and was tagged out. It was an inauspicious ending to a disappointing and brief career in Japan.

Regarding his departure from the team, the *Yomiuri Shimbun* quoted Dai Tokyo as saying simply, "... he wasn't feeling well, so we sent him home."[13] Jimmy boarded the *Taiyo Maru* on November 16 and returned home to the United States.

Japanese records show Bonner playing seven official games. He pitched in four of those games and finished with a win-loss record of 0-1 and an era of 9.90 in 9 and 2/3 innings pitched.[14] Against fifty-two batters, he walked fourteen (26.9 percent), and only struck out two. At the plate, he finished with eleven hits in twenty-four at bats for a .458 batting average. The Japanese assessment of Bonner was that he was not a good pitcher, not very good as a utility player on defense, but good at the plate. What we know from his games prior to and after Japan, is that he could be an effective and successful pitcher.

Historians are left wondering what may have accounted for Bonner's lack of success in Japan. One possible explanation is the quality of the Japanese batters. Baseball had been popular in Japan since the 1880s, and players trained hard in the basics like patience at the plate. In 1936, the average height of a Japanese male was 5 feet, 4 inches. This would likely result in a smaller strike zone than Bonner was used to.

Another factor could have been the ball itself. The Japanese baseball is slightly smaller than an American ball. Japanese American player Jiggs Yamada, who toured Japan in 1925, complained that the leather of the Japanese ball was slick. For a developing pitcher still working on control, these factors might have made a difference in his performance.

After returning home to his wife Lillian in Oakland in December 1936, Bonner began his career as a Pullman porter. He continued to play ball as his schedule allowed. He pitched well for the Berkeley Grays and California Yellow Jackets in 1937, and the California Colored Giants in 1938 through at least 1940. Bonner enlisted in the U.S. Army in 1943, and then later returned to the Pullman Company where he was employed as a porter until his death on May 10, 1963. He was fifty-two years old. His obituary says that he was active in baseball as a pitcher during the years 1935 and 1936 in Northern California and Japan, and that he was known as "Count Bonner" by his many friends and admirers.

Acknowledgements

I would like to thank Jeff Kusumoto, Bill Staples Jr., Yoichi Nagata, and Jeff Alcorn for their research assistance, Kota Morikawa, Dexter Thomas Jr., and Jeff Kusumoto for their translation work, and Lisa Bonner-Brown for her encouragement and support.

*   *   *

Sources:

Aielo, Thomas, *The Kings of Casino Park: Black Baseball in the Lost Season of 1932* (University of Alabama Press, 2011), 51.

Guttmann, Allen and Lee Thompson, *Japanese Sports: A History* (University of Hawai'i Press, 2001), 137.

Japan Pro Baseball Encyclopedia (Baseball Magazine, 1985), 254-262.

Johnson, Daniel E., *Japanese Baseball: A Statistical Handbook* (McFarland & Co., 1999) 9-12.

Morioka, Hiroshi, *Biographical Dictionary of Japan Professional Baseball Players 1936 – 2003* (Nichigai Associates, 2003), 516.

Pearce, Ralph M., *From Asahi to Zebras: Japanese American Baseball in San Jose, California,* (Japanese American Museum of San Jose, 2005), 22.

Tramble, Thomas and Wilma Tramble, *The Pullman Porters and West Oakland* (Arcadia Publishing, 2007), 7, 33.

Yamato, Kyushi, *Pro Yakyu Sangokushi: Ogon-hen* (Baseball Magazine, 1957), 149-160.

"American Negro Here to Join Dai Tokyo," *The Japan Times and Mail,* October 7, 1936.

"Athen Elks Blanked," *Oakland Tribune,* May 19, 1936, 29.

"Black Sports Play Here Sunday, Monday," *The Times (Shreveport),* April 17, 1932, 18.

"The First Black Player to Play in Japan: Bonner's Contract in American Auction," *Sports Hochi*, January 28, 2013, 19.

"Here's How Players Will Bat Tonight," *Oakland Tribune*, September 2, 1936, 10.

"International League Leaders Face Trouble," *Berkeley Daily Gazette,* May 20, 1936.

"Lead Shifts Often," O*Oakland Tribune,* May 1, 1935, 13.

Oakland Tribune, April 20, 1937, 27.

Oakland Tribune, June 22, 1937, 24.

Oakland Tribune, November 23, 1938, 13.

Oakland Tribune, January 24, 1939, 14.

Oakland Tribune, October 17, 1939, 35.

Oakland Tribune, May 14, 1940, 37.

Oakland Tribune, May 21, 1940, 20.

Oakland Tribune, May 13, 1963, 28.

"Remarkable Black Pitcher Arrived," *Kokumin Shimbun,* October 6, 1936.

Yomiuri Shimbun, November 4, 1936.

Yomiuri Shimbun, November 5, 1936.

Yomiuri Shimbun, November 7, 1936.

Yomiuri Shimbun, November 10, 1936.

Yomiuri Shimbun, November 11, 1936.

Miyake, Daisuke, "Recollection of Star Players," *Baseball Magazine,* June 1949, 22-25.

Ancestry, www.ancestry.com

Ashwill, Gary. "Jimmy Bonner," Agate Type, http://agatetype.typepad.com/agate_type/2014/10/jimmy-bonner.html

Auther, Ronald. "Negro League Baseball: Judge Bussey, Sunny Jim Bonner and Joe Dimaggio," The Shadow Ball Express, https://shadowballexpress.wordpress.com/2015/03/02/negro-league-baseball-judge-john-bussey-sunny-jim-bonner-and-joe-dimaggio/

Thomas, Dexter, Jr., "Japan's First Black Baseball Player," Those People, https://medium.com/thsppl/japans-first-black-baseball-player-7c3e203e1f7

Whirty, Ryan, "World Series: During the Great Depression, a Wild Experiment in Baseball History Defied Segregation," SFWeekly, https://archives.sfweekly.com/sanfrancisco/berkeley-international-league-baseball-byron-speed-reilly/Content?oid=3188878

Notes

1. From Certificate of Death, State of California Department of Public Health.

2. Auther, Ronald. "Negro League Baseball: Judge Bussey, Sunny Jim Bonner and Joe Dimaggio," The Shadow Ball Express.

3. Ashwill, Gary. "Jimmy Bonner," Agate Type.

4. Whirty, Ryan, "World Series: During the Great Depression, a Wild Experiment in Baseball History Defied Segregation," SFWeekly.

5. Ashwill.

6. Kono financed the Japan tour of a Caucasian team in 1931, and would finance a Japanese American all-star tour of Japan in 1937.

7. From original contract between Dai Tokyo Baseball Club and James E. Bonner.

8. "The First Black Player to Play in Japan: Bonner's Contract in American Auction," *Sports Hochi*, January 28, 2013, 19.

9. Through Japanese American player Jimmy Horio (Tokyo Giants, Hankyu), Nagoya successfully contracted with four American players from semi-professional teams in Los Angeles.

10. Thomas, Dexter, Jr., "Japan's First Black Baseball Player," Those People.

11. Yamato, Kyushi, *Pro Yakyu Sangokushi: Ogon-hen* (Baseball Magazine, 1957), 149-160.

12. Ibid.

13. "The First Black Player to Play in Japan: Bonner's Contract in American Auction."

14. Morioka, Hiroshi, *Biographical Dictionary of Japan Professional Baseball Players 1936 – 2003* (Nichigai Associates, 2003), 516.

野球

Appendix J: Biz Mackey: Catcher, Manager, Mentor Extraordinaire

by Bob Luke

Abstract

Considered the best defensive catcher in the Negro leagues, who nailed base stealers without standing up, James Raleigh "Biz" Mackey switch-hit for a career average over .300, displayed an uncommon agility for a big man, played every position, and taught the game to two generations of players. Monte Irvin called him "the dean of teachers." His most famous protégés included fellow Hall of Famers Irvin, Roy Campanella, and Larry Doby. He played on the first Negro League team to visit Japan and Hawaii in the late 1920s. The Hall of Fame opened its doors to him in 2006. This article reviews his career and offers the reader a comparison between Mackey and the Negro Leagues' other superb catcher, Josh Gibson.

"THE TEAM LOOKS VERY GOOD. Games this week should determine if we win the pennant. Mackey is a story all by himself. It is really remarkable the ball he is playing, and the response he is getting from the team. He admits to being 47." So wrote Effa Manley, business manager of the Newark Eagles, to veteran sportswriter Art Carter of the *Baltimore Afro-American* on August 22, 1945.[1] In truth, Biz Mackey, the Eagles' player-manager, was a year older than he admitted. He was also the team's heaviest player, wearing a size 50 uniform shirt.[2] Despite his age and size, Effa Manley counted on Mackey in the clutch, saying, "When it was late in the game and the pitcher [had] stopped all our good hitters, and just one hit was needed, I'd say, 'Mackey, go in there and hit that ball.' I've seen him go in there and get a hit."[3] Mackey's reliability at age 48 was just one example of his durability. He managed as well as he played, piloting the Washington and Baltimore Elite Giants and the Newark Eagles. He developed many young players into stars, most notably Roy Campanella. Mackey excelled as a player, manager, and mentor in the Negro Leagues throughout his 24-year career from 1920 to 1947, which included four years away from the league.

Though he came up as a shortstop, Mackey was primarily a catcher, with a rocket for an arm. A switch-hitter, he hit well over .300 throughout his career, registering .335 against Negro League opponents and .326 against major league pitching in exhibition games.[4] For all his power, Mackey could also lay down a bunt when he had to. Right-handed pitcher Franklin "Doc" Sykes played against Mackey in the 1920s and remembered him laying down a perfect bunt to bring home the winning run, when everyone thought he would swing away. "He had a whole lot of baseball sense," Sykes declared.[5] Mackey enjoyed his work. "He was funny," said Negro League outfielder Crush Holloway, one of Mackey's best friends since their days with the San Antonio Black Aces. "He was jolly; especially with those fast men who said they were going to steal on him. When he'd throw them out, he'd get such a big kick out of it, he'd fall down laughing."[6] Mackey distracted batters with a stream of jabber and earned his nickname "Biz" for giving batters "the business." He enjoyed himself off the field too, and often partied into the wee hours, but without sacrificing his performance on the field.

Although the subject of numerous articles and headlines in the African American press during his career, Mackey lived in obscurity after his retirement from baseball in 1949 until his death in 1965, save for a 1952 *Pittsburgh Courier* poll that ranked him as the Negro Leagues' second-best catcher behind Josh Gibson. Long overdue recognition of his contributions to professional baseball came in July 2006, when he was inducted into the National Baseball Hall of Fame and joined the other legends in Cooperstown. Yet, for all his accomplishments, little has been written about Mackey.

James Raleigh Mackey was born July 27, 1897, to Ernest and Beulah Mackey in rural Caldwell County, Texas, northeast of San Antonio. The family sharecropped a small cotton farm. Raleigh had four older siblings: two brothers, Ernest and Ray, and two sisters, Eula and Clero. Sometime between 1900 and 1910, Beulah Mackey remarried to a man named Montgomery Meriwether and moved the family 90 miles south to his farm in Guadalupe, Texas. Even as a young boy, Raleigh worked in the cotton fields, hoeing the rows in spring, pulling weeds during the hot Texas summer, and filling burlap bags with the white fibers at harvest time. When their work was done, Raleigh and his brothers met up with other local boys and played ball until it was too dark to see.[7] The three brothers played semi-pro ball together in 1915 with a Prairie League team in the San Antonio area. Biz next played two years with the Luling Oilers, then in 1918 with the Dallas Black Giants, and in 1919 with the Waco Black Navigators.[8] Mackey's first taste of professional ball came with the San

Antonio Black Aces in the Texas Colored League, where the 21-year-old started at catcher and also pitched occasionally for two seasons, 1919–1920. Jesse Hubbard, his teammate on the Black Aces in 1919, remembered that Mackey "had that underhand curve ball and an over-hand drop ball, and he could throw hard."[9] Hubbard would know. He saw Mackey pitch a shutout on the day after Labor Day against the Austin Black Senators. Weeks later, Hubbard also saw Mackey pitch in relief in the last game of the 1919 Texas Colored League World Series to save the game and the championship for the Aces over the Dallas Black Marines.[10]

When the Aces played the Senators in Austin, a teenager sought out Mackey and pleaded with him, "Let me carry your bat. Let me carry your glove. Anything." The boy wanted to watch the games, but all the free seats and tree limbs outside the park were usually spoken for when he arrived from his home across town. Mackey always found something for the youngster to do.[11] The teenager was Willie Wells, who later joined Mackey as a teammate and was inducted into the National Baseball Hall of Fame in 1997, nine years before his childhood hero.

By 1920, Mackey's talents attracted the attention of Indianapolis ABCs manager C.I. Taylor, who signed him and half a dozen other Black Aces, including Henry Blackman. The ABCs were charter members of Rube Foster's newly formed Negro National League (NNL).[12] Mackey flourished as both catcher and infielder under Taylor, whose ability to mold players' skills and character was considered second only to Foster. Biz no doubt also picked up pointers from teammates and future Hall of Famers Oscar Charleston and Ben Taylor, C.I.'s brother.

Mackey soon impressed the local sportswriters. Shortly after he joined the ABCs, the *Muncie (IN) Star* praised Mackey's defense: "He does a clever a job of backstopping as is ever seen, and his throwing is nothing less than marvelous. Base runners have no business monkeying with his arm. To make the would-be base stealers look worse, he waits until they are halfway to their objective and then his whip catches them several feet away. Four [Kansas City Monarchs] came to grief in this manner, and they were caught so far off that they didn't even slide."[13] Mackey's arm and agility earned him an occasional start at shortstop, where he performed credibly. But when he had a rare bad day at short, his miscues came in bunches, such as the three errors he committed in a July 24, 1922, game against the same Kansas City Monarchs, whose base stealers he had previously mowed down with such ease.[14]

During the winter of 1920–1921, Mackey made his first appearance in the California Winter League (CWL), the nation's first integrated professional league, based in Los Angeles, where Mackey would eventually establish his permanent residence. He played eighteen seasons in the CWL, more than any other Negro Leaguer, amassing a .366 batting average through 272 games.[15]

Mackey's play drew the interest of Ed Bolden, owner of the Eastern Colored League (ECL) Hilldale Giants, based in Darby, Pennsylvania, just west of Philadelphia. In the spring of 1923, Bolden "raided" Mackey from Indianapolis, angering Rube Foster, who had given a measure of structure to black baseball by establishing the NNL in 1920 partly to prevent such incursions. Nevertheless, with the move, Mackey began a thirteen-year stay in the Philadelphia area.

With Hilldale in 1923, Mackey again alternated between short and catcher, backing up two aging future Hall of Famers: the legendary shortstop John Henry "Pop" Lloyd and catcher Louis Santop, whom one reporter called "a Philadelphia tradition like scrapple and political corruption."[16] Mackey also occasionally played second and first because Bolden wanted his bat in the lineup since Mackey led ECL hitters and "play[ed] the game with all the enthusiasm of a schoolboy."[17] Perhaps his enthusiasm prompted *Pittsburgh Courier* sportswriter and Negro League executive W. Rollo Wilson to give him the nickname "Baby Doll."[18]

After Bolden released Lloyd in 1924 for causing dissention on the team, Mackey shared the shortstop role with Jake Stephens. This was an unusual position for a player of Mackey's size: six feet, three inches tall and weighing over 200 pounds. Most shortstops were of slighter build because of the agility the position required, yet Mackey performed well, frequently drawing rave reviews even though he was still prone to an occasional error-filled game. Stephens, himself a pretty fair shortstop, said, "Mackey didn't have the range I had, but he was a better shortstop than I was. He never threw the ball harder than he had to. A hard hit ball came to Mackey and he'd take and bounce it down on the ground and throw the man out."[19]

Stephens also noted that Mackey liked his liquor and occasionally played drunk, "with his eyes rolling around in his head. But," Stephens added, "it didn't affect his fielding or his hitting." Pitcher Chet Brewer concurred, saying "[Mackey would] party all night and go out to the ball park [at] ten o'clock in the morning, take a shower, come out and catch a doubleheader." Mackey's only other known weakness while with Hilldale was his tendency to dwell over an umpire's bad call to the point where it affected the team. In those instances, Hilldale third baseman and future Hall of Famer Judy Johnson called time and talked to Mackey about girls or their plans for after the game until Biz collected himself.[20]

An example of Mackey's good days at short occurred early in the 1924 season on April 20 against a semi-pro team, the Farmer's Club of Brooklyn, New York. Mackey, a reporter wrote, "drew rounds of applause from the stands when he flung himself at full-length on the ground and took Allen's bad throw, hooking the bag in time to force Shannon at second."[21] But then six weeks later, Mackey came up the goat when he booted four balls on June 7 against the New York Lincoln Giants. A local scribe reported, "Biz Mackey was the chief offender on the Hilldale squad. The big shortstop kicked in with a quartet of glaring miscues that aided materially in the New York team's run making."[22] The newsworthiness of Mackey's errors was enhanced by the fact that he was trying to fill the shoes of veteran shortstop Pop Lloyd, who had led the Giants to the 1923 Eastern Colored League pennant.[23] Shortly before the 1924 season began, one reporter predicted, "Biz's work will be watched with interest by the fans."[24]

Mackey filled Lloyd's shoes well enough to lead the Giants to the ECL pennant and a World Series date with the NNL Monarchs. Both teams had won their league's pennant the year before, but hard feelings between league presidents Foster and Bolden prevented a World Series in 1923. By the fall of 1924, Foster said he would be willing "for the sake of peace" to allow those players who jumped to the ECL to remain with their current teams if the Eastern owners would sign an agreement promising to refrain from future raids on Negro National League teams.[25] It is not known whether the Eastern owners signed such an agreement, but Hilldale and the Monarchs played a nine-game championship series with games in Chicago, Baltimore, Philadelphia, and Kansas City.

After seven games, the series was tied: each team had claimed three wins, and one game had ended in a tie. In the eighth game, Hilldale was up 2–0 going into the ninth inning, when Santop dropped a pop-up foul from Monarchs catcher Frank Duncan.

Seizing the opportunity, Duncan stepped back into the box to hit what baseball historian John Holway called "a scorcher but a sure out to Biz at [third]." According to Holway, the ball zoomed through Mackey's legs, allowing two runs to score, but historian Larry Lester offers a different scenario, saying that "Duncan rapped a bloop single past ... Mackey at third."[26] The box score shows the only error charged to Santop. In any case, two runs scored, and Kansas City won the game 3–2, then went on to win the next game to take the series 5 to 3.[27] Hilldale manager Frank Warfield delivered a tongue lashing to Santop that made the big catcher cry.[28] Following the series, Mackey left for Cuba to play for the Almendares during the 1924–25 winter season, his only appearance in Latin America.[29]

Santop's error and his age, 35, convinced Bolden to put Mackey behind the plate and use Santop as his backup and pinch hitter for the 1925 season. The local press welcomed the move, and one sportswriter announced, "receiving, by the grace of manager Bolden, will be Biz Mackey, an all-round player but a catcher by nature and a darned good one at that."[30] Mackey responded with a "sterling performance behind the plate." The newly anointed catcher led the Giants to another ECL title and a World Series rematch against the

Monarchs. This time Hilldale won the series, thanks in part to Mackey's work behind the plate and his .360 batting average, second only to teammate Otto Briggs at .429. Mackey scored the last run of the series in the seventh inning of the last game, "banging a terrific blow over the right field fence."[31]

In 1926, Mackey continued playing brilliantly behind the plate as Hilldale's regular catcher. He finished the season with a .333 batting average, good for second place on the team behind George Carr's .355. The Giants did not repeat as league champions and finished in third place.

Opponents and teammates praised Mackey's throwing ability. Bill Holland, pitcher for the New York Lincoln Giants in the late 1920s, said, "Mackey had a great arm. Didn't have to stride and throw. He'd just raise up and that ball would go down to second."[32] Jake Stephens recalled Mackey throwing out the International League's (a white minor league) leading base stealer, Snooks Dowd of Newark, seven times in a three-game series. "He shot you out," Stephens declared. "Listen. Please believe me; nobody could catch as much baseball as Mackey. Mickey Cochrane couldn't carry his glove."[33] Also a Hall of Famer, Cochrane caught for Connie Mack's Philadelphia Athletics (1925–1933) and the Detroit Tigers (1934–1937). Like Mackey, Cochrane possessed great ability both behind the plate and at bat. Even though both catchers played for Philadelphia teams, no record exists of them facing each other.[34] However, Roy Campanella saw both in their prime and said, "For real catching skills, I didn't think Cochrane was the master of defense that Mackey was."[35]

During his stay with Hilldale, Mackey liked to show off his arm and sometimes teamed with second baseman Frank Warfield to put on a show during infield practice between innings. Mackey would make one of his patented throws to second, and Warfield would shout, "Ow! Mackey, you're gonna kill somebody."[36]

Mackey's name does not appear in a 1927 box score until July 24 because he and eleven other members of the California Winter League's Philadelphia Royal Giants jumped their Negro League teams to barnstorm in Japan. They were the first black team to play in Asia.[37] Mackey's move was not unexpected. In January, false rumors had surfaced that Bolden was planning to trade Mackey. By early March, newspapers correctly reported that Mackey was "unofficially, considering a trip to Japan with a touring outfit."[38] Upon hearing the report, several owners said they would take drastic action against any player opting for Japan. *Philadelphia Tribune* columnist J.M. Moss echoed their statement: "It is unreasonable for the players to expect that they could ramble around in the Orient and then report to their teams."[39] Throughout the existence of the Negro Leagues, owners were bedeviled by players jumping their contracts. In futile efforts to prevent the practice, owners threatened suspensions and fines. Mackey himself faced a five-year suspension. As a reporter for the

Philadelphia Tribune put it, "Undoubtedly, [players who go to Japan] will be numbered as A.W.O.L. when the roll is called for the league season. 'Tis then that the five-year penalty from organized ball will give the wayward ones time to tour Siberia and Madagascar."[40] However, players—not owners—fill seats at the ballparks, and one reporter predicted, "Hilldale needs Mackey.... The East will most likely find some way to wink at the new rule and put Mackey back in good graces."[41]

Wink they did. Ed Bolden gave Mackey only a two-month suspension, starting from his return to the United States on May 20 to his first game on July 24 against the Bacharachs. This light treatment tempted Mackey's teammate pitcher Phil Cockrell to jump Hilldale and join the Lincoln Giants for postseason play. In the opinion of veteran sportswriter F.A. Young, Bolden was getting a taste of his own medicine.[42] Long-time sports editor for the *Chicago Defender*, Young also served as secretary to the Negro American League for a decade.

The reporter who said Hilldale needed Mackey had it right. His departure for Japan reportedly "[fell] like a bombshell in the ranks of Hilldale fans." The team, which had recently won three pennants, was "taking it on the chin" during Mackey's absence. Morale was fading, and Bolden suspended Nip Winters, George Carr, and Namon Washington in early June for lack of discipline and indifferent play. A month later, Bolden replaced Warfield with Otto Briggs as team captain. All that changed with Mackey's return.[43] Even during his suspension, fans and players alike perked up just seeing Mackey sitting in the stands. His presence as a spectator was so important that one reporter credited him for inspiring the team to take two games from the league-leading Bacharachs.[44] Once back in the lineup, Mackey led Hilldale to a 19–17 record for the second half of the season, a vast improvement over the team's dismal 17–28 record for the first half.[45]

In an August 4 home game against the Cuban Stars, Mackey reminded people what he meant to the team. The battery of Nip Winters (now reinstated) and Mackey held the Cubans to two runs, and Mackey contributed five of Hilldale's nine runs by scoring two himself and driving in three more with a double and a triple.[46] On August 23, Mackey again led the way, but this time against the Bacharachs. Accounting for nine of the Giants' 22 runs, he smashed two homers and a triple, crossing the plate five times and driving in four more.[47] One of the homers was a grand slam, and fans expressed their appreciation for it a week later by giving Mackey $40,[48] a significant sum for a player earning $175 a month.[49]

Though Mackey was usually reliable at the plate, his bat sometimes failed him. On such occasions, he sometimes displayed peculiar rituals. During a game against the Lincoln Giants on May 27, 1928, he lost his bat swinging at the ball and missed the next one by a foot. To regain his composure, he called time, walked over to a grassy area, pulled up a piece of turf, replaced it, returned to the batter's box, and put the next pitch into right field for a single. Mackey relied on his "grass" to bring him luck.[50]

The travel bug bit Mackey again in the spring of 1929, when he decided to play in Hawaii for two months along with his Hilldale teammate "Ping" Gardner and George Carr of the Bacharach Giants. This time Bolden decided to only suspend the absent players one day for every day they were gone. Bolden stated, "League mandates must be obeyed."[51] Mackey did serve a suspension upon his return, but shorter than Bolden initially proposed. On June 15 the *Chicago Defender* reported that Mackey had returned and would be eligible to play on June 24.[52] Mackey remained with Hilldale for the duration of the 1929 season, and his return, along with Gardner, gave the team a much needed boost. The Giants had posted a 15–20 record for the first half of the season while the two were in Honolulu but rebounded with a second half record of 24–15.[53]

Against the backdrop of the Great Depression, 1930 and 1931 were turbulent times for the country and the Negro Leagues. In 1930 Bolden sold the ECL Hilldale club to John Drew, a businessman who ran a bus line from Darby to Philadelphia. Drew called the team the Hilldale Daisies. Bolden then formed a new independent team that he named the

Biz Mackey with teammates from the Hilldale Giants. From left: Jess Hubbard, Mackey, John Beckwith, and Rap Dixon (Sotheby's).

Hilldale Giants. Mackey stayed with the Giants until September 1930, when he struck up a one-month association with the Baltimore Black Sox.

As the 1931 season approached, Bolden was still running the Hilldale Giants with many of his former regulars: Mackey, Martin Dihigo, Walter Cannady, Jake Stephens, and Bill Yancey.[54] Bolden's Giants had a good year, posting a 42–13 record,[55] but not good enough to lure Mackey back for 1932. Instead, he again toured abroad with the Philadelphia Royal Giants, playing games in Japan, Hawaii, and the Philippines.

In 1933 Bolden refashioned his team as the Philadelphia Stars, and Mackey was one of the first to sign on. Bolden touted Mackey to the press as "a big catcher who is known throughout the country for his uncanny throwing arm and destructive batting." To avoid any misunderstanding about Mackey's intentions for 1933, Bolden asked a notary public to witness his signature on the contract. Others who signed with Bolden's Stars included Dick Lundy, Jud Wilson, Jake Stephens, Chaney White, and Rap Dixon. Bolden started the 1933 season with a promise to Philadelphia fans: "We expect to land a team that will make this city forget its baseball headaches of recent seasons."[56] He named Lundy as team manager and Mackey as captain.[57]

In addition to captaining the Stars, Mackey maintained his throwing prowess. He delighted in luring Pittsburgh Crawford Cool Papa Bell, the Negro Leagues' fastest base runner, into a steal attempt and then nailing him. Right-handed pitcher Webster McDonald remembered Mackey saying, "Mac, let's get Cool" and calling for three curves. Bell took off as soon as the third curve ball was on its way, and Mackey threw him out.[58]

As an associate member of the NNL in 1933, Bolden's Stars did well enough that the league accepted the team as a full member for the 1934 season. Mackey returned along with the nucleus of the 1933 team, namely Wilson, White, Stephens, and Dixon. Bolden tried to trade Dixon to the Pittsburgh Crawfords for Josh Gibson, but the Craws "hee-hawed" his proposal.[59] Bolden replaced Lundy as manager with Webster McDonald, known as the "Gentleman of Negro Baseball." With this lineup, 1934 would be a good year for the Stars, though Mackey would struggle.

Philadelphia fans did not have to wait for opening day to see many of the Stars in action. On Easter Sunday, Mackey led a group of Stars against Charles Henry's Zulu Giants. Decked out in grass skirts, war paint, and headdresses, the Zulus went by such names as Wawhoo, Limpopo, Nyassa, and Bangweold. A reporter noted before the game, "It remains to be seen if people like their baseball presented by a team dressed in jungle garb." Before a crowd of 1,500, Mackey's All-Stars won 3–2, and Biz himself drove in two of the runs.[60] No references show additional games between the Zulus and Stars, though the Zulus continued barnstorming against other clubs for the next several years.

The Stars brought the 1934 NNL championship home to Philadelphia, but with only limited help from Mackey. An arm injury relegated him to occasional appearances and only at first or third. Mickey Casey filled in as the Star's backstop. Before the next season, Bolden sent Mackey to Hot Springs, Arkansas, to take the "full course of treatment" for his arm. The full course consisted of "twenty-one baths and a good boiling out process."[61] The treatment worked, at least temporarily.

Bolden opened spring training in 1935 by announcing, "A championship pennant has been donated by the National Negro League and my men, ever conscious of the title they won last year, will go forward with a new determination to conquer." To help them succeed, Bolden outfitted them in new uniforms featuring red and blue jerseys and stockings with red, white, and blue stripes. Mackey caught the Stars' 1935 season opener against the Brooklyn Royals, contributing one hit and four putouts.[62] But he played sparingly after that as his arm continued giving him trouble. Two years is a long time for a team to carry an injured player, even one of Mackey's stature. After the Giants finished their disappointing 1935 season with a 24–27 record, Bolden announced that players who did not produce in 1935 need not look for 1936 contracts.[63] That included Mackey, whom Bolden traded to the Columbus Elite Giants, soon to become the Washington Elite Giants, for outfielder Roy Parnell and pitcher Sam Thompson.[64]

Shortly after the trade, Mackey's arm regained its old form, and during spring training he played "his best game of ball in some years" against the Montgomery Grey Sox.[65] Mackey continued to play well with Washington, and in mid–July a reporter for the *Washington Tribune* proclaimed, "Mackey has been a bulwark of power on defense and offense. He continued his heavy hitting in [a doubleheader against the Pittsburgh Crawfords] by smacking a homer in the second tilt."[66]

Mackey had served as team captain with Hilldale, but in 1936 he took the helm as Washington's interim manager for three weeks when manager "Candy" Jim Taylor, another of C.I.'s brothers, took four of the Elites (Schoolboy Griffith, Sammy Hughes, Felton Snow, and "Wild Bill" Wright) to Denver to join a Negro all-star team in the *Denver Post* Tournament.[67] The next year, Taylor left the Elites for the Chicago American Giants, and Mackey replaced him as Washington's player/manager. Sportswriter Art Carter welcomed the news: "Mackey, once the hardest hitting backstop in the game ... today is a dangerous hitter at all times, [and] ranks with the best in handling pitchers."[68] Mackey continued to hit with authority, leading regulars at the plate with a .375 average.[69] Fans acknowledged his managerial expertise by electing him to manage the East squad in the 1937 East–West All-Star game. Mackey beat out Oscar Charleston, regarded by many as the Negro Leagues' best player, who had managed the East team in 1934 and 1936 and the West in 1935.[70]

Mackey stayed with Tom Wilson's Elite Giants as the team relocated to Baltimore. During the 1938 season, he started at catcher and managed the team, but his biggest contribution was his mentoring of a teenage rookie catcher from Philadelphia, Roy Campanella. Mackey met Campanella in the spring of 1938. Tom Dixon of the Atlantic City Bacharachs, for whom Campanella was playing on weekends, introduced the two outside the Woodside Hotel at 141st Street and Broadway in Harlem. There, Mackey asked Campanella to join the Elites. The two agreed to meet the following week at the Attucks Hotel in Philadelphia, where Mackey gave Campanella a Giants' uniform and a contract for $60 per month. This was less than he was earning with Bacharachs, but it was the big time.[71]

Mackey took young Campanella under his wing and taught him what he needed to know to become one of the finest catchers in the Negro Leagues and after integration in the major leagues. "He just asked me to sit beside him," Campanella said. "He helped me to learn everything. I tried to be the image of Biz Mackey. He was the master." Mackey advised the rookie how to handle pitchers: "You got to scold some. You got to flatter some. You got to bribe some. You've got to think for some, and you got to mother them all. If you can do all those things, son, you'll be the biggest man in the league."[72] Campanella learned to do all those things, but the learning did not come easily. "Biz wasn't satisfied for me to do just one or two things good," Campanella said. "He wanted me to do everything good. And the onliest way I was going to improve myself was by working at the game working, working, working. There were times when Biz made me cry with his constant dogging. But nobody ever had a better teacher."[73]

In 1938 Wilson replaced Mackey as manager with George Scales, and in June 1939 sold the veteran catcher to Effa Manley's Newark Eagles as part of a youth movement for the Elites. The Newark Herald cheered the news of his arrival: "he has long been known to be the best developer of young hurlers and, with only one veteran pitcher, Leon Day, on the staff, the services of Mackey are badly needed."[74] The writer may have been thinking about Mackey's tutelage of left-handed pitcher Slim Jones, who went 13–1 in 1934 and led the Philadelphia Stars to their Negro League World Series win over the Chicago American Giants.[75]

For the remainder of the 1939 season and for all of 1940, Mackey continued his outstanding play while developing the Eagles' young pitchers. In August 1940 Effa Manley installed him as team manager, replacing Dick Lundy.[76] That same year Mackey received one of his rare fines and ejections. Umpire Fred D. McCrary put Biz out of the game for calling him names and for conduct unbecoming to ballplayers. The umpire ordered that ten dollars be "kept out of Eagles money for a fine for Mackey."[77]

Mackey returned as the Eagles' player/manager for the 1941 campaign. Now 44 years old, he had slowed down a bit on the field, but players still spoke well of his throwing ability. Future Hall of Fame pitcher Leon Day said at the time, "I don't see how he threw at all. His fingers were all broken on his right hand, all messed up."[78] Campanella remembered Mackey's hands the same way: "To look at his hands, you'd say, 'This guy must have been a butcher the way his fingers were curved and broken from foul tips.'"[79] In Mackey's day, catchers made a fist of their non-glove hand and held it level with their glove. Later, catchers began holding their non-glove hand behind their backs to avoid injuries.

In 1942, Mackey had a misunderstanding with Effa Manley, who replaced him as manager with Willie Wells.[80] Manley informed Mackey of the change by letter, saying that Wells planned to return and that she "always missed [Wells] off the club, and of course [wanted] him back." She continued, "I also want him to manage the team. I do not know whether or not this will surprise you, but when you left Newark last year without seeing me, I was of the opinion that you were not anxious to manage ... and a manager should have been interested in discussing plans for the next season, at the close of the last." After assuring him that "Wells and I both want you to stay," she said, "I would like you to take

Mackey, right, shakes hands with Joe DiMaggio, circa 1944. New York Black Yankees owner James Semler stands between the players (courtesy Sotheby's Auction House).

charge of driving the bus," for which she promised him additional pay and the driving assistance of teammate Ed Stone.[81]

Mackey would have returned as player/bus driver had it not been for a misunderstanding over money. Instead, he stayed in Los Angeles from 1942–1944 playing in the CWL and holding down a good-paying defense job with North American Aviation that Manley grudgingly helped him obtain. In a May 6, 1942, letter she told Mackey she received a letter from the company requesting a letter of recommendation for him. She promised to write the letter if Mackey returned the money she had sent him to cover his travel expenses to return East, which Mackey did not do. In his May 17 reply Mackey said, "I would have returned had you sent me the other money I ask for. I couldn't walk back there so I had to do the next best thing ... get a job." He promised to return the money: "I have played ball twenty two years and I haven't taken a nickle [sic] from no one but they have taken plenty away from me ... don't worry you will get your money back."[82]

Mackey returned to the Eagles in 1945 and replaced Willie Wells as player/manager after a disagreement between Wells and Effa Manley. Mackey kept the position through the 1947 season. In 1946 he managed the Eagles to their only World Series championship, defeating the Kansas City Monarchs four games to three. Though he was no longer the Eagles' starting catcher, his ability to work with pitchers and call a game when he did play often meant wins for the team. In the first inning of a game against the Baltimore Elite Giants, Newark pitcher Max Manning kept shaking off Mackey's signs for a curveball to Felton Snow. Mackey called time, walked to the mound, and told Manning, "Don't shake me off, I know these guys." Manning agreed and fed a steady stream of curve balls to Snow, who struck out four times that day. After the fourth time, Snow slumped on the bench and shook his head. Mackey yelled over to him, "It's a good thing you're not coming up again 'cause we'd do it again for a fifth time."[83]

On July 27, 1947, Mackey's 50th birthday, he was once again manager for the East squad in the East–West All-Star Game and even entered the game as a player. Wendell Smith, long-time sports editor for the *Pittsburgh Courier*, wrote, "The paunchy 50 year old manager of the East got into the fray. He picked up a bat in the eighth and hit for [Philadelphia Stars pitcher Henry] Miller and [Cleveland Buckeye Chet] Brewer gave him an intentional walk. Then Vic Harris of the Grays ran for him."[84]

The Eagles did not repeat as champions in 1947, and Effa Manley gave Mackey his unconditional release "to make the team a real pennant contender."[85] Now 51, he returned home to Los Angeles and barnstormed for a year with the San Francisco Sea Lions. Newspaper ads for the team's appearances always mentioned Mackey as the Sea Lions' best-known player, but they also touted "Little Sammy, The Wonder Boy," whose "exhibition of batting, catching, throwing, and daredevil sliding has amazed fans the country over." This player's arms were missing below his elbow, and his legs were missing below his knees. The Sea Lions traveled extensively, performing in such cities as Eau Claire, Wisconsin; Helena, Montana; Charleston, West Virginia; and Lethbridge, Alberta, Canada.[86]

Following his year with the Sea Lions, Mackey held a night job at Stauffer's Chemical Company in Los Angeles,[87] where he earned a salary "sufficient to ably support his wife and maintain a comfortable home."[88] Nevertheless, he rued the money that might have been. In 1951 he told an interviewer, "The fact that I'm not around now that Negro ballplayers are getting a break bothers me no little. Think of the salary I, along with a lot of other colored guys might have made with the hustle which was typical of our time."[89] With the Newark Eagles in 1946–1947, Mackey had received $375 per month, or about $2,250 for the season.[90] By comparison, in 1954 Junior Gilliam, who had played in the Negro Leagues with the Baltimore Elite Giants from 1946 to 1951, signed a contract with the Brooklyn Dodgers for $10,000 a year.[91]

Biz Mackey died on September 22, 1965, in Los Angeles and was buried in Evergreen Memorial Park. The Negro Leagues died about the same time. By 1965 major league baseball was signing the best African American players, drawing fans away from the black ballparks to major league stadiums.

Robert Peterson's classic history *Only the Ball Was White* (1970) marked the beginning of what has become a substantial body of literature on the Negro Leagues. Among the issues discussed are the relative merits of the leagues' star players. When historians debate the Negro Leagues' best catcher, the argument comes down to Josh Gibson and Biz Mackey. In 1952, the *Pittsburgh Courier* selected both catchers for an all-time Negro League all-star team. The decision panel included sportswriters and players from before 1945. Gibson received the most votes for catcher, 23, followed by Mackey with 15 votes.[92]

Most fans and players gave Gibson the nod based on his consistent ability to smash awe-inspiring home runs that often traveled more than 400 feet. Yancey and Johnson agreed that Mackey's hitting was not in Gibson's class. "He'd sting the ball, but the pitchers didn't fear him. They wouldn't walk him to get to somebody else," Johnson said.[93] Hall of Famer Monte Irvin, who played against Gibson and against and with Mackey, said, "Biz was a good line drive hitter— lots of singles and doubles and homers once in a while."[94]

While Gibson was unquestionably the most feared hitter of the two, Mackey had the edge defensively, though both had world-class arms. Irvin said of their defensive talents, "Josh was good at blocking the ball, but he wasn't the best receiver. He didn't like foul balls. He'd call for the first or third baseman to catch them. Campy [Roy Campanella] and Biz loved to run down the lines after 'em."[95] When asked to describe Mackey, players often noted his mental skills. Manning said Mackey "was one of the smartest catchers I ever threw to." Webster McDonald, Mackey's teammate on the Hilldale Giants and Philadelphia Stars, said he "was the best in baseball bar none. He was an artist behind the plate."[96]

*   *   *

My comparison of these two Hall of Famers is not meant to denigrate Gibson, but to elevate Mackey. Gibson will forever be remembered as a durable catcher with a wicked arm who hit more home runs and hit them further than any other Negro Leaguer and perhaps any major leaguer. Between 1929 and 1946, he spent seventeen seasons in the Negro Leagues and two (1940 and 1941) in Mexico with Vera Cruz. Had he not been felled by a stroke at age 35, Gibson may well have played another seven years to match Mackey's twenty-four Negro League seasons. That having been said, Negro League executive Cum Posey, who saw both catchers in their prime, voiced his assessment: "For combined hitting, thinking, throwing, and physical endowment, there has never been another like Biz Mackey."[97]

Notes

1.   Art Carter Papers, Box 170–16 File 9, Manuscript Division, Moorland-Spingarn Research Center, Howard University, Washington, DC.

2.   James Overmyer, *Queen of the Negro Leagues: Effa Manley and the Newark Eagles* (Lanham, MD: Scarecrow, 1998), 192.

3.   John Holway, *Blackball Stars: Negro League Pioneers* (Westport, CT: Meckler Books, 1988), 231.

4.   David L. Porter, *Biographical Dictionary of American Sports* (Westport, CT: Greenwood Press, 2000), 964.

5.   Holway, *Blackball Stars*, 231.

6.   John Maher, "Mackey Due for a Place in the Hall of Fame," *Cox News Service,* February 15, 2001.

7.   Mackey entered this birth date and location on his World War I draft registration card. Other biographical information comes from his brothers' draft registration cards and the 1900 and 1910 U.S. Federal Census records. David King discusses Mackey's Luling, Texas, experiences in the *San Antonio Express News*, July 29, 2006.

8.   Porter, *Biographical Dictionary of American Sports*, 964. Larry Lester contributed additional information about Mackey's association with the Black Giants and Black Navigators.

9.   Holway, *Blackball Stars*, 220.

10.   David King, *San Antonio at Bat* (College Station: Texas A & M University Press, 2004), 51–52.

11. Kirk Bohls, "Crafty Shortstop is Content in Austin, but He Remains Absent in Cooperstown," *Austin American-Statesman.* HOF file. No date.

12. James A. Riley, *The Biographical Encyclopedia of the Negro Baseball Leagues* (New York: Carroll & Graf, 1994), 763.

13. Holway, *Blackball Stars,* 220.

14. "Monarchs Stop A.B.C.'s in Two Straight Games," *Chicago Defender,* July 1, 1922.

15. William F. McNeil, The California Winter League: America's First Integrated Professional Baseball League (Jefferson, NC: McFarland, 2002), 257.

16. "Philadelphia Has Strong Ball Team," *Chicago Defender,* May 4, 1935.

17. "He's to Cover Short for Hilldale," *Philadelphia Tribune,* April 5, 1924.

18. W. Rollo Wilson, "Sports Shots," *Pittsburgh Courier,* April 5, 1927, 5.

19. Holway, Blackball Stars, 222.

20. Holway, Blackball Stars, 221–2.

21. "Mackey Stars as Hilldale Defeats Farmers, 7–4," *Philadelphia Tribune,* April 26, 1924.

22. "Player Hits Umpire and Draws Fine," *Chicago Defender,* June 14, 1924.

23. Riley, The Biographical Encyclopedia of the Negro Baseball Leagues, 488.

24. "Lincoln Giants and Hilldale Have the Edge on Other Eastern Clubs in 'Hot Corner' Guardians," *Philadelphia Tribune,* April 5, 1924.

25. "Contract Jumpers Greatest Menace to Negro Baseball: Leagues Should Check Evil," *Philadelphia Tribune,* September 6, 1924.

26. Larry Lester, *Baseball's First Colored World Series: The 1924 Meeting of the Hilldale Giants and the Kansas City Monarchs* (Jefferson, NC: McFarland, 2006), 163.

27. Holway, *Blackball Stars,* 92.

28. Riley, *The Biographical Encyclopedia of the Negro Baseball Leagues,* 697.

29. "Sport Squibs," *Chicago Defender,* January 17, 1925.

30. *Philadelphia Tribune,* April 25, 1925.

31. "Hilldale Defeats Kansas City Five Games to One for Baseball Supremacy," *Philadelphia Tribune,* October 17, 1925.

32. Holway, *Blackball Stars,* 224.

33. Ibid.

34. The Hilldale Giants, with Mackey as catcher, beat the Philadelphia Athletics 5 games out of 6 in a 1926 postseason series, but Cochrane did not play.

35. Lawrence D. Hogan, *Shades of Glory: The Negro Leagues and the Story of African-American Baseball* (Washington, DC: National Geographic, 2006), 158.

36. Thom Loverro, *The Encyclopedia of Negro League Baseball* (New York: Facts on File, 2003), 186.

37. In addition to Mackey, the touring team included manager Lonnie Goodwin; Negro Leaguers Rap Dixon, Andy Cooper, and Neal Pullen; and "local players, pitchers Evans, Johnson, and Tucker; Pagon on second, Riddle on third, and outfielders Cade and Groon." "Four Major League Players Decide to Jump Teams for Oriental Four [sic]," *Pittsburgh Courier,* March 12, 1927.

38. "Charleston with Grays Is First of Season's Major League Baseball Deals," *Philadelphia Tribune,* January 8, 1927; *Philadelphia Tribune,* March 5, 1927.

39. J.M. Moss, "Sidelights," *Philadelphia Tribune,* March 12, 1927.

40. Lloyd P. Thompson, "Charleston in Fold. Mackey Sails East," *Philadelphia Tribune,* March 19, 1927.

41. "The Montalvo Case," *The Chicago Defender,* May 14, 1927.

42. "FAY Says," *Chicago Defender,* October 8, 1927.

43. "Biz Mackey and Dixon Are Headed Home," *The Philadelphia Tribune,* July 14, 1927.

44. "Otto Briggs Made Captain of Hilldale, Replacing Warfield," *Chicago Defender,* July 9, 1927; "Hilldale Players Fined," Chicago Defender, June 11, 1927; "Whole of Last Year's Squad with the Exception of 'Biz' Mackey Have Signed for the Season," T*he Philadelphia Tribune,* April 2, 1927.

45. Dick Clark and Larry Lester, *The Negro Leagues Book* (Cleveland, OH: SABR, 1994), 162.

46. "Biz Mackey Clouts Game to Hilldale," *Chicago Defender,* August 13, 1927.

47. "Orgy of Hits and Runs is Daisy Parade," *Chicago Defender,* September 3, 1927.

48. *Philadelphia Tribune,* August 29, 1929.

49. Hilldale Ledgers, Cash-Thompson Collection, Box 1, The African-American Museum in Philadelphia.

50. Randy Dixon, "Daisies Smother Rivals Under Barrage of Heavy Hitting: Score 10–6," *Philadelphia Tribune,* June 2, 1928, 10.

51. "Biz Mackey Missing As Daisies Make Ready For Lincolns This Saturday," *Philadelphia Tribune,* April 25, 1929; "Eastern Baseball Men Plan Trades at Friday's Confab," *The Chicago Defender,* May 18, 1929.

52. "Lincoln Giants Are Big Surprise in Amer. League," *Chicago Defender,* June 15, 1929.

53. Clark and Lester, *The Negro Leagues Book,* 162.

54. "Chaney White, Judy Johnson, Cannady to Play for Hilldale." *Chicago Defender,* April 11, 1931.

55. Clark and Lester, *The Negro Leagues Book,* 162.

56. Immigration problems prevented future Hall of Famer Martin Dihigo from leaving Venezuela to join Bolden's new squad. Randy Dixon, "Galaxy of Baseball Aces to Play for Ed Bolden's Phila. Stars This Season," *Philadelphia Tribune,* March 16, 1933.

57. "Mackey Picked As Captain of Philly Stars," *Philadelphia Tribune,* March 6, 1933.

58. Holway, *Blackball Stars,* 221.

59. Randy Dixon, "Wide Representation as Baseball Moguls Launch Plans For Real League," *Philadelphia Tribune,* February 15, 1934.

60. "Zulu Gts. Play Mackey's Stars Easter Monday [sic]," *Philadelphia Tribune,* March 29, 1934; "Zulus Bow to All Stars By 3 to 2 Count," *Philadelphia Tribune,* April 5, 1934.

61. "Biz Mackey Goes to Hot Springs," *Philadelphia Tribune,* April 4, 1935.

62. Ed R. Harris, "Stars Meet Brooklyn for 3 Tilts," *Philadelphia Tribune,* May 16, 1935.

63. "Bolden's Plans for Next Year Still Mystery," *Philadelphia Tribune,* September 12, 1935.

64. Ed. R. Harris, "Greenlee Absent As Meetings Start Late," *The Philadelphia Tribune,* January 30, 1936.

65. "Big Men Wanted for Elite Giants, Says Tom Wilson," *Afro-American,* April 18, 1936.

66. "Elites Win First Half Loop Championship," *Washington Tribune,* July 17, 1936.

67. "Mackey at Manager's Post as Elites Face Newark," *Washington Tribune,* July 31, 1936.

68. Art Carter, "Mackey Succeeds Taylor as Elite Giants Manager," *Washington Tribune,* April 3, 1937.

69. John Holway, *The Complete Book of Baseball's Negro Leagues: The Other Half of Baseball History* (Fern Park, FL: Hastings House, 2001), 343.

70. "Mackey Directs East's Team in the All-Star Game," *Chicago Defender,* August 7, 1937.

71. Roy Campanella, *It's Good to be Alive* (Boston: Little Brown, 1959), 58–59.

72. *Ibid.,* 67.

73. *Ibid.,* 165.

74. "Eagles Sign Biz Mackey," *Newark Herald,* July 22, 1939.

75. David King, *San Antonio Express News,* July 29, 2006.

76. "Newark's Team to Florida," *Chicago Defender,* April 5, 1941.

77. 1940 note, Newark Eagles Files, Newark Public Library, Newark, NJ.

78. Holway, *Blackball Stars,* 231. 79. Ibid., 228.

80. Effa Manley to Raleigh Mackey, February 19, 1942, Newark Eagles Papers, Newark Public Library, Newark, NJ.

81. Effa Manley to Raleigh Mackey, February 19, 1942, Newark Eagles Papers, Newark Public Library, Newark, NJ.

82. Effa Manley to Mr. J. Raleigh Mackey, May 6, 1942; James Raleigh Mackey to Mrs Manley, May 17, 1942, Newark Eagles Files, Newark Public Library, Newark, NJ.

83. Monte Irvin, personal interview, January 17, 2007.

84. Wendell Smith, "National League Helpless in Classic," *Pittsburgh Courier,* August 2, 1947.

85. "Newark Fires Manager Biz Mackey," *New York Amsterdam News,* January 31, 1948.

86. "Sea Lions Lose," *Chicago Defender,* June 19, 1948; "Cincinnati, 'Frisco' Negro Teams Here," Charleston (WV) Daily Mail, July 10, 1948; "S.F. Lions Challenge Strong Crescents Here," Charleston Daily Mail, July 1, 1948; "Touring San Francisco Sea Lions," The Independent Record (Helena, MT), August 21, 1948; "A Colorful Clan," Lethbridge Herald (Alberta, Canada), August 18, 1948; and "Little Sammy," Lethbridge Herald (Alberta, Canada), August 19, 1948.

87. From Mackey's death certificate, as relayed by Larry Lester in a telephone conversation on December 18, 2007.

88. "Do You Remember Biz Mackey?" *Negro Digest*, February, 1951, 36. Most accounts of Mackey's personal life say he was single. Jerome Kessler, the Eagles' publicist, wrote in 1940 that "Mackey was a confirmed bachelor." However, his bachelorhood apparently ended in the early 1940s. Mackey closed a December 23, 1943, letter to Effa Manley with a word about his wife: "You should see Lucille. She is too fat for words. She says hello." In a March 24, 1945, letter to Effa discussing his travel plans to come East, Mackey wrote, "Just send two tickets for me and wife." His death certificate gives his marital status as divorced. The Kessler statement and both letters are in the Newark Eagles Files at the Newark Public Library, Newark, NJ.

89. "Do You Remember Biz Mackey?" *Negro Digest*, February, 1951, 36.

90. Eagles Pay Scales, Newark Eagles Papers, Newark Public Library, Newark, NJ.

91. "Gilliam Gets '54 Pay Boost," *Pittsburgh Courier,* February 21, 1954.

92. "Experts' Dream Team," *Pittsburgh Courier,* April 19, 1952.

93. Robert O. Peterson, Only the Ball Was White (New York: Prentice-Hall, 1970), 223.

94. Monte Irvin, personal interview, January 17, 2007.

95. *Ibid.*

96. Hogan, Shades of Glory, 158.

97. *Ibid.*

野球

Appendix K: 1927 Tour Scrapbook
(Japan, Korea, Hawaii)

The Nippu Jiji
December 21, 1926

NEGRO BASEBALL TEAM TO JAPAN

—

Fukuoka City Invites Los Angeles White Sox To Play Games

—

To stimulate interest in the Far Eastern Exposition to be staged in Fukuoka City, Japan, next spring, municipal authorities have concluded negotiations with prominent promoters in Los Angeles whereby a Negro baseball team of that city will be brought to the city for a series of exhibition games with Japanese teams.

The Negro nine is known as the White Sox and is rated fairly strong.

Present plans call for the team to arrive in Japan in May and tour the country for the next two months.

Source: Negro Baseball Team to Japan, The Nippu Jiji, December 21, 1926, pg. 2.

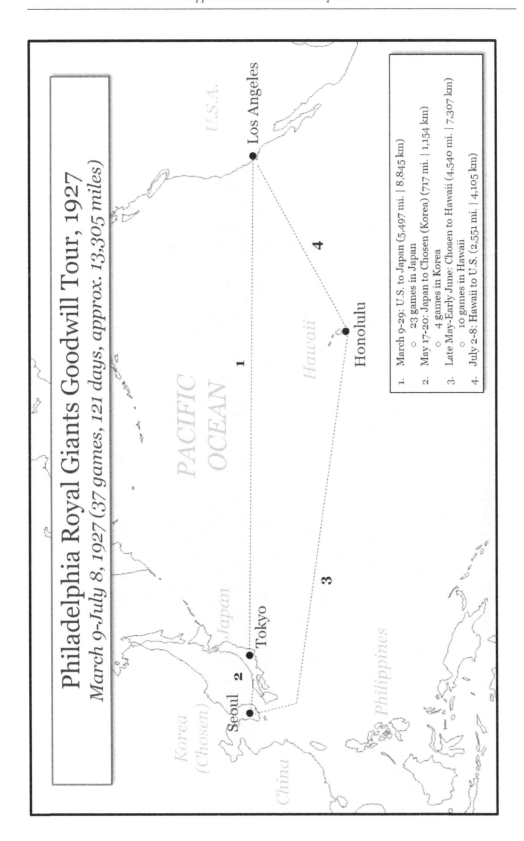

Philadelphia Royal Giants Goodwill Tour, 1927
March 9–July 8, 1927 (37 games, 121 days, approx. 13,305 miles)

1. March 9–29: U.S. to Japan (5,497 mi. | 8,845 km)
   - 23 games in Japan
2. May 17–20: Japan to Chosen (Korea) (717 mi. | 1,154 km)
   - 4 games in Korea
3. Late May–Early June: Chosen to Hawaii (4,540 mi. | 7,307 km)
   - 10 games in Hawaii
4. July 2–8: Hawaii to U.S. (2,551 mi. | 4,105 km)

Passenger Ship Record Summary: 1927 Philadelphia Royal Giants

Family Name	Given Name	Age	Sex	Married or Single	If native of US, Date and Place of Birth	Date of Papers	Address in US
Cade	Joe	25	M	M	Apr 5, 1900, Saint Louis, Mo	Passport: Feb 24, 1927	215 W. 14th St., Los Angeles, Calif.
Cooper	Andrew L.	32	M	S	April 24, 1896, Waco, Texas	Passport 328112, Feb 21, 1927	1342 E. Adams St., Los Angeles, Calif.
Dixon	Herbert	24	M	S	Sept 15, 1902, Kingston, Ga.	Passport 328825, Feb 23, 1927	1424 E. Adams St., Los Angeles, Calif.
Duncan	Frank	26	M	S	Feb 14, 1901, Kansas City, Mo.	Passport 330649, Feb 28, 1927	1907 Highland Ave., Kansas City, Mo.
Evans	Alexander	30	M	S	Oct 17, 1897, Charleston, S.C.	Passport 329123, Feb 24, 1927	3519 A. McKinley, Los Angeles, Calif.
Fagan	Robert	25	M	S	March 27 1902, Terre Haute, Ind.	Passport 327135 Feb 17, 1927	1204 E. 23 St., Los Angeles, Calif.
Goodwin	Lon A	48	M	M	March 15, 1879, Austin, Texas.	Passport # 328288, Feb 21, 1927	1424 E. Adams St., Los Angeles, Calif.
Green	Junior	27	M	M	June 25, 1900, Galveston, Texas	Passport 327332 / Feb 17, 1927	1186 E. Jefferson, Los Angeles, Calif.
Irie	George	41	M	M	June 15, 1885, Yamaguchi, Japan	R.P. 255314 Wash., Dec. 30, 1926	Calif. Los Angeles
Johnson	Ajay	26	M	S	Jan 23, 1901, Waco, Texas	USA Passport 327297 Feb 17, 1927	974 E. 36th St., Los Angeles, Calif.
Mackey	Raleigh	28	M	S	July 27, 1899, San Antonio, Texas	U.S. Passport 328566, Feb 21, 1927	1127 E. 27th St., Los Angeles, Calif.
Pullen	O'Neal	28	M	M	Sept 8, 1899, Beaumont, Texas	U.S. Passport 328553, Feb 21, 1927	1651 Essex St., Los Angeles, Calif.
Riddle	John	26	M	S	Dec 9, 1900, Columbus, Ohio	U.S. Passport 328554, Feb 21, 1927	346 Stevenson St., Los Angeles, Calif.
Tucker	Eugene	28	M	S	July 5, 1897, West Point, Georgia	P.P. --	55 New South St., Northhampton, Mass.
Walker	Jesse	22	M	S	Sept 10, 1904, Austin, Texas	US Passport 328563, Feb 21, 1927	1434 E. 48th St., Los Angeles, Calif.

The Royal Giants upon their arrival in Hawaii. (Left to right) Top row: Dixon, Goodwin, Cooper, Duncan, Johnson, Mackey, and Pullen. Bottom row: Fagen, Green, Cade, Walker, Riddle and Evans (Honolulu Star-Bulletin).

The Royal Giants at Jingu Stadium in Tokyo. (Left to right) Top row: Johnson, Mackey, Dixon, Duncan, Goodwin, Cooper, Walker, and Tucker. Bottom row: Pullen, Green, Riddle, Irie, Cade, Evans, and Fagen (Nisei Baseball Research Project).

The Afro-American
Mar 19, 1927

Goodwin Flays Big League Salaries On His Departure

LOS ANGELES, CAL, Mar., (P.C.N.B.) — "The National Negro and the Eastern Leagues are cutting salaries to a place where a baseball is not fairly paid for services rendered", is the parting shot hurled by Lonie Goodwin as he and hist team embarked Wednesday for the Orient on a Japanese steamer.

On is team he had Duncan and Cooper, National leaguers and Dixon and Mackey, Eastern leaguers. The blub will play its first games in Japan and stop in Manila and Honolulu on the return voyage. Sometime in June is the date the players are expected to return to the States.

The remainer of the team made up of locals, namely: Evans, Johnson and Tucker, pitchers; Fagon, 2nd base; Riddle, 3rd base; Cade, centerfield; Green, rightfield; and Pullen, catcher. Pullen, Fagen, and Evans formerly played in the East.

Source: Goodwin Flays Big League Salaries on His Departure; Afro-American, Mar 19, 1927, pg. 14.

*   *   *

The Chicago Defender
June 25, 1927

Royal Giants Won 26; Tied One on Their Japanese Tour

Honolulu, Hawaii, June 8. — The Philadelphia Royal Giants, and aggregation of baseball players of the first caliber, left the United States March 9 for a tour of Japan and the Orient.

After a very stormy 18-day trip and two days in which to get rid of their sea legs, they swung into a very strenuous schedule of games and travel against the teams of Japan and Chosen.

Baseball in the Orient, Japan and Chosen, is very good, much better than one would expect, considering the short length of time that they have been playing ball there. They were not, of course, in a class with this aggregation and stars, which includes among its personnel such men as captain Raliegh Mackey, shortstop; Herbert "Rap" Dixon, centerfield dirt delux, Andrew "Lefty" Cooper pitcher par excellent; Pullen, catcher; Duncan, the first baseman; Green, pitcher and right fielder, and one of the hardest hitting little men in present-day baseball.

The Royal Giants club is made up of Negro League baseball players, brought together every year in California, where they play in the professional Winter League under the management of Lon Goodwin.

The professional league is a five teamly composed of the cream of the white major and minor league ball players, except the Giants this year and last they were successful in winning the championship of the league, after many grueling and exciting games.

Truly an enviable record for any ballclub, considering the fact that most of the time while off the ballfield was spent in travel and then, too, quite a few of the games were played under some of the most adverse weather conditions, which are absolutely foreign to American baseball.

Following is the record against the leading teams of Japan and Korea:

At Tokio, April 1 – Royal Giants 2, Mita club 0. Battery, Cooper and Pullen.

At Tokio, April 2 – Royal Giants 10, Mita club 6. Battery, Mackey and Pullen.

Osaka, April 3 – Royal Giants 7, Diamond club 2. Battery, Green and Pullen.

Osaka, April 5 – Royal Giants 1, Diamond club 1. Battery, Mackey and Pullen.

Osaka, April 6 – Royal Giants 10, Daimai 2. Battery, Cooper and Pullen.

Osaka, April 7 – Royal Giants 6, Kansai Daigaku 0. Battery, Green and Pullen.

Kyoto, April 9 – Royal Giants 2, Doshiska Daigaku 0. Battery, Johnson and Pullen.

Kyoto, April 10 – Royal Giants 4, Diamond club 2. Battery, Johnson and Pullen.

Osaka, April 12 – Royal Giants 9, Prebus club 6. Battery, Evans and Pullen.

Takarazuka, April 13 – Royal Giants 4, Takarazuka 3. Battery, Green and Pullen.

Tokio, April 16 – Royal Giants 6, Tomon (Waseda) 2. Battery, Johnson and Pullen.

Tokio, April 17 – Royal Giants 9, Tomon (Waseda) 1. Battery, Evence and Pullen.

Tokio, April 20 – Royal Giants 9, Fresno club 1. Battery, Cooper and Pullen.

Tokio, April 25 – Royal Giants 8, Meiji 9. Battery, Johnson and Pullen.

Tokio, April 28 – Royal Giants 14, Rikkyo Daigaku 0. Battery, Johnson and Pullen.

Nagoya, April 29 – Royal Giants 4, Zenshinehu o. Battery, Cooper and Pullen.

Dogo Iyo, Japan. May 1 – Royal Giants 8, Iyo Tetsudo 1. Battery, Cooper and Pullen.

Hiroshima, Japan, May 4 – Royal Giants 17, Koryo Chugaku 1. Battery, Green and Pullen.

Kokura Fukuouka, Japan, May 7 – Royal Giants 11, Kokura All Stars 4. Battery, Evance and Pullen.

Saburo Yokozawa (1904-1995) was from Taipei and attended Meiji University, where he participated in a goodwill tour of the U.S. in 1924. In 1927 he played for Daimai, the team that tied the Royal Giants 1-1 on April 5. He later became an umpire in the Pacific League, and was named umpire-in-chief after WWII. In 1983 he was interviewed extensively by Kazuo Sayama for the book, *Gentle Black Giants.* Five years later, Yokuzawa was elected to the Japanese Baseball Hall of Fame (Prestige Collectibles).

Haka Fuquoka, Japan, May 8 – Royal Giants 12, Fukuoka All Stars 4. Battery, Cooper and Pullen.

Toyama, Japan, May 15 – Royal Giants 7, Kansai Daigaku 5. Battery, Johnson and Pullen.

Taikyu, Korea, May 19 – Royal Giants 14, Taiku All Stars 2. Battery, Dixson and Pullen.

Fusan, Korea, May 20 – Royal Giants 11, Fusan 0. Battery, Evance and Pullen.

Keijo, Korea, May 21 – Royal Giants 22, Shousan Bank 4. Battery, Evence and Pullen.

Keijo, Korea, May 21 – Royal Giants 6, Ryuzan R.R. club. Battery, Johnson and Pullen.

Keijo, Korea, May 22 – Royal Giants 17, Ryuzan R.R. club, Battery, Cooper and Pullen.

Source: Royal Giants Won 26; Tied One on Their Japanese Tour, The Chicago Defender, June 25, 1927, pg. 9.

*   *   *

Royal Giants - Run Differential, by game, Japan Tour

Date	Opposition	Pitcher	PRG Runs	Opp. Runs	Diff
1-Apr	Mita Club	Cooper	2	0	2
2-Apr	Mita Club	Mackey	10	6	4
3-Apr	Daimai	Green	7	2	5
5-Apr	Daimai	Mackey	1	1	0
6-Apr	Daimai	Cooper	10	2	8
7-Apr	Kansai Daigaku	Green	6	0	6
9-Apr	Doshika	Johnson	2	0	2
10-Apr	Diamond Club	Johnson	4	2	2
12-Apr	Brebus Club	Evans	9	6	3
13-Apr	Takarazuka	Green	4	3	1
16-Apr	Toma (Waseda)	Johnson	6	2	4
17-Apr	Tomon	Evans	9	1	8
20-Apr	Fresno	Cooper	9	1	8
25-Apr	Meiji	Johnson	9	8	1
28-Apr	Rikkyo Daigaku	Johnson	14	0	14
29-Apr	Zenshinehu	Cooper	4	0	4
1-May	Iyo Tetsudo	Cooper	8	1	7
4-May	Koryo Chugaku	Green	17	1	16

Date	Opposition	Pitcher	PRG Runs	Opp. Runs	Diff
7-May	Kokura All-Stars	Evans	11	4	7
8-May	Fukuoka All-Stars	Cooper	12	4	8
16-May	Kansai Daigaku	Cooper	7	5	2
17-May	Kansai Daigaku	Johnson	10	4	6
19-May	Taiku All-Stars	Dixon	14	2	12
20-May	Fusan	Evans	11	0	11
21-May	Shousan Bank	Evans	22	4	18
21-May	Ryuza RR Club	Johnson	6	0	6
22-May	Ryuza RR Club	Cooper	17	0	17
		Total	241	59	182
		AVG	9.27	2.27	7.00

*   *   *

Royal Giants - Individual Pitching, Runs Allowed, Japan tour

Pitcher	G	W	L	T	Runs allowed	Runs Per Game
Cooper	8	8	0	0	13	1.63
Johnson	7	7	0	0	16	2.29
Green	4	4	0	0	6	1.50
Evans	4	4	0	0	11	2.75
Mackey	2	1	0	1	7	3.50
Dixon	1	1	0	0	2	2.00
Total	26	25	0	1	55	2.12 AVG

Source: Royal Giants Won 26; Tied One on Their Japanese Tour. The Chicago Defender (National edition) (1921-1967), June 25, 1927.

Opposite, top: The Royal Giants were incorrectly identified as an American Indian team by some members of the Japanese media. The note on the back of this photo reflects that error. *Opposite, bottom:* Featured (left to right) are Ajay Johnson, Rap Dixon, Frank Duncan, Biz Mackey shaking hands with Tokyo Mayor Nishikubo Hiromichi, John Riddle (middle), Eugene Tucker, Andy Cooper, George Irie, and Jesse Walker (Courtesy of a private collector).

Left: In Taisho 14 (1925), Minoru Yamashita of the First Kobe Shinkou Commercial High School hit the longest ball ever witnessed in Koshien Stadium—a one-hopper to the wall that was well over 400 feet from home plate. This feat was surpassed in Showa 2 (1927) by the Royal Giants' Rap Dixon, who belted a line drive off the wall for a triple. *Right:* On April 29, Showa 2 (1927), Saburo Miyatake of Keio University hit a home run that many believed was the first ever at Jingu Stadium. However, thanks to the efforts of historian Kazuo Sayama, we now know that Royal Giants' Biz Mackey holds that distinction. On April 20 Mackey hit one over the fence, nine days before Miyatake's blast (Prestige Collectibles).

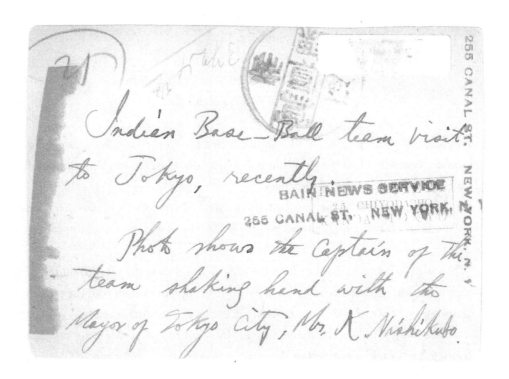

Indian Base—Ball team visit to Tokyo, recently.

Photo shows the Captain of the team shaking hand with the Mayor of Tokyo City, Mr. K. Nishikubo.

BAIN NEWS SERVICE
255 CANAL ST. NEW YORK.

The Chicago Defender
June 25, 1927

Royal Giants in 10 to 0 Win in Honolulu

Beat Asahis Before a Record Crowd

Honolulu, Hawaii, June 6. — The largest crowd ever turned out for a baseball game in Honolulu yesterday filled the grandstand and first-base leader of the Honolulu stadium and overflowed into the football bleachers.

Of course thousands of the fans had also come to see the game between the Braves and the Filipinos, but the main attraction of the afternoon was the initial appearance of the Giants.

When the Giants walked out of their dressing rooms during the seventh inning of the Braves-Filipino affray it was the occasion for a burst of applause which rival the plaudits of the multitudes who witnessed last year's football games in the same stadium.

Vieussens he's played some excellent ball, the pitching of young Moriyama being outstanding. He struck out several of the giant sluggers and acquitted himself with much credit for his bearing and ability to puzzle the giant batteries.

The Giants displayed some of the best baserunning and the fastest in fieldwork ever seen on local time. Evans, who Cotsen, certainly put the fear of his whip into the opposition when they saw him make one or two pegs to second base. Not a base was stolen by the Asahi's during their entire game.

Cooper, the giant picture, and his teammate, Dixon, who played shortstop, where the outstanding players of yesterday's game. Not only was their work affected, but with their clowning they kept the fan in a good humor and became mighty popular.

Dixon, who played shortstop, is about the fastest player seen here in sometime. His peculiar style of catching and throwing the ball and his tremendous speed enabled him to pull some stuff that is absolutely new in Honolulu, and while the sand could not help laughing at the same time that left them open mouth to see the speed with which his this big fellow scooped up and got rid of the old pill.

ASAHIS

	AB	R	H	P
Nagai ss …	3	0	1	3
Shizura 3b ..	4	0	2	1
Tokuda cf …	4	0	1	2

Mamiya rf ..	4	0	0	0
Arakawa 1b.	4	0	0	6
Nishihara lf	4	0	1	2
Moriyama 2b	4	0	0	3
Kozuki c	4	0	0	8
Moriyama p	2	0	0	0
Yoshida ss ..	1	0	0	2
Wakabashi p	0	0	0	0
Totals ...	34	0	5	27

ROYAL GIANTS

	AB	R	H	P
Duncan 1b ..	5	1	0	10
Green lf	4	2	2	2
Mackey ss ..	6	1	1	5
Dixon cf ...	5	1	2	1
Pullen c	4	1	3	7
Evans 2b ...	5	1	1	0
Cade rf	4	0	1	2
Walker 3b .	4	2	1	0
Cooper p ...	5	1	2	0
Totals ...	42	10	13	27

Royal Giants . . . 2 0 0 1 0 1 2 1 3 = 10

Asahis . . . . 0 0 0 0 0 0 0 0 0 = 0

Source: ROYAL GIANTS IN 10 TO 0 WIN IN HONOLULU, The Chicago Defender, June 25, 1927, pg. 9.

After facing the Philadelphia Royal Giants in Hawaii in 1927, Asahi pitcher Tadashi "Bozo" Wakabayashi would later join Hosei University and then became the ace for the Hanshin Tigers. During his 18 years in professional baseball, he recorded 237 wins, 144 loses, and 1,000 strikeouts. He was elected to the Japanese Baseball Hall of Fame in 1964 (Prestige Collectibles).

Honolulu Star-Bulletin
July 13, 1927

Royal Giants Defeated By Chinese; First Loss In 31 Contests Played

—

Kan Yen and You Chung Prove Too Much for Visitors; Giants Unable to Connect with Slow Ball

—

By LOUI LEONG HOP

The non-stop flight of the Royal Philadelphia Giants to attain an unblemished record in the Pacific lands was checked at the Honolulu Stadium yesterday afternoon when they were forced down by the Chinese, 3 to 1, in a piping-hot fracas before a huge baseball assemblage of more than 6000 persons.

The forced landing of the Giants in their intended non-defeat flight was made after they had traveled more than two and a half months (covering a distance better than 9500 miles), during which time they won 26 games and tied one out of 27 played in Japan, and thumped three local teams. In other words, the Giants' defeat yesterday was the first since taking off from the Pacific coast for the cherry blossom land.

Source: Royal Giants Defeated by Chinese, Honolulu Star-Bulletin, July 13, 1927, pg. 8.

Editor's note: This game occurred roughly two months after the first Trans-Atlantic flight accomplished by Charles Lindberg on May 21, 1927. Reporter Loui Leong Hop's article represents an early infusion of aviation terminology into baseball reporting.

Honolulu Star-Bulletin
July 13, 1927

Down Giants

GIANTS

	AB	R	H	PO	A	E
Duncan, 1b ..	4	0	1	11	0	1
Riddle, rf	4	0	1	0	0	0
Mackey, ss ..	4	0	0	0	3	0
Dixon, cf ...	4	1	1	1	0	0
Pullen, c	3	0	0	8	0	1
Green, lf ...	3	0	1	2	0	0
Evans, 2b....	2	0	0	0	1	0
Fagen, 2b....	2	0	1	0	1	0
Walker 3b .	3	0	0	2	0	0
Cooper, p ...	3	0	0	0	1	0
Totals ...	32	1	5	24	6	1

CHINESE

	AB	R	H	PO	A	E
En Sue, lf ..	4	1	2	0	0	0
Lin Fat, rf	3	0	1	2	0	0
Kai Luke, 2b ..	3	0	0	0	2	0
Kualii, 1b ...	4	1	1	10	0	0
Shipp Lo, cf...	2	0	0	2	0	o
Kan Yen, c ...	4	1	1	9	0	0
Bunn He, ss...	4	0	0	1	2	0
Lee Chong...	4	0	2	3	1	0
You Ching...	3	0	0	0	0	0
Totals ...	31	3	7	27	5	0

Runs by Innings

Giants . . . . 0 0 0 0 0 0 0 0 1 = 1
Chinese . . . . 1 0 0 2 0 0 0 0 0 = 3

Source: Royal Giants Defeated by Chinese, Honolulu Star-Bulletin, July 13, 1927, pg. 8.

The Afro-American
July 23, 1927

"Pros" Ask for Jonnie Riddle

Honolulu, H.T. (PCNB) – John Riddle, a graduate of the University of California, an architect by profession and an all-round athlete, has been asked to play football this winter with a professional Hawaiian team.

Riddle, playing baseball with the Philadelphia Royal Giants here while in route to California after a tour of Japan and Korea had not been in the city and hour before a former white schoolmate, now a resident of the island, made him an offer. In addition to his football playing Riddle, if he excepts will be given a position in an architect's office.

Source: "Pros" Ask for Jonnie Riddle, The Afro-American, July 23, 1927, pg. 14.

Before he was a member of the Royal Giants, Johnnie "Up-the-Middle" Riddle, was a fullback for the USC Trojans (University of Southern California, University Archivist & Manuscripts Librarian, Doheny Memorial Library).

The Afro-American
July 9, 1927

30 Day Suspension for Four Players

CHICAGO, Ill—At the meeting of the directors of the National League held here several days ago, it was voted to add a $200 fine to the thirty-day suspension netted our to the players who took the trip to Japan, namely Frank Duncan, Monarchs catcher and Lefty Cooper, Detroit pitcher.

The other two men, Dixon of Harrisburg and Mackey of Hilldale will be accorded the same treatment in the Eastern League if the agreement between the two organizations hold.

Secretary Q.J. Gilmore notified President Nutter of the eastern Mutual Baseball Association of the ruling immediately after it had been decided.

Source: 30 Day Suspensions for Four Players, The Afro-American, July 9, 1927, pg. 15.

*   *   *

The Chicago Defender
September 24, 1927

Fay Says—Mackey Jumped

"...Hilldale violated an agreement with the West when it was voted to fine and suspend the players that jumped the league and went to California, but Hilldale played Mackey as soon as he could get into a uniform on his return. Harrisburg did the same with Dixon and Detroit did the same with Cooper.

Only one owner lived up to the agreement. He was J.L. Wilkerson of the Kansas City Monarchs (regarding Frank Duncan)."

Source: Fays Says—Mackey Jumped, The Chicago Defender, September 24, 1927, pg. 8.

Honolulu Star-Bulletin
December 3, 1927

Negro All-Stars Agree to Play Here Next Year

... the coming of the negro all-star outfit is made possible by the Hawaii Undokai Sha which made the invitation through Kanichi Takigawa, publisher of the "Sports of Hawaii," a Japanese monthly magazine devoted to athletics.

Source: Negro All-Stars Agree to Play Here Next Year, Honolulu Star-Bulletin (Honolulu, Hawaii), December 3, 1927, pg. 8.

* * *

Catcher O'Neal Pullen and pitcher Ajay Johnson in Hawaii on June 5, at the end of the Philadelphia Royal Giants 1927 tour (Negro Leagues Baseball Museum).

Only the Ball was Small:
Birth of the Royal Giants 1927 Tour

by Bill Staples, Jr.

Editor's note: The following is an excerpt from the book, Kenichi Zenimura, Japanese American Baseball Pioneer (McFarland, 2011).

> "In our baseball, if you walked to first base, you stole second,
> they'd bunt you over to third and you stole home.... Actually
> scored runs without a hit. This was our baseball."[1]
> —Buck O'Neil, Negro Leagues baseball patriarch

The 1925 Season

On Sunday September 6, 1925, Kenichi Zenimura and his Fresno Athletic Club (FAC) traveled to Los Angeles to play a doubleheader, first starting with a contest against the Diamond club, an L.A.-based Japanese club, and then an afternoon contest with the all-black semi-pro Los Angeles White Sox, led by manager Lon Goodwin. All of the games were to be played at the White Sox Park, located on the corner of Compton and 35th in Los Angeles.[19] Coming off of a dominating four-game win streak, the Los Angeles White Sox were ready to tackle the Fresno Athletic Club.

The White Sox had developed a reputation as one of the fastest semipro teams in LosAngeles. Armed with his longtime friend and teammate from Hawaii, Kenso "The Boy Wonder" Nushida, Zenimura felt good about his chances against Goodwin's White Sox Fresno defeated the White Sox on the Los Angeles diamond, 5 to 4. Three thousand fans witnessed the contest.[20] In addition to his 2 for 5 day at the plate, Zenimura recorded a stolen base. The Fresno Athletic Club's victory over the White Sox stunned everyone.

The victory marked the second time in baseball history for an all–Japanese team to defeat an all-black team—the first was the FAC over the Oakland Pierce Giants in 1923.[21] Virtually all the members of the White Sox had some experience playing in organized black baseball in the east or in the California Winter League against major league and PCL-level talent.

Leading off for the White Sox was pitcher/outfielder Bill Foote, long-time member of the club and former player on the California Winter League (CWL) Alexander Giants in 1920. Outfielder Azel Savage was a member of the 1924–25 CWL White Sox who once recorded a 2–4 day at the plate against Detroit Tigers pitcher Pug Cavet.

Catcher O'Neal Pullen was a Negro-League journeyman from Texas who spent time with the Brooklyn Royal Giants, the New York Lincolns, and Hilldale, in 1920. After the '20 season, he accompanied Bill Pettus to the West Coast to play in the CWL. He fell in love with California and decided to stay and play with the L.A. White Sox during the regular season and in the CWL during the winter months. This encounter marked the beginning of a lifelong professional relationship between Pullen and Zenimura.

Third baseman John Riddle joined the L.A. White Sox in 1920 as a high school student. He later attended the University of Southern California (USC) and studied to become an architect. Considered an all-round athlete, he played football for the Trojans as well. His nickname was "Up the Middle Riddle" and he was described in 1921 as "Trojan Fullback, a dark, handsome gentleman of power and skill." Riddle became the first African American from USC to play in the Rose Bowl when the Trojans defeated Penn State 14–3 in 1923.

Second baseman Robert Fagan was a familiar face to Zenimura. Fagan was a member of the 25th Infantry Wreckers stationed at Scholfield Barracks in Hawaii up until 1918. He was also one of the players signed by the Kansas City Monarchs during the charter year of the Negro National League in 1920. Fagan participated in several CWL clubs, including the LA White Sox in 1920, Colored All-Stars in 1921, St. Louis All-Stars in 1922–23 and St. Louis Stars in 1923–24.

Like Goodwin and Pullen, pitcher Ajay Deforest Johnson was a native Texan. Described as a lanky right hander (6'0", 165 lbs), he attended L.A. High School where he pitched and played outfield. After completing school it's believed that he traveled east to join the Peoria Black Devils in 1920. And when that team folded he spent a brief stint with the Dayton Marcos club, led by Candy Jim Taylor. Johnson's mother passed away in the early 1920s, and it's believed that he returned home to California to help his father raise his younger siblings. He would eventually join the Los Angeles Police Department (LAPD) as a beat patrol officer and continue to pitch for Goodwin's semipro White Sox. Johnson would eventually join the Philadelphia Royal Giants in the 1927 California Winter League season and accompany the club on its tour to Japan, Korea and Hawaii. He became the number-two ace behind lefty Andy Cooper and helped lead the Royal Giants to a phenomenal 25–0–1 record against competition in Japan and Korea. Once out of baseball, Johnson dedicated himself to his career as a police officer, and in 1943 earned the distinction of becoming one of the first black uniformed patrol lieutenants and sergeants in LAPD history.[22]

Manager Lon Goodwin shifted his focus from the semipro Golden State Southern California Baseball League (GSCBL) season to another California Winter League (CWL) season with the addition of some of the top talent in the Negro Leagues from the east. Historically Goodwin carried his GSCBL team name of L.A. White Sox into the winter league season. Perhaps the timing is coincidental, but immediately after his loss to Zenimura's FAC in September 1925, he changed the name of his CWL team to the Philadelphia Royal Giants.[23] Joining Goodwin for the '25-'26 Winter League season were Crush Holloway, Tank Carr, Jess Hubbard, Biz Mackey, Joe Rogan, Connie Day, Rap Dixon, O'Neal Pullen, Newt Allen, Bob Hudspeth, Rube Currie and George Britton. Mackey, Dixon and Pullen, along with Los Angeles White Sox teammates Fagan, Riddle and Johnson, would all later join Goodwin for a tour of Japan in 1927.

In addition to the competition on the field, the ballpark configuration of the momentous FAC-White Sox game was also a challenge for Zenimura and his ballclub. Often compared in structure to Sulpher Dell Field, the "Improbable Ball Park" located in Nashville, Tennessee, White Sox Ball Park could be described as a field "where the second baseman and the right fielder play the same position." The fence in right field was approximately 270 feet from the home plate. Those familiar with Sulpher Dell said that right field was so close that the outfielder backed up first for overthrows on a grounder with no men on base, instead of the catcher. To further convey the odd dimensions of the field, it was said that the "right fielder ordinarily plays so close to the second baseman that he's virtually breathing down his neck and they have been known to throw out men at first on balls through that side of the infield."[24]

The 1926 Season

Zenimura and Goodwin scheduled a rematch of their 1925 meeting to take place in Fresno. It was decided that if the L.A. White Sox were going to travel over 200 miles north for baseball, they should make it worth their while and play two. So a two-game rematch was scheduled for the Fourth of July weekend, except this time Goodwin's men would not to play against the All-Japanese FAC, but against a Fresno all-star team comprised of the top stars from the Japanese, Police and Fire Department teams and managed by Johnny Steinhauer.

The Fresno All-Stars defeated the Los Angeles White Sox, 9 to 4. The game was "featured by heavy hitting and spectacular fielding on the part of the local aggregation.... The colored boys outhit the locals, but their batting rallies were repeatedly halted by flashy fielding stunts. The All Stars played through without making an error, while the visitors turned in four."35 An unexpected highlight then followed: "Zenimura hit a home run with one man on in the fourth inning. The boss of the Fresno Athletic Club's baseball outfit was the star of the day, getting three hits and playing a fine game at short."36 The man best known for playing "small ball" had surprisingly belted a home run. Years later Zenimura's son Howard commented that he thought his dad's 1926 Fourth of July home run must have been an inside-the-parker. "I don't think he could hit the ball that far," said Zeni's son. "It must have gone over somebody's head or landed inside the baseline. And he's so fast that he just ran around the bases."37

The next day the Fresno All-Stars defeated the L.A. team again by the score of 4 to 3. "A single in the ninth inning by Iwata with Hill on base, followed by an error by Fagen (sic), gave the Fresno All-Stars a victory."38 With the exception of Evans pitching for Los Angeles and Sako pitching for Fresno, the lineups remained unchanged from the previous day.39 Based on the precedent of inviting the Oakland Pierce Giants to a social and dance during their weekend visit back in 1923, this Fourth of July weekend visit to Fresno by the L.A. White Sox provides the greatest scenario as the time and place when Zenimura and Goodwin first discussed a joint tour to Japan for 1927. The tour to Japan was still more than eight months away and there was still a lot of baseball to be played—and still more barriers to break.

The 1927 Season

In January, the FAC announced its arrangements to make a second tour of Asia in March with 40 games in Japan scheduled and plans to take the team to China and Korea with a stop in Honolulu on the way home. There were a number of new players on the team.51 Not included in the initial news wire was the fact that the FAC were visiting Japan at the invitation of Meiji University, or more specifically, Zenimura's cousin, friend and colleague, Takizo Matsumoto, the man formerly known as Frank Narushima, one of the cofounders of the FAC.

In February, the Japanese American newspaper *Rafu Shimpo* announced similar news about Lon Goodwin and his Philadelphia Royal Giants.52 According to historian Kazuo

Sayama, the Philadelphia Royal Giants traveled to Japan on its own budget and "on recommendation by a certain Japanese American entrepreneur in California."53 Although he is never mentioned by name, historians believe that the entrepreneurial Californian is Zenimura based on his previous interactions with Goodwin and their teams throughout the 1925–26 seasons.

Records in Japan indicate that Goodwin attempted to bring his entire winter league roster on the tour. However, because of their contractual obligations to Negro League clubs back east, the majority of the players declined the offer. When Goodwin's men arrived in Yokohama on March 28, the local press reported the incoming guests as the complete Philadelphia Royal Giants 1926-27 California Winter League roster.

According to Kyoko Yoshida, baseball historian and professor at Keio University, the roster was telegraphed by Royal Giants interpreter George Irie to the Japanese media and promoters prior to their arrival. It is unknown why Irie did not modify the roster before leaving Los Angeles.[54] What is known is that Goodwin became persona non grata with the Negro Leagues for taking their stars Mackey, Cooper and Dixon away for part of the regular season.[55]

In April 1927, Kenichi Zenimura (bottom row, third from left) and the Fresno Athletic Club embarked on their second Goodwill Tour of Asia. Competing against the best semipro, industrial and college teams in Japan, China, Korea and Hawaii, the FAC finished with a 40–8–2 record, an .800 winning percentage (Nisei Baseball Research Project).

Rematch in Japan

On April 20, 1927, the FAC and Philadelphia Royal Giants met head-to-head in the newly constructed Meiji Shrine Stadium in Tokyo. Captain Zenimura shared with reporters his eagerness and excitement to play the upcoming game with Goodwin's club. "The Fresno players, who have defeated the invading Royal Giants in America in baseball, will have the opportunity of demonstrating their superiority over the same nine when they cross bats in their first game in Japan on Friday afternoon at the Meiji Shrine Field. This match ought to attract a huge attendance as both teams have shown great strength in their contests against the local nines."[63]

According to Japanese historian Kazuo Sayama, Zenimura's comments about previously defeating the Royal Giants caused quite a stir with several of the black players, especially Mackey, Dixon and Cooper. They openly expressed their disappointment with the FAC and wondered why the Japanese players from Fresno would lie about beating the Royal Giants, when they knew for a fact that they had never played one another.[64] More than 80 years later, we now see the historic misunderstanding that unfolded between Zenimura and Mackey.

Based on his comments to the Japanese press, it appears that Zenimura was under the impression that the Negro League team he was scheduled to play in Tokyo was comprised of players from the 1925–26 L.A. White Sox, the squad he had help defeat three times prior to the tour. Zeni had no idea that the Royal Giants team that boarded the ship in April was actually comprised of two different rosters: Cooper, Dixon, Duncan, Pullen and Mackey from Goodwin's 1926–27 CWL team, and select members of Goodwin's 1926 L.A. White Sox of the semipro GSCBL.

While the misunderstanding was unfortunate, it worked in favor of the Royal Giants. Who knows, perhaps Goodwin was a mastermind when it came to motivating his players? Either way, Biz Mackey channeled his anger into his bat and more than 10,000 baseball fans at Meiji Shrine Field witnessed the future hall of famer singlehandedly defeat Fresno 9–1.[65] "Mackey, the star shortstop of his team, was the heaviest slugger of the day, getting three safeties on four official trips to the diamond, one being a four-ply wallop, and the other two, a three sacker and a double." He was a single shy of hitting for the cycle.[66]

His historic home run, the first ever hit at Meiji Shrine Stadium, whistled through the air and landed in the center field bleachers.[67] The ball then rolled out of sight some hundred feet into a clump of trees, setting a record for the first and longest home run since the stadium opened.[68]

According to reports, the game was actually much closer than reflected by the final 9–1 score. It was still anyone's ball game after the sixth inning with a 2 to 0 score, but the Royal

Giants "blew the lid off" the game by scoring four runs in the seventh and then adding three more runs in the eighth. The Fresno club was able to get on the board in the ninth inning on a double by Jud Simons and a run batted in by pinch-hitter Sam Yamasaki.[69]

After the game it was reported that the Fresno Japanese would have a chance to "wreak their sweet revenge upon the boastful Colored nine" in a follow-up game scheduled for Friday.[70] Unfortunately, the game was rained out and never rescheduled. For the majority of players on both teams, they would have to wait until they returned to the U.S. for a rematch.

After the rained-out contest, each team went their separate ways to play the best semipro, industrial and college teams in the Japan, China, Korea and Hawaii. Both squads completed their respective tours with impressive winning records. The FAC finished with a 40–8–2 record, a solid .800 winning percentage. Playing against the same competition, the Philadelphia Royal Giants finished with a 35–2–1 record, an amazing .921 winning percentage.[71]

Perhaps more important than the wins and losses was the positive cross-cultural impact made by the tour. The Japanese players and fans were enamored with the Philadelphia Royal Giants, and the feeling was mutual. In Japan, both the Nisei and Negro players found sanctuary from the racism they faced back in America. And in the end, both teams were recognized by their Japanese hosts as true sportsmen and gracious ambassadors for the U.S. during the tour.[72]

In his book *Gentle Black Giants*, Japanese author and historian Kazuo Sayama credits the 1927 tour, especially Mackey and his Philadelphia Royal Giants teammates, as the inspiration for the start of professional baseball in Japan in 1936.[73] Sayama states that Japanese players and spectators knew about the racial segregation in professional sports in America and understood that, although they could not play in the Major Leagues, they were as good as, or even better than, the major league players. Saburo Yokozawa, a Japanese player, later described how the Royal Giants played each game gentlemanly, with warm pedagogical thoughtfulness toward the inexperienced Japanese players, while the All-American team (of 1934) sometimes treated the Japanese players with entertaining contempt during the actual games.[74]

This mutual respect is best exemplified in an exchange between Biz Mackey and a Japanese pitcher. Mackey was accidentally beaned with an inside pitch by a young Japanese player. The pitcher bowed to the burly switch-hitting catcher as a form of apology. Before taking his base, Mackey bowed back.[75]

Notes:

1. Kansas City Monarchs display, Negro Leagues Baseball Museum, Kansas City, MO.

19. "Star Jap Nine to Play Series Here," Los Angeles Times, September 6, 1925, A1.

20. "Fresno, 5; White Sox, 4," Los Angeles Times, September 7, 1925, 13.

21. Former Manzanar internee Rose Ochi recalls reading the headline "Japs Beat the Niggers." Email correspondence with Kerry Yo Nakagawa, May 30, 2006. Newspapers containing this headline have yet to surface.

22. Email correspondence with Glynn Martin, Executive Director, Los Angeles Police Historical Society, March 28, 2008.

23. McNeil, The California Winter League, 120.

24. "Sports of the Times," New York Times, Jun 3, 1956, 206.

25. Lincoln Sunday Star, January 31, 1926, A6.

26. "Shan Kilburn's Team to Tangle with FAC Team," Fresno Bee, February 7, 1926, 23.

27. "Hazelwood Defeat FAC in Fast Contest," Fresno Bee, February 8,

1926, 7.

28. "Japanese Baseball League Organized," Modesto News-Herald, March 6, 1926, II-1.

29. "Fresno Japanese Baseball Outfit Blanks Stockton," Fresno Bee, March 8, 1926, 7.

30. New Castle News (New Castle, PA), April 15, 1926, 19.

31. "Stockton Beats Fresno A.C. Team in Game Here, 8–6," Fresno Bee, May 3, 1926, 7.

32. "Fresno Athletic Club Beats Stockton Team in Japanese League, 5–2," Fresno Bee, May 10, 1926, 7.

33. "Sciots Win Game from F.A.C. by Score of 11 to 0," Fresno Bee, May

24, 1926, 8.

34. "FAC Defeats Sciot Ball Team by 8 to 3 Score, Fresno Bee, June 28, 1926, 11.

35. "Fresno All-Stars Beat Los Angeles Crack Team, 9 to 4," Fresno Bee, July 5, 1926, 10.

36. Ibid.

37. Interview with Kenso Zenimura, February 2008.

38. "Fresno All-Stars Win Again from L.A. Team, 4 to 3," Fresno Bee, July 6, 1926, 10.

39. Ibid.

40. "Postoffice Wins City League Flag," Fresno Bee, July 27, 1926, 13.

41. "Sako Holds the Printers to Two Hits," Fresno Bee, July 30, 1926, 13.

42. "Yoshikawa Hits Hard Enough to Beat Little Lake," Fresno Bee, August 3, 1926, 10.

43. "FAC Defeats Firemen's Team in Slugfest 14–11," Fresno Bee, July 26, 1926, 8.

44. "Around the Bases in the Twilight Leagues," Fresno Bee, August 25, 1926, 11.

45. "Fresno Athletic Club Loses to Alameda Pastim ers by 5–4 Count," Fresno Bee, October 4, 1926, 10.

46. "FAC Falls Before Pastimers from Capital City," Fresno Bee, October 11, 1926, 10.

47. "Fresno Fans to See Oakland's Best Here Today," Fresno Bee, October 31, 1926, 3D.

48. Ibid.

49. "Oakland Outfit Beats Locals in Fast Game, 5 to 4," Fresno Bee, November 1, 1926, 10.

50. "Stockton Pastimers Defeat FAC in Series Opener, 12 to 5," Fresno Bee, November 22, 1926, 10.

51. "Japanese Ball Club to Invade Orient Again," Fresno Bee, January 4, 1927, 10.

52. "Philadelphia Royal Giants Going to Japan," Rafu Shimpo, February 13, 1927.

53. Kazuo Sayama, Black Baseball Heroes: The Rise and Fall of the "Nigro League" (Tokyo, Japan: Chuo Shin sho, 1994), 11–12.

54. Email correspondence with Kyoko Yoshida, 2007.

55. Comment 144, Hall of Merit Discussion: Biz Mackey, BaseballThink Factory Blog, comment posted April 15, 2005, http://www.baseballthink factory. org/ files/hall_of_merit/discussion/biz_mackey/P100.

62. "Rikkyo Baseball Team to Visit Southern, Central, Northern Calif.,"

January 12, 2010 news release, http: //www.hokubei.com/en/news/2010/01/Rikkyo- Baseball-Team-Visit-Southern-Central-Norther- Calif.

63. "Fresno Japanese Plays Basketball 1st Game April 20," Japan Times, April 14, 1927, from the Harvey Iwata 1927 Tour Scrapbook, National Baseball Hall of Fame.

64. Email correspondence with Kyoko Yoshida, 2007.

65. "Royal Giants Swamp Fresno Japanese 9–1," Japan Times, April 21, 1927, from the Harvey Iwata 1927 Tour Scrapbook, National Baseball Hall of Fame.

66. Ibid.

67. Ibid.

68. Ibid.

69. Ibid.

70. Ibid.

71. Stephen Ellsesser, "Black Giants Were Treated Like Royalty,"

MLB.com, February 23, 2007, http://mlb.com/news/article.jsp?ymd=20070

223&content_id= 1812798 &vkey=news +mlb&fext=.jsp&cid=mlb.

72. "Royal Giants Won 26, Tied One on Their Japanese Tour," Chicago Defender, June 25, 1927, 9.

73. David King, "Finally Getting His Due," San Antonio Express-News, July 30, 2006, 1C.

74. Kazuo Sayama, Black Baseball Heroes: The Rise and Fall of the "Nigro League" (Tokyo, Japan: Chuo Shinsho, 1994), 11–12.

75. Stephen Ellsesser, "Black Giants Were Treated Like Royalty," MLB.com, February 23, 2007, http://mlb. com/news/article.jsp?ymd=20070223&content_id=1812798&vkey=news+mlb&fext=.jsp&cid=mlb.

*   *   *

Barnstorming the Empire: The 1927 Philadelphia Royal Giants Visit Colonial Korea

by Kyoko Yoshida

Editor's Note: The following article is based on a presentation delivered by Kyoko Yoshida, professor at Ritsumeikan University in Kyoto, Japan, during the "Playing Americas: Sports and Nations" session at The International American Studies Association 7th World Congress, The American Studies Association of Korea 50th International Conference, Seoul, South Korea, August 17-19, 2015.

In the spring of 1927, an all-star Negro baseball team named the Philadelphia Royal Giants embarked on a Goodwill Tour to Asia. Their journey included a total of 27 games against local teams in Japan and colonial Korea. This article will focus on the four games in Seoul. By taking a closer look at the context of the Seoul games, we see how this particular setting benefitted the Americans and the Japanese involved, and how baseball was instrumental in imposing Japanese supremacy in colonial Korea.

1927 Tour Overview

The 1927 Philadelphia Royal Giants was a joint team of the Philadelphia Royal Giants from the California Winter League and a local semi-professional Black team called the Los Angeles White Sox (also referred to as "Bear Cats" in the media), managed by Alonzo "Lonnie" Goodwin. The California Winter League was the first racially integrated professional baseball league in American history. It started in the early 20th century and continued on in Los Angeles in different configurations until 1947. From around 1920, it became a staple for the California Winter League to have an African-American team.

One such team was the Philadelphia Royal Giants, which in the late '20s and the early '30s, regularly conquered the league championship, overpowering the white teams comprised of active major and minor Leaguers. The winter season of 1926-27 was no exception. The team boasted a batting average of .360 and a fielding average of .980. The captain of the team was Raleigh "Biz" Mackey, often dubbed as the all-time best defensive catcher in the Negro League history. In 2006, Mackey and the Royal Giants' ace pitcher Andy Cooper were inducted into the Baseball Hall of Fame in Cooperstown.

The Royal Giants arrived at the port of Yokohama on March 29, 1927. The first game played in Japan, against Keio University's alumni club, took place on April 1 at the new Meiji Jingu Stadium in Tokyo. Mayor Hiromichi Nishikubo tossed the first ceremonial pitch. The Giants won 2-0. From then on, their schedule was filled; by the time they left Seoul on May 22, the Giants had played 27 games at 15 different ballparks—with 26 wins and 1 draw. They filled the stadiums everywhere they traveled. They enjoyed the tour so much that they would return to Japan in 1932 and '34.

Black, Strong and Modest

The Royal Giants could not have visited Japan at a better time than in the late 1920s: it was a period of mutual fascination between African-American leaders and Japanese opinion makers from a wide ideological spectrum. Figures such as W.E.B. Du Bois, James Weldon Johnson, and Marcus Garvey's infatuation with Japan is now well known thanks to reassessments by Reginald Kearney, Marc Gallicchio, Etsuko Taketani, and others.

The African American public viewed the Japanese both as a hope for colored people's ascendance to a prominent international position of power, and a fellow darker race in the struggle against white oppression. This mood was especially strong in Los Angeles where African Americans and Japanese immigrants lived and operated their business side by side in the newly expanding but tightly zoned city.

In the Japanese view, African Americans were the primary victims of racial discrimination in the United States, from which their own emigrants were also suffering. The indignation about the U.S. Immigration Act of 1924 was still much in the air.

In the field of baseball, the Japanese fans were well aware of the racial ban in the Major Leagues and thus viewed the Negro Leaguers' sportsmanship with much sympathy. Suishu Tobita (1886-1965), the manager of Waseda University's baseball team, who played a major role in defining the Japanese way of baseball in its early period, shared his impression of Negro League games during his tour in the United States in 1925:

> An incredible power of the pitcher, line drives like shooting stars into the bleachers—it
> is no less different from games at the Big Leagues. The slightest difference between is the

color of their skins, between Black and White. [....] Yet this difference subjugated the Blacks into slavery and made the Whites so vainly arrogant as to even expel the Yellows.

[....] American Indians are allowed to join the Big Leagues, but people of African race are not. Just because they are Black, they are never treated as human beings. And therefore, some of them told me that once a war broke out between Japan and the United States, they would be on the Japanese side. (Translation & emphasis mine)

Tobita's remark represents a widely shared sentiment at the time—so racial solidarity was the undeniable factor of the Giants' tremendous success in Japan. It was also a huge attraction: most people had never laid eyes on people of African descent, which partly explains why the further away they traveled from Tokyo, the more enthusiastic their reception was and the more space did local newspapers devote to the exploits of the Black athletes.

The earliest research on the barnstorming tour of the Royal Giants was conducted by Kazuo Sayama in the 1980s. His understanding of the Giants well summarizes the reason of their success in Japan: they were black, strong, and modest, contrary to the Major Leaguers who were white, strong, and arrogant. His conclusion is mostly based on letters written by the ailing Yasuo Shimazu reminiscing the games he played with black and white athletes back in the 1920s:

> Several baseball teams visited Japan in those days from abroad. College teams, semi-pros and professionals. Each impressed us. We could hardly expect to defeat any one of them. So it would have been too much expectation to hope for their uttermost sincerity in all games. [....] Some players [...] made several kinds of funny shows. Some danced around before the spectators, and made strange sounds like those made by fowls. The players themselves! Those were the last acts we expected of players. The Royal Giants didn't display these kinds of deeds. [....] A member of the Giants, whose name I forgot, said to me, 'I like Japan and I like the Japanese people. There is no racial barrier here. What a wonderful country! I would like to come back here again.' I believe that this was manifestation of the true heart. [...] I'd like to emphasize that the players of the Royal Giants were true Gentlemen. [....]
>
> We heard that, though they [the Royal Giants] were not major leaguers, they were as strong as, or stronger than, the majors. I myself played in some games against them, and saw many of their games here. I know it was true. But I'm still in wonder. [....] Why was it that we felt we could nearly win? We had the feeling after the game against the Giants that if we had tried a little harder, we could have won. In the games against the major leaguers, we were treated like children. We were at their mercy. We

could do nothing. Babies against grownups—that was the impression we had. But in the games against the Giants, the whole impression is quite different. [....] [A]s a whole, they could not have been so far away from the major leaguers. Then why was it that we almost always had close games? Was their batting not so good? Look, they blasted long hits when they were needed. They seemed to be able to hit as they wished. (Trans. by Sayama, Emphasis mine).

Sayama takes on Shimazu's simile of Japanese baseball as a baby and praises the Royal Giants' gentle handling of the fragile infancy of the sport in order to argue that their nurturing attitude encouraged the Japanese to found their first professional league as early as 1936.

The tour maintained a euphorically amicable mood overall. The team left Kobe on May 17, arrived in Busan the morning after and played a game each in Daegu and Busan before arriving in Seoul on May 20. The Royal Giants literally received a royal treatment in Seoul as well. They stayed at the Chosun Hotel, their parade was filmed for a newsreel, and two welcome banquets were held on May 20 and 21. And at the game on May 20, U.S. Consul General Ransford Stevens Miller (1867-1932) even honored the Negro Leaguers with a ceremonial first pitch. I wonder if there was another such example of American officials acknowledging the Negro Leaguers at the time. It seems as if the welcoming red carpet continued on all the way to Seoul, but here, the song of racial harmony ever so slightly changed its tone.

Barnstorming the Colony

The games were organized by the *Keijo Nippo [Kyungsung Iibo]*, the Japanese language newspaper authorized by the government-general. The number of pages it devoted to the Royal Giants prior and after the games were of no comparison to any other local media's attention in Japan. The evening before the first game in Seoul the *Keijo Nippo* published a greeting from manager Alonzo Goodwin. His long comment was captioned "Manager Goodwin Speaks / of His Respect for Japan, the Figurehead of the Colored Peoples":

"It's been our longtime dream and wish to come visit Japan, the leader of us the colored peoples. [....] On top of the excitement of visiting Japan, we were curious to see how advanced the Japanese were in the arts of baseball, and we had imagined ballparks would be like those in American countryside, but against our expectations, we were delightedly surprised first at the Meiji Jingu Athletic Field and then at the Koshien Stadium in Osaka, whose facilities were as equipped as major ballparks in the United States, and we were also impressed how refined the teams and fans were. This is something Americans should learn from.

This time, we are paying a visit to the Keijo Nippo office, the newspaper of authority, not only to expand our views, but also to promote further friendship between Japan and the United States through sports. We are especially pleased with our visit to Chosun particularly because we are well aware that Count Soejima, the president of the *Keijo Nippo*, has been invited by Chicago University [baseball team] to the United States [in 1925] and that he is exceptionally well informed about the Japan-U.S. relationship. Mr. Kojima of your Osaka branch office enlightened us much about baseball in Chosun in advance, and we've heard that Kyungsung has a beautifully equipped baseball ground and that there hasn't been any record of over-the-fence hit yet, so we are confident to make the first record there as we did at Koshien and Meiji Jingu Stadiums." (Translation & emphases mine)

Goodwin had made similar remarks earlier in Japan, but this mixture of joyful impressions, cultural diplomacy, and wishful embellishment on the side of the newspaper reporter takes on a different connotation against the colonial backdrop. Just like Tobita and Shimazu quoted unnamed African-American athletes to underline their innocent mutual respect, Goodwin's discourse could be utilized to promote the rhetoric of racial harmony in Greater Asia under the Japanese leadership.

While the *Keijo Nippo* promoted the tour's last showdowns in Seoul, the "strongest teams" were chosen to play against the invincible Royal Giants, and those teams turned out to be two Japanese clubs from the Yongsan Railway and the Industrial Bank, both chartered companies in close relationship with the government-general. Korean athletes were entirely excluded from the contests.

The game with the Industrial Bank at the Kyungsung Ground on May 20 became a stage for diplomatic sociability—President Ariga of the Industrial Bank and its board members, Mayor Umano, managers of the Yongsan Railway and other high-rank bureaucrats of the government-general attended the game along with Consul General Miller and Deputy Consul Stevens [sp?]. Students from the expat community were mobilized, too. The game was preceded by a release of 50 white doves by four soldiers and Miller's ceremonial first pitch.

Consul General Miller had started as a missionary in Japan and then joined the diplomatic staff in Tokyo in 1895. He was the Chief of Division of Far Eastern Affairs at the time of the annexation of Korea in 1910, and was assigned to Seoul as Consulate General in 1919, right after the March-First Movement. He was in favor of the government-general's conciliation or so-called "cultural" policy of "promoting educational and other cultural enterprises and of improving industrial conditions" along with the strengthening of the police force, all of which had resulted, in his opinion, in a "domestic peace in Chosen". The Kyungsung Ground ceremonial on May 20 was, therefore, a token of his cooperation with the Japanese conciliation policy.

The presence of Miller much affected the setup of the three games as it endorsed both the government-general and the Negro Leaguers. For the government-general, the games were a means to validate their brand of colonial internationalism, and to demonstrate the Japanese supremacy in and through baseball to the Japanese and Korean fans; for the Negro Leaguers, it was a singular opportunity to show off their presence, power, and pride.

The scores eloquently reveal what was at stake for the Giants: in all of the four games, the Giants beats the local Japanese teams with wide margins. 11-0 against Fusan on May 20, 22-4 against the Industrial Bank on May 21, 6-0 against the Yongsan Railway on 21, and 17-2 against the Yongsan Railway on 22. These results clearly suggest that the Giants didn't treat the Railway and Bank boys as fragile babies. And neither were these teams powerless nor unskilled like some of the small town teams. Chartered companies in the colonies had some of the best teams. Player employees were recruited from elite baseball colleges such as Keio and Waseda. The intended spectators that the Giants needed to impress had changed in Korea: it was not just the Japanese baseball fans anymore. The Giants had something different to prove in front of Miller and the other dignitaries.

Creating a National Myth through Baseball

The reasons for which Japan was so receptive to baseball when it was introduced in 1872 are still debated. Some argue that its rituals and duals between a pitcher and a batter suited the samurai ethic; others argue that it was its newness that attracted elite students of the Meiji Era. I'd like to argue that the American origin of the game helped the Japanese redefine their modern national identity.

It never left Japanese ballplayers' mind that the game was American. Precisely for this reason, Japanese teams repeatedly toured the United States to study the game and improve their skills. On the other hand, they had to control their fascination with the American sport by making agonizing efforts to establish a baseball of their own kind, a baseball imbued with a Japanese spirit, a baseball that would beat Americans. The game was a means for the Japanese to adopt and assimilate to the West and to distinguish themselves as a unique people at the same time.

Baseball played a similar role among the immigrants and ethnic minorities in the United States in the early twentieth century. It was a symbol of both assimilation and their ethnic pride. Playing baseball meant to be part of the nation-building. Therefore, the Negro League professional baseball before Jackie Robinson bears a special significance as a political act, a tool of protest and resistance, paving the way for the civil rights movement as many veteran Negro Leaguers contend. It is precisely at this cross-road of dual desire to assimilate with and distinguish oneself from the dominant culture that the Japanese ballplayers and Negro Leaguers shared in the series of games they played against each other.

In his survey on sport imperialism, sport sociologist Allen Guttmann concludes that Thorstein Veblen's notion of "emulation" explains the diffusion of modern Anglo sports to the rest of the world better than the Marxist theory of "cultural imperialism" or the Gramscian idea of "cultural hegemony."

"In sports, more often probably than in any other domain, […] [o]nce successful emulation has shattered the ludic monopoly, the literal or metaphorical colonials have a splendid opportunity to enhance their self-esteem[….] Simultaneously, one signals allegiance […] and superiority […]."

For Korean ballplayers, the situation was similar but more complex. Baseball was introduced by American missionary Philip Loring Gillett in 1905, but, "Even as early as 1910, many Koreans perceived baseball to be a Japanese game or, if not strictly a Japanese game, then certainly a game the Japanese had embraced and mastered to a degree worth emulating. [….] the sport became a way for [Koreans] to both appease and challenge their occupiers". As soon as baseball was introduced in Korea, the Japanese appropriated the sport, and the contest was not between the introducer of the game and the residents, as Guttmann argues, but between the colonial ruler who was better at the game, and the colonized who still had a lot to learn. On top of that, when the African-American Philadelphia Royal Giants played in Seoul, the colonial chartered companies, with the help of the American consulate, staged a spectacle of

American missionary Philip Loring Gillett introduced baseball to Korea in 1905 (Springfield College, Babson Library, Archives and Special Collections).

racial harmony, imperial internationalism and colonial cosmopolitanism, in the absence of Korean athletes.

The narrative this pageant portrays is parallel to the one the Japanese empire deceptively told Greater Asia and, above all, themselves. The American game helped shape not only the Japanese identity but also its empire.

*   *   *

Yakyukai Magazine, Tokyo, Japan
May 1927

The May 1927 issue of *Yakyukai* magazine is one of the rarest and most sought after Japanese baseball publications. Only a few surviving copies are known to exist. In 2011, a copy sold in an online auction for over $3,000. The following pages feature all of the photos from that prized issue.

O'Neal Pullen and Shinji Hamazaki on the cover of *Yakyukai* magazine. The Royal Giants kicked off their tour of Japan with a two-game series against Hamazaki's Mita Club on April 1-2 at Jingu Stadium. The Royal Giants won 2-0 and 10-6, respectively. This famous photo was taken during that series (Prestige Collectibles).

Caption reads: The practice of the black team; (top right) pitcher Andy Cooper in motion; (top left) catcher O'Neal Pullen; (bottom) batting practice at Jingu Stadium (Prestige Collectibles).

三塁對黑人二回戦
（上圖）第四回ダンカン
中右間二塁打に出で、
フォーゲン二塁に迫ら
れ、ディクソンの右犠牲
飛に本塁なつき捕手落
球に生還した刹那ペヘ下
岡（第六回、二死後満塁
となり村川の一塁強襲
に三谷還り、新川つゞ
いて本塁な強襲して死
す。

Caption reads: Mita vs. Royal Giants, second game. (top photo) In the 4th inning, Duncan hit a double to right-center field; Fagen advanced to third. Next, Dixon hit a sacrifice fly to right, and as the runner slid into home the catcher dropped the ball. (bottom photo) In the 6th inning, two out, bases loaded. Murakami hit it a hard shot to the first baseman and brought Mitsuya home. Nitta also tried to score but was called out at home (Prestige Collectibles).

When not on the field playing ball, or in the city as tourists, the Royal Giants enjoyed playing billiards at the hotel. Left to right: Evans, Cooper, Tucker and Johnson. (Prestige Collectibles).

Captions read: (top) Black Team in Japan. Mayor Nishikubo throws the first pitch; (middle) Tochigiyama (Kasugano: Sumo Room) and executives of Black Team. Tochigiyama third from the right in the back row; (bottom) Black Team before the game with Mita Club (Prestige Collectibles).

（で口入場球宮神）容陣の團球野人黑

Caption reads: **Black Baseball Team Lineup (at the entrance of Jingu Stadium) (Prestige Collectibles).**

野球

Appendix L: 1928, 1929 & 1931 Hawaiian Tours Scrapbook

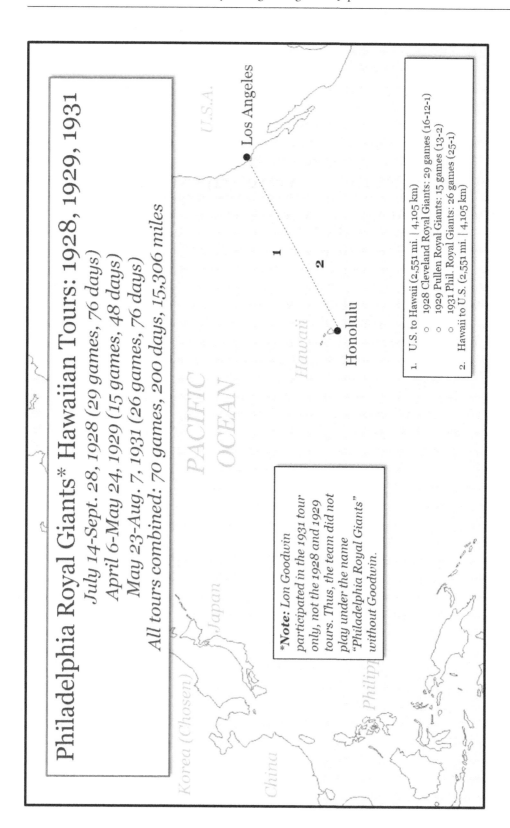

Philadelphia Royal Giants* Hawaiian Tours: 1928, 1929, 1931

July 14–Sept. 28, 1928 (29 games, 76 days)
April 6–May 24, 1929 (15 games, 48 days)
May 23–Aug. 7, 1931 (26 games, 76 days)
All tours combined: 70 games, 200 days, 15,306 miles

*Note: Lon Goodwin participated in the 1931 tour only, not the 1928 and 1929 tours. Thus, the team did not play under the name "Philadelphia Royal Giants" without Goodwin.

1. U.S. to Hawaii (2,551 mi. | 4,105 km)
    o   1928 Cleveland Royal Giants: 29 games (16-12-1)
    o   1929 Pullen Royal Giants: 15 games (13-2)
    o   1931 Phil. Royal Giants: 26 games (25-1)
2. Hawaii to U.S. (2,551 mi. | 4,105 km)

Los Angeles

Honolulu

U.S.A.

Hawaii

PACIFIC
OCEAN

Japan

Korea (Chosen)

China

S. S. City of Los Angeles Voyage 70 ___ *sailing from* ___ Los Angeles Harbor, California July 14th, 19 28.

No. on List.	NAME IN FULL. Family Name.	Given Name.	AGE. Yrs.	Mos.	Sex.	Married or Single	IF NATIVE OF UNITED STATES INSULAR POSSESSION OR IF NATIVE OF UNITED STATES, GIVE DATE AND PLACE OF BIRTH (CITY OR TOWN AND STATE).	IF NA
1	Alcaide	Frank	21		M	S	June 10, 1908	Honolulu, Hawaiian Islands	
2	Bullen	Leonard	21		M	S	Dec 25, 1906	New York City, New York	
3	Coles	Sam	30		M	S	Sept 5, 1899	Augusta, Ga	
4	Cade	Joe	27		M	S	Apr 5, 1901	Saint Louis, Mo	
5	Cooper	Samuel	30		M	M	Dec 5, 1897	New York City, New York	
6	Day	Connie	28		M	M	Dec 30, 1899	Lima, Ohio	
7	Evans	Alexander	33		M	M	Oct 17, 1895	Charleston, S.J.	
8	Eschright	Laura	43		F	M	Apr 10, 1885	Waterbury, Connecticut	
9	Eschright	Albert	2		M	S	Jan 25, 1926	Los Angeles, California	
10	Fagan	Robert	26		M	M	Mar 27, 1902	Terre Haute, Ind	
11	Guevara	Ernest	36		M	M	Mar 9, 1892	Santa Barbara, California	
12	Green	John	29		M	M	June 25, 1899	Galveston, Texas	
13	Hall	Alice	21		F	S	Oct 21, 1906	Honolulu, Hawaiian Islands	
14	Hennessey	James	44		M	M	Oct 12, 1883	Holden, Mass	
15	Ing	Clarence	28		F	M	Mar 8, 1900	Hilo, Hawaiian Islands	
16	Jenkins	Katurah	54		F	M	Dec 31, 1873	Springfield, Ohio	
17	Jenkins	William	64		M	M	June 18, 1863	Springfield, Ohio	
18	Morris	Harvey	27		M	M	Feb 24, 1901	Oakland, California	
19	Moore	Henry	37		M	M	Apr 20, 1890	New Orleans, La.	
20	Massey	Ivan	21		M	S	Mar 21, 1907	Elsinore, Mo	
21	Magurio	Takeo	20		M	S	Nov 21, 1905	Honolulu, Hawaiian Islands	
22	Pullen	O'Neal	34		M	M	Sept 8, 1894	Beamont, Texas	
23	Savage	Asel	30		M	S	Apr 16, 1897	Macon, Ga.	Distr
24	Schmidt	John	53		M	S	Dec 25, 1875		Ulste
25	Uyeno	Imao	23		M	S	Sept 27, 1905	Honolulu, Hawaiian Islands	
26	Walker	Jesse	24		M	M	Sept 10, 1904	Austin, Texas	
27	Zenimura	Kenso	1	2	M	S	May 16, 1927	Fresno, California	
28	Zenimura	Lillian	21		F	M	June 12, 1907	Fresno, California	
29	THIS LINE AND SUBSEQUENT LINES NOT USED								

Above is a partial record of the S.S. *City of Los Angeles* sailing to Honolulu in July 14, 1928. Among those on board are 10 members of the Royal Giants and the Zenimura family—Kenichi (not listed above), wife Lillian Kyoko, and infant son, Howard Kenso. Ninety years later, the stars would align for Kenso to write the foreword to this book about the Royal Giants (Honolulu, Hawaii, Passenger and Crew Lists, 1900-1959).

Honolulu Star-Bulletin
July 18, 1928

Source: Honolulu Star-Bulletin (Honolulu, Hawaii), July 18, 1928, pg. 8.

* * *

Honolulu Star-Bulletin
July 21, 1928

Source: Honolulu Star-Bulletin (Honolulu, Hawaii), July 21, 1928, pg. 11.

Honolulu Star-Bulletin
September 20, 1928

Royal Giants Sail Saturday
The Cleveland Giants Close Their Series of Games Here; a Popular Team

By Pete Doster

Yesterday marked the close of the series of games played at the Honoulu Stadium by the Cleveland Giants, the negro baseball team that has been furnishing much entertainment for baseball fans duing the past two months or more.

This is the second negro team that J. Ashman Beavan has brought to Honolulu to play against local teams. Both of them have won the larger portion of their games here.

The Cleveland Giants, who include in their ranks some of the players who visited here last year with the Philadelphia Royal Giants have been a popular team. The fact that the baseball season has been somewhat lengthy has cut down the attendance to a great extant, but the fans who still faithfully attend the games at the stadium seem to get a great deal of enjoyment from watching these negroes play baseball.

The Giants have played a total of 29 games. They have lost 12 of them, tied one, and won the remainder. They have furnished local baseball fans with much good entertainment, and whether or not they are as popular as the team that visited Honoulu last year, the fact remains that the baseball season has been better for their visit.

Source: Honolulu Star-Bulletin (Honolulu, Hawaii), September 20, 1928, pg. 58.

*   *   *

Honolulu Star-Advertiser
September 22, 1928

HOOMALIMALI, by Red McQueen

ALOHA CLEVELAND GIANTS

THE LASSCO liner City of Los Angeles take out the members of the Cleveland Giants team this morning. The Giants are returning to Los Angeles, their home town.

To every member of the squad, we say ALOHA. You have been in our midst for two months; you won more than half of your games. You did not get going until you dropped several encounters. After that, you came back and showed the fans that you were the goods.

Last year the Royal Giants were here. They, too, made a noble showing. After watching you fellows work in you first few games we, as well as the fans thought you would be a complete flop. You juggled your lineup several times until you hit a combination that worked like the money and certainly was a tough squad to down.

We have our doubts whether the Royal Giants were superior to you fellows. They were a more colorful team. In Mackey and Green, they had a duo that would decidely gain the favor of the fans in any town—and they were real ball players. Outside of these two boys, they didn't have a thing on you fellows.

Connie Day certainly will leave a host of friends here. In fact, everyone of you have Honolulu baseball world in your corner.

You were keen sports and took a couple of bad breaks in an honest-to-goodness sportsmanlike manner. Baseball will have to take the gate in favor of football. Our season is over and you fellows brought it to a very successful close.

So, so long, fellows! We would like to see you back here again next year for a series. Again ALOHA!

Source: Honolulu Star-Advertiser (Honolulu, Hawaii), September 22, 1928, pg. 10.

*   *   *

Honolulu Star-Bulletin
April 3, 1929

PULLEN GIANTS WILL INVADE HONOLULU FOR SERIES NEXT MONTH

Pullen's Giants, a team of colored baseball players, managed by O'Neal Pullen, will arrive here from the mainland next month for a series of games with Hawaii league teams. Players in group picture, left to right—O'Neal Pullen, c; Bert Dixon, cf; George Carr, 1b; Jess Walker, utility; Alex. Evans, p; Joe Cade, p; Sam Conley, p; Butch Spencer, lf; Buddy Anderson, rf. Players coming (not in picture)—John Beckwith, 3b; Connie Day, 2b; George W. Wilson, rf; Sung Dink, lf; Ping Gardner, p, and "Lefty" Shaw, p.

Source: Honolulu Star-Bulletin, April 3, 1929, pg. 10.

Honolulu Star-Bulletin
April 10, 1929

Source: Honolulu Star-Bulletin, April 10, 1929, pg. 10.

Honolulu Star-Bulletin
April 12, 1929

FANS WILL LIKE HIM HERE

Regularly makes "All-Star" rating as first baseman. Pullen says George Carr will show Honolulu fans some of the classiest initial sacking ever seen here. Atlantic City, N. J., is his regular big time team, and he was given permission to make the trip to Honolulu only on condition that he reports in good condition on June 1 when the regular league season opens at the famous Atlantic resort. You will talk about Carr long after the 1929 Giants series is a thing of the past. He throws right but, like Mackey, is a demon slugger with either left or right.

Source: Honolulu Star-Bulletin, April 12, 1929, pg. 19.

Honolulu Star-Bulletin
April 13, 1929

Pullen Giants Hit Port

THREE PULLEN GIANTS STARS—Left is "Butch" Spencer, outfielder who is doubling for Dixon. He showed plenty of class in practice yesterday. At center we have Alec Evans, hurling ace of both the '27 and '28 teams. Evans is enjoying one of his best seasons and is expected to divide the important mound assignments with "Ping" Gardner (right), who is reputed as one of the greatest colored pitchers in the business today.

"BUTCH" SPENCER

"PING" GARDNER

ALEC EVANS

Note: Outfielder Spencer Butcher is incorrectly called "Butch Spencer" above.

Source: Honolulu Star-Bulletin (Honolulu, Hawaii), April 13, 1929, pg. 10.

Honolulu Star-Bulletin
May 4, 1929

GIANT CAPTAIN HAS .419 MARK; MADE 3 HOMERS
Giants Way Ahead of Local Teams in Both Hitting and Fielding

By Loui Leong Hop

Raleigh Mackey, whose cudgel appears to have been loaded with T.N.T. and which exploded in the face of several of our best pitchers here, is leading Pullen & Co. team in individual bludgeoning with the healthy figure of .419 for the eight games which he played at the Honolulu Stadium, according to the data released this morning by William ("Bill") Rapoza, official scorer. Mackey spanked the apple for 13 hits in 31 treks to the rubber. Five of the 13 hits went for extra bases, distributed as follows: three home runs and two twin baggers.

Source: Honolulu Star-Bulletin (Honolulu, Hawaii), May 4, 1929, pg. 8.

*   *   *

Honolulu Star-Bulletin
May 17, 1929

PULLEN GIANTS BATTING RECORDS

		G	AB	R	H	TB	Pct.
Cooker	....	5	15	2	7	10	0.467
Mackey	....	14	53	13	21	36	0.396
Day	....	15	53	17	17	22	0.321
Walker	....	15	59	14	18	31	0.305
Pullen	....	14	64	8	18	24	0.281
Anderson	....	15	54	9	14	18	0.259
Gardner	....	5	16	2	4	6	0.250
Evans	....	7	26	4	6	10	0.231
Dunn	....	15	60	14	13	17	0.217
Carr	....	14	57	9	12	22	0.211
Butcher	....	14	50	11	8	11	0.160
Cade	....	5	18	1	2	5	0.111
Giants	....	**15**	**525**	**104**	**140**	**212**	**0.267**

Source: Honolulu Star-Bulletin (Honolulu, Hawaii), May 17, 1929, pg. 35.

Honolulu Star-Bulletin
April 14, 1929

Note: Cartoonist's Preview of the multi-cultural 1929 Hawaiian League.

Source: Honolulu Star-Bulletin, April 14, 1929, pg. 9.

Honolulu Star-Bulletin
May 17, 1929

Versatile Negro Ace Has Average of .396 For the 14 Games He Performed
Pullen Giants Batted .267 as a Team and Fielded .959; Anderson, Cooker Fielded Perfectly

By Loui Leong Hop

RALEIGH MACKEY, the versatile star with the Pullen Giants who completed an exhibition series in Honolulu Wednesday, will leave tomorrow on the City of Honolulu bound for the mainland with the best batting record. During the 14 games he played, Mackey made 21 hits in 53 times up for an average of .396. Of the total knocks he rapped out against local pitchers, four went for homers, three for double and 14 for singles.

During the 15-game series here, the Giants won 13 games, lost two. They have amassed a batting average of .267 collectively and fielded .959 as a unit. The only team to outhit the Giants was the Naval Air nine which collected 10 hits but went under a 10-0 beating.

Two Giants when through the series without an error. They are Buddy Anderson the hustling left gardner, and Sam Cooker, the saliva ball pitcher. Cooker led the pitchers in hitting, making seven smashines in 15 treks to the plan in the four games he played.

Source: Honolulu Star-Bulletin (Honolulu, Hawaii), May 17, 1929, pg. 10.

*   *   *

Honolulu Star-Advertiser
May 30, 1931

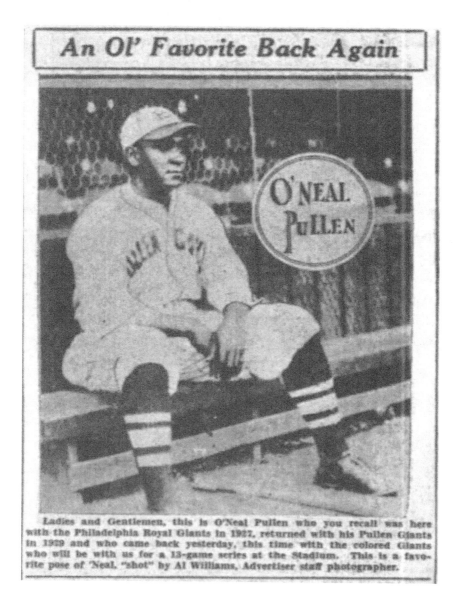

Source: *Honolulu Star-Advertiser (Honolulu, Hawaii), May 30, 1931, pg. 8.*

The Chicago Defender
July 4, 1931

Royal Giants Nip Hawaiian Braves 5-0
Ross Hurls U.S. Outfit to 8th Victory

(Chicago Defender Foreign News Service) HONOLULU, June 26. – Manager Lonnie Goodwin's Philadelphia Giants handed the Hawaiian Braves a 5 to 0 defeat here behind the good pitching of Ross, formerly of the Pittsburgh Homestead Grays. Ross gave up only four hits, one in the first, one in the second, one in the seventh and one in the ninth. The Giants got 12 bingles off the delivery of Nalua and Teetai, bunching for in the second inning to score four runs.

The Royal Giants arrived here from the United States on May 29 from Los Angeles, Calif., where they played in the Winter league. They defeated the Braves here in the first game, 5 to 4, the game going 12 innings. The Braves won the second game of the series by a score of 2 to 1. Andy Cooper was on the hill for the Giants and should have won the game but the breaks were against him.

This is the second time Goodwin has brought a club over here from the States, his first trip being in 1927 and at that time all the local fans thought he had the best club available. But the bunch he has with him this season far outclasses that of 1927.

Andy Cooper and Ted Shaw of the Detroit Stars and William Ross of the Homestead Grays are three of the leading hurlers with the team seen here since the days of Bullet Rogan. The Giants have played nine games, won eight and lost one. They won seven of them in a row, three being shutouts.

HAWAIIANS

	AB	R	H	P
Meyer c-rf..	4	0	0	1
Harrison cf .	3	0	1	4
Steward 2b.	4	0	1	1
Mark'm 1b-c	4	0	1	9
Gleason ss..	3	0	0	2
T. Nobriga 3b	4	0	1	1
A. No'a rf-1b	3	0	0	3
J. Kau lf ...	3	0	0	3
Nalau p-lf..	2	0	0	0
Teetai p....	0	0	0	0

(continued)

Pilka 3b	1	0	0	0
Totals ...	31	0	4	24

ROYAL GIANTS

	AB	R	H	P
Delgado cf.	3	1	1	2
Carr rf	3	0	2	2
Santaella 3b	4	0	2	0
Perez 2b ...	3	0	1	2
Dunn lf	6	1	2	3
Pullen c....	3	1	1	3
Bland ss...	4	1	1	1
Miranda 1b	3	1	0	11
Ross p.....	4	0	2	0
Cooper 1b..	0	0	0	3
Totals ...	33	5	12	27

Score by inning:

Hawaiians	0	0	0	0	0	0	0	0	0 = 0
Royal Giants	0	4	0	0	0	0	1	0	x = 5

Source: ROYAL GIANTS NIP HAWAIIAN BRAVES, 5-0, The Chicago Defender, July 4, 1931, pg. 9.

*   *   *

Honolulu Star-Bulletin
July 25, 1931

Lon Goodwin Recognized as Greatest Colored Baseball Team Manager

Boss of Giants Once Hurled and Slugger of Note
Since Becoming Manager Goodwin's Aim Has Been to Develop Players

Why is it that the Philadelphia Royal Giants are such a great team? Why is it that they pummel the ball so much harder than local players?

Why is it that they are so good defensively? Why do they beat some of our best teams by such overwhelming scores?

And yes, why this and what that? Well, folks take it easy and we'll tell you.

The reason, Lon Goodwin, recognized as the leading manager in the negro baseball universe. And remember some of the colored teams are just as good as the major leaguers.

Goodwin is 50 years old. He has played and managed ball teams in almost every part of the United States where they play high brand negro ball. He was a star player himself, and has developed some of the greatest colored ball players known. And he is still developing them and aims to do so always. Wonder then why the Giants are so powerful?

Likes California

Although Goodwin has been places, California is his choice and for that reason, he lives here. He played on the Waco Yellow Jackets for six years, beginning 1905. While there was a star pitcher and fine hitter.

From 1916 to 1920, Goodwin managed a semi-pro team in Los Angeles White Sox. And from 1929 to 1931, he managed the famous Philadelphia Royal Giants. During this decade the Giants won six out of seven pennants of the California Winter league.

And at one stage of its success, the team won 47 of 49 played. The team stacked up against major leaguers, make a great showing against them.

While in Honolulu in 1927, they lost only to the Chinese and Hawaiians in their series of games. And this year, 1931, the Asahis were the only ones to defeat them. The Giants also cleaned up in its barnstorming tour of Japan in 1927. In two trips to Hawaii, the Giants have won 36 of 39 games.

Some of the boys that he developed and have been seen by Honolulu fans are O'Neal Pullen, catcher; Raleigh Mackay, pitcher, catcher and infielder; Connie Day, second sacker; Ralph Dixon, the sensational center fielder; George Carr, first baseman, Andrew Cooper, Duncan of the 1927 team, and Bland, 1931 shortstop.

Developed Carr, Pullen

Pullen, in his prime was a much better backstop than now. George Carr, in his prime a couple years ago, was known as the colored "Babe Ruth," home run swatter.

Then Duncan, the catcher, was rated as one of the best catchers living. And as for Mackay, Connie Day and Ralph Dixon, fans who have seen them, need not be told that they are superb players.

Goodwin also developed Oscar Charleston, center fielder, and rated as good as the famous Tris Speaker, the While Eagle of the Cleveland team of the American league.

Charleston was a wonderful fly chaser and hitter, besides being fleet of foot.

Right now, Goodwin sees prospects in Bland and Dunn, star shortstop and outfielder on the team. He thinks they will fairly sparkle with a couple more seasons of right coaching and experience. Bland is 20 years old and was graduated this year from the University of Southern California.

Source: Lon Goodwin Recognized as Greatest Colored Baseball Team Manager, Honolulu Star-Bulletin (Honolulu, Hawaii), July 25, 1931, pg. 9.

*   *   *

Honolulu Star-Bulletin
July 31, 1931

Some Jabs

Lon Goodwin, manager of the Negro Giants, said that he never threw a ball game in his life and won't as long as he has any connection with the national pastime.

# # #

Of course, Lonnie was not referring to a certain person who went to him twice here and asked him to toss games. "What is a few hundred dollars made when you have a reputation to uphold?" Goodwin asks.

Source: Honolulu Star-Bulletin (Honolulu, Hawaii), July 31, 1931, pg. 40.

Presenting Manager Lon Goodwin's 1931 Negro Giants who made an auspicious local diamond debut by defeating Coach George Haneberg's Braves by the close count of 5 to 4 in a 12-inning battle waged yesterday afternoon at the Honolulu stadium. Today at 3:15 p. m., the Dixie diamond troupe will oppose Coach Jimmy Moriyama's Asahis, four-time champions of the Hawaii senior league, in the nightcap of the Sabbath doubleheader at the stadium. Kneeling left to right: Sanatella, Blaine, Miranda, Manager Lon Goodwin, Borges, Shaw, Ross, Bralee. Standing: Pullen, Perez, Carr, Cooper, Gonzalez, Delgado, Dunn.

The 1931 Royal Giants included future Hall of Famer Andy Cooper and former Boston Red Sox infielder Miguel Gonzales —one of the few players to join a Negro Leagues team after leaving the major leagues (Nippu Jiji, May 31, 1931, pg. 12).

Honolulu Star-Bulletin
July 22, 1931

Dunn Best Giant Hitter

GIANT SERIES — HAWAII LEAGUE

Individual Batting

	G	AB	R	H	2B	3B	HR	TB	SH	SB	BB	SO	HP	Pct.
Dunn	16	71	18	30	6	2	2	46	1	4	2	8	0	0.423
Santaella	17	71	17	24	3	3	1	36	0	5	10	3	2	0.338
Pullen	16	66	8	22	3	2	1	32	0	2	6	3	0	0.333
Perez	18	76	20	23	4	1	1	32	1	12	5	4	0	0.303
Shaw	9	18	3	5	1	0	1	6	1	0	3	3	0	0.278
Bland	17	67	11	18	3	1	0	26	0	5	3	8	0	0.269
Miranda	18	63	7	15	2	1	0	19	1	2	5	2	2	0.238
Borges	13	42	11	10	2	0	0	12	5	3	8	4	3	0.238
Gonzales	5	21	1	5	1	0	3	6	0	2	1	4	0	0.238
Carr	12	43	9	10	1	1	0	22	0	1	2	5	1	0.233
Delgado	16	79	14	18	2	2	0	24	1	2	9	6	3	0.228
Ross	7	26	0	5	1	0	0	6	0	1	0	10	0	0.192
Cooper	9	23	1	2	0	0	0	2	1	0	2	7	0	0.087
Brulee	2	5	0	0	0	0	0	0	0	0	1	1	0	0.000
Giants	18	671	120	187	29	13	9	269	11	39	57	68	11	0.279

Individual Fielding

	G	PO	A	E	TC	Pct.
Dunn	16	20	7	0	27	1.000
Shaw	9	2	8	0	10	1.000
Gonzalez	5	18	5	0	23	1.000
Brulee	2	4	0	0	4	1.000
Pullen	16	110	10	1	121	0.992
Miranda	18	186	7	3	196	0.985
Perez	18	61	72	4	137	0.971
Delgado	16	23	0	1	24	0.958
Cooper	9	3	12	1	16	0.938
Borges	13	13	1	1	15	0.933
Santaella	17	26	39	8	73	0.890
Bland	17	23	32	8	63	0.873
Carr	12	17	8	4	29	0.862
Ross	7	0	13	3	16	0.813
Giants	18	506	214	34	754	0.955

Source: Honolulu Star-Bulletin (Honolulu, Hawaii), July 22, 1931, pg. 8.

Honolulu Star-Advertiser
August 1, 1931

'Big Hips' Shaw and His Boss

Action photo of Ted Shaw, southpaw pitcher of the Los Angeles Negro Giants, one of the best ever to show in these islands. The insert below is Lon Goodwin, manager of the team and an old ball player himself. The Giants sail today for America.—Photo by Al Williams.

Source: Honolulu Star-Advertiser (Honolulu, Hawaii), Aug 1, 1931, pg. 8.

Honolulu Star-Bulletin
July 28, 1938

Long Hops with Loui

They're still talking about that baseball turnout last Sunday afternoon at the Honolulu Stadium. In point of paid admissions it was the seventh largest in the history of the stadium.

The major league all-stars brought here in 1931 by Herb Hunter set the record at slightly over 9,200. Last Sunday's crowd totaled 6,040 customers. The second biggest paid attendance was registered in 1934 when Connie Mack's stars performed here. There was a turnout of 8,186. Babe Ruth's visit in 1933, sponsored by Herb Hunter, drew the third largest house, 8,171 ... The Philadelphia Royal Giants of 1927, in their opening tussle, lured 6,865 through the gates for the sixth largest gate. Incidentally, the colored diamondeers of Raleigh Mackay, O'Neil Pullen, Jack Dixon & Co. brought 25,702 customers to the ball orchard in six games. Following are the figures on single game and six game series crowds:

YEAR	TEAM	SINGLE GAME	SERIES TOTAL
1927	Royal Giants	6,065	25,702
1927	Waseda University	5,372	19,039
1927	Manila All-Star	4,157	13,746
1928	Keio University	7,867	29,070
1928	Royal Giants	4,076	15,778
1929	Royal Giants	4,271	14,689
1929	Hosei University	3,386	11,799
1931	Hunter's Major Leaguers	9,200	9,200
1932	Rikkyo University	2,287	8,721
1932	Waseda University	6,098	19,421
1933	Santo Tomas	4,867	13,753
1933	Kwansai University	2,458	10,113
1933	Babe Ruth exhibition	8,171	8,171
1934	Connie Mack's Stars	8,186	8,186
1934	Meiji University	5,504	13,014
1935	Dai Nippons	5,040	15,814
1936	Kwansai University	2,994	9,820
	TOTAL		229,688

The above data was compiled by J. Ashman Beaven, director and superintendent of the stadium.

Source: Honolulu Star-Bulletin (Honolulu, Hawaii), July 28, 1938, pg. 10.

野球

Appendix M: 1932-33 Tour Scrapbook (Hawaii, Japan, Korea, China, Philippines)

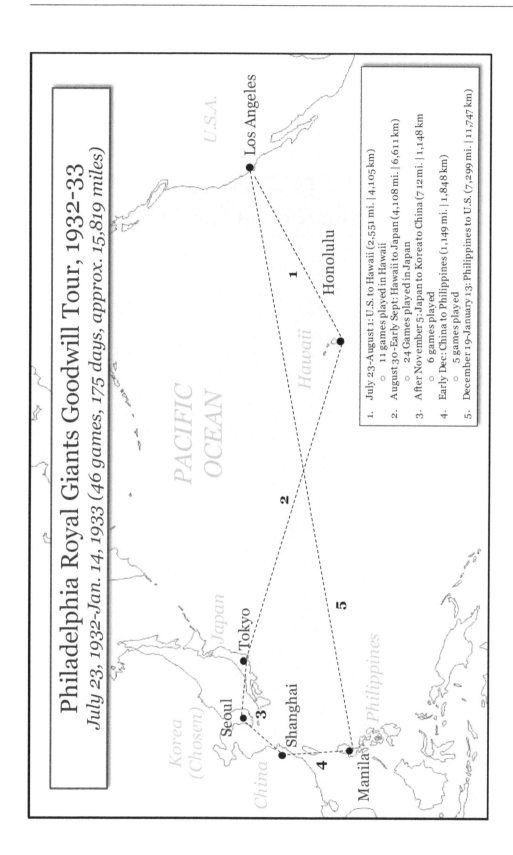

Philadelphia Royal Giants Goodwill Tour, 1932-33

July 23, 1932-Jan. 14, 1933 (46 games, 175 days, approx. 15,819 miles)

U.S.A.

Los Angeles

PACIFIC OCEAN

Hawaii

Honolulu

1

2

5

Japan

Tokyo

Korea (Chosen)

Seoul

3

Shanghai

China

4

Manila

Philippines

1. July 23-August 1: U.S. to Hawaii (2,551 mi. | 4,105 km)
   o 11 games played in Hawaii
2. August 30-Early Sept: Hawaii to Japan (4,108 mi. | 6,611 km)
   o 24 Games played in Japan
3. After November 5: Japan to Korea to China (712 mi. | 1,148 km)
   o 6 games played
4. Early Dec: China to Philippines (1,149 mi. | 1,848 km)
   o 5 games played
5. December 19-January 13: Philippines to U.S. (7,299 mi. | 11,747 km)

Passenger Ship Record Summary: 1932-33 Philadelphia Royal Giants

Family Name	Given Name	Age	Sex	Married or Single	If native of US, Date and Place of Birth	Address in US
Baker	Julius Miller	35	M	M	January 11, 1897, Gallantin, Tenn.	1721 E. 53rd St., Los Angeles, Calif.
Bland	Alfred Peter	20	M	S	September 10, 1908, New Orleans, LA	726 E. 52nd St., Los Angeles, Calif.
Carr	George Henry	36	M	M	September 2, 1896, Atlanta, Georgia	1465 Hooper Ave., Los Angeles, Calif.
Cooper	Andrew Lewis	36	M	S	April 24, 1896, Waco, Texas	811 E. 31st St., Los Angeles, Calif.
Delgado	Clemente Cruz	27	M	S	1906, Havana, Cuba	n/a
Evans	Alexander	38	M	M	October 17, 1894, Charleston, S.C.	1322 3/4 E. Adams St., Los Angeles, Calif.
Gamiz-Ramirez	Virginio	34	M	S	1899, Havana, Cuba	n/a
Goodwin	Lon A.	54	M	M	March, 15, 1879, Austin, Texas.	1424 E. Adams St., Los Angeles, Calif.
Hardin	Halley Claire	28	M	S	November 13, 1904, Wichita, Kansas	900 E. Adams St., Los Angeles, Calif.
Mackey	Raleigh	38	M	S	July 27, 1899, San Antonio, Texas	1127 E. 27th St., Los Angeles, Calif.
Martin	Wilson	33	M	M	Feb 12, 1899, Cairo, Illinois.	671 Willow St., San Francisco
Noda	Gikaku	40	M	M	Feb 16, 1892, Honolulu, Hawaii	
Perez	Javier	25	M	M	1908, Havana, Cuba	n/a
Ross	William	38	M	M	October 5, 1893, Corrigan, Texas	1372 E. 21st St., Los Angeles, Calif.

The Royal Giants and the Mitsuhiko Fujita Baseball Collection

On Saturday, November 5, 1932, the Philadelphia Royal Giants defeated the Kobe Diamond Club, 8-3, at the Kobe Ground. Among the fans that day was 21-year-old Mitsuhiko Fujita, a baseball enthusiast whose hobbies included taking photos at ballgames, having the images developed the same day, and returning to the ball park to have them signed by the players.

At this game he captured over a dozen images of the Philadelphia Royal Giants, and even had a ball signed by the team. In 2007, Fujita's family auctioned off his baseball collection, and for the first time the world was able to view his treasured baseball memories. Several of those images are featured throughout this chapter, courtesy of Sotheby's.

Below is a brief profile of Fujita from the Sotheby's catalog, *Important Sports Memorabilia and Cards, New York, June 5, 2007*:

"Born into the distinguished family of his grandfather Baron Denzaburo Fujita in 1911, Mitsuhiko Fujita grew up watching and playing baseball in Kobe, Japan. Through his grandfather's connections, young Mitsuhiko gained access to many areas in which the general public was not allowed. Always taking his camera on the ball field, Mitsuhiko took many photographs of Japanese baseball players and American Tour Team players ... He loved baseball to the very end of his life, cherishing these unique items that he collected, which still present an unparalleled window into the most glorious eras of both Japanese and American Baseball in Japan."

Photos of young Mitsuhiko Fujita (Sotheby's).

From the Mitsuhiko Fujita collectin, the Royal Giants pose for a team photo as Japanese fans look on. *Left to right:* (Back row) Halley Harding, Alfred Bland, Andy Cooper, George Carr, Lon Goodwin, Javier Perez, Stack Martin, Alexander Evans, and William Ross; (Front row) Steere Noda, Mizoguchi, Raleigh Mackey, Virginio "Chico" Gamiz, Clemente Delgado, and Jesse Baker (Sotheby's).

Hawai Hōchi, Honolulu, Hawaii
August 8, 1932

ROYAL GIANTS TRIM ASAHIS EASILY BY 5 TO 1

"... Among the features of yesterday's game was the playing of Raleigh Mackey in nine positions, from catcher to infield to outfield to pitcher."

GIANTS

	AB	R	BH	PO	A	E
Chico, 3b, c	4	1	0	4	2	0
Carr, 1b, 2b	4	0	1	0	1	0
Delgado, cf, lf	4	0	0	1	0	0
Mackey c, 1b, 2b, 3b, ss, lf, cf, rf, p	5	1	3	2	2	0
Perez, 2b, c	5	1	3	2	2	0
Martin, rf, c	4	0	0	4	1	0
Harding, lf, ss	4	1	1	2	1	0
Bland, ss, 3b	4	1	1	2	2	0
Ross, p	4	0	2	0	0	1
Baker, c	0	0	0	1	0	0
Totals	38	5	11	27	11	1

ASAHIS

	AB	R	BH	PO	A	E
Nakayama, lf	4	1	1	4	0	0
Itoga, rf	4	0	1	1	0	0
Enomoto, ss	4	0	1	2	2	0
Nakamichi, lf	3	0	0	1	0	0
Mamiya, 1b	4	0	1	11	0	2
Shinegawa, 3b	3	0	0	0	0	0
Yoshioka, c	3	0	0	4	1	0
Manabe, 2b	3	0	0	4	2	0
Shibata, p	2	0	1	0	1	0
S. Kameda, p	0	0	0	0	0	0
Matsuno, p	1	0	0	0	0	1
Totals	38	1	5	27	6	3

Score by inning:
Giants . . . . 1 2 0 0 1 0 0 0 1 = 5
Asahis . . . . 0 0 0 0 0 1 0 0 0 = 1

Sources: Article: Hawai Hōchi (Honolulu, Hawaii), August 8, 1932, pg. 12.
Box score: The Honolulu Advertiser, August 8, 1932, pg. 7.

Biz Mackey in batting practice, from the Mitsuhiko Fujita collection (Sotheby's).

Honolulu Star-Advertiser
August 16, 1932

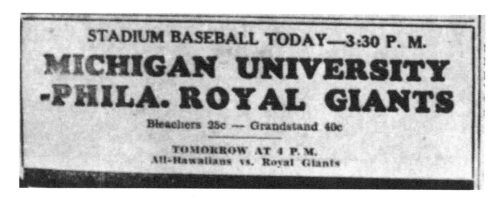

Source: Honolulu Star-Advertiser (Honolulu, Hawaii), August 16, 1932, pg. 18.

*   *   *

Honolulu Star-Bulletin
August 17, 1932

GIANTS TAKE ON HAWAIIANS IN 7TH GAME

The Royal Giants are scheduled to play their seventh game against members of the Hawaii league circuit this afternoon at 4 o'clock at the Honolulu stadium when they meet the All-Hawaiians for the second time.

In their last tangle, the colored stars bumped off the Native Sons when Andy (Smiling) Cooper limited them to but three hits.

Mr. Cooper was beaten by the University of Michigan nine Tuesday and indications are that Right Hander Evans will do the chucking for the Giants this afternoon.

Charlie Teetai will probably receive the pitching assignment from Boss Lang Akana.

Source: Honolulu Star-Bulletin (Honolulu, Hawaii), August 17, 1932, pg. 22.

*   *   *

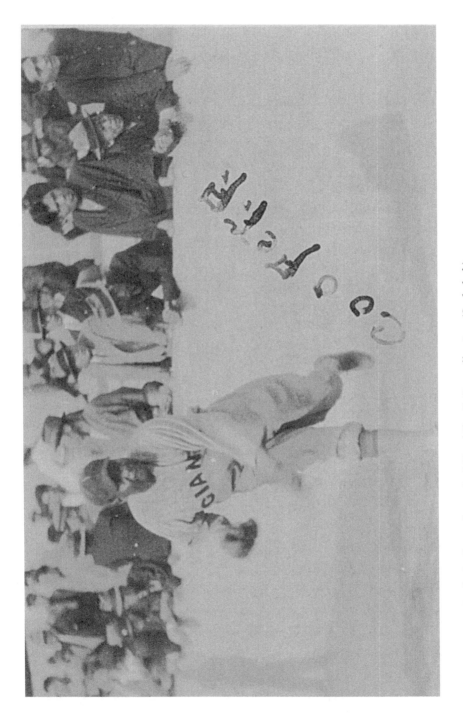

Andy Cooper warming up in the bullpen, from the Mitsuhiko Fujita collection (Sotheby's).

Philadelphia Tribune
September 8, 1932

Nine Straight For Royal Gts. Over Haw'ians

HONOLULU, Hawaii. – Lonnie Goodwin and his Philadelphia Royal Giants have just finished their nine-game series here and they won every game. They proved too much for the boys of the Island. The Giants have one of the best clubs that has ever played on these islands and when we say this we are not forgetting the American All-Stars played here last year after the World Series. In Cooper, Ross and Evans the Giants are well taken care of in the pitching department, and all other positions are well taken care of by some of the best in the business.

The line-up and batting percentages of the players are as follows:

Name, Position	AB	H	Pct.
Hallie Hardin, ss	42	12	.285
George Carr, 1b	38	16	.421
V. Checo, rf	33	11	.333
Rauligh Mackey, c	42	20	.476
J. Perez, 2b	39	17	.436
Stack Martin, lf	36	11	.306
Clemente Delgardo, cf	36	9	.250
Alfred Bland, 3b	40	13	.325
Andrew Cooper, p	15	4	.267
Slow Time Evan, p	7	0	.000
William Ross, p	11	4	.364
Baker, utility	8	3	.375

Will tour the Orient

The Giants were scheduled to sail for Japan on August 30, where they will play 20 games. They also played 10 Games in China and then sail for the Philippine Islands where they will play 30 games. It will be sometime next year before the Giants return to Los Angeles, California. Anyone wishing to get in touch with any member of the team may reach him at the Joshuya Hotel Yokohama, Japan.

Source: Nine Straight for Royal Gts. Over Haw'ians, Philadelphia Tribune, September 8, 1932, pg. 9.

Biz Mackey (top) and Lon Goodwin (bottom), from the Mitsuhiko Fujita collection (Sotheby's).

The Chicago Defender
September 10, 1932

PHILLY GIANTS UNDEFEATED ON HAWAIIAN SOIL

```
                                       R. H. E.
Giants .........033 100 020—9 12  2
Navy ..........000 000 010—1  8  5
   Batteries—Cooper and Mackel; Pa-
terson and Wills.
                                       R. H. E.
Giants .........110 120 000—5  9  2
Wanderers ......010 010 100—3  7  3
   Batteries — Evans and Mackey;
Shaw and Heiser.
                                       R. H. E.
Giants .........120 010 001—5 11  1
Asahis .........000 001 000—1  5  3
   Batteries—Ross and Mackey; Shi-
bata, Wameda and Yoshioka.
                                       R. H. E.
Giants .........000 040 102—7  9  0
Hawaiians ......000 000 010—1  3  4
   Batteries—Cooper and Mackey; Teti
and Morris.
                                       R. H. E.
Giants .........110 010 000—3  8  0
Chinese .........000 000 000—0  5  1
   Batteries — Evans and Mackey;
Keer and Chai.
                                       R. H. E.
Giants .........300 040 140—12 17  0
Braves .........100 000 200— 3  7  2
   Batteries—Ross and Mackey; Jac-
kuki and Cabrinha.
                                       R. H. E.
Giants .........012 000 003—6 10  3
Navy ..........020 000 021—5  7  4
   Batteries—Ross and Baker; Scher-
ruble and Downs.
                                       R. H. E.
Giants .........000 330 300—9 10  2
Braves .........000 000 000—0  6  3
   Batteries — Cooper and Mackey;
Williams and Cabrinha.
                                       R. H. E.
Giants .........000 000 001—1  4  0
Hawaiians ......000 000 000—0  1  0
   Batteries—Ross and Mackey; Tee-
tia and Meyer.
```

Source: Philly Giants Undefeated on Hawaiian Soil, The Chicago Defender, September 10, 1932, pg. 9.

Andy Cooper and William Ross (top), Alexander Evans and Alfred Bland (bottom), from the Mitsuhiko Fujita collection (Sotheby's).

Royal Giants 1932 Tour Schedule & Game Results in Japan

DATE	LOCATION	OPPONENT	SCORE
9/13	Yokohama Park Stadium	Yokohama Commercial H.S. OB Club	5 -3
9/18	Totsuka Ground	Tomon Club	10-7
9/18	Yokosuka Naval Port Mikasa Ground	Kashima Club	4x-1
9/19	Odawara Komine Ground	Unknown	13-1
9/20	Jingu Stadium	Mita Club	6x-5
9/25	Star Ground	Kumagaya Star Club	8-4
10/1	Takarazuka Ground*	Osaka Railway Office	5x-3
10/2	Takarazuka Ground*	Star Club	11x-1
10/2	Takarazuka Ground*	Kansai Mita Club	5x-0
10/4	Kurashiki Ground	Yonago Railway Office	10x-2
10/5	Chugoku Ground	Hiroshima Tobacco & Salt	3-4
10/5	Unknown	Moji Railway Office	9x-1
10/8	Keijo Ground	Korean Telegram & Telephone	3x-1
10/14	Chofu Ground	Moji Railway Office	5x-1
10/15	Suizenji Ground	Kumamoto Railway Office	15x-2
10/17	Otani Ground	Yahata Steel	16x-2
10/18	Unknown	Yahata Steel	10x-3
10/20	Meizen Middle School	All Kurume	28x5
10/22	Beppu Ground	Moji Railway Office	18x-2
10/26	Kokura Ground	Moji Railway Office	9x-7
10/27	Shin-Kashii Ground	Yahata Steel	19x-5
11/3	Neyagawa Ground	Kansai Sundai Club	13x-2
11/3	Unknown Kansai	Mita Club	20x-0
11/5	Kobe Ground**	Kobe Diamond	8-3

* See ticket for these games on next page.
** The day of Mitsuhiko Fujita's photographs.

Source: Compiled by Kyoko Yoshida, from Sayama publications 1986 and 1994.

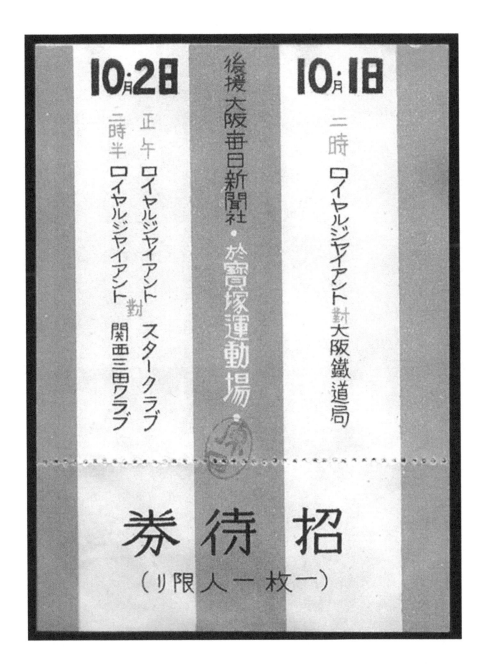

Unused ticket from the 1932 Philadelphia Royal Giants Tour of Japan. This ticket is for the games against the Osaka Railway Club and Mita Club held on October 1 and October 2 at the Takarazuka Ground. Translation by Kyoko Yoshida (PrestigeCollectibles.com).

Halley Harding (top), Virginio "Chicho" Gamiz and Javier Perez (bottom), from the Mitsuhiko Fujita collection (Sotheby's).

The Chicago Defender
December 10, 1932

Royal Giants Are Home From Japan

Manila, P.I., December 1 – Lon Goodwin and his Philadelphia Royal Giants, who have been playing baseball for the past two months in Japan, China and Chosen, sail today with one of the best records ever established in Japan. They played 30 games and only lost one, which is far better than any records set here before. They defeated the best teams with ease that could possibly be put together over here. They proved far too much for any team that meant.

The only game they lost was 10 innings, 4 to 3, and Pereze [sic], their second baseman, pitched the game. Their pitching staff, Ross, Cooper and Evans, was all anyone could wish. Ross seemed to be unbeatable, having won 16 straight games since the club sailed from the states. He won five straight shutouts and fanned 63 batters in his last five games. They will play in Manila until the latter part of January.

Home Soon

They will sail for Los Angeles, Calif., where they will play winter ball. The batting record of each member of the club includes 30 Games in Japan, China and Chosen, and 11 in Hawaii, 41 and all:

How They Hit

Harding, ss	.321	Bland, 3b	.298
Chico, rf	.333	Delgado, cf	.296
Carr, 1b	.355	Cooper, p	.342
Mackey, c	.388	Evans, p	.203
Perez, 2b	.362	Baker, c	.275
Martin, lf	.362	Ross, p	.331

Source: Royal Giants Are Home From Japan, The Chicago Defender, December 10, 1932, pg. 11.

Clemente Delgado and George Carr (top), Wilson "Stack" Martin and Julius Baker (bottom), from the Mitsuhiko Fujita collection (Sotheby's).

The Chicago Defender
January 14, 1933

PHILLY GIANTS COP MANILA BASEBALL TITLE
COOPER'S ARM GIVES 'EM WIN IN FINAL GAME
RECORD CROWD SEES FIVE CONTESTS

Manila, Philippines. January 13—Battering Bertulfo and Bautista, All-Filipino hurlers, for a total of 14 hits, which included three doubles, the Philadelphia Royal Giants, on a barnstorming tour of the far east, Sunday wound up their five-game series with the Philippine Baseball league without a defeat. Yesterday's score: Giants 8, All-Filipinos 2.

Casimiro Francisco, All-Filipino left fielder, was taken to the Philippine General Hospital after severely wrenching his right hip in the first inning straining after a fly ball hit into left by Harding, lead off man for the Giants, in the last half of the first. Casimiro will be X-rayed this morning as it was too badly swollen yesterday to allow an X-ray to be taken.

Some 6,500 spectators yesterday watched the Giants drive out at least one hit in every inning except the fifth. Bertulfo was yanked after 5 1/3 innings in which time the Giants nicked his offering for nine hits and six runs. Bautista fared a little better, the Giants pounding him for five hits, which meant an additional brace of runs for them.

ALL FILIPINOS

	AB	R	H	P
Tiangro lf..	3	1	0	3
Casimiro lf.	1	0	0	0
Cruz 3b	4	0	1	0
Saberon c ...	4	0	0	3
Rivera cf ...	4	1	3	3
Estorba rf ..	4	0	0	3
Diser 2b	4	0	1	3
Escamos 1b ..	1	0	0	2
Regia 1b	3	0	1	6
Bernales ss.	3	0	1	1
Bautista p ..	1	0	0	0
Bertulfo p ..	2	0	0	0
Totals ...	34	2	7	24

ROYAL GIANTS

	AB	R	H	P
Harding ss.	4	1	1	3
Gomez rf ...	5	1	2	0
Carr 1b	3	1	0	9
Mackey c ..	3	0	3	4
Perez 2b ...	5	1	1	4
Martin lf ..	5	2	2	3
Bland 3b ...	4	0	0	1
Delgado cf ..	4	2	2	2
Cooper p ...	4	0	3	1
Totals ...	37	8	14	27

Score by inning:

All Filipinos   0 0 0 1 0 0 0 1 0 = 2
Royal Giants   0 2 2 0 0 2 0 2 x = 8

Source: Philly Giants Cop Manila Baseball Title, The Chicago Defender, January 14, 1933, pg. 11.

*   *   *

Baseball signed by the 1932 Philadelphia Royal Giants, from the Mitsuhiko Fujita collection (Sotheby's).

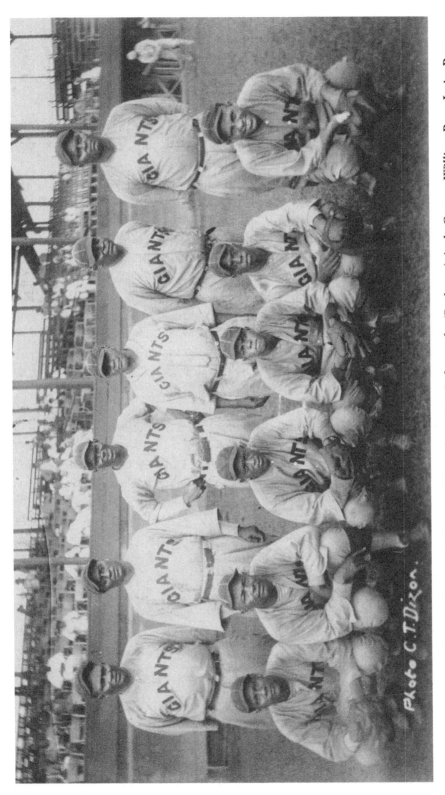

The Philadelphia Royal Giants in Manila, Philippines, December 1932. *Left to right:* (Back row) Andy Cooper, William Ross, Javier Perez, Lon Goodwin, George Carr, Biz Mackey; (Front row) Clemente Delgado, Alexander Evans, Julius Baker, Alfred Bland, Chico Gamiz, and Halley Harding. Not pictured: Stack Martin (Christies.com).

Afro-American
February 4, 1933

Royal Giants Nine Return to U.S. with Only Two Defeats in 52 Games
Bizz Mackey, Hallie Harding, Andy Cooper Among Those Returning

LOS ANGELES, (WS) — The Philadelphia Royal Giants baseball tossers returned to the United States last week after a lengthy trip to the Orienty where they won 49 games, lost two and tied one.

The trip which lasted for six months, carried them to Hawaii, Japan, Korea, and the Philippine Islands. The team won eight games and lost one in Honolulu. The lone loss sustained was at the hand of the University of Michigan team which stopped there on its trip to the Orient. In Hilo (Hawaiian Islands) they won two and lost none; in Japan they won 28 and lost one at (at Hiroshima); in Manila they won 9 and tied one, and in Korea won two and lost none.

Players who made the trip are: Hallie Harding, shortstop; George Carr, one time first baseman for the Bacharach Giants; Bizz Mackey, hard-hitting catcher of Hilldale; Wilson Martin, left fielder of the Indianapolis A.B.C.; Alfred Bland, third baseman from New Orleans University; Andy Cooper, pitcher of the Kansas City Monarchs; Roy Evans, pitcher; Nagadoches Ross, pitcher of the Homestead Grays; and Baker, a catcher.

TWO GET JOBS
Bland, Third Baseman, Gets Post Teaching Chemistry at Manila School

All of the players returned to the States except Martin and Bland. The former secured work at the Cavite Navy Yard near Manila, and Bland, who is a graduate of New Orleans University, and at the time of the departure was a student at the University of Southern California, has secured a position as assistant professor of chemistry at the University of Santo Tomas in Manila.

The Giants are scheduled to play a series of baseball games with the El Paso Mexicans at the White Sox park here. The Mexican team finished second in the winter league last season and was only beaten consistently by Tom Wilson's Elite Giants. After the series there may be another with Joe Pirrone's All-Stars.

Source: Royal Giants Nine Return to U.S. with Only Two Defeats in 52 Games, Afro-American, February 4, 1933, pg. 16.

野球

Appendix N: 1933-34 Tour Scrapbook (Japan, China, Philippines, Hawaii)

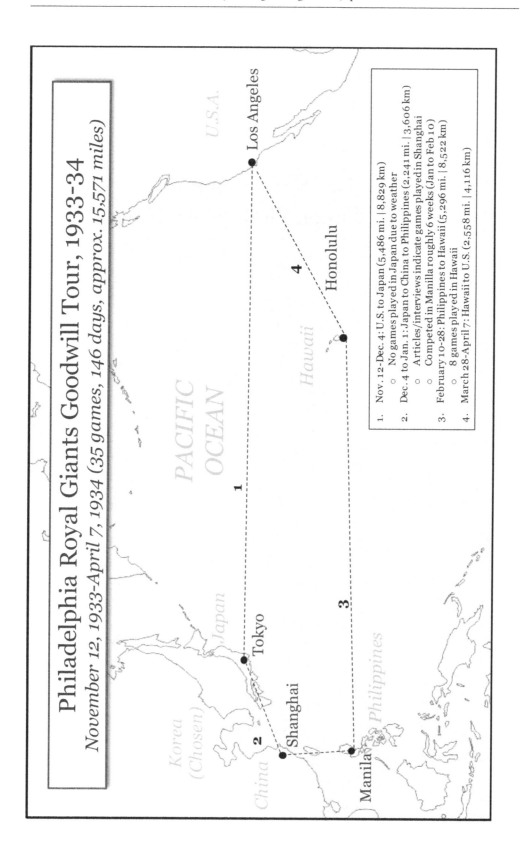

Philadelphia Royal Giants Goodwill Tour, 1933-34

November 12, 1933-April 7, 1934 (35 games, 146 days, approx. 15,571 miles)

1. Nov. 12-Dec. 4: U.S. to Japan (5,486 mi. | 8,829 km)
   - No games played in Japan due to weather
2. Dec. 4 to Jan. 1: Japan to China to Philippines (2,241 mi. | 3,606 km)
   - Articles/interviews indicate games played in Shanghai
   - Competed in Manila roughly 6 weeks (Jan to Feb 10)
3. February 10-28: Philippines to Hawaii (5,296 mi. | 8,522 km)
   - 8 games played in Hawaii
4. March 28-April 7: Hawaii to U.S. (2,558 mi. | 4,116 km)

Passenger Ship Record Summary: 1933-34 Philadelphia Royal Giants

Family Name	Given Name	Age	Sex	Married or Single	If native of US, Date and Place of Birth	Address in US
Allen	Newton Henry	31	M	S	May 19, 1903, Austin, Texas	2403 Tracy Ave., Kansas City, MO.
Brewer	Chester Arthur	27	M	M	January 14, 1907, Levenworth, Conn.	716 Third Ave., Levenworth, Conn.
Brown	James	25	M	S	Sept 11, 1908, San Antonio, Texas	1171 E. 40 St., Los Angeles, Calif.
Cooper	Andrew Lewis	38	M	M	April 24, 1896, Waco, Texas	4627 Compton Ave., Los Angeles
Daniels	Adam D.	22	M	S	August 16, 1911 Clearview, OK.	1430 E. 23 St., Los Angeles, Calif.
Gamiz-Ramirez	Virginio	26	M	S	1908, Havana, Cuba	N/A
Goodwin	Lon A.	56	M	M	March, 15, 1879, Austin, Texas.	1424 E. Adams, Los Angeles, Calif.
Martin	Wilson	35	M	M	February 12, 1899, Cairo, IL	671 Willow St., San Francisco, Calif.
Mothell	Carroll Ray	36	M	S	August 13, 1897, Topeka, Kansas	1506 Quincy St., Topeka, Kansas
Pullen	O'Neal	39	M	M	Sept 8, 1899, Beaumont, Texas	9326 Baird Ave., Los Angeles, Calif.
Rogan	Wilbur	44	M	M	July 28, 1889, Oklahoma City, OK.	1308 Michigan St., Kansas City, MO.
Rogers	Earl	20	M	S	May 6, 1913, Elko, Nevada	22 Fourth St., Richmond, Calif.
Ross	William	40	M	M	October 5, 1893, Corrigan, Texas	1372 E. 21 St., Los Angeles, Calif.
Young	Thomas Jefferson	30	M	M	June 10, 1903, Wichita, Kansas	1236 Pitt St., Wichita, Kansas

The Chicago Defender
July 29, 1933

Bland Off on a Tour of Orient

Los Angeles, California, July 28. – Alfred Bland, well-known professional, left here for Manila, P.I. last Thursday night after months visit with his parents of 835 E. 28th St. Before this visit he had been in the Philippines for the last year, teaching at the University of Santo Thomas and playing baseball.

He departed for San Francisco by train and was slated to embark on the President Coolidge of the dollar line last Friday afternoon. Bland left here in 1932 with the Philadelphia Royal Giants baseball team to tour the Orient. Biz Mackey, George Carr, Nagodoches Ross, Hallie Harding, and others made the trip, but they decided to return to the states. Bland, however, remained in Manila, where he had been given a position as instructor.

Source: Bland Off on a Tour of Orient, The Chicago Defender, July 29, 1933, pg. 5.

*   *   *

The Chicago Defender
Oct 14, 1933

Royal Giants Nine to Play in Hawaii

Los Angeles Calif., Oct. 13 – Lon Goodwin, owner and manager of the Philadelphia Royal Giants of this city and Capt. William Ross, formerly of the St. Louis Stars and Homestead Grays, are fast whipping their club in shape for their second Oriental tour.

Last year the Giants spent six months in the Orient playing in Hawaii, Japan, Korea, China and the Philippine Islands. They had a successful trip winning 4o games, losing two and tying one and the Oriental fans are demanding their return.

They will sale Nov. 12 on the S.S. President Pierce from Manila P.I. where they are booked for two months play. On the way back they will play in China in Hawaii. Here are some of the stars that will make the trip, Ross, Cooper, George Carr, Mackey, Perez, Gomez, Flenor and others. And all the Giants will play about 35 games and will be away about four months. Watch this paper for the returns of their games while playing abroad.

Source: Royal Giants Nine to Play in Hawaii, The Chicago Defender, Oct. 14, 1933, pg. 8.

Wilbur "Bullet Joe" Rogan, was a star pitcher and utility player for the 25th Infantry Wreckers between 1915 and 1920 in Honolulu. Rogan's return to Hawaii was celebrated in March 1934 when the Royal Giants stopped in the islands for a series of games on their return trip home from Asia (Fort Huachuca Museum).

The Chicago Defender
November 25, 1933

Royal Giants Off For Stay In Manila, P. I.

Los Angeles, Calif. – Lonnie Goodwin and his Philadelphia All-Stars baseball team sailed for Manila P.I. Sunday. The following players made up the trip that will last for several weeks: William Ross, Captain Andrew Cooper, Chuck Brewer, Bullet Rogan, Stack Martin, Virginia Gomez, James Brown, Newton Allen, A.D. Daniels, Dink Mothall, T.J. Young, Neil Pullen and William Rogers.

Source: Royal Giants Off For Stay In Manila, P. I., The Chicago Defender, Nov. 25, 1933, pg. 9.

*   *   *

The Chicago Defender
December 30, 1933

Japs Honor Philly Royal Giants Nine

Yokohama, Japan. December 30. – Lon Goodwin and his Philadelphia Royal Giants arrived here this morning and were escorted to the Yokohama Hotel where they were given a big banquet in their honor. They are on their way to Manila, PI. Where they will play a series of games with the best clubs in the Philippine Islands.

The Giants are great favorites in Yokohama because of the wonderful playing of last year when I spent two months playing in all the large cities in Japan and Korea. They proved to be the best ball club to ever visit Japan and they are well-liked by all Japan.

Captain William Ross, who has proven to be one of the brainiest baseball man ever to handle a team on the field here was called on to make a lecture on baseball, and after he finished he received one of the greatest ovations ever extended a ball player. All the leading newspapers of the Yokohama carried his lecture the following day, and all the baseball lovers of Japan are sorry because they want to have a chance to see this wonderful club in action this year as they are booked to return to Hawaii as soon as their engagements in Manila are finished but the leading baseball men of Yokohama are trying to book them for an appearance here in 1935.

Source: Japs Honor Philly Royal Giants Nine, The Chicago Defender, Dec. 30, 1933, pg. 9.

Honolulu Star-Bulletin
March 1, 1934

WILBUR ROGAN
Will Play With

THE PHILADELPHIA ROYAL GIANTS
Baseball Team at

HONOLULU STADIUM
SCHEDULE:

SATURDAY, MARCH 3
1:30—Univ. of Hawaii   vs.   Mutual Tel. Co.
3:15—BRAVES   vs.   ROYAL GIANTS

SUNDAY, MARCH 4
1:30—Haw'n Electric   vs.   Liberty House
3:15—WANDERERS   vs.   ROYAL GIANTS

SATURDAY, MARCH 10
1:30—Electric Shop   vs.   Mutual Tel. Co.
3:15—NAVY   vs.   ROYAL GIANTS

SUNDAY, MARCH 11
1:30—Moiliili   vs.   Wahiawa
3:15—BRAVES   vs.   ROYAL GIANTS

SATURDAY, MARCH 17
1:30—Univ. of Hawaii   vs.   Haw'n Electric
3:15—ALL HAWAIIAN   vs.   ROYAL GIANTS

SUNDAY, MARCH 18
1:30—Palama   vs.   Koyu
3:15—ALL JAPANESE   vs.   ROYAL GIANTS

SATURDAY, MARCH 24
1:30—Haw'n Electric   vs.   Electric Shop
3:15—WANDERERS   vs.   ROYAL GIANTS

SUNDAY, MARCH 25
1:30—Seibu   vs.   Moiliili
3:15—ALL CHINESE   vs.   ROYAL GIANTS

POPULAR LOW PRICES

Reserved	Grandstand	Bleachers
75c	50c	25c

Including Taxes
PHONE 3400 FOR RESERVATIONS

Source: Honolulu Star-Bulletin (Honolulu, Hawaii), March 1, 1934, pg. 16.

CRACK NEGRO GIANT OUTFIT HERE FOR GAMES

Introducing the members of the latest model of the Philadelphia Royal Giants, crack Negro baseball aggregation, which is here for a series of games in the Honolulu stadium. Wilbur (Bullet) Rogan, who starred here with the 25th Infantry back in 1914-1916, is sixth from the left in the back row. Picture of the team taken aboard the President Lincoln shows from the left, front row, Pep Young, Newton Allen, J. Ashman Beaven, L. A. Goodwin, Adam Ornellas, A. D. Daniels and Dick Mothel. Back row—Chester Brewer, O'Neal Pullen, S. Martin, James Brown, Earl Rogers, "Bullet" Rogan, Andy Cooper, William Ross and Yagina Gamez.—Star-Bulletin photo.

Source: Honolulu Star-Bulletin (Honolulu, Hawaii), March 3, 1934, pg. 8.

Honolulu Advertiser
March 28, 1934

Martin Best Sticker on the Giant Team
Amasses Average of .438; Scorer Roposo Releases Figures

Wilson Martin was the best hitter on the Royal Giants team, which concluded its series here against local teams last Sunday, with an average of .438, according to the averages released yesterday by Bill Raposo, official scorer. Martin went to bat 32 times and lashed out 14 hits.

Wilbur Rogan, center fielder, and Newt Allen, shortstop, followed with averages .345 and .324, respectively. Mothel, amassed an average of .323. The following are the averages:

GIANTS BATTING AVERAGES

	AB	R	H	TB	SH	SB	Pct.
Young	10	3	6	11	0	0	.600
Ross	5	0	3	3	0	1	.600
Martin	32	11	14	18	1	8	.438
Rogan	29	8	10	18	0	2	.345
Allen	37	9	12	12	0	8	.324
Mothel	31	6	10	12	3	3	.323
Daniels	22	2	6	7	0	2	.273
Brown	35	1	8	10	0	0	.229
Gamez	33	9	7	10	0	2	.212
Rogers	20	2	4	4	0	0	.200
Pullen	15	0	3	3	0	0	.200
Cooper	20	0	3	3	1	0	.150
Brewer	5	0	0	0	0	0	.000
Total	294	51	86	1	5	26	.293

FIELDING AVERAGES

	G	PO	A	E	TC	Pct.
Martin	8	18	5	0	23	1.000
Rogan	8	11	2	0	13	1.000
Rogers	7	6	2	0	8	1.000
Cooper	6	4	4	0	8	1.000
Young	2	9	1	0	10	1.000

Brewer	1	0	2	0	2	1.000
Ross	2	0	1	0	1	1.000
Allen	8	31	24	2	57	0.965
Gamez	8	21	21	2	44	0.955
Brown	8	66	1	5	72	0.931
Mothel	8	17	18	3	38	0.921
Daniels	6	7	3	1	11	0.909
Pullen	5	26	2	3	31	0.903

Source: Honolulu Star-Bulletin (Honolulu, Hawaii), March 28, 1934, pg. 8.

*　　*　　*

The Chicago Defender
March 24, 1934

ROYAL GIANTS BALL CLUB NOW EN ROUTE
BACK TO THE STATES

Honolulu, Hawaii, March 20 – Pop Lon Goodwin and his famous Royal Giants baseball team arrived here on the S.S. President Lincoln from Manila, P.I. where they have been playing for the past three months. According to Captain William Ross, all the gang are in splendid condition. They are scheduled to sail for the USA March 28 arriving in Los Angeles April 6.

Pop Goodwin has always brought a first-class club to the islands. The Giants are composed of the following players: pitchers Bullet Rogan, Lefty Andrew Cooper, Chuck Brewer and Captain William Ross. Ross has pitched here for the past four seasons and has never tasted defeat. He's the only pitcher to win 23 games over here without a loss. The infield has Brown, Dink Mothell, Gomez and Newt Allen. The outfield, Stack Martin, A.D. Daniels and Rogers. The catching is taken care of by T.J. Young and O'Neil Pullen.

Source: ROYAL GIANTS BALL CLUB NOW EN ROUTE BACK TO THE STATES, The Chicago Defender, March 24, 1934, pg. A5.

野球

Appendix O:
Hall of Fame Spotlight

Editor's note: Five members of the Philadelphia Royal Giants have been honored by the National Baseball Hall of Fame in Cooperstown, New York. "Bullet Joe" Rogan was inducted in 1998. Biz Mackey and Andy Cooper were inducted in 2006, and two others—Rap Dixon and Chet Brewer—were nominated for induction the same year. All five Hall of Fame Royal Giants are celebrated below.

*   *   *

CHARLES WILBER ROGAN

Nicknames(s): Bullet Joe, Cap
Born: July 28, 1893 in Oklahoma City, OK
Died: March 4, 1967 in Kansas City, MO
Bats: Right   Threw: Right
Height: 5'7"   Weight: 180 lbs.

Teams:
- 25th Infantry Wreckers (1914–1920)
- All Nations (1917)
- Kansas City Monarchs (1920–1938)
- ***Philadelphia Royal Giants (1933-34)
  Japan, China, Philippines, Hawaii***
- Kansas City Monarchs (1926–1934, 1936), *manager*

Inducted into the National Baseball Hall of Fame: 1998

HALL OF FAME BIOGRAPHY

Bullet Joe Rogan was not only one of the best pitchers to have played in the Negro Leagues, but he was also one of the best hitters. By not beginning his Negro League career until his mid 20s, Rogan got a late start. Nevertheless, he excelled during his 19 seasons with the Kansas City Monarchs, after beginning his baseball career as a part of the Army, playing for a team in the all-black 25th Infantry.

One statistical compilation records the hurler as winning more games than any other in the history of the Negro National League. He went 119-50 in his pitching career, with a 3.68 ERA, completing 132 of the 209 games that he started while using his repertoire of curveballs, spitballs, palm balls, forkballs and fastballs to strike out 855.

Splitting his time between the mound and the outfield, Rogan also ranks fourth in the league in career average, at .338. Rogan held a .515 slugging percentage with 45 home runs to go with 99 stolen bases and 361 runs. The slugger also notched 251 RBI, and led the Negro National League with 13 homers in 1922.

Rogan helped the Monarchs win three straight pennants from 1923-1925, and a Negro League World Series championship in 1924. During the championship season, Rogan hit .395 and had an 18-6 record on the mound. In the first Black World Series, he led his team with 13 hits and won two games for Kansas City as the Monarchs took down the Hilldale Daisies.

While Rogan's pitching was often compared to that of Satchel Paige, his son Wilber pointed out that there was at least one difference. "I do know that Satchel needed a designated hitter when he was on the mound," the younger Rogan said of his father. "When dad was on the mound, he was batting cleanup."

Source: National Baseball Hall of Fame, Bullet Rogan profile, baseballhall.org.

*   *   *

ANDREW LEWIS COOPER

Nickname(s): Andy, Lefty

Born: April 24, 1898 in Waco, TX

Died: June 3, 1941 in Waco, TX

Batted: Right   Threw: Left

Height: 6'2"   Weight: 220 lbs.

Teams:

- Detroit Stars (1920–1927, 1930)
- ***Philadelphia Royal Giants (1925-1934)***
  Japan, China, Korea, Philippines, Hawaii
- Kansas City Monarchs (1928–1929, 1931–1939)
- Kansas City Monarchs (1937–1940), *manager*

Inducted into the National Baseball Hall of Fame: 2006

HALL OF FAME BIOGRAPHY

A baseball player who spent the entirety of his playing career in the shadows of the major league due to the color of his skin, Andy Cooper made a name for himself in black baseball due to his mound mastery. Negro leagues historian Dick Clark once said of Cooper, "In my estimation, the greatest black pitcher ever to pitch for Detroit—that's for the Stars or the Tigers."

Born in Waco, Tex. in 1898, the thickly built Cooper, all 6-foot-2 and roughly 220 pounds of him, spent the majority of his Negro leagues career as a durable and consistent left-handed hurler with the Detroit Stars and Kansas City Monarchs over a two-decade career that spanned the 1920s and '30s.

Included among Cooper's many accolades and accomplishments during his playing days was a 43-inning stretch with the Stars in which he didn't issue a base on balls, winning twice as many games as he lost with both the Stars and Monarchs, helping lead Kansas City to the Negro National League pennant in 1929, once pitching 17 innings in a 1937 playoff game against the Chicago American Giants, and taking the mound in the 1936 East-West All-Star Game at the age of 40.

According to a scouting report prepared by famed Negro leagues player and manager Buck O'Neil, Cooper had a live arm with a total command of all of his pitches, which included a running fastball, tight curveball and biting screwball.

"Andy never possessed the fine assortment of curves held in the supple arms of other pitchers. However, he did have what so many pitchers lack—sterling control," wrote Russ J. Cowans in 1941 in The *Chicago Defender*, one of the top black newspapers of the day. "Cooper could almost put the ball any place he wanted it to go.

"In addition, Cooper had a keen knowledge of batters. He knew the weakness of every batter in the league and would pitch to that weakness when he was on the mound." A top starting pitcher early in his career who became a valuable reliever near the end, Cooper would also turn to managing, leading the Monarchs to three pennants between 1937 and 1940.

"Cooper was a smart manager and a great, great teacher," said Monarchs pitcher and fellow Hall of Famer Hilton Smith. After Cooper's death in 1941, The *Chicago Defender* wrote, "he not only won glory on the hurling mound but also won the respect and praise of the fans through his deportment off the field."

Source: National Baseball Hall of Fame, Andy Cooper profile, baseballhall.org.

*   *   *

JAMES RALEIGH MACKEY

Nickname: Biz
Born: July 27, 1897 in Caldwell County, TX
Died: September 22, 1965 in Los Angeles, CA
Batted: Switch   Threw: Right
Height: 6'0"   Weight: 200 lbs.

Teams:
- Dallas Black Giants (1918)
- Dallas Black Marines (1919)
- Waco Black Navigators (1919)
- San Antonio Black Aces (1919-20)
- Indianapolis ABC's (1921-22)
- Hilldale Daisies (1923-31)
- ***Philadelphia Royal Giants (1925-34)***
  Japan, China, Korea, Philippines, Hawaii
- Philadelphia Stars (1933-1935)
- Newark Dodgers (1935)
- Washington Elite Giants (1936-37)
- Baltimore Elite Giants (1938-39)
- Newark Eagles (1939-41, 1945-47, 1950)

Inducted into the National Baseball Hall of Fame: 2006

HALL OF FAME BIOGRAPHY

Though somewhat overshadowed by such legendary names as Josh Gibson and Roy Campanella, when black baseball's top catchers are discussed, Biz Mackey should be considered one of the great players of his era.

"Actually, as much as I admired Campanella as a catcher, all-around, and Gibson as a hitter," said Hall of Famer Cool Papa Bell, a veteran of the Negro leagues, "I believe Biz Mackey was the best catcher I ever saw." In fact, a 1954 Pittsburgh Courier poll saw Mackey edge Gibson as the greatest Negro league catcher.

Mackey would don the tools of ignorance in a career that spanned almost 30 years, from the late 1910s to the mid-40s. Whether while a member of the Hilldale Giants, Philadelphia Stars, Newark Eagles, Indianapolis ABCs or the Baltimore/Washington Elite Giants, he always proved to be a leader behind the plate or later as a manager. Fellow Hall of Famer Cum Posey, a longtime Negro league executive, once said, "For combined hitting, thinking, throwing and physical endowment, there has never been another like Biz Mackey. A tremendous hitter, a fierce competitor...he is the standout among catchers."

A line drive hitter whose batting average rarely strayed below .300, Mackey, named to five East-West All-Star teams, was a favorite receiver among pitchers and had a strong throwing arm.

"I've pitched to some great catchers, but my goodness, that Mackey was to my idea the best one I pitched to," said Hall of Fame hurler Hilton Smith. "The way he handled you, the way he just built you up, believing in yourself. He was marvelous."

Mackey has been given credit for furthering the development of a number of Negro leaguers who would go on to success in the major leagues, such as Campanella, Monte Irvin and Larry Doby.

"In my opinion, Biz Mackey was the master of defense of all catchers," Campanella said. "When I was a kid in Philadelphia, I saw both Mackey and Mickey Cochrane in their primes, but for real catching skills, I don't think Cochrane was the master of defense that Mackey was."

Source: National Baseball Hall of Fame, Biz Mackey profile, baseballhall.org.

*   *   *

HERBERT ALPHONSO DIXON

Nickname: Rap

Born: Sept. 15, 1902 in Kingston, GA

Died: July 20, 1944 in Detroit, MI

Batted: Right   Threw: Right

Height: 6'0"   Weight: 185 lbs.

Teams:

* Harrisburg Giants (1922–1927)
* ***Philadelphia Royal Giants (1927), Japan, Korea, Hawaii***
* Philadelphia Tigers (1928)
* Baltimore Black Sox (1928–1930)
* Chicago American Giants (1930)
* Hilldale Club (1931)
* Pittsburgh Crawfords (1932, 1934)
* Philadelphia Stars (1933)
* Baltimore Black Sox (1934)
* Concordia Eagles (1934)
* Brooklyn Eagles (1935)
* Homestead Grays (1936)
* Newark Eagles (1936)
* Pittsburgh Crawfords (1937)
* Santo Domingo All-Stars (1937)
* Harrisburg Giants (1942), *integrated team, manager*

National Baseball Hall of Fame ballot: 2006

HALL OF FAME BIO

After Satchel Paige, Josh Gibson and Buck Leonard were inducted into the National Baseball Hall of Fame in 1972, Richard Powell, former general manager of the Baltimore Elite Giants, told the *Pittsburgh Courier* that there was still more room for Negro League greats in Cooperstown. On his list of outfielders still be honored was Herbert "Rap" Dixon. "When you see fellows like Lou Brock, Frank Robinson, Roberto Clemente and such today, you are seeing a carbon copy of Rap Dixon...," said Powell.

Dixon was a five-tool athlete from Steelton High School in Pennsylvania who, as a teenager, competed on the local adult team, the Keystone Giants. During summers he worked in the local steel mill where legend has it he developed his tremendous arm and shoulder strength by "throwing pig iron billets at the crane operators."

In 1922, he joined the Harrisburg Giants, a semi-pro club that entered the elite Eastern Colored League two seasons later. For the next 14 years, Dixon performed at the highest levels of the Negro Leagues. During this period, he hit .331 and averaged 20 home runs and 25 steals for every 150 games played. He was also a five-time all-star (selected in 1925, 1929, 1933, 1934, and 1935). Highlights from his impressive career include:

- Between 1924-27, he was a member of arguably the greatest outfield in Negro Leagues history, playing with Oscar Charleston and Fats Jenkins.
- In 1927 he participated in a goodwill tour to Asia with the Philadelphia Royal Giants, with stops in Japan, Korea, China and Hawaii. While in Japan, he was honored for hitting the longest ball ever recorded in Koshien Stadium, and later he and his team were invited to meet with Emperor Hirohito of Japan.
- In 1929, he recorded 14 consecutive base hits, surpassing the MLB record of 12.
- On July 5, 1930, he became the first African American to hit a home run in Yankee Stadium, and finished the day with three home runs during a double header (a feat that not even Babe Ruth would accomplish at Yankee Stadium.)

After his death in 1944, Dixon was named to the list of all-time Negro League greats by several of his peers, including Oscar Charleston, Cool Papa Bell, Leon Day, and Larry Doby.

In 2006, the Hall of Fame followed Richard Powell's advice and held a special election for Negro Leaguers. Despite falling a few votes short of induction, Dixon is still considered one of the greatest outfielders to ever play the game. His day in Cooperstown will come—it's just a matter of time

Sources: Ted Knorr, Rap Dixon historian; SABR Negro Leagues Research Committee.

*   *   *

CHESTER ARTHUR BREWER

Nickname: Chet

Born: January 14, 1907 in Leavenworth, KS

Died: March 26, 1990 in Whittier, CA

Batted: Both   Threw: Right

Height: 6'4"   Weight: 176 lbs.

Teams:

- Brown's Tennessee Rats (1922-23)
- Capital City Giants (1923)
- Des Moines Cubs (1924)
- Glikerson Union Giants (1924)
- K.C. Monarchs (1925-31, 1932-35, 1937, 1940-41)
- Phil. Royal Giants (1926-27, 1929-31, 1937-38), *Cal. Winter League (CWL)*
- Cleveland Giants (1928-29), *CWL*
- Habana Leones (1930), *Cuba*
- Crookston, Minn. (1931), *Integrated*
- Washington Pilots (1932)
- ***Philadelphia Royal Giants (1933-34), Japan, China, Philippines, Hawaii***
- Jamestown Red Sox (1934)
- Brooklyn Royal Giants (1935)
- Wilson Elite Giants (1935-37), *CWL*
- Bismarck, N.D. (1935-36)
- New York Cubans (1936)
- Pittsburgh Crawfords (1937)
- Santiago Aguilas Cibaenas, (1937), *D.R.*
- Trujillo All Stars (1937)
- Baltimore Elite Giants (1938)
- Tampico Tamaulipas (1938-39), *Mexico*
- Memphis Red Sox (1940)
- Philadelphia Stars (1941)
- Royal Giants (1941-42), *CWL*
- Cleveland Buckeyes (1942-43)
- Kansas City Royals (1943-46), *CWL*
- Mexico City Diablos Rojos (1944), *Mexico*
- Bonds All-Stars (1945), *SoCal Semi-Pro*
- Satchel Paige All-Stars (1945)
- Chicago American Giants (1946)
- Cleveland/Louisville Buckeyes (1946-48)
- Chesterfield Smokers (1948-49), *Panama*
- Michigan City Cubs (1949, 1950)
- St. Jean's Braves (1949), *Canada*
- Carta Vieja Yankees (1949-50), *Panama*
- Indian Head Rockets (1951), *Canada*
- Sceptre Nixons/Panthers (1951), *Canada*
- Riverside Comets (1952), *Player/mgr.*
- Riverside-Porterville Padres (1952)
- Porterville Comets (1952), *Player/mgr.*
- Visalia Cubs (1952)
- Carman Cardinals (1953), *Canada, mgr.*
- Hollywood Stars (1957), *Coach/scout*
- Pittsburgh Pirates (1960s), *Scout/coach*
- Major League Scouting Bureau (1970s)

National Baseball Hall of Fame ballot: 2006

HALL OF FAME BIO

Chet Brewer is arguably one of the most important figures in Negro Leagues baseball history yet to be enshrined in the National Baseball Hall of Fame. On the field he was a phenomenal pitcher who dominated opponents for three decades. He was described by the press as a "curve ball artist with remarkable control." Later in life, opponents said he was "like Koufax, only right handed." Historian John Holway argues that Brewer was just as good as Satchel Paige.

"There was no better teammate than Chet Brewer," said James "Cool Papa" Bell. "He wanted to win so bad. He'll do anything to win. All of the fellows respected him for that. There's no one like him. There were games he just refused to lose. He was so strong-willed. He had total concentration on the mound."

In addition to his great playing ability, Brewer was an early and outspoken advocate for the integration of organized baseball during the 1930s and 40s. His frustrations with the lack of progress in eliminating the color line often resulted in him competing abroad, where he and his teammates were treated with the dignity and respect they deserved. International baseball was, in some regards, an act of protest for Brewer.

Despite the "gentleman's agreement" that kept him out of the majors, Brewer received several opportunities to prove he was major-league material. He compiled a 13-2 (.867) record against major league competition. In one victory against the Philadelphia Athletics, future Hall of Famer Jimmie Foxx popped up four times against Brewer's tricky pitches.

Former Commissioner Bowie Kuhn described Brewer and his Negro Leagues peers as pioneers. "They paved the way for the Willie Mayes and Hank Aarons to become the superstars they have become. Their place is important. They should not be forgotten."

In 1987, writer and historian Joe Reichler served on the 18-member committee responsible for selecting Negro Leagues players to the Hall of Fame. At the time, Reichler said the most deserving players still alive were Chet Brewer, Leon Day and Willie Wells. Today, Brewer is the only player on that elite list yet to be honored in Cooperstown.

Despite the HOF oversight, his legacy still resonates in the game today. Long before MLB launched the Reviving Baseball in Inner Cities (RBI) Program, Brewer organized leagues, camps and clinics for at-risk youth in the Los Angeles area. His efforts helped develop future big leaguers like Eddie Murray, Ellis Valentine, Bob Watson, Dock Ellis, Enos Cabell, Bobby Tolan, and Reggie Smith. "He was a huge influence, especially as it related to becoming a professional," said Smith, who in 2019 still coaches players and teams around the world. "(Chet Brewer) taught what it was all about in terms of expectations. We gained more experience than any 18 year old playing today."

Sources: Sporting News, Center for Negro Leagues Baseball Research, CooperstownExpert.com, ReggieSmithBaseball.com.

野球

Appendix P: Negro Leagues Trans-Pacific Barnstormers Summary & Bios

NEGRO LEAGUES TRANS-PACIFIC BARNSTORMERS SUMMARY

Total Number of Tours: 6 (1927, 1928, 1929, 1931, 1932-33, 1933-34)
Total Days, All-Tours Combined: 641 days (approx. 21 months or 1.76 years)
Total Distance, All-Tours Combined: 52,348 miles
Total Participants: 47 individuals (44 players, 1 manager, 2 promoters)

Most Active Participants, Ranked by Total Days on Tour:

NAME	TOTAL DAYS	% TOTAL
Goodwin, Lon	517	80.7%
Cooper, Andy	517	80.7%
Pullen, O'Neal	466	72.7%
Evans, Alexander	420	65.5%
Gamiz, Virginio	396	61.8%
Ross, William	396	61.8%
Mackey, Biz	344	53.7%
Carr, George	299	46.6%
Delgado, Clemente	251	39.2%
Perez, Javier	251	39.2%
Bland, Alfred	251	39.2%
Cade, Joe	245	38.2%
Walker, Jesse	245	38.2%
Fagen, Robert	197	30.7%

Baker, Julius	175	27.3%
Harding, Halley	175	27.3%
Noda, Steere G.	175	27.3%*
Allen, Newt	145	22.6%
Brewer, Chet	145	22.6%
Brown, James	145	22.6%
Daniels, A.D.	145	22.6%
Martin, Stack	145	22.6%
Mothell, Dink	145	22.6%
Rogan, Wilbur	145	22.6%
Rogers, Earl	145	22.6%
Young, T.J.	145	22.6%
Dixon, Rap	134	20.9%
Cooper, Samuel	124	19.3%
Day, Connie	124	19.3%
Duncan, Frank	121	18.9%
Irie, George	121	18.9%*
Johnson, Ajay	121	18.9%
Riddle, John	121	18.9%
Borges, Manual	76	11.9%
Brulee, Louis	76	11.9%
Gonzales, Eusebio	76	11.9%
Green, Julius	76	11.9%
Miranda, Elias	76	11.9%
Morris, Harold	76	11.9%
Santaello, Anastario	76	11.9%
Savage, Azel	76	11.9%
Shaw, Ted	76	11.9%
Tucker, Eugene	60	9.4%**
Anderson, Buddy	48	7.5%
Butcher, Spencer	48	7.5%
Dunn, Jake	48	7.5%
Gardner, Ping	48	7.5%

* *Served as promoter and translator during the tour.*

***Approximate, participated in 1927 tour but stayed behind in China due to illness.*

Negro Leagues Trans-Pacific Barnstormers, by Tour (1927-1934)

YEAR(S)	1927	1928	1929	1931	1932-33	1933-34
TEAM NAME	Philadelphia Royal Giants	Cleveland Royal Giants	Pullen Royal Giants	Philadelphia Royal Giants	Philadelphia Royal Giants	Philadelphia Royal Giants
DESTINATION(S)	Japan, Korea, Hawaii	Hawaii	Hawaii	Hawaii	Hawaii, Japan, Korea, China, Philippines	Japan, Philippines, Hawaii
DEPARTURE	March 9, 1927	July 14, 1928	April 6, 1929	May 23, 1931	July 23, 1932	November 12, 1933
RETURN	July 8, 1927	September 28, 1928	May 24, 1929	August 7, 1931	January 14, 1933	April 7, 1934
DURATION #DAYS	121	76	48	76	175	145
APPROX. MONTHS	4.03	2.53	1.60	2.53	5.83	4.83
MILES	13,305	2,551	2,551	2,551	15,819	15,689
MANAGER	Goodwin, Lon	Pullen, O'Neal	Pullen, O'Neal	Goodwin, Lon	Goodwin, Lon	Goodwin, Lon
PARTICIPANTS	Cade, Joe Cooper, Andrew Dixon, Herbert Duncan, Frank Evans, Alexander Fagen, Robert Green, Julius Irie, George Johnson, Ajay Mackey, Raleigh* Pullen, O'Neal Riddle, John Tucker, Eugene Walker, Jesse	Cade, Joe Cooper, Samuel Day, Connie Evans, Alexander Fagen, Robert Green, Julius Morris, Harold Savage, Azel Walker, Jesse	Anderson, Buddy Butcher, Spencer Cade, Joe Carr, George Cooper, Samuel Day, Connie Dunn, Jake Evans, Alexander Gardner, Kenneth Mackey, Raleigh* Walker, Jesse	Bland, Alfred Borges, Manual Brulee, Louis Carr, George Cooper, Andrew Delgado, Clemente Gamiz, Virginio Gonzales, Eusebio Miranda, Elias Perez, Javier Pullen, O'Neal Ross, William Santaello, Anastario Shaw, Ted[1]	Baker, Julius Bland, Alfred [2] Carr, George Cooper, Andrew Delgado, Clemente Evans, Alexander Gamiz, Virginio Harding, Halley Mackey, Raleigh* Martin, Wilson Noda, Steere G. Perez, Javier Ross, William	Allen, Newt Brewer, Chet Brown, James Cooper, Andrew Daniels, A.D. Gamiz, Virginio[3] Martin, Wilson Mothell, Carrol Pullen, O'Neal Rogan, Wilbur Rogers, Earl [3] Ross, William* Young, T.J.
# PARTICIPANTS	15	10	12	15	14	14

*Team captain   [1] Stayed in Hawaii   [2] Stayed in P.I.   [3] Stayed in Hawaii

PLAYER BIOS

ALLEN, NEWT
Newton Henry Allen (Colt)
Born: May 19, 1901, Austin, TX   Died: June 9, 1988, Cincinnati, OH
Bats: R Throws: R   Ht: 5'8" Wt: 160
Position: 2B   Tours: 1933-34
Highlights: Allen was among the Royal Giants' top hitters during the 1933-34 tour, batting
.324 in the closing series in Hawaii. He played second base in the Negro Leagues for many
years, mostly with the Kansas City Monarchs. In 1941 he as named interim-manager for
the Monarchs when Andy Cooper fell ill, and took over at the helm when Cooper died in
June 1941.

ANDERSON, BUDDY
Leroy Anderson (Buddy)
Born: July 26, 1901, Los Angeles, CA   Died: June 7, 1968, Los Angeles, CA
Bats: R Throws: R   Ht: 5'8" Wt: 190
Position: LF   Tours: 1929
Highlights: During the 15-game series in Hawaii, Anderson batted over .300 and played
error-free ball in 16 chances in left field, the only non-pitcher to field a perfect 1.000 for
the Royal Giants.

BAKER, JULIUS
Julius Miller Baker
Born: Jan. 11, 1897, Gallatin, TN   Died: Jan. 15, 1976, Los Angeles, CA
Bats: R Throws: R   Ht: Wt:
Position: C   Tours: 1932-33
Highlights: Baker served as the backup catcher behind Biz Mackey during the 1932-33 tour.
In limited action, he batted .275 during the entire tour, with a strong .325 performance
(3-for-8) during the 11-game series in Hawaii.

BLAND, ALFRED
Alfred Peter Bland
Born: Sep. 10, 1907, New Orleans, LA   Died: July 18, 1974, Los Angeles, CA
Bats: R Throws: R   Ht: Wt:
Positions: 2B, 3B   Tours: 1931, 1932-33
Highlights: During the 1931 Hawaiian tour, Bland went 2-for-4 with a home run and 4
runs batted in during a 10-1 route of the All-Chinese club. He batted .298 for the Royal

Giants during the 1932-33 tour. A graduate of the University of Southern California, he remained in the Philippines where he was hired as an assistant professor of chemistry at the University of St. Thomas in Manila.

BORGES, MANUEL

Manuel Borges-Areguila
Born: 1901 in Havana, Cuba   Died: Unknown
Bats: R Throws: R   Ht: Wt:
Position: LF   Tours: 1931
Highlights: Of Portuguese-Cuban descent, Borges played baseball in San Antonio, Texas in 1928-1930. During the 1931 tour, with the game tied 4-4 in the 9th inning, he walked and then scored the go-ahead run in a 6-4 victory over the Hawaiians on July 11.

BREWER, CHET

Chester Arthur Brewer (Chet)
Born: Jan. 14, 1907, Leavenworth, KS   Died: March 26, 1990, Whittier, CA
Bats: R Throws: R   Ht: 6'4" Wt: 176
Position: P   Tours: 1933-34
Highlights: Enjoyed a long career in the Negro Leagues, and is celebrated in the Los Angeles area as a pioneering coach who prepared many African American players for the majors. After retiring from baseball, he was a major-league scout and instructor for the Pittsburgh Pirates for almost thirty years (1957-1974), developing a very close relationship with Roberto Clemente, and later worked with the Major League Scouting Bureau. Later in life, in recognition of his contributions to baseball, Chet Brewer Field in Los Angeles was dedicated in his honor. For more career details, see Appendix O: Hall of Fame Spotlight.

BROWN, JAMES

James Willis Brown
Born Sept. 11, 1908, San Antonio, TX   Died: June 23, 1990, Seattle, WA
Bats: Throws: Ht: 5'9" Wt: 160
Position: 1B, C, P, SS   Tours: 1933-34
Highlights: Brown played first base and batted 7th in the lineup for the Royal Giants during the 1933-34 tour. On March 3 he went 3-for-5 in a 12-1 victory over the Braves. In 1940, he joined forces again with teammates O'Neal Pullen and A.D. Daniels as a member of the Bakersfield Cubs.

BRULEE, LOUIS

Louis Mitchel Brulee
Born: Sept. 29, 1909, New Orleans, LA   Died: Feb. 1, 1985, Los Angeles, CA
Bats: Throws: Ht: 5'7" Wt: 140
Positions: OF, UT (bat boy?)   Tours: 1931
Highlights: Brulee went hitless in five at-bats in two games during the Royal Giants 1931 tour to Hawaii. The press referred to him as the team's bat boy when Goodwin put him in

to play during their 9-2 victory over the Chinese ball club. Given Brulee's limited playing time and performance, "bat boy" may very well have been his role.

BUTCHER, SPENCER
Spencer Butcher (Butch)
Born: Sept. 3, 1896, Galveston, TX   Died: April 13, 1967, Los Angeles, CA
Bats: Throws: Ht: 5'9" Wt:: 160
Position: RF   Tours: 1929
Highlights: Butcher was a Texan who moved to the West Coast sometime between 1910 and 1920. He was a member of the semipro Los Angeles White Sox who was picked up by the Alexander Giants and Philadelphia Royal Giants in the CWL between 1920 and 1928. He was a veteran of WWI and buried in Golden Gate National Cemetery.

CADE, JOE
Joseph Nathan Cade
Born: April 5, 1900, Saint Louis, MO   Died: Unknown
Bats: Throws: R   Ht: Wt:
Positions: RF, P, C   Tours: 1927, 1928, 1929
Highlights: Cade also worked as a firefighter. He served in the U.S. Navy, played ball on the All-Navy team in Hawaii and was very popular with the fans in the islands during the Royal Giants' tours.

CARR, GEORGE
George Henry Carr (Tank)
Born: Sept. 2, 1894, Atlanta, GA   Died: Jan. 14, 1948, McPherson, KS
Bats: B Throws: R   Ht: 6'1" Wt: 210
Position: 1B   Tours: 1929, 1931, 1932-33
Highlights: Carr was a dangerous switch hitter who could hit for power and a high average. For a large man he possessed exceptional speed and was an excellent base stealer. Early in his career he was reportedly timed at 10 seconds flat for the 100 yard dash. During the 1932-33 tour he played first and second base for the Royal Giants, and was among the team's top hitters, batting .421 (16-for-38) during the nine-game series in Hawaii, and .355 for the overall 41-game tour to Asia.

COOPER, ANDY
Andrew Lewis Cooper
Born: April 4, 1896, Wash. Co., TX   Died: June 3, 1941 in Waco, TX
Bats: R Throws: L   Ht: 5'10" Wt: 200
Position: P   Tours: 1927, 1931, 1932-33, 1933-34
Highlights: Cooper pitched in the Negro Leagues from 1920 to 1941, compiling a record of 121–54 (.691). He recorded a 22–6 (.786) record in the California Winter League between 1922–31. Between 1927 and 1934, he was among the most active Trans-Pacific barnstormers in Negro League history, spending 517 days traveling across the ocean and playing abroad. He managed the Kansas City Monarchs until his death in 1941. Cooper

was elected to the National Baseball Hall of Fame in 2006. For more career details, see Appendix O: Hall of Fame Spotlight.

COOPER, SAM

Born: Dec. 5, 1897 in Brooklyn, NY	Died: Unknown
Bats: Throws: R	Ht: Wt:
Position: P	Tours: 1928, 1929

Highlights: Negro League pitcher with nine years experience with several teams in the east, including the Baltimore Black Sox and Homestead Grays. During the 1928 Hawaiian tour, he won 19 of 23 games.

DANIELS, A.D.

Adam D. Daniels *(Possibly born Adam D. Brown)*

Born August 10, 1910, Clearview, OK	Died: Feb. 28, 1983, San Diego, CA
Bats: R Throws: R	Ht: 5' 7" Wt: 185
Positions: OF, P	Tours: 1933-34

Highlights: Daniels was a pitcher and CF for the Royal Giants. In six games in Hawaii, he hit .273 (6-for-22). In 1930, he worked on his grandparents' farm (David & Lula Brown), in Kern Co., CA. In 1939, he joined the Bakersfield Cubs with Pullen and James Brown.

DAY, CONNIE

Wilson Connie Day (Dummy)

Born: Dec. 30, 1897, Lima, OH	Died: June 23, 1961, Indianapolis, IN
Bats: R Throws: R	Ht: 5'8" Wt: 160
Positions: 2B, SS, P	Tours: 1928, 1929

Highlights: Day was a sensational defensive middle-infielder in the Negro Leagues for 13 years. During the 1928 tour to Hawaii he was billed as "Baseball's Wonder Comedian." In 1929, hit batted .321 (17-for-53) in 15 games for the Royal Giants during their visit to Hawaii.

DELGADO, CLEMENTE

Clemente de la Cruz Delgado

Born 1906, Havana, Cuba	Died: Unknown
Bats: R Throws: R	Ht: 5'8" Wt:
Position: CF	Tours: 1931, 1932-33

Highlights: Delgado was the lead-off hitter and played center field for the Royal Giants, batting .296 during the 1932-33 tour of Asia. He and teammate Manuel Borges played in Texas between 1928-30, and returned to play there or in Mexico as late as 1938. He also played in the Mexican League for Nuevo Laredo in 1940 and Monterrey in 1942.

DIXON, HERBERT

Herbert Alphonso Dixon (Rap)

Born: Sept. 15, 1902, Kingston, GA	Died: July 20, 1944, Detroit, MI
Bats: R Throws: R	Ht: 6'0" Wt: 185

Position: OF   Tours: 1927, 1929*

Dixon was an outstanding all-round player in the Negro Leagues from 1922 to 1937. He hit .326 in five seasons in the California Winter League, including a .380 clip with the 1927–28 Royal Giants. He attempted to participate in the 1929 tour of Hawaii but could not remain because his mother became ill and he had to return home. Dixon was a candidate on the ballot for the National Baseball Hall of Fame election in 2006. For more career details, see Appendix O: Hall of Fame Spotlight.

DUNCAN, FRANK

Frank Lee Duncan Jr.

Born: Feb. 14, 1901, Kansas City, MO   Died: Dec. 4, 1973, Kansas City, MO
Bats: R Throws: R   Ht: 6'0" Wt: 175
Position: C   Tours: 1927

Highlights: Frank Duncan Jr. was one of the top catchers in the Negro Leagues between 1920 and 1948, playing mostly with the KC Monarchs. He was an average hitter, batting .268 in the Negro Leagues and .304 in two seasons in the California Winter League.

DUNN, JAY

Joseph P. Dunn Jr. (Jake)

Born: Dec. 5, 1908, Oklahoma City, OK Died: July 24, 1984, Los Angeles, CA
Bats: R Throws: R   Ht: 5'10" Wt: 190
Positions: CF, SS   Tours: 1929, 1931

Highlights: Dunn was a Negro Leaguer for a decade, making two All-Star teams. He got his start with the Detroit Stars in 1930. During the 1929 tour to Hawaii, he batted just .216. Two seasons later, he improved his hitting, working his way into the #5 spot in the batting order. Among his 1931 tour highlights was a 4-for-4 day at the plate in a 10-4 win over the Asahi. Dunn went on the become one of the top hitters in the CWL with a .335 career average, 8th all-time between Bullet Rogan and Tank Carr. He also served in the U.S. Military from 1942 to 1945.

EVANS, ALEXANDER

Charles Alexander Evans (Slowtime; Alec)

Born: Oct. 17, 1895, Charleston, SC   Died: Oct. 15, 1964, Los Angeles, CA
Bats: R Throws: R   Ht: Wt:
Positions: P, 2B   Tours: 1927, 1928, 1929, 1932-33

Highlights: Evans, a lont-time member of the L.A. White Sox, was among the most active Trans-Pacific barnstormers in baseball history, participating in four tours, and spending an estimated 420 days sailing the Pacific Ocean and competing abroad. According to the Honolulu press, he was also Biz Mackey's brother-in-law.

FAGEN, ROBERT

Robert William Fagen (note: Last name also spelled Fagan and Fagin)

Born: March 27, 1894, Henderson, KY   Died: Jan. 19, 1960 in Fort Worth, TX
Bats: R Throws: R   Ht: Wt:

Position: 2B   Tours: 1927, 1928
Highlights: Fagan was a member of the 25th Infantry team in Hawaii and Arizona who joined the KC Monarchs in 1920. He enjoyed a four-year career with Negro Leagues teams in the east before returning to California where he played and managed for the remainder of his career. See Appendix E for his insight as a baseball manager on the West Coast.

GAMIZ, VIRGINIO

Gamiz-Ramirez, Virginio (Chico, Chicho)
Born: Feb. 24, 1898, Havana, Cuba   Died: June 1967 in Honolulu, HI
Bats: R Throws: R   Ht: Wt:
Positions: 3B, RF, C   Tours: 1929, 1932-33, 1933-34
Highlights: Gamiz began his career in the Cuban leagues, and toured the U.S. in 1930. He settled in Honolulu after the Royal Giants 1933-34 tour, and became an active and respected coach in the baseball community. In 1952 he became the first Cuban manager in the Hawaiian Baseball League.

GARDNER, KENNETH

Kenneth Fuller Gardner (Ping)
Born: March 5, 1899, Washington, DC   Died: March 9, 1984, Charlottesville, VA
Bats: Throws: L   Ht: 5'9" Wt: 157
Position: P   Tours: 1929
Highlights: During the Royal Giants' 1929 tour of Hawaii, Gardner won 5 of the Royal Giants 15 victories, sharing pitching duties with Biz Mackey and Sam Cooper. Among his 5 wins was a one-hitter against the tough All-Chinese club on May 5.

GONZALES, EUSEBIO

Eusebio Miguel Gonzalez Lopez (Mike, Papo)
Born: July 13, 1892, Havana, Cuba   Died: Feb. 14, 1976, Havana, Cuba
Bats: R Throws: R   Ht: 5'10" Wt: 165
Position: 1B, 2B, 3B   Tours: 1931
Highlights: Gonzales is the only Royal Giants player to have also played major league baseball. After hitting .400 for Almendares against the Brooklyn Dodgers in Cuba in 1913, Gonzales was signed to play in the U.S. He joined the Troy Trojans in the New York State League in 1914, and later signed with Boston in 1917, at age 25. He played only three games with Babe Ruth and the Red Sox club, never to return to the majors. He went on to play in Toronto and Texas, and all points in between. According to the SABR BioProject, Gonzales disappeared from pro ball in 1928. We now know that three years later he was with the Royal Giants during their 1931 tour to Hawaii. He made headlines when he promised to buy a hat for every member of an opposing team who could defeat the Royal Giants. With his team down 2-1 in the 9th inning against the Braves, he almost had to make good on his bet. Instead, with a runner on third, he singled to right field to tie the game and sent it into extra innings. The Royal Giants went on to beat the Braves, 4-2.

GOODWIN, LON
Goodwin, Alonzo (L.A., Lonnie)
Born March, 15, 1878, Austin, TX   Died: Feb. 22, 1966, Los Angeles, CA
Bats: R Throws: R   Ht: 5'10" Wt: 200
Position: Manager (formerly SS, P)   Tours: 1927, 1931, 1932-33, 1933-34
Highlights: Former player with the Austin Reds and Waco Yellow Jackets who competed under the name "Lonnie Graves." See Goodwin's full biography in Appendix F

GREEN, JULIUS
Green, John (Junior, Junius)
Born: June, 25, 1900, Galveston, TX   Died: Unknown
Bats: Throws: R   Ht: Wt:
Position: OF, P   Tours: 1927, 1928
Highlights: *The Chicago Defender* described Julius Green as "one of the hardest hitting little men in present-day baseball." Before joining the Royal Giants, he competed with Lon Goodwin's LA White Sox. On the mound he won four of the teams 26 victories in Japan, allowing a total of 6 runs. He also was among the team leaders in batting with a .333 average in Hawaii during the 1927 tour.

HARDING, HALLEY
William Claire Harding
Born: Nov. 13, 1905, Wichita, KS   Died: April 1, 1967, Chicago, IL
Bats: B Throws: R   Ht: 5'9" Wt: 170
Positions: SS, 2B, OF   Tours: 1932-33
Highlights: Harding was a three-sport star in college and the pros who played for both the Kansas City Monarchs and one of the early Globetrotters basketball teams, tried out for the Chicago Cardinals, and appeared with Fritz Pollard's New York Brown Bombers (football team). He batted .321 during the Royal Giants tour of Asia in 1932-33.

IRIE, GEORGE
Joji "George" Irie (born Goichi Hajun Irie)
Born: June 15, 1885, Yamaguchi, Japan   Died: Unknown
Position: Promotor, translator   Tours: 1927
Highlights: See Irie's biography in Appendix G.

JOHNSON, AJAY
Ajay Deforest Johnson
Born: Jan. 23, 1901, Waco, Texas   Died: Oct. 12, 1996, Los Angeles, CA
Bats: R Throws: R   Ht: 6' 0" Wt: 170
Positions: P, OF   Tours: 1927
Highlights: Johnson began his career in 1924 with the L.A. White Sox. He joined the Royal Giants at the end of the 1926-27 California Winter League season when Bullet Joe Rogan declined Goodwin's offer to accompany the club on their upcoming tour. He became the number-two ace behind lefty Andy Cooper, winning seven of the teams' 25 victories. Once

out of baseball, Johnson became a police officer in L.A, and in 1943 earned the distinction of becoming one of the first black uniformed patrol lieutenants and sergeants in LAPD history.

MACKEY, RALEIGH
James Raleigh Mackey (Biz, Bizz)
Born: July 27, 1897, Caldwell Co., TX   Died: Sept. 22, 1965, Los Angeles, CA
Bats: B Throws: R   Ht: 6'0" Wt: 200
Position: SS, P, C   Tours: 1927, 1929, 1932-33
Highlights: For more career details, see Mackey's full bio in Appendix J and Appendix O: Hall of Fame Spotlight.

MARTIN, WILSON
Martin, Wilson (Stack)
Born: Feb. 12, 1895, Cairo, IL   Died: June 20, 1978, San Francisco, CA
Bats: R Throws: R   Ht: 6'0" Wt:
Position: OF   Tours: 1932-33, 1933-34
Highlights: Wilson was a versatile player who competed in the Negro Leagues as a pitcher, catcher, first baseman, third baseman, and outfielder. He got his start with the Washington Potomacs in 1925, and moved around to the Indianapolis ABCs, Dayton Marcos, and Detroit Stars in a five year span. After the 1932-33 tour, he stayed in the Philippines for a job in the Cavite Navy Yard. During the 1933-34 tour, Martin led the team in batting with a .438 average (14-for-38) during the 8-game series in Hawaii. He also finished with a perfect fielding percentage, committing no errors with 23 chances in the outfield.

MIRANDA, ELIAS
Born: 1898, Havana, Cuba   Died: Unknown
Bats: Throws: Ht: 5' 9" Wt:
Position: 1B   Tours: 1931
Highlights: Miranda played in the Texas and/or Mexican Leagues in the late 1920s. With the Royal Giants, he was a sure-fielding first baseman. With the score tied 2-2 in the 12th inning, his single to left field was key to the Royal Giants 4-2 victory over the Braves on July 12, 1931.

MORRIS, HAROLD
Harold Goodwin Morris (Yellowhorse, Dazzy, Hal)
Born: Feb. 24, 1902, Little Rock, AR   Died: Sept. 6, 1959, San Francisco, CA
Bats: R Throws: R   Ht: 5'9" Wt: 170
Position: P   Tours: 1928
Highlights: Morris was a respected pitcher with the Kansas City Monarchs, Detroit Stars and Chicago American Giants in the '20s and '30s. As a member of the 1924 KC Monarchs, he appeared in 18 games and helped the team to the first Colored World Series with a 6-4 record and 4.02 ERA. During the Royal Giants' 1928 tour of Hawaii, Morris pitched a 9-0 shut out against the tough Chinese ball club, and belted a home run during a 2-for-5 day at the plate. In 1946, Morris became the owner and manager of the San Francisco Sea

Lions of the West Coast Negro League. He was hired as a scout by the Chicago Cubs in early April 1949.

MOTHELL, DINK
Carroll Ray Mothell (Deke)
Born: August 13, 1897, Topeka, KS   Died: April 24, 1980, Topeka, KS
Bats: B Throws: R   Ht: Wt:
Position: C, Utility   Tours: 1933-34
Highlights: During the Royal Giants' 1933-34 tour, Mothell was among the top hitters on the club. In the 8-game series in Hawaii he hit .323 average (10-for-31). Among his hits was a triple off of former Royal Giants pitcher Ted Shaw that secured an 8-5 victory over the Hawaiian Mutual Telephone ball club on March 21.

NODA, STEERE
Steere Gikaku Noda
Born: Feb. 16, 1892, Honolulu, HI   Died: March 29, 1986, Honolulu, HI
Position: Promoter, translator   Tours: 1932-33
Highlights: Noda founded the famous Hawaiian Asahi Nisei ball club in 1905. He played first base and was the captain of the team until his retirement, and later served as team president. The Asahi first competed against Lon Goodwin's Royal Giants in 1927, and later Noda joined Goodwin and the team for their tour to Japan and the Philippines in 1932-33. In 1948 he was elected to the Hawaiian Territorial House of Representatives, and later served as a delegate to the first Hawaii State Constitutional Convention that led to statehood in 1959.

PEREZ, JAVIER
Javier Perez (Blue)
Born: 1908, Havana, Cuba   Died: Unknown
Bats: R Throws: R   Ht: 6'0" Wt: 175
Position: 2B, 3B, OF   Tours: 1931, 1932-33
Highlights: Perez was one of six Cuban players to join the Royal Giants for the 1931 tour, impressing Lon Goodwin enough to make him the clean up hitter by the end of the tour. He was also compared to Connie Day, for being known as the team comedian in '31. He returned to the club for the 1932-33 tour of Asia, where he tied for second in batting with Martin, hitting .362, just behind Mackey's leading .388 average. After the 1933 tour, Perez went East and joined the Atlantic City Bacharachs, New York Cubans, Brooklyn Eagles, Newark Eagles and Homestead Greys.

PULLEN, O'NEAL
Born: Sept. 8, 1892, Beaumont, TX   Died: April 19, 1944, Los Angeles, CA
Bats: R Throws: R   Ht: 6'0" Wt: 220
Position: C   Tours: 1927, 1928, 1929, 1931, 1933-34
Highlights: Pullen started his career in the Texas Negro Leagues with Silsbee in 1910, joined Beaumont in 1915, and missed two years of play due to service in WWI. He was a

solid defensive catcher who had a career .314 average in 127 games against PCL and major league talent in the California Winter League. He is among the most active Trans-Pacific barnstormers in Negro Leagues baseball history, participating in five different tours, and having spent an estimated 466 days crossing the ocean and competing abroad.

RIDDLE, JOHN
John Thomas Riddle, Sr.

Born Dec. 9, 1900, Columbus, Ohio   Died: Oct. 3, 1981, Los Angeles, CA
Bats: Throws: Ht: Wt:
Position: INF   Tours: 1927

Highlights: Riddle was a two-sport athlete at the University of Southern California. He starred at Pasadena High School as a halfback prior to joining the Trojans in 1922. Nicknamed "Up-the-middle Riddle," he played three seasons (1922–24) with USC and gained notoriety as the first African American for the Trojans to play in the Rose Bowl when USC defeated Penn State 14–3 in 1923. After the Royal Giants' 1927 tour he accepted a position as an architect in Hawaii, and also played baseball and football for local clubs in the islands.

ROGAN, "BULLET JOE"
Charles Wilber Rogan (Bullet Joe; Cap), middle name later spelled Wilbur

Born: July 28, 1893, Okla. City, OK   Died: March 4, 1967, Kansas City, MO
Bats: R Throws: R   Ht: 5'7" Wt: 160
Positions: P, OF   Tours: 1933-34

Highlights: Rogan played for the 25th Infantry Wreckers in Honolulu between 1913 and 1916, and was a fan favorite. He joined the Kansas City Monarchs in 1920 and enjoyed a long and successful career that led to his induction into the National Baseball Hall of Fame in 1998. For more career details, see Appendix O: Hall of Fame Spotlight.

ROGERS, EARL
William Earl Rogers (Stumpy)

Born May 6, 1913, Elko, NV   Died Nov. 1, 1966, Honolulu, HI
Bats: R Throws: R   Ht: 5'3" Wt: 175
Position: OF, INF, C   Tours: 1933-34

Highlights: Rogers platooned in the OF for the Royal Giants during the 1933-34 tour. During the Hawaiian series he struggled at the plate, hitting .200 (4-for-20), but helped the team with his glove with a 1.000 fielding average on defense. He moved to Hawaii after the tour and was later employed by the Mutual Telephone Co. in Honolulu.

ROSS, WILLIAM
William Ross (Nacogdoches)

Born: Oct. 5, 1893, Corrigan, TX   Died: Dec. 22, 1964 in Diboll, TX
Bats: Throws: R   Ht: 5'9" Wt: 170
Position: P, OF   Tours: 1931, 1932-33, 1933-34

Highlights: See Ross' full bio in Appendix H.

SANTAELLO, ANASTARIO

Born: 1903, Havana, Cuba   Died: Unknown
Bats: Throws: R   Ht: Wt:
Position: 3B   Tours: 1931

Highlights: Santaello was one of six Cubans to join the Royal Giants for the 1931 tour to Hawaii. He batted third in the lineup and finished the 18-game season with a .338 average (24-for-71), second best on the team behind Dunn's .423 performance.

SAVAGE, AZEL

Azel Savage (Ace)
Born: August 16, 1898, Macon, GA   Died: July 15, 1984, Portland, OR
Bats: Throws: R   Ht: Wt:
Position: OF   Tours: 1928

Highlights: He played for the Los Angeles White Sox with Pullen and Fagen during the 1920s. For the 1928 tour to Hawaii, it was reported that he was once a member of the Lincoln Giants. During the 1924-25 California Winter League season, he played right field for the White Sox, and once went 2-for-4 against former Detroit Tigers pitcher Pug Cavet. According to military records, Savage served during WWI, WWII, and the Korean War. He achieved the rank of Master Sargent with the U.S. Air Force, and is buried at the Willamette National Cemetery in Portland, OR.

SHAW, TED

John A. Shaw (Ted, Lefty, Big Hips, Duncan)
Born: Feb. 24, 1906, Monrovia, CA   Died: Feb. 2, 1966, Honolulu, HI
Bats: R Throws: L   Ht: Wt:
Position: P   Tours: 1929, 1931

Highlights: He was a Negro National League pitcher in the 1920s who moved to Hawaii in the 1930s after his tours with the Royal Giants. Between 1933 and 1937, the press reported that Shaw had a 38-game unbeaten streak as a pitcher in Hawaii. He continued playing ball in Honolulu into the 1940s with the Mutual Telephone Company, and was a beloved member of the baseball community.

TUCKER, EUGENE

Born July 5, 1897, West Point, GA   Died: Unknown
Bats: Throws: R   Ht: 5'11½" Wt: 145
Position: P   Tours: 1927

Highlights: Tucker is a WWI veteran who joined the Royal Giants for the 1927 tour, although he did not return with the team due to injury; stayed behind in Asia for medical treatment. Travel records from 1927 reflect Georgia as place of birth, whereas his WWII registration record indicates that he was born in Hawaii. Tucker had the middle finger on his pitching hand amputated. In the mid-1940s he resided in New York state, but worked in West Virginia at the state penitentiary in Moundsville.

WALKER, JESSE

Jesse Walker (Hoss, Deuce, Aussa)

Born: Sept. 10, 1904, Austin, TX   Died Jan. 26, 1984, San Antonio, TX

Bats: R Throws: R   Ht: 5'11" Wt: 190

Position: 3B   Tours: 1927, 1928, 1929

Highlights: Walker spent more than 20 years in the Negro Leagues and later managed the Indianapolis Clowns and Baltimore Elite Giants. In 1927, he was the youngest member of the Royal Giants during their tour of Asia. He batted .290 (9-for-31) in the 8-game series in Hawaii on the return trip to the U.S.

YOUNG, T.J.

Thomas Jefferson Young (T. J., Tom, Pep, Shack Pappy)

Born: Sept. 6, 1902, Wetumpka, AL   Died: Unknown

Bats: L Throws: R   Ht: 6'1" Wt: 210

Position: C   Tours: 1933-34

Highlights: Young played in the Negro National League between 1925 and 1941. He joined the Royal Giants for the 1933-34 tour to Asia where he served as the backup catcher behind O'Neal Pullen. He saw limited action, but when given the opportunity he excelled, hitting .600 (6-for-10) in the Philippines. In an exhibition game against Dizzy Dean's All-Star team, Young batted clean up and hit a double off of Dizzy and a triple off of brother Paul "Daffy" Dean. Young and Royal Giants teammate Chet Brewer played ball in Puerto Rico in the early 1940s. Young also worked at the Boeing Airplane Co. in Wichita, Kansas during WWII.

*   *   *

Sources: Ancestry.com, AgateType.com, Baseball-Reference.com, Seamheads.com, Newspapers.com, The Biographical Encyclopedia of the Negro Leagues Baseball, by James A. Riley; The California Winter League, by William McNeil, Center for Negro Leagues Baseball Research, Negro Leagues Baseball Museum and the National Baseball Hall of Fame.

野球

Index

野球

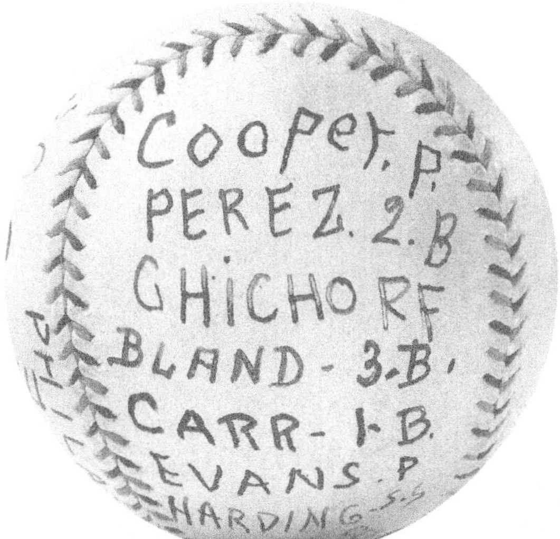
Cooper. P.
PEREZ. 2.B
GHICHO RF
BLAND - 3.B.
CARR - 1.B.
EVANS. P
HARDING S.S

59347407R00213

Made in the USA
Columbia, SC
03 June 2019